The Culture Trap

Advance Praise for *The Culture Trap*

"This is an important contribution to our understanding of how discourses and practices of racial representation work to shape and perpetuate ethnic inequalities in our schools. Wallace's comparative ethnography of schools in London and New York offers a unique insight into how ideas of culture and identity are formed historically and politically, and how these are lived by those caught in the trap of ethnic expectations. With a sharp eye for detail and an ear for the voices of young people, teachers, and parents, Wallace breathes new life into an old, and seemingly intractable, problem."

—Claire Alexander, Professor of Sociology, The University
of Manchester

"Cultural explanations of the achievement gap, such as culturally responsive and culturally relevant pedagogy, are popular within schools, colleges, and universities. This visionary, timely, engaging, and informative book describes the limits of cultural explanations and how culture, class, and context interact to influence academic achievement. It is a compelling and essential read."

—James A. Banks, Kerry and Linda Killinger Endowed Chair
in Diversity Studies Emeritus, University of Washington, Seattle

"This book is a masterpiece! It is anti-racist research at its best. This book dispels the myth of 'cultural difference' as the explanation for poor academic performance, and shows how the British state has created structural differences and misrepresented them as a matter of 'culture'. The fundamental role of teacher expectations, by comparison, jumps off the pages of this extraordinary study of the academic experiences of Black Caribbean children in large secondary schools in London and New York. This is a book worth reading and celebrating. It is good for teachers, school leaders, the Black community, the Caribbean community, and US and UK policymakers who want to be part of the solution."

—Bernard Coard, Educational activist and author of *How the West Indian
Child is Made Educationally Subnormal in the British School System*

"*The Culture Trap* exemplifies the beauty of cross-national research by deftly illuminating both the general and the particular of social forces across contexts. Wallace sharpens our understanding of the ways that different racial formations in the U.S. and Britain intersect with ethnic and class identity of Black Caribbean youth and permeate the walls of schools and classrooms. It's a compelling ethnography of the everyday lived experiences of second-generation immigrant students, which illuminates how 'ethnic expectations' influence their educational well-being. Many scholars and teachers of culture, race, ethnicity, and education will appreciate the informative, useful nature of Wallace's work."

—Prudence L. Carter, Sarah and Joseph Jr. Dowling Professor of Sociology, Brown University

"Derron Wallace has written a field-defining book. Comparing Black Caribbeans in London and New York, he shows how ethnic expectations, rooted in history, colonialism, and the proliferation of U.S. media culture, influence the incorporation and academic outcomes of second-generation Black Caribbean youth. Bursting with rich narrative accounts, powerful theoretical insights, and exceptional writing, this book will shape the sociology and education discourse on Black Caribbean students for years to come. Everyone who cares about race, ethnicity, education, and immigration should read this book."

—John B. Diamond, Professor of Sociology and Education Policy, Brown University

"How to explain the markedly different educational experiences and levels of achievement of African-Caribbean youth in London and New York? Conceptual clarity alongside careful listening to the voices of Black youth, parents, and teachers is at the heart of Derron Wallace's timely and thoughtful analysis of the 'ethnic expectations' which serve as an alibi for racisms and reinforce inequalities."

—Catherine Hall, Chair of the Centre for the Study of the Legacies of British Slavery, University College London

"This fascinating book takes us into two schools—one in New York City and one in London—where teachers use cultural narratives on the essential elements of Caribbean heritage towards very different goals—to highlight Black students' endless talents and possibilities in one setting and to stress the limited potential of Black adolescents in another. Beautifully written, gripping, and deeply interesting, *The Culture Trap* sheds new light on the mechanisms through which inequality is sustained. Highly recommended!"

—Annette Lareau, Professor of Sociology, University of Pennsylvania

"This brave, brilliant book takes no hostages. Beautifully evocative and richly theorized, *The Culture Trap* sets out a compelling argument for why culture should not be prioritized over structure in understandings of educational achievement. Weaving wonderful ethnographic narratives with stunning insights, the book brings a welcome clarity to the messy and highly contested morass that culture has become. For much-needed illumination, this is the book to read—it is both an enormous pleasure and a revelation."

—Diane Reay, Professor of Education, University of Cambridge

"*The Culture Trap* is a wonderful contribution to the comparative analysis of the ways in which Black youth have been the subject of unequal schooling. Through a nuanced and detailed analysis, Wallace illustrates how Black Caribbean youth have been subjected to persistent and deeply embedded unequal treatment in the school systems of the UK and US."

—John Solomos, Professor of Sociology, University of Warwick

"*The Culture Trap* is an insightful study of the experiences of Afro-Caribbean youth in New York City and London schools. Wallace's careful look at how schools create 'culture traps' through essentializing ethnic expectations of their Afro-Caribbean students is sure to become an instant classic. The book demonstrates how positive expectations go hand in hand with negative expectations, and how the history of colonialism shapes ethnic stereotypes in the US and Britain. Beyond the school, Wallace also shows how students themselves respond to the ethnic expectations they experience. Never reductive, Wallace uses 'storytelling sociology,' providing a vivid and convincing account of the lived experiences of the communities he observed, with deep respect, care, and curiosity. This book is a must-read for anyone interested in immigration, education, and the African diaspora."

—Natasha Warikoo, Lenore Stern Professor in the
Social Sciences and Professor of Sociology, Tufts University

The Culture Trap

*Ethnic Expectations and Unequal Schooling
for Black Youth*

DERRON WALLACE

OXFORD
UNIVERSITY PRESS

OXFORD
UNIVERSITY PRESS

Oxford University Press is a department of the University of Oxford. It furthers
the University's objective of excellence in research, scholarship, and education
by publishing worldwide. Oxford is a registered trade mark of Oxford University
Press in the UK and certain other countries.

Published in the United States of America by Oxford University Press
198 Madison Avenue, New York, NY 10016, United States of America.

Library of Congress Cataloging-in-Publication Data
Names: Wallace, Derron., author.
Title: The culture trap : ethnic expectations and unequal schooling for Black youth /
Derron Wallace.
Description: New York : Oxford University Press, 2023. |
Includes bibliographical references and index.
Identifiers: LCCN 2022034999 (print) | LCCN 2022035000 (ebook) |
ISBN 9780197531471 (paperback) | ISBN 9780197531464 (hardback) |
ISBN 9780197531495 (epub)
Subjects: LCSH: Children, Black—Education—New York (State)—New York. |
Children, Black—Education—England—London. | Immigrant children—
Education—New York (State)—New York. | Immigrant children—Education—England—London. |
Children of immigrants—Education—New York (State)—New York. | Children of immigrants—
Education—England—London. | Academic achievement—Social aspects—New York (State)—
New York. | Academic achievement—Social aspects—England—London. | Educational equalization—
New York (State)—New York. | Educational equalization—England—London.
Classification: LCC LC3733.N5 W35 2023 (print) |
LCC LC3733.N5 (ebook) | DDC 371.829/9697290097471—dc23/eng/20221007
LC record available at https://lccn.loc.gov/2022034999
LC ebook record available at https://lccn.loc.gov/2022035000

DOI: 10.1093/oso/9780197531464.001.0001

Paperback printed by Marquis, Canada
Hardback printed by Bridgeport National Bindery, Inc., United States of America

To my children, Jeremiah and Jamilia Wallace,
To my parents, Amaneita Samuels Wallace and Derrick Wallace Sr.,
and
To my beloved uncle, Ronald Johnson,
who died in the early stages of the COVID-19 pandemic.
This book is your legacy, too.

Contents

Acknowledgments

Too often, acknowledgments come at the very end of a book, and loved ones come last in such tributes. The preferred order of praise salutes mentors and advisors first; colleagues, friends, and editors next; and loved ones last. But love is at the root of this work, so I begin with those who sustained my being, becoming, and thinking long before any theory assisted me in making sense of the world.

First and foremost, I thank God. God's unfailing love afforded me the strength of mind and heart to truly listen to people as an exercise in care, respect, and love. I am compelled to acknowledge and thank my partner in love and laughter, Danya O'Meally Wallace, who first urged me to leave the halls of the University of Cambridge and abandon abstract theoretical musings to connect with Black youth in South London who were being disproportionately excluded from schools. Her searching questions about Black life in Britain affirmed my own about Black life in the United States and brought clarity to my understanding of diaspora as both noun and verb. It is in the company of Black youth, and with Danya's guidance, that I acquired a truly higher education.

I first learned to love Black youth from watching my parents love me, my siblings, and young people in various sites of schooling in Jamaica—from churches and community centers to street corners and playgrounds. My parents, Amaneita Samuels Wallace and Derrick Wallace Sr., taught me that listening, questioning, and learning are sacred methods bequeathed to us by our foremothers and forefathers as strategies worth pursuing and promoting in order to change the world. This book is an attempt to articulate the lessons I have gleaned from years of listening to the voices and views of Black Caribbean young people on both sides of the Atlantic. I owe my parents and the Black youth whose voices animate this book an enormous debt of gratitude.

During the course of this project, my life was gifted with two precious treasures—my children, Jeremiah and Jamilia. With each smile and giggle, they've made my world whole, and made me whole for the world. Playing with them often seems like just what my soul needs to exhale. While they have scribbled on, colored, and torn up several drafts of this book manuscript, they have also inspired me to complete the project with a clear-eyed sense that the ultimate purpose of this ethnography is not to flood the academic production line with intrigue, but to contribute to the development of a more just world in which Black children and young people, no matter where they are, flourish in freedom.

The completion of this book was made possible by a generous community of relatives, friends, and colleagues. Some of you came to visit me in Boston, with and without warning. You all make me smile from my heart. This book, and my life, are all the better because of your probing questions, soul-stirring prayers, comforting meals, and downright hilarious jokes. I pledge to return the favor (and your food containers) soon. Until then, rest assured that I am so grateful for your expressions of faith and love.

The cover of this book bears my name, but there are many other names I hope readers keep in mind whenever they see mine: Danya O'Meally Wallace, Jeremiah Wallace, Jamilia Wallace, Amaneita Samuels Wallace, Derrick Wallace Sr., Ivy Samuels, Harold Samuels, Esther Wallace, James Wallace, Ronald Johnson, Nola Barnes, Georgianna Samuels, Janet McNeil, Hopeton Samuels, Cecil Samuels, Kenneth Wallace, Clarence Wallace, Sophia Bell, Allisia Walker, Andre Walker, Hopeton Bell, Derrick Wallace Jr., Elexia Wright Clunis, Valerie Wallace Malcolm, Delroy Wallace, Veronica Samuels, Dean McNeil, Donte McNeil, Jason Campbell, Janice Campbell Dougie, Alvin Campbell, Janet Campbell Cameron, Jamie McClymont, Melisha Malcolm, Shanice Wallace, Joan Sawer, Ishmael Sawer, Mark O'Meally, Jomar O'Meally, Jomarda O'Meally, Sarah Scarlett, Pierre Robinson, Jermaine Robinson, Jaimee Robinson, Anita Walker, Bes Walker, BJ Bell, Lamia Bell, Chaz Bell, Lynzi Reynolds Bell, Taylor Wallace, Nia Wallace, Stephen Simpson, Jermaine Thomas, and Dwayne Kelly. These loved ones have never published a book, but they all believed I could, and frequently reminded me that I should. This work, this life, mean nothing at all without you.

This project would have been impossible without the generosity of time and spirit shown by the parents and teachers of Black Caribbean students. I am especially grateful to the mothers and fathers who peppered me with questions about my study's intent, insisted that I include adults' perspectives, and welcomed me into their homes, churches, coffee shops, sports games, parties, and community gatherings to witness, as one mother put it, "how we fight fi get the best education fi wi pickney dem [for our children]." This is a common struggle with local particularities across the Black Atlantic.

The generosity of spirit participants showed reminds me of the richness and depth a relational ethic of care affords—and why, to any ethnographer, relationships matter.

Fellowships from the Citizens & Scholars Foundation (formerly the Woodrow Wilson Foundation), the Stuart Hall Foundation, the W.E.B. Du Bois Research Institute at the Hutchins Center for African & African American Research at Harvard University, and Brandeis University afforded me time away from teaching responsibilities to devote my energy to the manuscript. I found my time at the Hutchins Center to be a deeply refreshing reminder that African diaspora studies and sociology are unmistakably political articulations of the world as it was, as it is, and as it ought to be. My study of race, culture, and education on both sides of the Atlantic finds its inspiration and interventions in these formative fields. It is my hope that this book honors the leadership and legacy of the fellowships' namesake, particularly outsider sociologists W. E. B. Du Bois and Stuart Hall, who are finally receiving the acclaim they always deserved.

I am very grateful for my colleagues, mentors, friends, and scholar-siblings on both sides of the Atlantic for their kindness, care, and support during this book-writing process: Hugo Ceron-Anaya, Travis Bristol, Tolani Britton, Bedelia Richards, Marcelle Medford, Orly Clergé, Shameka Powell, Jarvis Givens, Joshua Bennett, Bianca Baldridge, Joseph Nelson, Chezare Warren, Roderick Carey, Cory Hunter, Jessie Abrahams, Nicola Ingram, Shirley Ann Tate, Remi Joseph-Salisbury, Krystal Strong, Arathi Sriprakash, Sharon Walker, Leon Tikly, Crain Soudien, Susan Burch, Satnam Virdee, Vilna Bashi, Nicola Rollock, Daniel Laurison, Kassie Freeman, Ernest Morrell, Hank Levin, Carla Shedd, Pere Ayling, Jason Arday, Chantelle Lewis, Nadena Doharty, Vikki Boliver, Will Baker, Saida Grundy, Sally Nuamah, Jacqueline Forbes, Raúl Pérez, Anthony O'Campo, Milton Vickerman, Michelle Harris, Harvey Charles, Richard Reddick, Javier Treviño, Kersti Yllö, Hyun Kim, Suzanne Model, Phil Kasinitz, Reuel Rogers, Christina Greer, Shirley Collado, David Perez II, Norm Jones, Barbara Ofosu-Somuah, Augusta Irele, Carl Manalo, Kepler Jeudy, Ryan Letada, Jonathan Berhanu, Donte McGuire, Keon McGuire, Rishi Mediratta, Jordan Harrison, Mezgebu Hailu, Sumer Mehmet, and most of all, my brothers and friends, Derrick Wallace Jr., and Dwayne Kelly.

I thank my companions in graduate school, Thabo Msibi, Siza Mtimbiri, Edward Davis, Garth Stahl, Emel Thomas, Maia Chankseliani, and Oakleigh Welply for supporting my study of race and culture, even when it was unpopular and at times controversial to do so at the University of Cambridge.

Debbie Bial and The Posse Foundation have been constant sources of inspiration for me throughout my career. Thank you, Debbie and Posse, for believing in me from high school until now.

At Brandeis, I am especially appreciative of Faith Smith, Greg Childs, Jasmine Johnson, Carina Ray, Marya Levenson, David Cunningham, Wendy Cadge, Elizabeth Ferry, Robin Miller, Sarah Lamb, Leah Gordon, Joe Reimer, Rachel Kramer Theodorou, Manuel Tuan, Eileen Kell, Joe and Carol Fahey, Dennis Tyrell, Susan Eaton, Raj Sampath, Siri Suh, Gowri Vijayakumar, Michael Nooy-Strand, Cheri Hansen, Daniel Kryder, Erika Smith, Elaine Wong, Kim Godsoe, Susan Birren, Lisa Lynch, and Ron Liebowitz. I've found a home at Brandeis because of each of you—and the brilliant students I've been so honored to teach.

I thank Prudence Carter, John Diamond, Karolyn Tyson, and Natasha Warikoo from the bottom of my heart for offering sound advice and critical comments that helped to make the manuscript stronger. My gratitude abounds for Jenny LaFleur, Zora Haque, Sylvia Stewart, Kevin Thomas, Diana Witt, Adam Musser, Lauren Nichols, Ashleigh Cartwright, Denezia Fahie, and Elinor Eggers for the technical assistance they provided throughout. Grey Osterud has been a wonderful mentor. She listened to me and supported me on very difficult days, and through it all, reminded me that good writing is about re-writing.

Diane Reay, Claire Alexander, Tiffany Joseph, Julie Kleinman, Annette Lareau, Aaron Pallas, Nancy Foner, Freeden Blume Oeur, Andrew Smith, Adam Gamoran, L'Heureux Lewis-McCoy, Lisa McCormick, Louise Archer, John Solomos, and Joseph Ferrare read rough drafts of chapters and still believed in the promise of this project. The support of James Cook, my editor at Oxford University Press, assisted me in completing this book. I thank the anonymous reviewers who read my manuscript carefully and offered important advice for improving it. You all invite reflections on the goodness of kindness. I am profoundly grateful to each of you for believing in me and this work. Thank you!

So I close as I began, with love. I honor Danya O'Meally Wallace, the brightest light in my life, who with unmistakable faith has prayed me through seasons of doubt and disappointment, and with unparalleled grace has reminded me time and time again that writing a book starts with a dream and ends well with hard work. I thank God the dream has finally come true.

Preface

Although it was morning, the dreary London skies suggested otherwise. The gray all around seemed to dull the red double-decker bus I boarded in Brixton heading to a primary school in another part of South London.[1] During the 40-minute journey, I pressed my head against the window on the upper deck and observed the changing landscape beyond it—from the rows of Victorian terraced houses with big bay windows, the evergreen trees swaying in the breeze, and the rubbish bins lying on their backs along the pavement, to the multistory blocks of flats towering over convenience stores and fruit stalls, the police officers striding up and down the road, and the teenagers alighting at bus stops en route to school. In time, I hopped off the bus and rushed down the road to see students I had worked with for nearly a year in my capacity as a community organizer—young people of Caribbean, African, Asian, European, and multiethnic heritage who reflect Britain's 'new diversity.'

When I arrived at the school, a Black teacher with salt-and-pepper hair, parted and plaited with a timeless arithmetic, welcomed me with a warm embrace. Ms. Bell reminded me, as she always did, that she has been teaching for as long as I have been alive. On our way up the stairs to her class, Ms. Bell asked about my work. I told her, among other things, that I studied at the University of Cambridge. "And you're Caribbean?" she asked with an unmistakably sharp Jamaican accent, as she spun around with knitted brows, squinted eyes, and the look my mother gives me if I dare tell a lie in her hearing. I responded in the affirmative, and for what felt like all too long, Ms. Bell searched my face intently, as if in disbelief.

"Caribbean people don't get into Cambridge," she continued. "Africans maybe, but not Caribbean young people."

I slowed my strides.

I had completed secondary school and university in the United States, and heard reports of Caribbean success with considerable frequency in and out of schools—often with unbearable annoyance.[2]

"In the US, Caribbean people usually do well," I said.

Ms. Bell took me by the hand to hasten my footsteps, pointed down the hall to her classroom, and said "Not in Englan', mi fren'!" An awkward silence followed us down the hallway until a group of eight- and nine-year-olds shouted, "Mister Wallace! Mister Wallace!" As I stepped into the classroom to plan the next steps in a local street safety campaign, I couldn't help but wonder if Ms. Bell's perceptions were true.

Immediately following my meeting with the students that December day in 2010, I pulled my phone from my back pocket and searched the internet for evidence of what Ms. Bell had asserted about Black Caribbean people in Britain. As a newcomer to England, it had not dawned on me that Caribbean students did not fare well in British schools writ large. Nor did I realize that the individual experiences of Caribbean girls and boys I knew who struggled in schools were indicative of a wider pattern in the British educational system. How, I wondered, could this be? When did this happen?

I soon stumbled upon an article written just days before by David Lammy, a Member of Parliament and former Minister of Higher Education, decrying what he called "the Oxbridge whitewash."[3] In his opinion editorial, Lammy, a second-generation Black Caribbean politician who represents Tottenham in North London, declared: "Just one British Black Caribbean student was admitted to Oxford last year. That is not a misprint: one student."[4] Though Lammy's critique was consistent with my own awareness of the limited racial and ethnic diversity at the University of Cambridge, I attributed the controversy to a recent report on inequalities in elite British higher education. Nevertheless, I could not stop thinking about Ms. Bell's assertions—and mine. What should I make of the paradoxical positions of Black Caribbean people in Britain and the United States? How would I experience this diaspora dilemma as a Jamaican-born US citizen studying in England? Furthermore, what historical factors and political conditions shaped the divergent representations of Caribbean achievement? I tried to quiet these and related questions surfacing in my mind, but they would not leave me.

Days later, I recalled a fiery debate I read about in *The New York Times* at the end of my first year in university. The title grabbed my attention: "Top Colleges Take More Blacks, but Which Ones?"[5] At a gathering of Harvard's Black alumni, Professors Lani Guinier and Henry Louis Gates Jr. pointed out that most alumni in attendance were not of African American heritage, but were Black immigrants or the children of Black immigrants from the Caribbean and sub-Saharan Africa.[6] Guinier's and Gates's observations about Black ethnic diversity were also applicable to Black student enrollment at a host of other elite universities. Results from the National Longitudinal Survey of Freshmen revealed that Black Caribbeans and Black Africans were overrepresented at Ivy League and other selective institutions, while African Americans were underrepresented.[7] A subsequent study found that Black Caribbean and Black African immigrants and their children accounted for 41 percent of Black undergraduates at Ivy League institutions even though they made up less than 10 percent of the Black population in the United States.[8] Somehow Black Caribbean students in the United States seemed to have quite a different experience than African Americans—and a very different experience from Black Caribbean students in Britain. As it turned out, and as this book explains, there are significant differences in the educational discourses about Black Caribbean students in Britain and the United States. In both national contexts, educators often saw Black Caribbean 'culture' as the heart of the matter.

When I next met Ms. Bell, this time outside of a church near Clapham Common where she codirected a Saturday supplementary school, she seemed perplexed by our previous conversation too.[9] "Is what you told me about Black Caribbean people in the US really a thing?" she asked. Confessing that she had never heard claims of Caribbean success in the United States, she wondered aloud, "What caused Caribbean people to be successful there and not here?" I insisted that Caribbean success in the United States was not universal, but contextual at best. I told Ms. Bell that in cities like New York, Black Caribbean people developed and defended a reputation of being hardworking and committed to education, all in pursuit of the American Dream. Perhaps dissatisfied with my reply, Ms. Bell again expressed her confusion about the contrasting statuses of Black Caribbean people in the United States and Britain. I eventually admitted my uncertainty about their differing reputations in two global empires linked by history, language, and laws.[10]

I then questioned her about Caribbean disadvantage in Britain and its causes. I thought that if I understood more about the education of Black Caribbean people in Britain, I could perhaps venture a satisfactory explanation to assuage Ms. Bell's concerns, if only momentarily. Ms. Bell suggested that when she had arrived in England in the 1970s, Caribbean disadvantage was clearly due to institutional racism. The contemporary challenges, however, seemed to be low parental involvement, limited role models, and a lack of academic aspirations among Caribbean students. "But that can't be it," I replied. "What is stopping Black Caribbean kids from achieving?"

"They keep talking about what's bad about Caribbean culture and Caribbean people," she said. Eyes wide. Right arm akimbo.

"But how could it be our culture when people with Caribbean culture have different results in different countries?" I asked.

"Ah dat mi a wondah [That's what I'm wondering]!" Ms. Bell replied.[11]

"Mi nuh tink culture hav' nutin' fi do wid it [I don't think culture has anything to do with it]!" I said, with the kind of impassioned patois you hear from me if you step on my toes or touch my food without my consent.

"Then what is it?" Ms. Bell asked.

This cultural dilemma captivated me. Something about the curious paradox of Caribbean achievement gave me clarity and sparked restless curiosity. During my walk to the train station following my conversation with Ms. Bell, I decided to pursue this line of inquiry further. In a few short days, I changed my doctoral research from a study of economic development to a cultural analysis of racial inequalities in British and American schools as experienced by Black Caribbean young people. I needed to understand, if only for myself, the unexamined differences among Black Caribbean pupils in the London and New York City educational systems. What, if anything, does culture have to do with shaping Black Caribbean youth's social and scholastic experiences? In comparison to whom, and according to whom, were Black Caribbean young people 'high-achieving' in the United States and 'underachieving' in Britain? *The Culture Trap: Ethnic Expectations and Unequal Schooling for Black Youth* is the result of that moving, memorable exchange with Ms. Bell and the questions our discussions provoked.

This ethnography is centrally concerned with a perplexing paradox among Black Caribbean youth in British and American society, which has been shaped discursively and comparatively from the early 20th century to the present. Since the 1920s, Black Caribbean people in the United States have been considered a high-achieving Black model minority. In contrast, since the 1950s, Black Caribbean people in Britain have been regarded as a chronically underachieving minority. In both national contexts, however, it is often suggested that Caribbean culture informs their status, whether as a celebrated or degraded group. This book reveals the relationship between race and culture in education within and beyond national particularities, highlights the connections between narratives of culture and histories of structural inequality, and points to new possibilities for equity and justice in and out of schools.

To ascertain the influence of culture in shaping the educational experiences of Black Caribbean youth in global cities, I carried out a multisited ethnography. I returned to secondary schools I was familiar with from my experiences as a community organizer in South London and as a former student in a New York City public school. The relationships I had built with school leaders, teachers, and students long before I began this study afforded me meaningful access to these schools, which I detail in the appendix. In *The Culture Trap*, I draw on a total of 16 months of ethnographic fieldwork in two of the largest high schools in London and New York City, school and community-based archival materials, and focus group and one-on-one interviews with Black Caribbean pupils, their teachers, and parents to elucidate the limits and liabilities of the cultural narratives that are used to justify the achievement levels of Black Caribbean youth in the United States and Britain. As this ethnography reveals, educators at times rely too heavily on culture as the chief explanation for the disparate social and educational positions of Black Caribbean people on both sides of the Atlantic. On their own, cultural explanations oversimplify an inherently complex phenomenon. Regarding culture as the fundamental determinant of Caribbean youth's educational experiences undermines the impact of national context, social class, and (post)colonial conditions on group outcomes in schools.

In truth, this ethnography is as much a critical account of culture's influence as it is a critique of my previous perspectives on culture's insignificance. As my exchange with Ms. Bell near Clapham Common makes clear, I initially held fast to the view that culture was entirely inconsequential to the educational experiences of Black Caribbean young people.[12] I had grown leery of 'culture' as a zombie, catch-all category, a politicized explanation for all forms of social ills, and a code for blaming individuals and groups for their ways of living and being, rather than attending to the structures of power that foment racial and ethnic inequalities.[13] But the singular emphasis on culture and my staunch resistance to cultural explanations are perhaps two sides of the same coin. Both are excessively deterministic and limit the visibility of the wide range of experiences among ethnic groups.[14] Based on in-depth research, *The Culture Trap* examines how and why structural forces *and* cultural constructions matter for Black Caribbean youth in schools in ways that call prevailing societal views and my initial perspectives into question.

For Black Caribbean people on both sides of the Atlantic, the confluence of culture, class, and context in nations with peculiar racial histories of slavery and colonialism informs the differing experiences and expectations of Black Caribbean youth.[15] How ethno-racial groups like Black Caribbeans (re)imagine, articulate, and practice cultures is contingent on their situated contexts and their positioning within them.[16] Moreover, the specific cultural strategies ethno-racial groups marshal to signify their status are informed by their structural positions and social circumstances in the host society.[17] These nuances are often elided in public and educational discourses. But these complex perspectives are necessary for challenging the preponderance of cultural claims in schools that neglect the variation within groups and promote a fixed formula about which groups achieve and why. Overreliance on and oversimplification of ethnic cultures to explain success or failure is a trap.

This ethnography explores the significance of what I call *the culture trap* for Black Caribbean young people in London and New York in two different but related ways. I define the culture trap as an alluring yet ensnaring set of logics that draws on ethnic culture to decipher ethno-racial minority students' success, but instead distorts and misinterprets it. The culture trap treats ethnic culture as group description *and* prescription. I unpack these and related points in *The Culture Trap*. In the first part of the book, I analyze the historical factors and institutional practices that create the constraints of the culture trap for second-generation Black Caribbean pupils, from the different structures of academic 'ability' grouping in London and New York to the role of the US media in shaping negative perceptions of urban public schools in the United States and the influence of colonialism in fostering positive perceptions about the power of British schooling. I illuminate ethnic expectations as routine forms of the culture trap that teachers, parents, and Black Caribbean youth reinforce directly and indirectly in schools. In the second part of the book, I highlight how Black Caribbean young people experience the culture trap, reproducing it even as they resist it. In both sections of the book, I provide more comprehensive and nuanced answers to Ms. Bell's searching questions than I could muster when she first posed them.

That grim, gray day when Ms. Bell met me at the school gate will be forever etched into my consciousness as a moment of deep intellectual awakening. Her comments and questions ushered my mind down a previously unfamiliar corridor and motivated this comparative ethnography. Were Ms. Bell's assertions correct? Were mine? More importantly, how can popular perceptions of Black Caribbean students' achievement help, hinder, or harm students like those who greeted me with bright, broad smiles at the entrance of Ms. Bell's classroom? This ethnography provides critical and original perspectives to elucidate a complex cultural and structural phenomenon. Amidst ongoing discussions about racial inequalities in education and institutional racism in British and American schools, this ethnography points to the urgent need to challenge the conscious and unconscious cultural assumptions that teachers, school leaders, parents, and pupils at times use to assess students' success.

Introduction

The Power of the Culture Trap

No one expected such a hot day in April in New York City—at least, not so soon. Time seemed to crawl when the sudden, sweltering heat drove away the cool of spring. I wished for a gush of rain to waft cool air through the open window into the muggy classroom at Newlands High School where I sat with 24 teenagers studying American literature.[1] From the back of Mr. Sterling's 10th grade Honors English class, I watched a few students fashion makeshift paper fans, while others rested their heads. Some wrote feverishly. A couple took notes slowly with one hand, dangling the other from their desks.

"Yo Mister!" Tom said, "When we gonna get AC in class like the principal and teachers got in the office?" Mr. Sterling, a veteran white teacher, ignored Tom—a usually provocative voice among his peers known for his wisecracks and defensive skills on the soccer field. "Mister! Yo, Misteeer!" Tom continued. "It's hot as hell in here. Turn on the AC, man."

"You'll get AC when you get A's instead of C's."

"Oooooooohhhh!!!" students said in swelling unison.

"Don't worry about my C's, Mister. Worry about that river runnin' from them [arm] pits you got."

"Oooooooohhhh!!!"

I chuckled. A good rebuttal never loses its power.

Mr. Sterling warned the class that one more outburst would be followed by a pop quiz. In due time, the room fell silent. "I just can't understand," Mr. Sterling continued, "why other West Indian [Black Caribbean] kids get A's and B's in my class, and you're here with C's and D's being a nuisance."[2]

"C ain't a bad grade, Mister," Tom said in hushed tones.

"It is if you're Caribbean."

I couldn't believe what I was hearing. During my time as a student attending a large New York City public high school, I heard teachers express high expectations of Black Caribbean students, but not so publicly, or so punitively.[3]

The Culture Trap. Derron Wallace, Oxford University Press. © Oxford University Press 2023.
DOI: 10.1093/oso/9780197531464.003.0001

"You are capable of more," Sterling added. "The other West Indian children are smart and you are too. . . . Your mother told me not to let you settle. You know how to work harder." Tom sucked his teeth, stood up, snatched the hall pass from Mr. Sterling's desk, walked out of the room, and slammed the door.[4]

I wish this were the only time I witnessed such an exchange at Newlands High School, but it was not. Most encounters between white teachers and Black Caribbean students I observed were not like what Tom experienced with Mr. Sterling, but for Tom and his peers, explicit and implicit beliefs about Caribbean students' exceptional capacity for high achievement and hard work were all too familiar.

Falling into the Culture Trap

Thousands of miles across the Atlantic, in a leafy section of South London with mature oak trees and neatly manicured grass, Caribbean students wrestled with weighty, yet quite different, expectations of their capacity for achievement. One encounter made this particularly clear.

On an unseasonably warm day at Londerville Secondary in South London, Akilah approached Ms. James, a white English Language teacher, about the "54%" scribbled in green at the top of her mock exam.[5] The Black Caribbean Year 10 student was known as a studious leader with a knack for reading, literary criticism, and debate. With a key assignment a few days away, Akilah found herself panicking about the lowest grade she had received since the start of the school year. When she saw me talking with Ms. James in the stairwell, Akilah pulled her perm into a ponytail, straightened her tie, and cleared her throat.

"Excuse me," she said as she approached. "Ms. James, can I talk to you about my last exam? I pretty much failed."

"Sure," Ms. James said. "Why don't you come by the staff room during lunch?"

"I will, Ms. It's just that I'm not used to this kind of grade, and so many people did well." Akilah's voice trembled and cracked.

Ms. James patted Akilah on the back. "Don't worry," she said. "Don't worry. Remember this is just one exam. You are already exceeding expectations."

"I don't understand, Ms. How come I'm exceeding expectations when I pretty much failed the exam?"

What Ms. James said in response left Akilah confused and disturbed. "Most students don't do as well as you, Akilah. Other Caribbean students don't do as well as you."

Akilah furrowed her brow. I squinted my eyes. "And what is that supposed to mean, Ms.?" Akilah asked politely.

"It's a compliment," Ms. James replied. "You're a very good student, Akilah."

Having worked in several London primary and secondary schools as a community organizer, I had grown accustomed to subtle, underhanded, yet well-meaning comments about Black Caribbean students underachieving and misbehaving. But this candid exchange between Akilah and Ms. James "took the cake and the biscuit," Akilah explained later. It was a moment of remarkable clarity about the low educational expectations Black Caribbean students faced at schools like Londerville.

"Stop by the staff room at lunch time," Ms. James said. Akilah agreed. After Akilah walked away, I couldn't help but seek clarification from Ms. James about what seemed like low expectations for Akilah and her Caribbean peers—a common pattern in British schools, particularly among white teachers like Ms. James.

"We have high expectations of all our students, Mr. Wallace, but not everyone can meet them. Caribbean students in particular struggle to do so. . . . This was true when I was in secondary school and it's still true now."

Ms. James's comments shocked me, as only two weeks earlier, standing in the same stairwell, she had told me that "we must believe in all our young people, no matter their background." What Ms. James said to Akilah seemed to be a contradiction between ideal aspirations and everyday expectations.[6]

Akilah's encounter with Ms. James and Tom's with Mr. Sterling are emblematic of the contrasting educational expectations of Black Caribbean young people navigating the education systems in two different institutional, geographical, and political contexts. These examples epitomize numerous moments in education when teachers and students are caught in *the culture trap*—instances in which loose understandings of ethnic culture distort perceptions of students' achievement. Frequent, casual commentary on Black Caribbean students' potential and performance shaped their experiences at Newlands High and Londerville Secondary. These judgments were often so naturalized and normative that they remained largely unquestioned and unchallenged. I call these assumptions about students' prospects for achievement based on their cultural heritage *ethnic expectations*—consequential expressions of the culture trap.

What Is the Culture Trap?

The success or failure of ethno-racial minorities in schools and society is often ascribed principally, and at times exclusively, to their distinct cultures. Though such observations of social difference may appear to be value-neutral, they are often value-laden expressions that reinforce racial hierarchies, privileging some groups as model minorities with 'good cultures' or 'cultures of success' and subordinating others as underachieving minorities with 'bad cultures' or 'cultures of poverty.'[7] Students like Akilah in London and Tom in New York are but two of the many ethno-racial minority youth, particularly Black youth, who find themselves caught in the culture trap—an alluring yet insidious way of understanding inequalities that frames racialized minorities' experiences and outcomes based on the perceived characteristics of their ethnic culture.

By overestimating the power of culture in everyday discussions and ignoring the influence of historical contexts and institutional structures, these assumptions reinforce long-standing stereotypes and limit fuller, more complex understandings of individuals' behavior and groups' positions. Teachers like Ms. James and Mr. Sterling are caught in the culture trap, too. They adhere to an essentialist interpretation of culture, treating it as a largely uniform orientation intrinsic to specific ethno-racial minority groups, and using it in order to predict students' likelihood of success. But, as we have just seen, the ways they interact with students based on those assumptions often backfire—heightening tensions in teacher–student interactions and shaping students' perceptions of teachers' expectations.

On both sides of the Atlantic, culture is an appealing explanation for differences in the identities, experiences, and status positions of ethno-racial minorities.[8] In contexts where appeals to a fixed, biological essence of specific ethno-racial groups are more widely understood as fraught, fictional, and racist, culture has re-emerged as an acceptable way of defining differences between groups and drawing distinctions within them. Culture functions as a seemingly race-neutral code, a way of obfuscating race while reproducing racial and ethnic hierarchies.[9] But the use of culture is not only tricky; it can be a trap. As sociologist Claire Alexander warns, "the role of culture in relation to issues of racial and ethnic identity remains an intellectual and political quicksand," in part because it is often unclear what exactly culture is and how it shapes social action and interaction.[10]

Culture is often loosely defined and strategically deployed to frame ethnoracial minorities in flattening, stereotypical ways. Culture can be understood broadly as material possessions and forms of expression, as sociologist R. Patrick Solomon contends,[11] or knowledge, behavioral norms, attitudes, and choices based on shared beliefs, as sociologists Orlando Patterson and Ethan Fosse suggest.[12] Additionally, culture has been articulated as discourse that shapes meaning-making, as sociologist Stuart Hall argued,[13] and examined as everyday social actions that reproduce inequalities, as sociologist Pierre Bourdieu explained.[14] But such varied notions of culture give rise to deep misunderstandings about what people mean when they refer to culture in day-to-day discussions.[15]

When examined in relation to social structure, culture can be a meaningful analytical frame for understanding social differences and identifying the implicit and explicit forces that shape educational inequalities. However, using culture to understand achievement can be a trap when culture is overemphasized as a definitive explanation of group educational and economic outcomes on one hand, and when culture is used loosely in public and everyday discourses that explicitly or implicitly "recode biological notions of race as 'culture'" and reinforce racial inequality,[16] on the other.

As this ethnography reveals, the culture trap is not simply a matter for theoretical debate in British and American sociology. It is experienced through cultural narratives in interpersonal and intergroup interactions as part of everyday life. The Black Caribbean young people at the heart of this ethnography describe the cultural constraints they encounter in schools as "culture racism," as teachers "using our culture against us," and as "a weird way to divide Black Caribbean students from African students." In this regard, the culture trap is an interpretive and experiential dilemma that has profound consequences for the educational experiences of students like Akilah and Tom in London and New York City public schools.

In this ethnography, I point out that the Black model minority myth, used to describe Black Caribbeans in the United States throughout the 20th century,[17] is an example of the culture trap. I assert that the culture of poverty myth, used in reference to Black Caribbeans in Britain (and African Americans in the United States) from the mid-20th century to date,[18] is also an example of the culture trap. At the heart of this book, I argue that there is another distinctive example of the culture trap that informs the educational experiences of Black Caribbean young people like Akilah and Tom in London and New York: ethnic expectations.

Ethnic Expectations as a Culture Trap

Ethnic expectations are casual, sometimes calculated, and at other times unconscious assumptions that rely on ethnicity as a proxy for predicting, interpreting, and justifying students' educational performance.[19] Ethnic expectations are dominant beliefs and routine, day-to-day estimations about what individuals in specific ethnic groups are capable of or likely to achieve. These distinct expectations treat ethnicity not merely as a descriptive category for students' cultural identities, but also as a prescriptive indicator of students' academic success or failure.[20] Educators at times assign meaning and value to students' achievement based on their ethnicity. Ethnic expectations also legitimate educators treating students differently because of their cultural backgrounds. In New York City, ethnic expectations reinforce perceptions of Black Caribbean young people as relatively high achievers, claims that date back to the early 20th century in the United States.[21] In London, by contrast, ethnic expectations reproduce claims that Black Caribbean youth are underachievers, a perspective that gained prominence in Britain from the mid-20th century to the present.[22]

Ethnic expectations are confining judgments. Yet they are more subtle, more varied, and broader in their operation than stereotypes, which impose a set of uniform images on individual members of ethnic groups. Ethnic expectations are not simply self-fulfilling prophecies in which students assume that their academic performance and behavior will confirm negative preconceptions of their group, which social psychologists Claude Steele and Joshua Aronson call "stereotype threat."[23] Neither are ethnic expectations merely perspectives that students will be seen more advantageously through the lens of positive assumptions about their ethnic group, which sociologists Jennifer Lee and Min Zhou call "stereotype promise."[24] Although both concepts acknowledge the weight of social and symbolic factors, they do not fully address the simultaneous operation of imposed and internalized expectations.

Ethnic expectations include both the intrinsic *and* the extrinsic perceptions that enhance or inhibit students' academic achievement, access to educational opportunities, and relationships to authority. Crucially, societal and institutional assumptions that some ethno-racial groups are likely to experience academic failure and others academic success, lead to unequal learning opportunities and disparate educational practices.[25] In this ethnography, I explore the academic and behavioral expectations for Black students and show how they differ based on ethnicity while reinforcing racial disparities.

The operation of ethnic expectations resembles what sociologist Cecilia Ridgeway calls "performance expectations,"[26] preconceptions about the competencies and capacities of individuals based on their gender, race, and class that influence everyday social relations. Not only do they contribute to specific groups' prestige and power, but they affect the resources and opportunities some groups are afforded and others are denied, reproducing social inequality. In Ridgeway's view, performance expectations are mainly products of unconscious biases, an explanation that, as critics have argued, underestimates the connections between the conscious and the taken-for-granted assumptions that shape perceptions of minoritized groups.[27]

While Ridgeway's research focuses primarily on gendered performance expectations, and sociologists Amanda Lewis and John Diamond examine racialized performance expectations, I focus on ethnic expectations, a version of performance expectations that centers ethnicity as the dominant frame through which to regulate the day-to-day educational experiences of Black Caribbean young people.[28] I show that ethnicity is used, strategically and situationally, to downplay—and inadvertently or deliberately reinforce—the significance of race and the prevalence of racism in schools.[29] Ethnic expectations invoke 'culture' as reason, resource, and remedy for racialized academic achievement.[30] In this regard, race is not incidental, but instrumental, to the development of ethnic expectations.[31] In *The Culture Trap*, I point out the ways in which culture is used as a seemingly race-neutral resource, and as an alibi for racism in a putatively post-racial society.

How Ethnic Expectations Trap Students and Teachers

Ethnic expectations result in three key outcomes. First, they reproduce dominant cultural beliefs, a set of well-rehearsed ideologies used to make inferential judgments about student achievement. Participants presumed that members of specific ethnic groups are hard-working or lazy, high-achieving or underachieving, well or poorly behaved. In Ms. James's interaction with

Akilah in London and Mr. Sterling's confrontation with Tom in New York City, both teachers drew on ethnicity to estimate their students' capacities and interpret their academic performance. These teachers' orienting beliefs are informed by viewpoints developed through and reinforced by everyday social interactions, historical narratives, popular media representations, and dominant achievement discourses in schools and society. Parents and pupils reinforce these cultural beliefs, too—even if they seldom state or act on them publicly in the ways Mr. Sterling and Ms. James did. As I show in this ethnography, when functioning as orienting cultural beliefs, ethnic expectations engender a sense of distinctiveness, of being different from or better than others, particularly as students in subordinate ethno-racial groups seek to elevate themselves above a more stigmatized group.

Second, ethnic expectations regulate behavior. Ethnic expectations are mobilized as a correction strategy to urge students to fulfill ideals that are shared by their ethnic group and the dominant society, pursue high academic achievement, and rise above racial and ethnic stereotypes that trap students in self-perpetuating patterns of underachievement. When Mr. Sterling and Ms. James drew on dominant perceptions of Caribbean ethnic identities during their discussions with Tom and Akilah, each teacher compared these individuals to Caribbean students in general to contextualize their low performance. The aim, at least according to Ms. James and Mr. Sterling, was to encourage students to perform better by highlighting the possibilities of success or failure based on the performance of their co-ethnic peers. In London, Ms. James drew on the common preconception of Black Caribbean underachievement to situate Akilah's usually excellent performance as exceptional. In New York City, in contrast, Mr. Sterling summoned intra-ethnic comparisons to motivate Tom not simply to 'pass' the exam, but to excel like the other students of Caribbean heritage in the class. In both settings, ethnic expectations functioned as what sociologist Diane Reay calls an "ideological whip" for motivating students to achieve academically.[32] The results of this study point out that ethnic expectations are also behavior and performance management strategies for disciplining students and encouraging them to behave deferentially toward those in authority.

Third, ethnic expectations reinforce the categorization of students—even as an unintended consequence of academic 'ability' grouping. As an organizing scheme invoked by teachers, pupils, and parents, wittingly and unwittingly, and reinforced by organizational arrangements like academic 'ability' grouping (setting in Britain and tracking in the United States), ethnic expectations position ethno-racial groups as model minorities, failing minorities, or somewhere between the two. Ethnic expectations flatten the varied experiences and capabilities of individuals based on group membership and reinforce hegemonic perceptions of ethno-racial groups' past achievements as guiding or even determining their future prospects. Teachers draw on representations of the group to shape their treatment of individuals. In New York, Mr. Sterling justified his ethnic expectations by mentioning Tom's mother's admonition to push Tom to do his best like "the other West Indian kids get[ting] A's and B's in my class." Ms. James, in contrast, tried to assuage Akilah's anxieties about her low performance on an exam by telling her that she is "exceeding expectations" relative to her Black Caribbean peers. As we will see, defiance emerges when individual students experience their ethnic identities as straitjackets or when teachers use students' ethnicities, consciously or unconsciously, as reasons for profiling or punishing them.[33]

My concept of ethnic expectations extends and deepens our understanding of the dynamics inside and outside of schools that distort perceptions of students' achievement because of their ethnic cultures. I consider both the subtle and implicit and the strategic and explicit articulations of expectations that Black students experience as pervasive features of their schooling. I add ethnicity to the standard trilogy of race, class, and gender as a dominant status characteristic used to make academic differentiations among Black youth. Moreover, I explore ethnic distinctions made by Black youth themselves—between Black Caribbeans and Africans in Britain; and between Black Caribbeans, Africans, and African Americans in the United States. These same ethnic distinctions are often used by school teachers and leaders to discount the influence of race and racism in schools.

This study highlights the structural and cultural life of ethnic expectations in both the homeland and the host society, within schools and families, and through the interactions of teachers, students, and parents. Its comparative perspectives illuminate the varied ways that students make meaning of, and respond to, the ethnic expectations they encounter. I pay particular attention to how Black Caribbean young people recognize, reproduce, and resist ethnic expectations in an attempt to free themselves from the culture trap. But as I show in this ethnography, the culture trap is a tricky snare from which it is difficult to escape. In fact, in the lived experiences of Black Caribbean young people in London and New York, freedom from the culture trap often requires trapping another group in it.

In school and policy contexts ostensibly committed to closing achievement and opportunity gaps, and supporting the success of all students, ethnic expectations identify some, but not other, Black students for concentrated attention and investment. Instead of relying on race, teachers, and school officials at times resort to ethnicity as a default device for predicting students' futures. In various parts of New York, Black Caribbean students are believed to be "more likely to live up to their potential than the typical African American or Latino kid," as one teacher put it. In London, the same assumption is increasingly made about West African students, but not Black Caribbeans.[34]

On both sides of the Atlantic, ethnic expectations are marked by an inherent irony: the strategy of selecting specific ethnic groups among Black students is a racial trick that reinforces myths of Black pathology, elevating a select Black group while maintaining the marginalization of the majority. Ethnic expectations legitimate the notion that racist perceptions of Blackness, structural constraints, and institutional racism do not limit students' advancement. Rather, as some scholars contend and the white public often believes, differing cultural resources and values, coupled with positive or negative orientations toward schools and hard work, shape Black students' outcomes.[35] *The Culture Trap* calls these and related claims into question.

Ethnic expectations matter because these judgments constrain students' educational experiences, distort the perceptions and representations of their cultural identities, and often impinge on their well-being—invoking frustration, anger, and stress. By examining the lived experiences of second-generation Black Caribbean young people in public schools, *The Culture Trap* illuminates the dynamics of what sociologist Ann Swidler referred to as "culture in action"[36] encountered by Black Caribbean students in London and New York City, showing how ethnic expectations function as a culture trap. This ethnography reveals the dominant beliefs, historical factors, and taken-for-granted school structures that limit educational equity and justice for Black students.

Cultural Explanations of Racial and Ethnic Inequalities

Racial and ethnic inequalities in schools remain stubborn barriers to equity and justice in society. For decades, researchers, policymakers, and educational leaders have tried to identify and eliminate the factors that reproduce unequal educational achievement, particularly on the basis of race, ethnicity, gender, and class.[37] Perspectives that center culture as a major contributing factor to racial and ethnic inequalities gained traction in Britain and the United States during the mid-20th century. The critical examination of these all-too-common explanations has afforded us important insights into the debates regarding the relative influence of culture versus structure in generating and perpetuating inequality;[38] the racialized misrepresentations of specific ethnic cultures from deficit perspectives;[39] and the strategies of reproduction and resistance adopted by ethno-racial minority students.[40] *The Culture Trap* builds on these key themes and highlights the interrelationship between culture and social structure.

The most widespread cultural explanation of racial and ethnic inequalities reveals the implications of prioritizing culture over structure as *the* principal factor determining educational achievement. The culture of poverty thesis popularized by US sociologist and politician Daniel Patrick Moynihan in 1965 has long misrepresented the impoverishment of African American families as a matter of pathological cultural patterns, rather than government policies and socioeconomic structures.[41] The same culture of poverty thesis emerged in Britain in the late 1960s and the 1970s following British politician Enoch Powell's attempts to explain the deprivation of immigrant and nonwhite families, especially those from the Caribbean.[42] Culturalists like Moynihan and Powell undermined the power of structure in shaping group experiences and outcomes. Structuralists, on the other hand, have questioned the outsized influence attributed to culture in generating inequality, but have inadvertently reproduced the misrepresentation they critiqued by underestimating the power of culture that informs groups' distinct social experiences.[43]

The structure-versus-culture dichotomy in public debates limits our understanding of the interrelated factors that shape and reproduce the educational underachievement of historically disadvantaged groups. In this book, I show how historical forces, school structures, *and* cultural meaning-making strategies matter in the lived experiences of Black youth. This analysis suggests that we must pursue solutions that transform both structure and culture.

Another key cultural explanation contends that inequality is exacerbated by framing select Asian and European ethnic cultures as assets while frequently representing a monolithic Black culture as a liability linked to oppositional, anti-school orientations. Asian and European ethnic cultures are associated with the 'power of different cultures,' whereas Black ethnic cultures are frequently tied to the 'problem of different cultures.'[44] This contrast is depicted and unpacked in British anthropologist Susan Benson's classic essay, "Asians Have Culture, West Indians Have Problems."[45]

Perhaps the clearest and most common example of this theme is the ongoing reinforcement of the model minority myth[46]—a claim that Chinese, Korean, Japanese, and Indian people in Britain and the United States are exemplary minorities with 'good cultures' because of their academic and occupational success. Like ethnic expectations, the model minority myth is an example of the culture trap. Although it is clear that these groups, as well as the individuals within them, differ in their levels of educational and economic attainment, the model minority myth inspires widely accepted, false notions of what can be expected of Asians in general.[47]

In contrast, discussions of academic achievement gaps routinely frame Black students, particularly African American students in the United States and Black Caribbeans in Britain, as underachieving minorities with 'bad cultures' relative to their white and Asian counterparts—or, in the words of sociologist Antonia Randolph, as "the wrong kind of different."[48] Such perspectives reinforce low expectations of Black students, especially historically disadvantaged groups like African Americans in the United States and Black Caribbeans in Britain.[49]

These discourses do not consistently account for the relationship between purportedly 'model groups' and 'failing groups,' much less recognize that the framing of a model group is often contingent on the presence of a failing one. Furthermore, the complex expectations shaping ethno-racial groups that do not fit neatly into these discursive categories remain largely unrecognized. In order to capture the mix of elevation and demotion that ethno-racial groups negotiate, we need a less dichotomous conceptual frame. Ethnic expectations account for these nuances, which are often unaddressed by scholars even though they loom large to those directly affected by them. This cross-national ethnography illustrates how the differing historical and political contexts in Britain and the United States inform the historically opposing representations of Caribbean culture, as a liability in one case and an asset in the other.

Another significant cultural explanation of racial and ethnic inequalities in education focuses on the practices of conformity or resistance adopted by minoritized groups in schools and society. These perspectives aim to account for the attitudes, behaviors, and orientations that shape how minoritized racial, ethnic, and class groups experience public schools as state institutions.[50] Anthropologists John Ogbu and Signithia Fordham's theory of oppositional culture is emblematic of frameworks used to make meaning of Black youth's responses to inequality in schools.[51] Like sociologists Pierre Bourdieu and Stuart Hall, Ogbu and Fordham maintain that as marginalized youth resist inequalities in their schools through oppositional stances toward authority, they inadvertently reinforce and reproduce them.[52] In this ethnography, I show that resistance is not an ethnic orientation, but a strategic, situational response to unequal institutional arrangements in London and New York.

By exploring Black Caribbean young people's experiences of ethnic expectations, this book extends our understanding of how cultural explanations of racial and ethnic inequalities affect schooling. In the lived experiences of Black Caribbean young people in London and New York City, ethnic expectations are signature features of a nefarious process of splintering Black youth by ethnicity, and establishing status hierarchies among them that reinforce educational inequalities.[53] Caught in the culture trap, Akilah, Tom, and their Black Caribbean peers challenge the default, common-sense association between *their own* Black identities and expectations of both academic failure and achievement that lead educators to underinvest in these students and overemphasize correcting their behavior.

Beyond 'Good Cultures' and 'Bad Cultures'

The Culture Trap challenges the interpretations of 'good cultures' and 'bad cultures' in Britain and the United States—interpretations that fail to consider the differing contexts in which cultures develop.[54] The comparison of Black Caribbeans in the United States and Britain brings into vivid focus the power of context in shaping perceptions of culture, challenging essentialist interpretations that represent ethnic cultures as singular or static. In the United States, Caribbean culture has historically functioned as a reputational resource—even an ethnic credit—in an attempt to displace racial stereotypes and delineate ethnic distinctions among Blacks.[55] In public discourse, Black Caribbeans have garnered positive recognition for their industriousness, immigrant 'grit,' and investment in education in the United States.[56] In Britain, by contrast, Black Caribbean culture is often presented negatively, as an ethnic penalty.[57]

Just as Paul Willis signaled in *Learning to Labor*,[58] a study of how white working-class young people in a British comprehensive secondary school got working-class jobs in the 1970s, Black Caribbeans in Britain are the reference group from which other disadvantaged groups often seek to distance themselves.[59] Willis asserted: "Certainly in the case of some young second generation West Indians, their cultural responses and processes can be likened to those of 'the lads,'" a group of white working-class boys with strong anti-school attitudes. "They also . . . inherit from the West Indies a culture of wagelessness and poverty. It appears to them as if there is a viable possibility of surviving without wages." In Britain, "as structural unemployment becomes a permanent feature of this society and some sections of white youth are forced into long term unemployment, there may well develop a white ethnic culture of wagelessness (borrowing very likely from the West Indian one)."[60]

Such perspectives, offered in one of the most celebrated British ethnographies of class, power, and schooling, shored up the culture of poverty thesis developing rapidly in 1970s Britain and reinforced dominant representations of British-born second-generation Black Caribbeans.[61] Inadvertently, Willis's account frames Caribbean and Caribbean diasporic cultures in deficit terms and reduces the experiences of second-generation Black Caribbean young people to a set of stereotypes.

Sociologist Mary Waters's *Black Identities*, perhaps the most popular, in-depth study of Black Caribbeans in New York, unwittingly reinforces negative representations of African American youth, albeit in a subtler manner than Willis's representation of Black Caribbean youth. Critics have suggested that Waters framed African Americans in deficit terms in her interview-based study, even as she explores the cultural identities and experiences of Black Caribbean immigrants and their children.[62] Commenting on Waters's book, anthropologist Jemima Pierre argued that "her insistence on linking all African Americans to discussions of 'poverty,' the 'underclass,' the 'ghetto,' and as having an 'oppositional culture' perpetuates the most vulgar stereotypes."[63]

While Paul Willis's *Learning to Labor*, Mary Waters's *Black Identities*, Claire Alexander's *The Art of Being Black*, and Natasha Warikoo's *Balancing Acts* explore the cultural expressions and educational experiences of second-generation Black Caribbean youth in London and/or New York schools, these studies pay little or no attention to how memories of schooling in the (post) colonial Caribbean influence the children of immigrants in the diaspora.[64]

The Culture Trap points out that perceptions of schooling in the diaspora are shaped by formidable colonial empires in the homeland. Furthermore, *The Culture Trap* shows that combining the differing perspectives of teachers, administrators, parents, and students offers us fuller understandings of Black young people's cultural worlds.

To date, cross-national ethnographic analyses of Black youth in global cities remain sparse.[65] This is particularly curious given the predominance of the local/global frame in critical youth studies that elucidates the operation of global dynamics in local contexts. Cross-national studies of Black youth are of considerable political import because they challenge assumptions about the universality of local cultural conditions, question the durability of normative achievement hierarchies, and gesture toward the global architecture of racism within and beyond national particularities. Cross-national ethnographies of Black youth invite critical reflections on the productive ties and tensions between global phenomena and their local manifestations, between narratives of culture and the histories of structural inequality that often shape the future. *The Culture Trap* examines the cross-national character of racial and ethnic inequalities in public education as experienced by Black Caribbean youth, along with the limitations of explanations used to rationalize achievement outcomes as indicative of ethnic culture.

Examining the Cultural Politics of Schooling

Inspired by my discussion with Ms. Bell about the differences in Black Caribbean achievement in the United States and Britain (recounted in the preface), I collected rich empirical data at one of the most important cultural anchor institutions in global cities: public schools. No other public institution is as consistently influential in the lives of young people.[66] It is in schools that Black Caribbean students learn what Stuart Hall calls the power of culture,[67] and what Pierre Bourdieu regards as the culture of power.[68] I pursued a comparative ethnography in two of the largest public schools in London and New York City. Ethnography is a particularly valuable approach to understanding the beliefs and behaviors of Black Caribbean youth in the diaspora, the meaning-making that governs their worlds, and the rhythms of everyday life as these Black youth envisage and experience them. In this setting, we can see how the real and fictitious formulations of 'Caribbean culture' shape the social experiences and academic advancement of second-generation Black Caribbean youth.

During a total of 16 months of ethnographic fieldwork, I conducted 50 focus group interviews with second-generation Black Caribbean students and 134 one-on-one, in-depth interviews (60 with students, 40 with parents, 16 with teachers, and 18 with school administrators). Based on these diverse sources, *The Culture Trap* elucidates the limits of cultural narratives used as an analytical shorthand and politicized proxy for gauging and explaining the achievement of Black Caribbean youth in London and New York City. I focused on Black Caribbean people in London and New York City because of their history and demographics in these global cities. According to the 2011 UK Census, while Black Caribbeans constituted 1.1 percent of the British population, over 50 percent of them live in London.[69] And while statistical data on immigrant and second-generation Black Caribbeans as a share of the US population are hard to come by, the 2010 US Census indicated that more immigrant and second-generation Black Caribbeans live in New York City than in any other US city.[70] These data points guided my decision to focus on Black Caribbeans in London and New York City.

I began fieldwork in London and New York City wishing to paint rich, social portraits of urban schools in the lives of Black Caribbean young people, but left with fuller understandings of schools as racialized sites of power that influence the trajectories of second-generation youth negotiating their parents' host society as their homeland. I focused on two schools with substantial proportions of Black Caribbean students. Using pseudonyms to protect individual privacy and institutional confidentiality, I call them Newlands High School in New York City and Londerville Secondary School in London. The description of each school that follows aims to be sufficiently specific to contextualize what I observed and heard there, but sufficiently general to prevent either from being identified and perhaps suffering embarrassment and reprisals.

Newlands High in New York

Newlands High School is one of the largest public secondary schools in New York City. With a student body of over 1,000 and an average class size of 30, the school is located in a working-class neighborhood with middle-class pockets. Historically white Irish and Jewish, the area now has a consider-able number of Black Caribbean residents. In 2012, approximately 55 per-cent of its students identified as Black, a large proportion of whom were of Caribbean heritage; 2 percent were Asian; 1 percent were white; and the remaining 42 percent were Hispanic, primarily from Puerto Rico and the Dominican Republic. Approximately two-thirds of students were eligible for free school lunches, well above the state average of 55 percent. Thus, a sizable proportion of students came from economically disadvantaged households. Although the school was originally designed to draw pupils mainly from the local area, it pulled students from other sections of the borough because of its location and size.

In a city where dismantling large schools and turning them into 'small learning communities' is increasingly popular, Newlands High's size and structure make it a distinctive educational environment. This secondary school, like the handful of other large schools across the city, is not selec-tive. No special, subject-specific exams are required for admission; neither is prior high achievement in primary (K–5) and middle school (grades 6–8). With over 120 teachers, 8 assistant principals, and a seasoned, long-serving principal, the school offers a variety of specialized educational programs and courses that vary in rigor. Newlands is marked by a significant academic hi-erarchy, in which students are ranked according to students' scholastic per-formance, academic preparedness, and intellectual interests. From high school transition classes, special educational needs provisions, and language proficiency courses to pre-collegiate programs and Advanced Placement seminars in mathematics, the social sciences and humanities, the school caters to a wide range of students from grades 9 to 12.

Londerville Secondary in London

Londerville Secondary shares some demographic and structural features with Newlands High. Londerville is one of the largest co-educational, com-prehensive schools in London. Secondary schools in the borough have an average of 700 students from Year 7 to 11,[71] but Londerville has over 1,000. Though Londerville Secondary and its surrounding area have tradition-ally served the white working class, there has been a marked increase in the number of Black Caribbeans and Africans living in the area over the past 20 years. In 2012, the student body was majority white (50.5 percent), but rapidly diversifying. Members of ethno-racial minority groups constituted 46.2 percent of the student body, with students of Caribbean descent forming the largest single group. In 2012, one-third of the pupils were eligible for free school meals, well above the national average of 18 percent. Similar to Newlands, the surrounding neighborhood has a mix of working-class and middle-class residents. The school draws students from South London. Londerville's high proportion of Black Caribbean and economically disadvantaged pupils makes it comparable to Newlands in New York.

Londerville is a non-selective school, as its admission requirements are non-academic. Like Newlands, it has over 100 teachers, 9 assistant and deputy headteachers, and a long-serving headteacher. The academic hierarchy among students is even more distinct at Londerville than at Newlands. This stratification has a significant impact on the student body and peer relations. Most students are divided by Years (7–11) and ranked by sets according to GCSE subject preferences and educational attainment.[72] The curriculum is marked not only by considerable breadth, but also by varying degrees of rigor, as special needs classes and remedial sessions were offered in a number of subject areas. The diversity of the students and course offerings leaves room for a wide range of social, cultural, and scholastic experiences.

Comparing Contexts

Given the marked similarities between Londerville Secondary and Newlands High in size, structure, demographic composition, and location within their respective cities, these schools are appropriate sites for a comparative analysis of the cultural and educational experiences of Black Caribbean students. Throughout this work, context refers not only to social space, but also to the historical, cultural, and political dynamics that give these settings such multiplex meanings. As cultural geographer Jon Anderson points out, "Context can influence what actions we choose to make and how we choose to make them, it can influence how these actions are judged by ourselves and others, and thus how successful and significant they turn out to be. Context is therefore vital to take notice of and understand, yet in everyday life it is something we often ignore."[73] As this ethnography reveals, context influences and is influenced by the cultural identification and sense-making strategies of Black Caribbean young people.[74] Moreover, this book illuminates *how* school context matters differently for Black Caribbean youth in London and New York

City public schools by calling attention to institutional mechanisms such as academic 'ability' grouping that differ in their formulation and function.

The analyses of Londerville Secondary in London and Newlands High in New York advanced in this ethnography build upon and extend Stuart Hall's critical consideration of race, culture, and diaspora by considering schools as central sites of cultural construction and contestation. They also draw on and deepen Pierre Bourdieu's conceptualization of the reproduction of cultural and class inequalities in schools by exploring race as an always already contributing dimension of class relations.[75] The fusion of these two theoretical perspectives affords us a critical sociology of culture that is just as sensitive to race and racialization as it is to class and social positioning. By comparing different public schools in London and New York City, this book demonstrates why scholars, policymakers, and educators must address racial and ethnic inequalities in relation to their sociocultural context.

Form, Voice, and the Power of Cultural Flexibility

The Culture Trap is written in a tradition of storytelling sociology, a mode of writing that invites readers to *listen* to participants' stories for themselves, to consider participants' own words and sense-making, and to appreciate how Black Caribbean young people, their parents, peers, and teachers voice critical perspectives about schools and society in their everyday lives.[76] In this regard, this book is not a traditional academic text. In keeping with this storytelling tradition, I quote participants at length, layer their sometimes-colorful comments in one-on-one and focus group interviews with systematic observations, and enrich these perspectives with archival records to tell a multidimensional story about the historical and contemporary complexities of ethnic expectations.

In its richest and most substantive form, listening requires close, careful attention to substance and style, voices and viewpoints, arguments and accents in the analytical and sonic registers. This kind of listening is a method that Stuart Hall considered necessary for understanding the social world and those who traverse it, as noted in his provocative *Familiar Stranger: A Life Between Two Islands*.[77] Storytelling sociology also proved to be a method of analytical engagement for Pierre Bourdieu, and is perhaps best exemplified in his popular *The Weight of the World*, which draws on close readings of individual narratives to illuminate structural and institutional conditions.[78] But truth be told, Stuart Hall and Pierre Bourdieu did not provide the impetus for my use of storytelling sociology in this book. I marshal this analytical strategy to honor the voices and (counter)cultural views of Black Caribbean young people and their parents on both sides of the Atlantic.

Throughout my fieldwork, I noticed that storytelling proved a key method for describing, debating, and deconstructing ethnic expectations between parents and teachers, between teachers and pupils, and between Black Caribbean pupils and their co-ethnic peers. Storytelling was not merely an articulation of specific racialized accounts; it was also an accessible strategy for negotiating and resisting ethnic expectations in everyday life. It seemed fitting, then, to take my cue from Black Caribbean parents and young people, and marshal storytelling as a key feature of this cross-national account. I also deploy storytelling to exemplify what Caribbean anthropologist David Scott refers to as "practicing discerning and engaged thinking-with-others."[79] This approach invites readers not only to be privy to the co-construction of meanings in social situations, but also, as Caribbean anthropologist Deborah Thomas puts it, "to bear witness with all its attendant complexities and complications" through hearing, sensing, and feeling what participants experience in their daily lives.[80]

Central to my work as an ethnographer, storyteller, and writer is the power of cultural flexibility—the strategic cultural and political practice of adjusting language, attitude, and behavior according to our audiences, circumstances, and settings. At its core, cultural flexibility is an exercise of power, creativity, and social awareness often used in everyday life to negotiate the nuances of race and culture. For me and the Black Caribbean participants whose voices animate these chapters, the choice of whose form of English to speak; which English grammar to follow; which Caribbean language or dialect to use; which accent to summon; and which styles, tastes, and expressions to draw on (Caribbean, American, British, African, standard, vernacular, or otherwise) often depends on local and situational contexts.

In this book, I have strategically retained the original linguistic, attitudinal, and behavioral expressions of participants—without doctoring them to conform to formal academic conventions for rendering speaking as if it were writing—in order to invite readers into participants' ways of being and knowing across cultural, institutional, and diasporic settings. In my use of storytelling and cultural flexibility throughout The Culture Trap, I address a perennial question that animated Stuart Hall's and Pierre Bourdieu's work: what is the relationship between the personal and the political, between the public and the private, between the past and the present, and belief and behavior? This ethnography suggests that the answers to this question are rooted in how a person is *positioned* in society.

I am positioned in this work, too. As a Black Caribbean man born and raised in Jamaica who moved to New York City during adolescence and later studied in Cambridge, England, and worked in London, I experienced ethnic expectations from teachers during my time as a public high school student in New York, but didn't have the language to name it. Teachers made occasional public references to my 'Caribbean background' as the reason for my 'good behavior' and 'hard work.' Some issued biting critiques of second-generation Black Caribbean students underperforming in classes and praised others who excelled. But it was the subtle, under- or unstated expectations from teachers that I would get top marks in honors classes and that my parents and my Caribbean friends' parents would be hard-nosed disciplinarians that struck me then. Teachers and students at Newlands reported hearing similar comments. Yet the piercing, public remarks from teachers like Mr. Sterling seemed more intense. I undertook school-based ethnographic fieldwork and 500 hours of classroom observations to better understand the dynamics associated with ethnic expectations.

Throughout the course of my fieldwork, I straddled the boundary between being an insider and an outsider.[81] I often occupied a 'third space' at their intersection, which Stuart Hall referred to as being "a familiar stranger."[82] At times I nursed a sense of being in and of Jamaica, New York, and London, but at other points, I did not—or not enough. Even though the shifting positions entailed in hybridity often felt like a painful surprise, accompanied by periods of cultural disorientation, the experience was also a gift, enabling me to float between constituencies of varying power, between pupils and parents, schools and streets, homeland and diaspora. As I explain in the appendix, I am also different from most school ethnographers because I was first a community organizer who, through personal and professional connections, developed relationships with students and teachers at Londerville Secondary in London and Newlands High in New York before I even conceived this study. The relationships I had with students, teachers, and leaders in both schools affected the kind and quality of access I gained to sites ranging from classrooms to sports fields, where discussions of culture occurred as part of students' everyday lives. My role as a community organizer-turned-school ethnographer prepared me for the ethnographic journey this book recounts.

Roadmap for the Ethnographic Journey

In *The Culture Trap*, I examine how Black Caribbean students' achievement prospects in London and New York City are imagined by educators, understood by parents, and experienced by students. I pursue this analysis in two specific ways. In Part I of the book, "Constructing the Culture Trap," Chapters 1, 2, and 3, I examine the historical and political context in which ethnic expectations emerged. Chapter 1 traces the development and dynamics of ethnic expectations through public and educational discourses about Black Caribbean people as model minorities in the United States and failing minorities in Britain. I examine the significant political and historical differences in the public representation and social positioning of Black Caribbeans in the United States and Britain. I show that the positioning of Black Caribbean people in Britain and the United States was at times a strategic exercise of the state—not merely the result of culture, as is often assumed.

Chapter 2 highlights the perceptions of schooling that Black Caribbean immigrant parents brought to their new host societies based on the colonial architecture of British schooling in the Caribbean. In the United States, parents considered schooling in the Caribbean more intellectually intensive than in New York, with more required classes, more advanced assignments, more stringent grading, and stricter rules for behavior. Caribbean parents held high expectations of their American-born children, pushing them to excel in school because they often presumed that the US educational system is inferior to that on the islands based on dominant media representations of failing urban public schools. In contrast, Caribbean immigrant parents in London expected better educational opportunities for their children and felt prepared to pursue them because of their familiarity with British schooling through colonialism. The familiarity they assumed, along with the quality of the facilities they observed, made them initially more excited, less vigilant, and less assertive about the education of their children in London than their counterparts in New York.

For second-generation Black Caribbean young people on both sides of the Atlantic, ethnic expectations in schools are reproduced through academic 'ability' grouping. Chapter 3 analyzes the differing 'ability' grouping mechanisms that shape students' educational experiences. In New York, students are grouped by their perceived ability in a relatively flexible subject-by-subject tracking process, which allows Caribbean students access to advanced classes and content in a range of courses and grades. Although the 'ability' grouping process in London—referred to as setting in Britain—is flexible in principle, in practice Caribbean students experienced it as a rigid process, sorting them into sets in core subjects over multiple years. I demonstrate that 'ability' grouping is a significant mediating factor in the reproduction of ethnic expectations and educational inequality.

In Part II, "Negotiating the Culture Trap," Chapters 4, 5, and 6, I explore the cultural worlds of second-generation Black Caribbean youth and examine how they make sense of ethnic expectations. I show how ethnic expectations reproduce dominant cultural beliefs about ethno-racial groups. I begin by considering the perceived value of *distinctiveness*, an orienting belief and strategic resource that Black Caribbean students summon to resist stigmatization and reposition themselves individually or collectively to attain higher status, positive recognition, and power. These students attribute meritocratic ideals to Caribbean culture, often conflating class privileges with cultural heritage. This chapter highlights the ways in which social class has a secret life in representations of ethnic culture that is often ignored in public discourse.

The next chapter explores the importance of *deference*—a commitment to 'good attitudes' and 'proper behavior' in order to earn positive recognition from school officials and showcase their stellar character as Black students. Students who adhere to this strategy prioritize their parents' teachings on 'having manners,' 'being obedient,' and 'respecting your elders.' But in the lived experiences of Black Caribbean students, deference is shaped by racialized gender norms. In both London and New York City, Black Caribbean males who practice deference are recognized by educators as exemplary Black boys, while Black Caribbean females who subscribe to the same orientation are undermined by their teachers and peers, who dismiss these qualities displayed by Black Caribbean girls as them "just being girls." Not only does this chapter highlight how ethnic expectations regulate behavior, but it also shows how racialized gender norms are often concealed under the guise of 'Caribbean culture.'

Chapter 6 considers *defiance* as understood by Black Caribbean young people who actively challenge negative stereotypes of their race and ethnicity. They raise questions about racism in schools and point out that ethnic expectations contribute to inequality. But even as these students call attention to the relationship between ethnic expectations and cultural racism when it is harmful to them, they are seldom critical when they benefit from it—when ethnic expectations position them as better than a more marginalized group.

These contradictions often influence life in a range of ethnic communities and in a host of social institutions. This chapter reveals how ethnic expectations in schools reinforce the categorization of students based on race and ethnicity.

The Culture Trap concludes with a conversation with Ms. Bell about the importance of considering culture and structure in the educational experiences of Black Caribbean youth. After synthesizing the key findings of this study, I highlight the cultural, structural, and political challenges faced by school teachers and administrators in London and New York City that lead to the reproduction of inequalities, even when educators strive to provide equal opportunities for all. Addressing these and related factors effectively is vital for dismantling the culture trap—instead of simply freeing some from its snare.

PART I

CONSTRUCTING
THE CULTURE TRAP

1

Model and Failing Minorities?

Divergent Representations of Black Caribbean Achievement

"Pastor Williams, this is the young man I was telling you about," Ms. Bell said. The Reverend stood up from his chair, pushed his glasses from the tip of his nose to the top of its bridge and gave me a firm handshake.

"Oooh, this is the young man from America!" he said.

"I'm actually from Jamaica, Pastor Williams!"

He laughed and said, "Me too! Which part ah yaad yuh com' fram [Which part of Jamaica are you from]?"

Later, Reverend Williams, Ms. Bell, and I reminisced about the Jamaica we remembered; about how much we missed Julie mangoes, naseberries, and Otaheite apples; and about how much we longed for warm weather year-round. It was a bonding ritual of nostalgia common among immigrants in the Caribbean diaspora.

I had joined Ms. Bell for her Saturday school near Clapham Common, held in the social hall of Reverend Williams's church. Ms. Bell invited me to "work with our young people, and meet some of the parents to hear what's really going on in our schools." Her invitation to visit her supplementary school was a priceless gift. It was a backstage pass to the interior worlds of Black education for Caribbean young people in Britain—a world beyond the purview of the state where veteran Black teachers; passionate parent volunteers; and driven though sometimes chatty Black Caribbean and ethnic minority young people gathered for hours at a time to learn, study, and support one another.

"You're going to work with some of our Caribbean boys, right?" Reverend Williams asked.

"Yes man!" Ms. Bell said. This was news to me.

"Good!" Reverend Williams replied.

"I'm happy to help out," I said.

Before I could finish telling the elderly pastor about my plans to understand the educational experiences of Black Caribbean children in London,

The Culture Trap. Derron Wallace, Oxford University Press. © Oxford University Press 2023.
DOI: 10.1093/oso/9780197531464.003.0002

Ms. Bell chimed in and recounted what I had told her about the education of Black Caribbean children in the United States.

He paused. I watched him move his eyes from left to right over and over again, seemingly deep in thought. "That's really interesting," he eventually remarked.

"Mi tink so tu [I think so too]," Ms. Bell said.

"A wah cause dat [What caused that]?" he continued, referring to the differing experiences of Black Caribbean people in the United States and Britain.

"A dat mi wah fyn' out [That's what I'd like to find out]," Ms. Bell added.

I told them that I planned on spending a year in schools in London and New York in order to understand the contradictory representations of Black Caribbean young people. Pastor Williams gave me his own bit of advice: "Make sure you study our history. There is a lot that we forget about education for Caribbean people in this country." When he began reeling off names of books, activists, and authors, I took out another notebook and wrote down what he suggested I read, including youth worker Bernard Coard's *How the West Indian Child Is Made Educationally Sub-normal in the British School System*.[1]

"Subnormal? Ah wah dat yuh jus' seh [What is that you just said]?" I asked.

"Yes," Reverend Williams and Ms. Bell replied in unison.

"That's what the government used to call us when I just came here," Reverend Williams continued.

"What?! Fi real? How com' nuh bady neva tell mi dis before [For real? How come nobody told me about this before]?

"You have a lot to learn, young man," Reverend Williams replied.

After my time at Londerville Secondary in London and Newlands High School in New York, I realized that Pastor Williams's comments were as relevant to the United States as they were to Britain. I had a lot to learn—and history would be an important teacher. This chapter points to the historical and contemporary uses of culture as an interpretive tool to explain Black Caribbean educational achievement. The chapter may initially seem like a detour from the contemporary situation, but looking at the past reveals the sources and signature features of the divergent social constructions and political representations of Black Caribbean culture and identities.

Divergent Representations

In what follows, I critically examine cultural narratives of Black Caribbeans as a Black model minority in the United States and as an underachieving Black minority in Britain. Immigration policies, racialized educational practices, and politically charged public discourses shaped the divergent representations of Black Caribbean young people on different sides of the Black Atlantic.[2] Placing these contrasting perspectives on Black Caribbean achievement in historical context offers sensitizing insights into the origins and operation of these claims, and attunes us to the ways in which common-sense conceptions "create the folklore of the future," as sociologist Stuart Hall suggested.[3]

I do not mean to suggest that these cultural narratives were the only ones advanced about Black Caribbeans in either country during the 20th century. Indeed, at various junctures, competing, disconfirming perspectives emerged based on the structural racism, targeted nativism, and overt xenophobia that Black Caribbeans encountered in British and American society.[4] During the 1980s and 1990s, for instance, US media and government agencies at the local and national levels paid considerable attention to dismantling 'Jamaican Posses' in New York City. Sociologist Philip Kasinitz maintains that, in response to violent crime by 'ethnic gangs' in Caribbean enclaves of New York City, the police targeted Black Caribbean youth and depicted Black Caribbean men as particularly dangerous.[5] These representations trouble the Black model minority trope, the claim that Black Caribbean people in the United States are a model of success among Black people, distinguished from African Americans based on their occupational and educational attainment.[6] Similarly, in Britain, recent immigrants from the Caribbean have occasionally been praised as an exemplary group. Sociologist David Gillborn highlights the brief celebration of Caribbean immigrant pupils from Montserrat who, after fleeing their homeland due to the eruptions of the Soufriere Hills volcano in 1995, resettled in Britain and excelled in select London schools.[7] But these views were only intermittent interruptions of the long-standing master narratives about Caribbean achievement in the two countries, whose historical significance, lingering presence, and embeddedness in schooling gives them enduring power today.[8]

Model Minorities? Narratives of Caribbean Achievement in the United States

Black Caribbean immigrants were never model minorities. They were *Black* model minorities, compared largely, if not exclusively, to other Black ethnic groups.[9] The Black model minority thesis emerged in the late 20th century to explain the relative socioeconomic success of Black Caribbean immigrants,[10] who outpaced their African American counterparts in employment, earnings, and education.[11] Yet myths about Black Caribbean ethnic distinctiveness have figured in public discourses since the 1880s, and have been used symbolically and strategically to undermine claims about the significance of racism.[12] What often appeared to Black Caribbean immigrants as objective attempts to account for differences in their accents, achievements, and supposed command of the Queen's English as an expression of 'highbrow' cultural taste served a racialized purpose. In this regard, ethnicity functioned as a source of what sociologist Pierre Bourdieu referred to as "distinction" to differentiate Black people.[13] Narratives of ethnic distinctiveness were often used to splinter Black political power, maintain white supremacy, advance claims of the purported cultural deficiency of African Americans, and deflect attention from the varied forms of anti-Black discrimination that African Americans and Black immigrants both endured.[14]

US census records show that Black Caribbeans, who constitute the largest share of Black immigrants in the United States to date, have traveled to the United States involuntarily and voluntarily since the early 17th century, albeit in limited numbers prior to 1900.[15] Most Black Caribbeans in the United States before the 20th century were highly skilled professionals—doctors, teachers, skilled artisans, entrepreneurs, clergy, and lawyers.[16] Some arrived as students, such as the noted abolitionist and publisher John B. Russwurm, from Port Antonio, Jamaica, who is widely regarded as "one of the first three black people to graduate from an American college" in 1826,[17] and recognized as the co-founder of "the first Afro-American newspaper in 1827."[18] Other distinguished Black Caribbeans were elected to the US Congress during Reconstruction.[19] The visibility of well-educated and accomplished Black Caribbeans contributed to the skewed public perceptions of Black Caribbeans as a Black model minority, misrepresenting these immigrants' class advantages as the products of, or synonymous with, their ethnic culture.[20]

These views gained strength as the flow and diversity of Black Caribbean immigrants increased markedly after the turn of the 20th century.[21] The vast majority settled along the northeastern seaboard, particularly in Harlem, which the *Amsterdam News* called "the largest West Indian city in the world" besides Kingston, Jamaica.[22] In New York City, and in the company of their African American counterparts—who had been systematically marginalized through centuries-long enslavement, Jim Crow segregation, and legalized educational, and occupational disadvantage—Black Caribbeans contributed to a dynamic Black diasporic society formed at the crossroads of migration and immigration, (anti)colonialism and (anti)capitalism, white supremacy as a cardinal feature of US nation building, and the pursuit of Black liberation as an international political project.[23]

Owing to their rapid establishment of mutual aid and benevolent associations, civic and employment alliances, small businesses, and religious organizations in New York City during the early 20th century, Black Caribbean people were stereotyped as 'business geniuses,' 'cultural heroes,' 'social lions,' 'paragons of intelligence,' and 'representative Negroes' whose accomplishments challenged white preconceptions of Black inferiority.[24] Recognition of their wide-ranging contributions to the literary, creative and performing arts, business, politics, and academia amid widespread anti-Black racism and xenophobia led noted African American poet Fenton Johnson to assert that "in every field of our American life we find the West Indian pushing ahead and doing all in his power to uphold the dignity of the Negro race. In every industry, in every profession, in every trade, we find this son of the islands holding aloft the banner of Ethiopia."[25] In praise of Black Caribbeans' radical activism along with their professional and economic achievements, renowned poet Langston Hughes asserted that Black Caribbeans were "warm, rambunctious, sassy . . . [with] tropical dreams on their tongue."[26]

One of the most prominent articulations of Black Caribbean achievement in the United States came from pioneering African American sociologist W. E B. Du Bois, who in 1923 told Jamaican activist-journalist Wilfred A. Domingo that "I, myself, am of West Indian descent and am proud of that fact."[27] Commenting on the presence and contributions of Black Caribbeans to multiethnic Black Harlem in the September 1920 issue of *The Crisis* magazine, Du Bois wrote:

> It is this mass of peasants, uplifted by war and migration that is today beginning to assert itself at home and abroad and their new cry of 'Africa for the Africans' strikes with a startling surprise upon America's darker millions.

The movement is as yet inchoate and indefinite, but it is tremendously human, piteously sincere and built in the souls of hardworking, thrifty, independent people who while long deprived of higher training nevertheless have among them very few illiterates or criminals. It is not beyond possibility that this new Ethiopia of the Isles may yet stretch out hands of helpfulness to the 12 million black men of America.[28]

In assessing the meaning and merits of Du Bois's assertion, Black feminist historian Irma Watkins-Owens asks, "But who were these newcomers whom Du Bois described as 'this mass of peasants'?"[29]

Obscuring Class

Although the majority of Black Caribbean immigrants who arrived in New York City in the early 20th century were literate working-class men and women, others were members of the middle classes with economic, cultural, and social capital that aided their incorporation into American society.[30] If Du Bois's comments are not properly situated in context, they can be considered a form of ethnic distinctiveness that renders Caribbean immigrants exceptional in character relative to their US–born Black peers. In fact, however, Du Bois's comments express his internationalist politics and deep commitment to the inclusion of all Black people throughout the African diaspora, including the full range of cultural and class backgrounds that informed their lives in colonial contexts. His recognition of "this new Ethiopia of the Isles" came, as literary scholar Louis Parascandola pointed out, just a few weeks after the inaugural convention of the pan-Africanist United Negro Improvement Association led by Marcus Garvey and Amy Ashwood, both of whom were Jamaican.[31] Du Bois's praise was predicated on the emergence of Black Caribbeans in New York City as a political force. While Du Bois recognized the contributions of the nearly 37,000 Black Caribbean immigrants to the political struggle for racial justice in the United States and celebrated their radical commitment to Black freedom locally and globally,[32] his remarks inadvertently contributed to a discursive tradition of celebrating high achievement among Black Caribbeans in the United States without fully acknowledging the social and political conditions that shaped who came and how they were received.

Noted civil rights activist and poet James Weldon Johnson, who was of Bahamian and African American parentage and is best known for authoring "Lift Every Voice and Sing," praised Black Caribbeans in *Black Manhattan*.[33] He argued that these immigrants "are characteristically sober-minded and have something of a genius for business, differing almost totally in these respects from the average rural Negro from the south."[34] Claims like Johnson's reinforce the power of the culture trap. These appeals ascribe the performance of ethnic groups to their distinct cultures without accounting for the social conditions that shape them. Johnson attributed Caribbean success to there being "practically no illiteracy among them" with many having "a sound common school education."[35] Yet the high literacy rate among Black Caribbean immigrants was the result of the 1917 Immigration Act, which made literacy a prerequisite for admission to the United States. As cultural historian Winston James asserts, that policy "ensured that the early stream of Caribbean migrants would be selected from a narrow stratum of Caribbean society," which typically included highly skilled workers of a generally high socioeconomic status.[36] State policies created class distinctions between Caribbean immigrants and African Americans, which were then misrepresented as evidence of cultural differences. Without a sense of the policies that shaped the positions of Black Caribbeans, we run the risk of overemphasizing the role of culture, obscuring the influence of social class and failing to recognize the impact of social structure.

Tracing early 20th-century narratives of Black Caribbean educational history in the United States, historian Winston James highlights how the pre-migration class advantages of Jamaican immigrants such as J. Alexander Somerville, who became the first Black graduate of the University of Southern California with a degree in dentistry, and Ira Ferguson, who graduated from Columbia University with a doctoral degree in clinical psychology, contributed to their success.

Both Somerville and Ferguson were of solid Jamaican middle-class background, and thus received an excellent secondary education. It was not from scratch, but from this sound educational foundation that they ascended in the United States. That—their class and educational background—was the key distinction between them and the Afro-American population generally, not their Caribbean "culture," per se.[37]

That fact was evident to contemporaneous Black observers. Carter G. Woodson, African American historian and founder of Negro History Week, which we now know as Black History Month, emphasized the role of Black Caribbeans' educational backgrounds in enabling their advancement. In *The Negro Professional Man and the Community*, Woodson argued that Caribbean immigrants' education in the islands "had a telling effect in the advantage which these West Indian trained students have had over Negro medical students who have been handicapped by the lack of thorough training in the backward parts of this country."[38]

These comparisons were made during the immigration of the first major wave of Black Caribbeans to New York City between 1890 and 1930 and the simultaneous migration of African Americans from the US South to Harlem,[39] which became the center of Black cultural production and political organizing in New York.[40] Due to the power of residential segregation, cultural narratives of Black Caribbean success emerged largely as a peculiar New York story with a national reach. Notions of Black Caribbean ethnic distinctiveness developed in this global city through comparisons with African Americans laboring for decades under the constraints of Jim Crow.[41] At this time, Black Caribbeans were lauded as an exemplary Black minority worthy of emulation, creating what sociologist Cecilia Ridgeway calls "performance expectations,"[42] which when based on ethnicity, I call ethnic expectations. Although praise narratives about Black Caribbeans have varied throughout the 20th century, representations of Caribbean ethnic distinctiveness were sustained, at least in part, by the commentary of Black political leaders and the centuries-long serial stigmatization and structural subordination of African Americans.

As the second major stream of Caribbean immigrants arrived between 1932 and 1965, Black Caribbean success became the focus of social scientific research.[43] In his pathbreaking work, *The Negro Immigrant: His Background Characteristics and Social Adjustment, 1899–1937*, sociologist Ira De A. Reid examined the demographic composition, social life, and economic contributions of Black Caribbeans.[44] Reid described Black Caribbean immigrants as more 'entrepreneurial', 'radical', 'scholarly', and 'diligent' than native-born Black Americans. He pointed out that as many as one-third of New York's Black professionals, including doctors and lawyers, were born in the Caribbean. Rather than offering a cultural explanation, Reid maintained that "the selective migration of the better educated West Indians has been a factor in the relatively high proportion of honors they have obtained in schools of the United States."[45] Nonetheless, Reid's inadvertent conclusion contributed to a line of social scientific research that continued to privilege Black Caribbeans with a positive ethnic reputation, a reputation often based on their class advantages.[46]

Using Culture to Obscure Racism

The celebration of Black Caribbean immigrants in the early to mid-20th century was not simply about the recognition of Black ethnic diversity, as was arguably the case for Du Bois. Claims of ethnic distinctiveness were marshaled as part of ongoing projects of racial uplift in ways comparable to the strategy of pronouncing well-off and well-educated Black people as a 'credit to the race.'[47] Caribbean immigrants' economic success, institution building, and political leadership in New York City were summoned as examples of what Blacks were capable of under different structural conditions, from different national contexts, and with different 'cultural values.' Ethnic distinctiveness was used to thwart anti-Blackness, but as we shall soon see, ethnic distinctiveness reinforced racism even as it aimed to resist it.

As the third and largest wave of Black Caribbean immigration to the United States began in the 1960s, an influential body of scholarship expanded the popular depiction of Black Caribbeans as a 'success story.'[48] Nathan Glazer and Daniel Patrick Moynihan's *Beyond the Melting Pot: The Negroes, Puerto Ricans, Jews, Italians and Irish* offered a controversial culturalist exploration of the demographic, social, and political transformation of New York City.[49] In their analysis, Glazer and Moynihan made interethnic comparisons that highlighted the differing representations of African Americans and Black Caribbeans. They argued that "the ethos of the West Indians, in contrast to the Southern Negro, emphasized saving, hard work, investment and education."[50] These highly polemical contrasts ignore the different structural factors and class conditions that shaped the trajectories of African Americans and Black Caribbeans in the United States. Glazer and Moynihan cited the success of Black Caribbeans as evidence of racism's declining significance, the power of culture for racial uplift, and the importance of holding mainstream values for determining group trajectories. For white conservatives like Glazer and Moynihan, these comparisons of cultures helped to legitimate political arguments about the limited value and efficacy of race-based public policies and helped to shore up white resistance to Black political and economic progress.[51]

Conservative African American economist Thomas Sowell extended Glazer and Moynihan's claims about Black Caribbean success with his article, "Ethnicity: Three Black Histories."[52] He emphasized cultural differences as the source and symptom of disparities among Black ethnic groups and downplayed the consequences of racial discrimination.[53] Sowell treated Black Caribbeans as an exemplary Black minority whose success resulted from their strong work ethic, male-headed two-parent families, economic self-reliance, and investment in education. In *Race and Economics*, Sowell highlighted Black Caribbeans' capacity for self-control, which he contrasted with representations of African Americans' 'characteristic' impulsivity, emotional expressiveness, and musicality. He asserted:

> West Indians emphasized such traits as work, thrift and education—more generally achievements involving planning and working for the future, implying the emotional control for self-denial in the present and emphasizing the logical and mundane over the emotional, the imaginative, and the heroic. The opposite characteristics can be seen among . . . American Negroes, where advancement can be achieved in . . . oratory, lyric literature and music.[54]

The distinction he accorded Black Caribbeans was predicated on the cultural degradation of African Americans. This trick is at the heart of the culture trap, and still has consequences for Black youth in schools today. These claims about the cultural differences between Black Caribbeans and African Americans proved both ideologically significant and politically expedient. Black Caribbeans function as a key reference case for conservatives seeking to downplay racism as a barrier to the advancement of Black people in the United States. If these immigrants and their children succeeded in similar contexts and under comparable racial conditions to African Americans, Sowell asserted, racism could hardly be the causal force. Instead, immigrant and second-generation Black Caribbeans served as "a test case of the explanatory importance of color, as such, in analyzing socioeconomic progress in the American economy and society, as compared to the importance of the cultural traditions of the American Negro."[55] Therefore, state-sponsored policies and programs addressing discrimination, like affirmative action, were arguably unnecessary—a key argument advanced by neoconservatives in the ongoing debate about the causes of racial inequality and the need for societal remedies. Like Glazer and Moynihan, Sowell marshaled the relative success of Black Caribbean immigrants as evidence of the declining significance of racism in the post-civil rights United States and pointed to culture as the decisive force that limited the advancement of African Americans.[56]

These controversial works fed into a political agenda that identified the 'culture of poverty' as chiefly responsible for the educational and economic disadvantages of African Americans.[57] Conservative commentators downplayed the significance of systemic racism,[58] reducing disadvantage to cultural pathologies exhibited by individuals and groups, rather than acknowledging that differential socioeconomic positions were a consequence of historical social forces.[59] As Black Caribbeans vied for elevated status in a context of anti-Black racism, they emphasized these patterns of employment, education, and political participation as signs of their ethnic distinctiveness. Some invested in being regarded as model minorities or as hard-working immigrants, often without realizing that these discursive formulations are selective suppositions or gross generalizations.[60]

With their claims of distinctiveness, Black Caribbeans exhibited what anthropologist J. Lorand Matory calls a "mode of schadenfreude, whereby a stigmatized population seeks relief from stigma by identifying a neighboring group as more worthy of the stigma."[61] As sociologist Vilna Bashi Treitler contends, claims of exceptionalism are features of "ethnic marketing campaigns" used to strategically alter racial perceptions.[62] It is from this politicized context that Black Caribbeans emerged as Black model minorities for whom there were distinct ethnic expectations.

These dubious assertions were bolstered by the fact that "every census of the US population since 1970 has shown that . . . black immigrants from the English-speaking Caribbean (West Indies) have higher labor force participation rates, higher employment rates and higher earnings than US–born Blacks."[63] These results have all too frequently been interpreted as reflections of cultural differences, rather than as expressions of immigrant selectivity, the order and timing of immigration, and educational disparities among Black people in the British and American Empires.[64] What is more, the educational attainment of Black Caribbeans was treated as both cause and consequence of their success in the labor market, when it is unclear whether or not their modest advantages in segments of the labor market necessarily reflect their levels of schooling.[65]

There is little empirical evidence to justify the claim that Black Caribbeans are high-achieving minorities in education, since US school districts analyze achievement data by race and seldom make ethnic distinctions among Black students. And of the available data from the Current Population Survey, as shown in Figure 1.1 for instance, the differences in educational attainment between Black Caribbeans and African Americans are either minor or non-existent. Despite this, the Black model minority myth has been powered for decades by perceptions of Caribbeans' economic and educational success.

Recent scholarship has questioned and contextualized this model of Black Caribbean success by calling attention to the role of uneven group comparisons in shoring up the myth. Political scientist Christina Greer, for instance, argues that Black Caribbeans are not model minorities, but elevated Black minorities; they are exceptional only when compared to the African American poor and working classes, not to Asians or whites.[66] Despite real and imagined cultural differences among Black ethnics, their realities are not substantially dissimilar within the ethno-racial order, given what political scientist Michael Dawson regards as the overarching 'linked fates' of Blacks in the US polity.[67] In her critique of the Black model minority myth, sociologist Suzanne Model reasons that success is "a consequence of choosing to move, not a consequence of Caribbean birth."[68] The positive selection of skilled and well-educated Black Caribbean immigrants, along with the ambition and drive shown by movers, should be carefully considered when comparing Black Caribbeans to African Americans.[69] In this view, Black

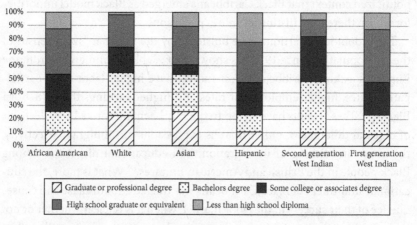

Figure 1.1   2017/2018 Educational attainment of New York City residents, Current Population Survey

Caribbean success is not due to their ethno-cultural heritage, but a result of their immigrant advantages.

Examining more recent data from the National Survey of American Life, sociologist Mosi Ifantunji finds similar patterns.[70] He points out that analyses emphasizing socioeconomic disparities are decontextualized and skewed. Sufficient attention is seldom paid to the fact that, unlike most immigrants to the United States, Black immigrants from the former British colonies in the Caribbean are native English speakers. When controlling for English language proficiency among Blacks, Ifantunji shows that Black Caribbeans do not necessarily fare better than their immigrant counterparts from Anglophone Africa.[71] What they possess is an *early* advantage over English-speaking Africans, which is based on Caribbeans' strong, long-standing networks and cultural institutions in places like New York City.[72] In light of these perspectives, it is clear that the measured success of Black Caribbeans in the United States is not a product of Black Caribbean culture, but an expression of their class background and an early advantage in positive contexts of reception.

The Black model minority thesis, then, is a symbolic distinction constructed on ideological lines and deployed for political purposes. It is an explicit reformulation of the myth long used to describe select groups of Asian Americans as success stories.[73] Yet the very use of the qualifier 'Black' signifies the unmistakable racial logics and limits of the term. The 'Black' preceding 'model minority' demarcates difference. On the other hand, 'Black' can also be mobilized as a diminishing or largely negative signifier as part of a linguistic maneuver reinforcing racialized hierarchies of intelligence. In both cases, whether provisional or pathological, the category 'Black' attached to model minority is an exercise in racialization, a rearticulation rather than a rejection of racial hierarchies.[74]

The Black model minority thesis finds its power from its appeal to various groups' interests: Black Caribbean immigrants' desire to maintain ethnic distinctiveness and resist negative stereotypes associated with economically disadvantaged African Americans; public fascination with the socioeconomic achievement and modest political prominence of Black Caribbeans throughout the 20th century; the conservative promotion of Black Caribbeans as exemplars whose existence confirms the diminishing significance of racism; and mounting public interest in the power of culture in shaping group success. These overlapping ideological struggles for recognition and the redistribution of resources, which emerge as competing ethno-nationalisms, erase the complexities of Black Caribbeans' experiences in the United States and undercut resurgent radical politics of Black solidarity.[75]

* * *

In order to further unsettle preconceptions of the role of culture in Black Caribbeans' educational and economic status, I turn to the development of the notion that Black Caribbeans in Britain are an underachieving minority. The differences between these traditions of representation and trajectories of achievement call attention to the power of national, local, and policy contexts in shaping the experiences of the second-generation Black Caribbean young people I focus on in this ethnography.

* * *

Failing Minorities? Narratives of Caribbean Underachievement in Britain

For much of the 20th century, representations of Black Caribbean young people as an underachieving minority in schools have been anchored in the minds of the British public.[76] To be sure, these constructions came to the fore of public consciousness in the second half of the 20th century. Despite substantial evidence challenging Black Caribbean underachievement as a fixed formula and a reflection on the cultural character of Black Caribbean people, conceptions of Black Caribbean underachievement remain prominent and powerful in British schools and society. Education policymakers and media personalities regularly point out that Black Caribbeans in Britain are more than three times as likely to be permanently excluded from schools as their white counterparts,[77] and they are disproportionately identified as having special educational needs,[78] and emotional and behavioral difficulties.[79] Moreover, as Figure 1.2 shows, Black Caribbean students had lower scores on national GCSE examinations than all other ethnic groups except for Gypsy/ Roma and Irish Travellers.[80]

These patterns are best understood by considering the historical, discursive, and policy contexts that inform the experiences of Black Caribbean people in Britain. To avoid despairing ahistorical analyses that render Caribbean underachievement a moral failure or a product of Caribbean culture, close attention to Caribbean immigration in mid-20th-century Britain is essential. This section moves beyond what historian Kennetta Hammond Perry identifies as

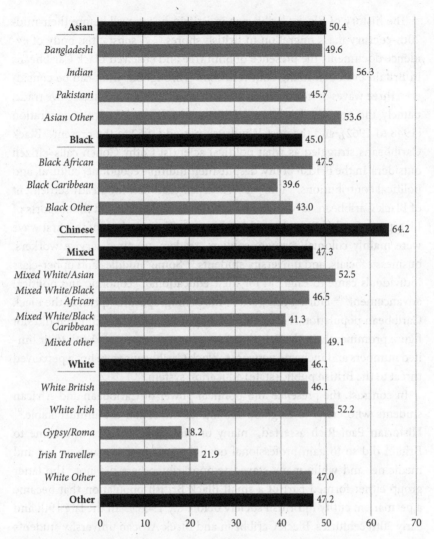

Figure 1.2 2018 General Certification of Secondary Education attainment by race and ethnicity

'tunnel histories' that focus exclusively on post-World War II migration from the Caribbean as the definitive inauguration of Black life in Britain.[81] Even before the 'Windrush moment,' by which I mean the post-1948 wave of Black Caribbeans to arrive in Britain, Black Caribbean immigrants and their children were " 'racial outcasts' amidst an outcast class."[82] The social construction of disadvantage through educational policy is a measure of state power, which becomes apparent by comparing pre- and post-Windrush historical accounts.

The history of Black Caribbeans in Britain began well before their mid-20th-century mass migration to British shores.[83] A substantial body of evidence documents the presence of both free and enslaved Black Caribbeans in Britain even before the 16th century.[84] Throughout what can be considered three waves of immigration after the abolition of the British slave trade, namely the pre-Windrush era (1880s to 1947), the Windrush generation (1948 to 1962), and the post-Windrush period (1962 to the present), Black Caribbeans struggled as what political scientist Cathy Cohen calls 'citizen outsiders' in the British polity, despite their multiple economic, cultural, and political contributions.[85] The pre-Windrush years saw the steady settlement of Black Caribbeans as well as Black Africans in London and the seaports of Liverpool, Cardiff, Bristol, and Manchester.[86] The members of this first wave were mainly colonial seamen, soldiers, traders, wartime service workers, business officials, and university students.[87] Some "middle- and upper-class individuals came to England for their educational, economic and political advancement."[88] During this period, the demographic footprint of the Black Caribbean population remained relatively small, and their children did not figure prominently in the British public education system.[89] With their limited numbers and inchoate networks, Black Caribbeans were not a perceived threat to the British public (state) education system.[90]

In contrast, the presence and political power of Caribbean and African students who came to England for higher education are unmistakable.[91] Historian Paul Rich asserted, "many of the Black students who came to Britain did so to gain professional qualifications in areas such as law and medicine, and while many stayed temporarily, others did not. The latter group either formed part of a small Black British population that became a permanent entity in British society before . . . 1948."[92] In the late 19th and early 20th centuries, Black Caribbean and Black African university students sustained transnational political coalitions such as the League of Coloured Peoples (LCP) and the Pan-African Federation in order to challenge de facto racial and class segregation, create spaces for the socialization of Black colonial subjects, and lobby the Colonial Office for structural change and political integration in and outside of universities.[93] These organizations sought to highlight the importance of education for racial uplift. The LCP drew attention to the academic achievements of "really great Africans and persons of African descent" from the Caribbean attending British universities in order to challenge pseudo-scientific claims of Black intellectual and cultural inferiority.[94] However, the male leaders of these organizations often failed to acknowledge the gender and class privileges that enabled their educational advancement.[95]

The education of Black Caribbean children and young people in Britain developed as a relatively small-scale initiative, with hardly any measurable impact on the British educational system prior to the 1950s.[96] Black Caribbeans were not perceived to be a threat—at least, not to the extent that they were later. While some gifted students, including Stuart Hall, were deliberately recruited from across the British Empire to study at British universities,[97] there was no systematic government-led organization of primary education for the children of Black ex-servicemen.[98] Such educational endeavors were often arranged on a case-by-case basis, and usually occurred alongside the British white working classes and Irish, German, and Jewish immigrants—cultural and political outcasts to the British mainstream.[99] At home as well as across the Empire, the state set up a complex racialized hierarchy of Britishness and belonging.

The Education Act of 1944 eliminated school fees and aimed to reduce the class inequalities that had previously limited access to schools, particularly for the white working classes. This sweeping policy measure sought to "remove the inequalities that remained in the system" by making secondary schooling free to all.[100] White fears intensified in and outside of schools when Black Caribbean adults and children arrived in larger numbers after World War II.[101]

Racial Tensions and Cultural Anxieties after World War II

The call for workers to aid in the reconstruction and economic redevelopment of Britain led to the arrival of a larger and more politically significant wave of Black Caribbeans. Under the British Nationality Act of 1948, which conferred Commonwealth citizenship on colonial subjects of the British Empire, 492 Black Caribbeans sailed to England on the SS Empire Windrush, arriving at the port of Tilbury in Kent on June 22, 1948, where they were greeted by curious crowds and some fanfare. Most sought greater opportunities than were available in the Caribbean, which was weathering the effects of increasing economic disinvestment and political disadvantage.[102]

A sizable contingent of the Windrush passengers had served in the British military and returned to the Caribbean afterward; now they came with their relatives, if they could afford the fare.[103] These Black Caribbeans eventually filled gaps in the labor market as farm workers, electricians, domestic and service staff, railway workers, plumbers, and in other working-class jobs, despite being qualified for positions as teachers and civil servants.[104] The intake of Black Caribbeans was initially limited to 1,000 per year, but after 1951 the number increased sharply.[105]

Britain's white majority grew increasingly fearful of the country's new 'coloured' minority from Commonwealth countries. Openly xenophobic and racial violence occurred in 1958 and 1959, when white working-class and middle-class Britons repeatedly attacked Black Caribbean, Indian, and Pakistani people and organizations.[106] Black Caribbean and South Asian immigrants were not only deemed a threat, but considered deficient by European standards.[107] Journalist Peter Fryer points out that the white British population regarded 'coloured' immigrants as "ignorant and illiterate, speaking strange languages, and lacking proper education."[108]

These deficit perspectives became evident in the educational policies and practices applied to Black Caribbeans and other ethno-racial minorities, as strategies were designed and enforced to promote their cultural, linguistic, and political assimilation.[109] At this political and historical moment, ethnic expectations emerged as an expression of the state. The fear expressed by white Britons about the country's 'colour problem' intensified the government's concern about immigration control, leading to the passage of the Commonwealth Immigrants Act on November 1, 1961, which limited the number of immigrants from across the Commonwealth and was officially implemented on July 31, 1962.[110] Rushing to gain entry before the enforcement of these legislative restrictions, Black Caribbean and other ethnic minority immigrants arrived in record numbers.[111]

Although the third wave of Caribbean immigration is much smaller than the previous one, its political significance for education is unmatched. From 1962 on, the narrative of Black Caribbean underachievement developed and strengthened, and Caribbean parents resisted its ill effects on their children's education.[112] As Black Caribbean immigrants sent their children to school, they confronted racial, cultural, and political tensions in a system that classified their children as "educationally subnormal."[113] To assuage white parents' concerns that Black Caribbean and South Asian immigrants "would affect detrimentally the educational performance of white students," local educational authorities instituted a practice of ethno-racial segregation through in-school and between-school academic 'ability' grouping.[114] With a government-endorsed mandate that "no one school should have more than 30 percent of immigrants," which resulted in an attempt to "distribute the problem," Black Caribbean children were bused across local districts to schools designated for the "educationally sub-normal" or disproportionately placed in separate classes for those perceived to have language and learning difficulties.[115]

The earliest, most influential critique of this deficit-based characterization of Black Caribbean school children in Britain is Grenadian educator Bernard Coard's *How the West Indian Child Is Made Educationally Subnormal in the British School System*.[116] Coard reported that in the special day schools for those classified as "educationally subnormal" by the Inner London Education Authority (ILEA), "over 28 percent of all the pupils" were immigrants, while immigrants comprised only 15 percent of pupils in the ILEA's ordinary schools. Coard's research indicated that "Three quarters of all immigrant children in these educationally sub-normal schools are West Indian, whereas West Indians are only half of the immigrant population in the ordinary schools."[117] Black Caribbeans were more likely than any other ethno-racial group to be assigned to separate learning environments.[118] Sensitive to the cultural, biological, and behavioral rationales used to account for the underachievement of Black Caribbeans and other ethno-racial minorities and to entangle them in a culture trap, Coard shifted attention from the self to the social structure, from ethnic minority individuals to educational institutions, and from the culture of Black Caribbean immigrants to the policies of the British state.[119]

Early Efforts to Escape the Culture Trap

Activists and community-based alliances joined Coard in working to change educational policy discourse from Black Caribbean students' supposed intellectual and behavioral inferiority to discrimination and disadvantage throughout the 1970s. Immigrant parents and women teachers pointed to the deficiencies in the schools, registered their discontent with public policies, and fashioned a Black female-led school movement as a practice of freedom and an exercise in belonging.[120] Black supplementary schools were designed to counter well-established myths of Black ineducability and Black working-class dependence on the state.[121]

Parents organized, funded, and sustained supplementary schools as organic grassroots institutions with after-school and weekend tutoring programs beyond the control of the British government. These schools prioritized the educational success, cross-cultural literacy, African diasporic consciousness, and political awareness of the next generation of Black youth in Britain.[122] In sum, Black supplementary schools functioned as "parallel discursive arenas where members of subordinated social groups invent and circulate counter-discourses, which in turn permit them to formulate oppositional interpretations of their identities, interests, and needs."[123]

In response to the protests of Black Caribbean, South Asian, and other ethno-racial minority parents against the discrimination their children encountered in public schools, the Labour Party government called for an independent investigation "into the causes of the underachievement of children of West Indian origin" in 1977.[124] Following a multiyear inquiry into six local educational authorities, the commission, led by Anthony Rampton, produced its first report in 1981, which highlighted the multilayered nature of racism in British schools. *West Indian Children in Our Schools*, popularly referred to as the Rampton Report, recognized dominant stereotypes about Black Caribbeans as a 'problem':

> We are convinced from the evidence that we have obtained that racism . . . has a direct and important bearing on the performance of West Indian children in our schools. . . . There seemed to be a fairly widespread opinion among teachers to whom we spoke that West Indian pupils inevitably caused difficulties. These pupils were, therefore, seen either as problems to be put up with or, at best, deserving sympathy.[125]

Documenting the racialized, structural limitations of schooling for Black Caribbeans in Britain, the report concluded that cultural biases in IQ tests, the lack of Black teachers, limited information on racial and ethnic diversity in teacher training programs, and consistently low teacher expectations contributed to the educational disadvantage of Black Caribbean pupils. Accordingly, it called for a transformation of teacher expectations, the diversification of the teaching profession, and the implementation of explicitly antiracist policies.[126]

The report and its recommendations were so controversial that the subsequent Conservative government, aiming for more "balanced" findings, replaced Anthony Rampton with Lord Michael Swann. The final report acknowledged interpersonal and institutional racism along with the "pervasive climate of racism" it creates.[127] Yet, rather than focusing on antiracist strategies in British schools, it called for an "inclusive multiculturalism" that sought the advancement of all members of British society.[128] The political purpose and focus of the Swann Report are perhaps best captured by its title—*Education for All.*

Despite its inclusive aims, this report made highly problematic claims about Caribbean culture as an impediment to academic success. Comparing the educational outcomes of Black Caribbeans with Asians, it suggested that racism was not the main obstacle to educational advancement:

> The performance of the totality of Asian children resembles on average the performance of White children. . . . The reasons for very different school performances of Asians and West Indians seem likely to lie deep within their respective cultures. . . . Asians are given to 'keeping their heads down' and adopting a 'low profile', thereby making it easier to succeed in a hostile environment. West Indians, by contrast, are given to 'protest' and a 'high profile', with reverse effect.[129]

Such perspectives reinforced the popular view that "Asians have culture, West Indians have problems," culturalist claims anthropologist Susan Benson critiqued.[130] Unlike the Rampton Report, which focused on racism as the primary barrier to Caribbean achievement, the Swann Report identified underachievement and poor behavior as the consequence of cultural differences.

In this perspective, culture emerged, not as a poisonous undercurrent in racial discourse, but as the central strategy to deflect claims of racism in British schools and society and to reinforce white domination. Urban education historian Ian Grosvenor contends that "by shifting the emphasis away from racism to class-cultural factors, the report effectively removed the responsibility for underachievement from the public education system."[131] This view of the import of culture was subsequently reinforced by colorblind, or more appropriately race-evasive, ideologies in schools promoting multiculturalism and cultural diversity and addressing class inequalities from the early 1990s to the present.[132]

Advancing "the postracial logic of culture and ethnicity,"[133] and consistently framing racism as a problem of the Empire, not the metropole, allows state and school officials to escape suspicion of implicit and explicit racial bias, even today. More than 70 years after the arrival of the SS *Empire Windrush*, Black Caribbean people remain a stigmatized minority in British schools. The institutional factors that constrained their educational success in the 1960s continue: racially biased curricula, limited recruitment of Black teachers and leaders, a dearth of culturally sustaining pedagogies, strained relations between Black Caribbean parents and educators, high rates of arbitrary school exclusions, and low teacher expectations.[134] In public discourse, culture still serves as a key explanation for Caribbean underachievement.

The Power and 'Problem' of Culture

At the 2011 London Schools & Our Children Conference, Secretary of State for Education Michael Gove offered sobering remarks on the performance of Black pupils and then said, "Black Caribbean parents can learn a lot from Africans, who do much better in education. There is much to be learned about the culture of Africans in this respect." Gove's emphasis on culture is not unusual. On August 4, 2008, for example, a *Times Educational Supplement* feature headline read, "More Caribbeans classified as EBD"—that is, as having emotional and behavioral difficulties that require special services. This announcement harks back to the long-standing discourse on Black Caribbean pupils' 'lack' of self-control.[135] Summarizing the results of a study of over six million British students, the article spotlights Black Caribbean pupils as "twice as likely as white pupils to be categorized as having behavioral, emotional and social difficulties," even after accounting for factors such as gender, age, and socioeconomic background.[136]

These findings, the *Times* piece points out, "go against theorists who like to talk about black and white, because this affects only black Caribbean children, not black African children. *So it's not about colour, it is more about culture.*"[137] This statement seems to reject the decades-old prejudice that race and biology explain differences in educational performance and social behavior.[138] Yet it builds upon a prevailing preoccupation with cultural deprivation, especially in relation to Black Caribbean students, without giving due attention to the historical, structural forces, discourses, and key actors that influence Black Caribbean young people's experiences in state schools. This, too, is an example of the culture trap.

In March 2021, the British government's independent Commission on Racial and Ethnic Disparities released a report, led by second-generation Black Caribbean Tony Sewell, which offered hotly contested perspectives on the state of race relations in 21st-century Britain. The Sewell report questioned the significance of institutional racism as a constitutive feature of British society, describing Britain as a model on race relations for Europe and other countries based on the academic, occupational, and social progress of Black and other ethno-racial minority groups. It identified education as "the single most emphatic success story of the British minority experience" and suggested that "all major ethnic groups perform better than White British pupils except for Black Caribbean pupils."[139] This report noted "with great concern the prevalence of family breakdown," with over 60 percent of Black Caribbean children "growing up in lone parent families," and pronounced it "the root of disadvantage."[140] Such perspectives shore up key tenets of the 'culture of poverty' thesis and tethers it to Black Caribbean ethno-racial identity, even in a putatively post-racial moment.[141]

For decades, narratives of Black Caribbean underachievement located the problem in the culture and character of Black Caribbean students and their families, not in the context and conditions of schooling that affect them. As the subsequent chapters show, discussions of Black Caribbean underachievement in Britain that overestimate the influence of culture and discount the significance of social structure have consequences. The normative narrative of Black Caribbeans as a failing minority informs perceptions in and outside of schools that they are less capable, less committed, and ultimately less meritorious than their other Black and ethno-racial minority peers.[142] These discourses construct Black Caribbeans as a hard-to-reach, low-performing underclass with significant attitudinal and behavioral problems.[143] Perspectives that attribute inordinate influence to culture—a manifestation of the culture trap—continue to hold sway in British public and educational discourses in the absence of more critical analyses.[144]

Comparative Perspectives on Structural and Cultural Differences

I return to the question that animated my discussion with a long-time educator in South London, Ms. Bell: How can Caribbean culture, as some commentators and participants contend, serve as the key reason for Black Caribbean young people's 'success' in the United States and 'failure' in Britain?

Five factors, taken together, contribute to the distinct educational expectations and experiences of Black Caribbean people in Britain and the

United States: the differing modes of incorporation for Black Caribbeans in British and American society, the order of migration, the timing of arrival, immigrant selectivity, and continuing transnational contacts. I explore each in turn.

Black Caribbeans' differing modes of incorporation into British and American societies are central to understanding the divergent perceptions of their capacities and situations. Anthropologists Margaret Gibson, Signithia Fordham, and John Ogbu provided original cross-national and cross-cultural comparisons that highlighted how ethno-racial groups' historical relationship to the host society (whether as forced or voluntary migrants) informs their trajectories and status positions.[145] Black Caribbeans entered Britain as political subjects of the British Empire by virtue of colonization.[146] Even before working-class and middle-class Black Caribbeans settled in Britain in large numbers, they were already identified as a degraded group in the popular British imaginary based on Black Caribbeans' subordinated position in the Empire as enslaved laborers and political dependents.[147] Black Caribbeans from British colonies who entered the United States, however, did so as voluntary economic migrants, not as enslaved subjects like African Americans who had labored for centuries under the legalized constraints of slavery, segregation, and state terror—features of structural racism.[148] These differences in the incorporation of Black Caribbeans in Britain and the United States contribute to their positions as elevated Black minorities in the United States and degraded Black minorities in Britain.[149]

The order of groups' arrival in the United States and Britain relative to other Black people also matters.[150] The presence and growing political power of African Americans have been advantageous for Black Caribbean people in the United States.[151] Beyond the support Black Caribbeans have often experienced from African Americans in residentially segregated neighborhoods based on their linked fates, Black immigrants and their children have benefited from social and educational policies established in response to the Civil Rights Movement.[152] Despite the recent retreat from school desegregation and affirmative action policies, these mandates created a favorable context for Black Caribbean immigrants in education and the labor market.[153]

In Britain, however, there was no large cohort of Blacks to ease the incorporation of Black Caribbean immigrants, as sociologist Nancy Foner argues.[154] Black Caribbean people who arrived between 1948 and 1962, along with their British-born children, represent the largest group of Blacks to enter the British educational system.[155] The political activism and educational organizing of Black Caribbean immigrants throughout the 1960s, 1970s, and 1980s through the Black Supplementary Schools Movement, the Black Parents Movement, and related coalitions, created a better, more inclusive nation-state in which subsequent Black ethnic groups, especially Black Africans, can thrive.[156] The order of Black migration underscores the power of a large preexisting Black group and its impact on the incorporation of new Black ethnic groups.

The timing of arrival also informs the contrasting achievements of Black Caribbean immigrants in the United States and Britain. The largest wave of Black Caribbean immigrants to the United States came under the auspices of the Hart-Celler Immigration and Nationality Act of 1965. This wave followed the Civil Rights Act of 1964, which banned discrimination in employment, and public accommodations based on race, color, religion, sex, or national origin; the Voting Rights Act of 1965; and the Fair Housing Act of 1968.[157] Despite the myriad, often successful efforts to thwart the full implementation of these laws, many Black Caribbean immigrants entered the United States after major policy shifts against racial discrimination and immigration restriction.

In contrast, Black Caribbean people in Britain experienced an increasingly hostile political context, especially after 1948. White Britons were ill-prepared for the diversity that accompanied Black Caribbean immigration and were deeply discomfited by the Empire coming 'home.'[158] Black Caribbeans in Britain were subjected to widespread discrimination in the labor market, the housing sector, and education, as well as in the immigration system.[159] Black African immigrants arrived en masse in Britain in the 1980s and 1990s following national investigations into and public acknowledgments of widespread institutional racism. Although these reports did not lead to the elimination of entrenched discrimination, they did create a more hospitable context of reception than that encountered by Black Caribbeans who arrived earlier.[160]

Class differences matter too. Although late 19th- and early 20th-century immigrants to Britain from the Caribbean were mainly middle class, those who arrived subsequently had more diverse class origins.[161] In recent decades, more middle-class Caribbean emigrants have chosen to go to the United States instead of Britain, in part because of its proximity to the Caribbean and their perception that the United States offers greater economic opportunities. Equally important, US immigration policies remain open to Black Caribbeans through family reunification and labor recruitment, while British policies have become more restrictive since the 1960s.[162]

These policy differences generated class differences in the cohorts of Black Caribbean immigrants to the two countries that shaped their subsequent trajectories.[163]

Differences in the volume and nature of immigration from the Caribbean to Britain and the United States also had consequences for the success of Black Caribbean immigrants in their respective host societies. In the United States, immigration from the English-speaking Caribbean to New York City remains strong, with the regular arrival of Caribbean students, workers, visitors, and permanent residents entering ethnic enclaves, religious and cultural organizations, and K–12 educational institutions.[164] Sociologist Tomás Jiménez refers to this phenomenon as 'replenished ethnicity.'[165] Ongoing immigration to New York City and other places with a strong Black Caribbean presence has stimulated cultural, religious, and political organizing that informs the identities and experiences of the second-generation.[166] With continued immigration and incorporation, recent arrivals help to sustain narratives of Caribbean people as aspirational and hard-working. The presence of new Caribbean immigrants socializes some second-generation Black Caribbean young people into Caribbean cultural patterns and adaptive strategies—even if these youth do not adhere to them consistently, and others disregard them.[167]

In Britain, by contrast, immigration from the Caribbean has slowed to a trickle, with just a small number of Caribbean immigrants coming to London or any other British city permanently for work or family reunification.[168] The comparatively few Caribbean immigrants who have arrived in recent decades are socialized by their third- and fourth-generation co-ethnics.[169] In this regard, the presence of a few Caribbean immigrants in Britain does not challenge dominant claims of Black Caribbean underachievement.

Despite the significance of the order and timing of arrival, immigrant selectivity, replenished ethnicity, and other macro-level factors in explaining the differences between Black Caribbeans in the United States and Britain, these explanations have generally neglected the power of school processes and educational discourses. Throughout this book, I argue that ethnic expectations are a key, frequently overlooked feature of Black Caribbean young people's cultural worlds in and outside of schools. When ethnic expectations are mobilized in educational institutions, teachers, administrators, parents, and pupils often ignore the significance of class resources, historical discourses, and policy contexts shaping the experiences of Black Caribbean pupils. Instead, they level undue weight to the power of culture in shaping

Black Caribbean young people's educational achievement. This, I argue, is the culture trap.

My History with History

I never had an opportunity to discuss the power of the culture trap and the influence of ethnic expectations with Pastor Williams, who first urged my serious consideration of the social and educational history of the Caribbean diaspora. By the time I finished my fieldwork he had retired to Jamaica. He was right about the power of history to help us understand the situation of contemporary Black Caribbean immigrants and their children. Although the predominant narratives about Black Caribbeans in Britain and the United States posit Caribbean culture as a key determining factor shaping group achievement, this trans-Atlantic comparison reveals that culture alone cannot have generated such different perceptions of Black Caribbeans in Britain and the United States and lays bare the culture trap involved. The overemphasis on 'culture' functions as a strategy to divert attention from racism and classism, which are systemic social forces.

Predominant perceptions of Black Caribbean culture shape ethnic expectations that differ markedly in different contexts but nonetheless distort the diversity within the group, and set up false distinctions between groups. Furthermore, the differences between the expectations of Black Caribbeans in the United States and Britain underscore the theoretical and political significance of Caribbean identity as a contextual construct—as "a 'production' which is never complete, always in process and always constituted within, not outside, representation," as Stuart Hall contends.[170]

The next chapter delves into these situated social constructions by examining the post-migration situations that Black Caribbean immigrant parents negotiate based on their pre-migration perceptions of urban public schools in the British and US Empires.

2

Black Caribbean Immigrants and the Legacies of Empire

"I didn't expect none of this in Englan," Karlene said, standing in front of her stove stirring brown stew chicken in a Dutch pot. That rainy October evening was my second visit to Karlene's home, a one-bedroom flat neatly arrayed with framed family photographs, white figurines on cotton crocheted doilies, black sofas with plush red cushions, thick red curtains with frills, a shiny clock shaped like the island of Jamaica, and other aesthetic signifiers of home in the Caribbean diaspora. She had invited me to have dinner with her and her family, including her son Odain, the clever Year 10 leader at Londerville Secondary whose searing comments about the state of schools often made me wonder about how he cultivated such views.[1]

When I asked Karlene about life and schooling in Britain since leaving Jamaica, she spoke of hopes dashed and deterred: "I thought Englan' was goin' to be better than this . . . Mi did really think the schools wouldah give him more opportunities than back home. But if I don't stan' up strong, Odain will just turn into another statistic in this school system."

As if the weight of her words—or the heat—suddenly rested on her, Karlene stepped away from the stove, leaned her lower back against the counter, shook her head, and sighed. "You have to fight for Caribbean children in these schools," she said, unconsciously echoing the voices of Black Caribbean mothers and fathers decades before who challenged the low educational expectations in British schools.[2]

"Why did you think schools would be better here?" I asked.

She stammered out a curious confession: "Well, well, a lot of reasons. The buildings dem look good, you don't have to pay, the teacher dem call yuh [you], textbooks are free. . . . We used to just have imitation British schools dem back home, so it must be better over here." I had heard such explanations from Caribbean parents at Londerville before, but their comments always unsettled me. I think Karlene saw me furrow my brow and perhaps presumed it was a sign of disbelief. She looked me in the eye, widened hers, and

The Culture Trap. Derron Wallace, Oxford University Press. © Oxford University Press 2023.
DOI: 10.1093/oso/9780197531464.003.0003

said loudly, "Like, this is big big Englan'. Queen Elizabeth Englan'. Mother country Englan'. . ."

"Mother country?!" Odain yelled, craning his neck from the dining table to stare at his mother in the kitchenette behind him. "Queen . . ." One look from Karlene silenced Odain.

Karlene continued: "Yuh know? Big Englan' . . . The real deal. . . . I didn't expect it to be a bed ah [of] roses, but this school ting over here is tricky bad. Tricky mi ah tell yuh [I am telling you]! . . . Dem don't expect much from the pickney [children] dem like Odain in school. . . . I have to constantly remind him, yeah, what he can do and push him . . . keep him belief and the confidence and the expectation dem high."

Once her two sons were seated at the dining table, Karlene said to them and to me: "I cannot give up on my children. . . . I have to fight for them, no matter what." She reached across the table, held her sons' hands, and smiled. "Mi [I] love them," she said. For many parents in London, love motivates their advocacy for their Black Caribbean children in school. That was also true for Black Caribbean parents like Lorraine in New York City, whose excitement about "coming to America" was shadowed with apprehension about its urban public schools.

Coming to America

Lorraine brought two ice-cold Malta drinks into her living room, gently placed them on the side table, and handed me a wooden coaster with an intricate design of the Grenadian flag. Its vivid red, green, and yellow seemed a sharp contrast to the off-white walls, crisp white sofas with tailor-made plastic covers to fit, a framed replica of the Last Supper with blond Jesus and his white disciples, along with a classic Caribbean poem on a wall mat that read:

> When you come here,
> What you see here,
> What you hear here,
> When you leave here,
> Let it stay here,
> Or don't come back here.

But Lorraine and I had a different agreement. Lorraine had invited me to her red-brick, two-story home to discuss "what goin' on at that school" I call Newlands High. We both swirled and sipped our frosty malt beverages as we battled the heat and humidity of mid-June. In time, she told me about her American dream—and that the "struggle to find good schools" for her son was "like a nightmare in the dream."

"I was excited about coming to America, especially New York. . . . But I was not looking forward to these public schools," she said.

"What do you mean? How come you weren't excited about the schools here?" I asked.

"I just think the school system here in New York is not like back home, where the kids learn to have manners, discipline, respect and the fear of God. . . . Back home they have to work really hard to get an A. But over here, it's just not hard."

"That's not true!" I said. "I went to high school in Jamaica and over here and teachers weren't giving away A's here. You had to work hard for them."

"You probably just had a different experience," she said. "But I know what I'm talking about at Newlands."

I placed the empty Malta bottle on the coaster, leaned forward in my seat, and said, "Give me an example," with a daring tone. She plopped her bottle down on the floor, wiped her hands, and replied: "What do you mean you're giving school children participation grade? What kind of stupidness is that?!" I laughed loudly.

"It's not a joke!" she insisted, chuckling while leaning back in her seat. "Back home, we don't give grades for attendance and participation. That is just the bare minimum. . . . The standards here is low! Why is Dwayne [her son] only taking six subjects in a semester? I love him, but he can do more. . . . I had 12 and 13 classes in secondary school back home." When I insisted that some US private high schools often offered a similar course load, she quipped: "Well, at least the private ones are not as bad like a lot of these American public schools in the news or on TV!" She sucked her teeth loudly and rolled her eyes. I pursed my lips for the sake of peace.

"So why did you allow Dwayne to go to Newlands?" I asked.

"Well, I wanted to get him to go to one of these private schools, but I just couldn't afford it and pay the mortgage. . . . But I wouldn't make him go to Newlands if I didn't think it was a decent school. He is definitely going away to college! . . . I love that boy. He makin' me so proud! But he would learn more if we was back home."

The Persistent Power of Schooling 'Back Home'

This chapter examines how Caribbean parents' understandings of school structures in the Caribbean shaped their perceptions of schooling in the diaspora. For Caribbean parents in London, British schooling functioned as a familiar stranger[3]—a historically distinct model of "excellent" schooling, which these parents had experienced in modified form in the postcolonial Caribbean but anticipated their children would encounter the best of in the "mother country." They assumed that schooling in England would be organized and conducted in a comparable way to schooling in the Caribbean and expressed particular appreciation for the material conditions of school buildings—or what sociologist Prudence Carter refers to as the hard structures of schools.[4] Like Karlene, Caribbean immigrant parents hoped "that things would be better for Caribbean children over here."

In New York City, by contrast, the Caribbean parents I spoke with considered schooling 'back home' more academically rigorous than the American educational system. They assumed that New York City's public high schools were of generally low quality, with lax grading, and a lack of appropriate discipline. Popular assumptions about the crisis of urban public schools based on Hollywood movies broadcast by US cable networks in the Caribbean made parents like Lorraine "protective" of their children. As Lorraine explained, "I was skeptical of these schools before I even come to this place!"

As I show in this chapter, Karlene's and Lorraine's perceptions of schooling in London and New York are rooted in the history and legacy of two competing Empires, and their differing relationships to the Anglophone Caribbean.[5] Immigrant Black Caribbean parents like Karlene and Lorraine seldom speak of colonialism in daily life.[6] Nevertheless, as a historical and ongoing political force, colonialism shapes the structure and substance of schooling in the Caribbean. This lingering structure of power has a profound "tutelary character," as sociologist Julian Go suggests, teaching its subjects about their place in the sovereign state and the global order.[7] Historical perspectives that examine the influence of colonialism can challenge culturalist claims that root achievement in the intrinsic character of ethno-racial groups without accounting for how colonial and state power influence those configurations.[8] In fact, such historical perspectives can serve as a counterforce to the culture trap and its guiding assumptions that ethnic cultures shape educational outcomes. At the heart of this chapter, I argue that experiences of (post)colonial schooling in the British Caribbean matter for parents' vision of schooling in the Caribbean diaspora.

Colonial Configurations of Schooling in the British Caribbean

Although Black Caribbean parents and their children are often framed as newcomers to Britain and its schools, such perspectives are worth interrogating. Britain's imperial relationship with the Caribbean and Black Caribbean people predates Britain's own formal existence.[9] The 1706–1707 Acts of Union, which formalized the legal partnership between England and Scotland and established Britain as a nation-state, came decades after the development of England's colonial, racial capitalist relationship with the people of Barbados, the Bahamas, Antigua, and Jamaica. As cultural historian James Cantres argues, rather than viewing mid-20th-century Black Caribbean citizen-subjects who came to Britain as beneficiaries of Britain's imperial benevolence, it may be more accurate to view Britain itself as a political formation shaped by its colonial project in the Caribbean and the dispossession of Black Caribbean people.[10] Black Caribbean people, then, are foundational to the British state, rather than peripheral to its development, despite what anti-immigrant discourses and status quo narratives in British schools and society at times assume.[11]

Schooling has been a key mechanism that facilitated British cultural and political-economic domination in the Anglophone Caribbean.[12] In countries as diverse as Guyana, Belize, Jamaica, and Trinidad and Tobago, schools functioned as central institutions of British colonialism.[13] In addition to orienting colonial subjects to the rules and values of the colonial state, colonial administrators established an organizational structure, a curricular formula, and an academic tradition that reflected schooling in the metropole.[14] British schooling in the Caribbean was first developed to provide cultural and curricular consistency for the children of white elites stationed there as agents of the Empire.[15] Indeed, from its foundations, the protocols and practices of formal schooling in the Caribbean constituted a racialized, classed, and gendered project that prioritized elite white males' cultural and political-economic self-interests.[16] In Caribbean plantation societies throughout the 18th and 19th centuries, educational expectations were unmistakably racialized, with the quality and scope of educational provision corresponding to the role of different racial groups in the labor force.[17]

Through the three centuries of British colonialism in the Anglophone Caribbean, hundreds of primary and secondary schools were established.[18] The first set of schools catered to the children of elite white colonial administrators and business owners.[19] Subsequently, schooling was extended to free mixed-race subjects, but not to the Black population, as "the rudimentary foundations of education were opposed by the planter class for whom the education of slaves constituted a dangerous precedent," as sociologists Christine Barrow and Rhoda Reddock argued.[20] In 1834, shortly after the passage of the Emancipation Act, which in principle ended chattel slavery, the Negro Education Grant Act extended formal schooling to formerly enslaved Black people.[21] Leaders of the British Empire realized that "the slaves' freedom and the slaves' education occupied two sides of the same coin."[22] According to historian Inge Dornan, "the role of elementary instruction as a tool of social discipline and moral reform to transform slaves into 'virtuous, enlightened and industrious' free British subjects largely explains the British government's decision to place the religious bodies in charge of establishing a system of elementary instruction in the colonies."[23]

Between 1835 and 1900, thousands of Black children and adults gained access to basic education.[24] But schooling was strategically curtailed to ensure that it did not constrain the growth of the plantation economy, cause social and political upheaval for the colonial state, disrupt economic gains it depended on, or threaten Great Britain's standing as a global superpower.[25] Through the remainder of the 19th century, missionaries and teachers were supported financially and politically by the British colonial state to establish schools, train foreign and native teachers, and supervise the development and administration of a curriculum that taught British subjects to revere God, Queen, and Mother Country.[26] A complex educational structure developed in the Caribbean that sustained Britain's colonial influence well into the 20th century. The purpose of colonial education across racial and class lines was to "teach the mutual intent of the mother-country and her dependencies, the rational basis of their connection, and the domestic and social duties of the coloured races."[27] At the time of national independence in a host of Caribbean countries, large swaths of the populace remained illiterate.[28]

The educational infrastructure was, in effect, a color-coded racialized system of teaching and learning that was fundamentally separate and unequal.[29] Its segregation was systemic and hierarchical. The children of white colonial administrators and businessmen attended the region's oldest and most elite schools, mixed-race pupils often accessed the best primary and some post-primary education, and the Black masses were subjected to basic schooling and vocational training that prioritized the development of boys more than girls and emphasized "moral training, practical education in agriculture or another manual pursuit, and basic literacy skills."[30] The system was grounded in the racialized economic hierarchy and featured differential access to schools and the resources within them.[31] In the rural and urban Caribbean, students were shuffled through what could be regarded as a between-school tracking system that aligned students by color, class, and gender with their assigned occupations based on biased perceptions of their abilities.[32]

Much of the decolonial effort in the Caribbean during the mid-20th century focused on providing equality of educational opportunity.[33] This initiative led to the establishment of more schools, the promotion of universal primary and secondary education, the recruitment of more Caribbean-born teachers, the expansion of a critical orientation to British imperial authority, the improvement of teacher training colleges, and the establishment of accredited regional universities.[34] Yet the structure and protocols of British colonial education persisted, from the organization, ranking, and curricular content of schools to corporal punishment and uniforms.[35] Consider the structural similarities between British and Caribbean schools to date, as shown in Table 2.1. Several decades after independence, the architecture of British colonial schooling remains largely intact in Caribbean nation-states.

The related histories and structures of British and Caribbean schools explain why Karlene experienced what she called "imitation British schools dem back home." Her schooling in the Anglophone Caribbean informed the lens through which she perceived schooling in Britain, as its structure sustains the impression that social life and schooling are better in the 'Mother Country' than 'back home' in the Caribbean.[36] What Stuart Hall called "the deep structure of affiliation" between Britain and the Caribbean is rooted in (post)colonialism, as imperial logics lingering in Caribbean immigrant parents' psychosocial worlds—even those who are part of the third wave of Caribbean immigrants to Britain, like the parents featured in this ethnography.[37] The illusory sense of home in England that "the deep structure of affiliation" created had serious implications for belonging and becoming once Black Caribbean parents settled in Britain. We now turn to Black Caribbean parents' expectations of schooling in England based on their experiences of schooling in the postcolonial Caribbean—critical perspectives on Black Caribbeans that Paul Willis's *Learning to Labor*,

Table 2.1 Comparison of Caribbean and British School Structures

Students' Age	Level of Schooling	Caribbean	Great Britain
3–4	Early Childhood	Nursery and Kindergarten	Nursery and Kindergarten
5–11	Primary School	Grades 1–6 *National Grade Six Achievement Test for secondary school placement*	Years 1–6 *Key Stage 1 and 2 Exams with secondary school placement by choice locally*
12–16	Secondary School	Grades 7–11 *Caribbean Secondary Ed Certificate Examination for Sixth Form and post-secondary placement*	Years 7–11 *National GCSE Exams for Sixth Form and post-secondary placement*
17–18	College/Sixth Form	Grades 12–13 *A-Level Examination*	Years 12–13 *A-Level Examination*
18–21	University	3 Years *Major typically based on A-level courses*	3 Years *Major typically based on A-level courses*

Mary Waters's *Black Identities*, Natasha Warikoo's *Balancing Acts*, Claire Alexander's *The Art of Being Black*, among other works, have missed to date.[38]

From Excitement to Disappointment in Britain

"I was so excited when I finally came to England!" Tiffany said exuberantly. She spoke with an easy confidence, a sense of self that always seemed fuller and stronger than her thin, high-pitched voice. "I learned so much about England in school, now I got to see it for myself!" This Antiguan-born mother of three and part-time project manager told me that coming to England was "sort of like coming home to a place you know very well, or you think you know very well, but you have never really been to." This impulse, I came to learn, was informed by cultural and political signifiers of British rule in the Caribbean—from the classroom with skewed histories of Columbus's "West Indies" to the contemporary courtroom following British laws and customs, from popular emphases on 'proper' pronunciation of the 'Queen's English' to the prolonged positioning of the Queen, and more recently the King, as Head of State.

Tiffany's initial excitement was rooted in a fundamental paradox that she described as "going abroad and going home." Her enthusiasm carried great expectations about the culture and character of British society based on training in the (post)colonial Caribbean. Tiffany said, "I know it's a different country, but I had been dreaming of this for so long. . . . I shouldn't say it, but I even practiced my British accent before I reach!" Her laugh boomed and bounced on the walls of the almost-empty café in Greenwich where we sat with cold drinks and croissants.

"That must have taken a lot of practice," I insisted.

"It wasn't hard because I knew how to speak proper English and some of the missionaries who visited my school came from England. We got to talk to them a lot."

The signifiers of Britishness were taught in her Antiguan secondary school, rehearsed and reinforced in religious and colonial encounters of the distant and recent past. Language, diction, and piety are part of the range of cultural orthodoxies attached to representations of Britain in the Caribbean. When explaining how eager she was to go back to school after she first settled in England in her late teens, Tiffany said the British schooling system was "what I was used to. I wasn't nervous about that." None of the Caribbean parents I spoke to in London were nervous about that, as they were familiar with the structure of British schools based on their schooling in the Caribbean.

"England is not Antigua," she continued. But "the way the schools are set up was generally similar." Or so she assumed. When I questioned her about why she made those assumptions, she pointed out that it was "reasonable" to do so "because Antiguan schools follow the British model." A close examination of the resemblance and relationship between British and Caribbean school structures indicates that her assumptions were indeed "reasonable." With an Antiguan curriculum that was British in structure and "Anglo-centric in content and emphasis,"[39] Tiffany felt "ready and excited for England." To be sure, Tiffany, like a number of Black Caribbean parents, insisted that she anticipated change as well as continuity. But she and other Caribbean women and men of her generation confronted situations they did not expect.

"I know Black children didn't do well here," she said. "But, I thought I could be different. . . . To me, it just seemed like you could do a good job here if you focused and worked hard. . . . I had discipline, manners, and excellent home training, and I was smart!" This resembled the individual distinctiveness some Black Caribbean children expressed about their success during my time at Londerville Secondary.

Other Black Caribbean mothers expressed similar appreciation for British-style schooling. Ann-Marie, a nursery school teacher from Barbados, said, "I got fairly good basic school and primary school education back home. . . . I expected some sort of racism when I came here, but I was just glad for the opportunity to be here and go to school here." Kay, a self-described homemaker from Jamaica who was preparing to move to her third flat in two years because of rent increases across London, said: "I heard so much about this place, even inna [in] school. . . . I was glad to come over here, but this place don't like faarin [foreign] people, even though Englan' rich because ah we [of us]. . . . I know, yeah, that even if England don't work out for me, I dream that it would work out for my children. . . . Mi love dem an' mi wah betta fi dem [I love them and I want better for them]."

For mothers like Kay, Tiffany, and Ann-Marie, schooling in the post-colonial Caribbean provided an orientation to schools in Britain that led them to anticipate success. When they encountered racism, classism, and xenophobia, they found hope in education—particularly for their second-generation children.[40]

School Structures and Their Limits in London

Most Black Caribbean immigrant parents described being impressed by school buildings and material resources when they first arrived in Britain. Tiffany, for instance, explained: "The schools looked so great . . . so much better than back home . . . and you didn't have to pay to go to school!" Harvey, a Guyanese business owner and father of two, said: "Man, when I see these schools had roofs that didn't leak and schools didn't ask for fees, I was like, this is it!" He flashed his hand and index finger up and down—a common way of signaling excitement in the Caribbean. In addition to the fact that some parents in the Anglophone Caribbean could not afford to cover tuition and buy uniforms, books, and supplies to send all their children to school, free public schools seemed to express the idea that in Britain all students were regarded as capable of academic success regardless of their parents' economic situation or residential location. For parents like Harvey, access to education was no longer contingent on wealth or even one's country of origin.

That boded well in a country otherwise marked by racial, ethnic, and class inequality.

Like other Black Caribbean parents I spoke with, Tiffany had discovered that schools' material resources cannot outweigh the impact of teacher-student relationships, peer support, and inter-group relations—what sociologist Prudence Carter refers to as the "soft structures of schools."[41] Tiffany said in pained tones: "I realized that the schools over here looked good, but maybe the schools back home were better for me and my children."

"Why do you think so?" I asked.

"Our teachers and schools cared about us. We were not less than anybody . . . It's just hard when schools here just expect so little from Caribbean young people and you know that's not the case back home." Tears filmed her eyes. At this point, rain began falling. Tiffany and I looked out the window and watched as the torrent sent school children and passersby scurrying for cover and the wailing winds sprayed water over those too stubborn to carry umbrellas.

"So why did you think schools back home are better?" I asked again.

She replied: "Back home, we trusted the schools, but you're a fool to do that here. . . . I used to do that, but not anymore! . . . I didn't find out until my son started failing! I didn't realize until it was too late." Tiffany's words echo a regularly repeated claim. The Black Caribbean parents I spoke with lost faith in British schools and society when their children failed—or, more precisely, when they believed schools failed their children.

As I sat across from Tiffany, I recalled what two fathers had told me a few days earlier. Jermaine, a construction worker, said, "I didn't decide to raise my children here in this country and send them to school here for underachievement. It just seem like our chances of success at school would be better back home!" Jermaine's passion often meant he could not hide his Grenadian accent, even if he tried. Harvey declared, his voice loud and firm: "If all you let these Caribbean young people know about themselves and their achievement in school is what they learn in this country and what they see in these schools, yeah, they will always think they are less capable than other people. . . it's different back home."[42]

In light of their children's negative experiences in British schools, Black Caribbean parents like Jermaine and Harvey summoned memories of schooling in the Caribbean to envision a world in which educational success for Black children was expected. Highlighting the high achievement that was common in their homelands, they sought to undermine the dominant narratives of Black Caribbean educational underachievement in Britain. Their nostalgia was arguably an attempt to escape the culture trap.

Over cups of tea later that rainy afternoon, Tiffany explained that her disappointment was not a knee-jerk response to the academic and social challenges Black Caribbean children faced in school. Rather, it developed gradually. Tiffany sought to explain away structural constraints and emphasize her own agency: "I tell myself, yeah, no, this place is not that bad. Racism here is not that big a deal anymore. Just work hard, be nice and polite, you know, show that stiff upper lip, and don't complain. But here I am," she said, her voice growing faint. "None of it worked for my son. It didn't help me and I couldn't even help him."

She recounted the schools' incremental disinvestment in and increasing punishment of her older son. He was consistently placed in low-ranked sets (tracks). Over several years, teachers did not give him the positive attention he deserved in class. He did not get support, but was labeled 'rude' and a 'troublemaker'. Tiffany and her partner felt guilty for trusting that schools would not fail her son. The five years since his permanent exclusion from a secondary school near Londerville did not blunt the sharpness of Tiffany's grief or lighten the weight of her disappointment. Yet the fault was not her own: punitive policies and practices render Black Caribbean young people more than three times as likely to experience school exclusion than their white peers.[43] From Tiffany's perspective, her son, like many Black Caribbean boys and girls, was deliberately neglected in schools that redirected time, encouragement, and resources away from failing and misbehaving students to those poised to succeed so that schools could succeed. "Now, I don't trust these schools," she said. "I make sure I go to parent-teacher meetings, school events, and make sure" her younger son "gets tuition [tutoring]. These schools alone cannot do our children any good."

The Black Caribbean mothers and fathers I spoke with described their children's schooling in Britain as "tough," "unfair," "a constant battle," "a nightmare," and "war." These perceptions reaffirm what Grenadian activist and youth worker Bernard Coard found in his 1971 book, *How the West Indian Child is Made Educationally Sub-normal in the British School System*. For Black Caribbean children and young people, public (state) schools too often functioned as sites of disadvantage and serial social suffering.[44]

Black Caribbean Parents in Britain and the Legacies
of the British Empire

The perspectives expressed by Tiffany, Harvey, and Jermaine were shared by other Black Caribbean parents as they negotiated what sociologist Les Back refers to as "hierarchies of belonging" in Britain.[45] They did not expect that their second-generation children would encounter such pervasive discrimination and exclusion in an educational system they regarded as more familiar than strange. Even though none of the Black Caribbean parents had been to Britain before emigrating, Britain's imperial logics lingered in their psychosocial worlds, creating an illusory sense of home in England, and shaping a mythical anthropology of the diaspora.[46] Under the British colonial regime, for instance, schools functioned as key sites of cultural and political socialization that made England *seem* like home, even to those living on faraway islands. In the Caribbean and across the British Empire, schools operated as extensions of imperial governance—culturally, economically, and politically. Like the Antiguan American novelist Jamaica Kincaid, Black Caribbean parents arguably "saw England for the first time . . . in school sitting at a desk" in a (post)colonial classroom—learning a language, geography, history, and culture that unsettled and usurped their own.[47]

Not unlike Harvey, Jermaine, and other Black Caribbean parents, Tiffany struggled to come to terms with the limits of her British dreams and the political constraints of British life. She tried to convince herself that "racism here is not a big deal anymore," until the structures of racial and ethnic inequality in school—in the extreme form of punitive exclusion from school—impeded her oldest son's advancement. Tiffany's initial appreciation for British schooling and cultural life, coupled with her determined efforts to prove herself a 'worthy' migrant, were insufficient to guarantee a sense of belonging in Britain.[48] Her oldest son's secondary school "pushed him out to a referral unit" without adequate counseling and support. Public schools, then, were not universal instruments of social uplift. For Black Caribbean young people in Britain, schools often operated as sites of confinement, punishment, and disadvantage.[49] Despite this, Black Caribbean parents continue to fight "so that we get the best for our children," as Harvey put it.

Harvey's, Jermaine's, and Tiffany's disappointment has considerable historical resonance for other Black Caribbean parents in Britain.[50] When the

British government disproportionately labeled Black Caribbean children "educationally subnormal" from the 1950s to the 1970s, Black Caribbean parents protested, organized civic alliances, established bookstores and publishing houses, and developed their own supplementary schools as a counterforce to the British state's racism.[51] Fifty years after the launch of the Black Parents' Movement in Britain in the early 1970s, Black Caribbean parents continue to resist through the same means and more, as their children are frequently labeled by school staff as having 'Emotional and Behavioral Difficulties', and are disproportionately placed in pupil referral units—arguably a contemporary iteration of schools for 'educationally subnormal' students that Black Caribbean parents vehemently protested. Black Caribbean parents' shift from excitement to disappointment allows us "to understand the transition experience as largely about the shattering of false illusions: a disenchantment which, although certainly not pleasurable, was necessary and in the end liberating," as Stuart Hall asserts.[52] The liberation Black Caribbean parents pursued was rooted in coming to terms with Britain as it is, so they could advocate for Britain as it should be.

* * *

In contrast to their counterparts in London, Black Caribbean parents in New York City expressed skepticism about US public education based on images of chaotic urban schools circulated by cable and news networks throughout the Caribbean. These expectations are entangled in a complex web of historical and structural forces that extends far beyond popular media culture and its invidious stereotypes of low-income Black and ethnic minority students, and the under-resourced schools in which they are often confined. Rather, Caribbean immigrant parents' expectations are shaped by their historical and contemporary encounters with British *and* US imperial governance. In the remainder of this chapter, I focus on Black Caribbean parents in New York City and their perceptions of the structural and cultural dissimilarities between Caribbean and US secondary schools. I point out how these differences are rooted in the United States' and Britain's different colonial relationships with Caribbean nation-states and their schools.

* * *

Colonial Formations in the 'American' Caribbean

The Caribbean was a central site of colonial conquest for the American as well as the British Empire. Although the formative role of British colonialism in Caribbean schooling is generally acknowledged, the sustained influence of US imperialism on schools in the Anglophone Caribbean is insufficiently recognized as a site of transnational political relations that ramify through the Caribbean diaspora. The historical analysis of colonialism that Mary Waters provides in *Black Identities* is illuminating, but limited based on its inattention to the colonial formation of schools in the Caribbean and the influence of such schooling on parents' and pupils' perceptions of schooling in the diaspora.[53] I contend that we must understand Black Caribbean parents' response to schooling in New York in the context of their perceptions and positioning in the British *and* US Empires before their immigration—perspectives on schooling that Waters largely overlooks.[54]

In its formation and scale, US colonialism has historically differed from British colonialism. Yet in its function and force as a mechanism of political control and cultural domination, US colonialism reflects and perpetuates patterns of power that are present in British colonial regimes.[55] The United States has directly governed and indirectly controlled Caribbean states to assert its economic and political interests. Whereas the British Empire included over a dozen territories in the region, the US Empire focuses mainly on Puerto Rico and part of the Virgin Islands. But its imperial power extends to other ostensibly independent nations, informing geopolitical ties, aid, and trade, and precipitating repeated political and military interventions.[56]

The influence of US colonial regimes on the structure of schools in the Caribbean, however, was largely confined to the territories the United States legally controlled. Under US rule, schools functioned as extensions of the state, socializing colonial subjects to the dominant mores and hierarchies of the US's racial capitalist society.[57] Accordingly, school systems in Puerto Rico and the US Virgin Islands have considerable structural similarities with the US school system. But there are considerable structural dissimilarities between the United States and most schools in the Anglophone Caribbean, as Table 2.2 shows.

US imperialism animates cultural and political life in the region.[58] Military invasions of Grenada, Cuba, Haiti, and Guyana throughout the 20th century

Table 2.2 Comparison of Caribbean and United States School Structures

Students' Age	Level of Schooling	Anglophone Caribbean	United States
3–4	Early Childhood	Nursery and Kindergarten	Pre-K and Kindergarten 1
5–11	Primary School	Grades 1–6	Kindergarten 2 and Grades 1–5
		National exams for regional secondary school placement	*State-based assessments in Grades 3 and 5*
12–16	Secondary School	Grades 7–11	Grades 6–8 (Middle School)
		Caribbean Secondary Exam Certificate	*State-based assessments in Grades 6, 7, and 8*
			Grades 9–12 (High School)
			Assessments vary from state to state
17–18	College/Sixth Form	Years 12–13	Continuation of High School
		A-Level Examinations	*No sixth form equivalent*
18–22	University	3 Years	4 Years
		Major typically based on A-level courses	*Major based on areas of interest*

contributed to the development of local governments both aligned with and resistant to US political-economic interests.[59] But US imperialism's historical force and contemporary influence are particularly visible in its persistent cultural dominance through expansive media technologies in the Caribbean.[60] Cable and satellite media shape the tastes, styles, and expressions that communicate power, privilege, and control.[61] Developed and expanded through transnational telecommunications networks based in the United States, the media circulate *selective* images of urban American life and schooling through movies, sitcoms, and news broadcasts that feature disfigured representations of African American culture and urban life rooted in deficit viewpoints.[62] Without context for recognizing the structural and cultural factors that shape life in the United States, Black Caribbean people acquired a limited or conflicted sense of urban public schools in the United States. In what follows, I explore how US imperialism through the US' dominant media culture in the Anglophone Caribbean shaped Black Caribbean parents' perceptions of schooling in New York City.

From Skepticism to Selective Excitement in the
United States

"I never really tink seh di [think that the] school dem woulda better inna
New York," Tony said, with doubt obvious in the tentative tone of his raspy
base voice. "Mi tink it would ah worse [I thought it would be worse], but I was
lookin' forward to faarin [foreign, i.e., the US], so mi come over still," he added.
Describing himself as a "man who was homeless, but now people work for me,"
he suggested that becoming a restaurant owner was the fulfillment of his own
American dream. Schooling for his children was another matter. This Jamaican
father of four praised his homeland's "quality schools" and shared what he called
"a sneaking suspicion" about New York City public schools that was common
among the Caribbean parents I spoke with. "These schools just look out of control! Dem mek mi skeptic [They made me skeptical]." Like other Newlands
parents, Tony said that his mistrust developed *prior* to immigrating to New York.

While sitting in the driver's seat of his old pickup truck, which he confessed
had been his home for years while getting his restaurant business off the
ground, Tony added depth to my understanding of one central mechanism in
the formation of "worry" and "concern" about New York City public schools
among immigrant Caribbean parents: the US media, which represents and
reproduces US cultural and political-economic dominance in the Caribbean
in the wake of what postcolonial theorist Frantz Fanon considered Britain's
"dying colonialism."[63] The media conveyed skewed portraits of the conditions
of schooling in the United States. These working-class and middle-class
parents remarked that Hollywood movies represented urban public schools
as "outta ahdah [out of order]," as Tony put it.

Tony offered perceptive insights into the social and political formation of
skepticism through the US media when he said, "You know how me really
learn 'bout America before mi reach [I reached]? TV! That's when mi [I] realize seh [that] American school dem bad, especially inna di [in the] inner-
city fi [for] Black American kids."

Black Caribbean parents tended to ascribe their generally low expectations
of US public schools to their seeing old movies and more recent television series such as *The Wire*, a gritty crime drama that showcases police corruption,
illegal drug dealing, and the aggressive neglect of African American youth
in schools and other public institutions in Baltimore, Maryland.[64] When
I asked about the movies that had contributed to that impression, he zoomed
in on the drama *Lean on Me*, which recounts how a tough-love, no-excuses

Black male principal turns around a largely disruptive and failing student body in a community marred by crime and drugs.[65] "Breddrin', di man haffi put chain pan di door dem fi keep out di drug dealer dem [Brethren/Brother, the man had to put chains on the doors to keep out the drug dealers]!" Tony was convinced that no school was "that bad in Jamaica."

"But, you know that show is about a school in [New] Jersey, not New York, right?" I said.

"Bredda [Brother], when mi watch it back home, mi never really see di difference."

"OK, but yuh know all of what they show you is a stereotype, right?" I asked.

"No, it's based on a true story!" he quipped.

"Yes, but how they show it in the movie is based on stereotype," I insisted.

"Well, stereotype or no stereotype, it ah show mi something!"

"Wah it show yuh?" I asked.

"Some ah dese schools dangerous fi yuh kids dem!" he replied.

"But not all or even most schools are like that. Have you ever seen a school like that?" I continued.

"No, but I don't want to . . . . Dat's why yuh affi watch dese schools [That's why you have to watch these schools]." Not only was Tony's wariness before his arrival in New York widely shared among Black Caribbean parents, but they too credited the media with making them dubious about the quality of public education in New York City.

At the height of new cable and telecommunication connections for households throughout the Caribbean in the 1980s and 1990s, Black Caribbean parents learned about US schools from Hollywood's misrepresentations.[66] Depictions of spectacularly unruly Black and Latinx students, disengaged parents, and crime-ridden neighborhoods played into white middle-class fantasies about the inner city and its schools, while yielding higher profits for the corporate movie industry.[67] Movies and television "both entertain and educate," serving as a form of what cultural critic Henry Giroux calls "public pedagogy."[68]

Giroux asserts that as the industry "reproduce[s] a magical combination of entertainment and fantasy," it "conceals the political and ideological nature of the pedagogical work it performs."[69] While inculcating private consumerism rather than the value of public schools as a public good among its international viewers, for its domestic audience it legitimizes cultural and financial disinvestments in public schools.[70] It focuses primarily on the behavioral and attitudinal problems of low-income and working-class African American and Latinx youth, rather than the prolonged histories of residential segregation, gentrification, un(der)employment and economic disinvestment that impact urban public schools.[71] Furthermore, these movies portray structural challenges largely as cultural problems in "those public schools."[72] Given the structural racism, residential segregation, social marginalization, and economic disadvantage that immigrant Black Caribbean parents often experienced upon arrival in New York City, some of "those public schools" became *their* public schools.[73]

Other Caribbean parents said that the news offered memorable portraits of crises in New York City's public schools, which during these years were convulsed by a struggle for power between educators and Black parents that included strikes and boycotts, as well as conflicts among students both in and out of school. Annett, a Barbadian nurse and mother of two, explained: the news "was never good about American schools in general, but especially the inner-city schools like in New York."

"How do you know it was New York?" I asked.

"They would say it. . . . and because my family was in Flatbush [Brooklyn], I used to pay attention to what the news was saying over there."

When I asked her to elaborate, she paused for a moment, and then recounted: "The news in New York was about the gangs in schools, fights, and that sort of thing. . . . They had colors and bandanas. It just seemed scary." She widened her brown eyes and folded her brow. "We don't have anything like that in Barbados. Nowhere back home is like that. . . . The children they have fights and all that, but gangs? In schools?"

I heard a similar report from Lorraine, a Grenadian nurse and parent leader at Newlands. She, too, had learned about New York public schools from the media. "I was glad to come over here, but I really had deep, deep concerns about these public schools in New York. . . . I know they are not all the same, but I didn't know which one I would get. Being here now, I realize maybe I didn't have to worry so much, but back then, I was just nervous because of what was on TV about these schools."

"Did you question what you were seeing or hearing about New York schools? I asked.

"No, well, I guess a little. I asked about my nieces and cousins, but they were young. . . . But when you see the news talking about gangs, fights, the police, metal detectors, and other things, what are you supposed to believe? I was like, I have to find a good part of the city to live in . . . like Queens!"

"The news only focuses on what's bad sometimes, or maybe you just remember the bad stuff," I said, anticipating a debate.

"Well, that's true," she said. "I did question things over here when Dwayne started going to school. I realized it wasn't as bad as I thought. And I fight to make sure he went to Newlands and not some of these other zone [local] schools."

"Right. I understand," I said.

"But to be honest," Lorraine continued, "when I realized New York schools are not like the movies, I couldn't stop thinking about how the schools back home were better than schools over here, still."

Tina, a soft-spoken Jamaican restaurant server and mother of two, put it a bit more pointedly: "I learn that New York schools are not bad, but not bad is not good enough for me. If Lisa [her daughter] was back home, she would be attending Immaculate, Andrew's, Holy Childhood, Wolmer's, or somewhere like that. That's the kind of school we have back home!" she said, brimming with pride.

The Jamaican secondary schools Tina named are among the oldest and most prestigious institutions founded for elite girls during the colonial period. The skepticism about New York public schools that parents like Tina expressed had its roots both in their *selective memories* of schools in the Caribbean, during a *particular time* in Caribbean history, and in the *surplus meanings* constructed by media representations of US urban public schools. The scripts showcased in the popular US media encode racialized messages about cities and the people who inhabit them. Black Caribbeans adopted ethnic expectations of African Americans as "not working hard enough," a description that Tina adduced. This derogatory culturalist claim ignores the long history of structural and institutional disadvantage in African American education.[74] As Black Caribbean parents absorbed media images of US urban life prior to immigration, they became skeptical about US urban public schools without any direct knowledge of them.

School Structures and Their Consequences in New York City

Though they arrived in the United States with ideas about schools already framed, Caribbean parents also drew on their own experiences in New York to suggest that school structures had harmful effects on students' learning.

When Tony parked his truck in front of his Jamaican restaurant, he was in the middle of trying to convince me that schools were "better back home." He conceded that schools in New York had "more money, better computers and bigger buildings than back home . . . and some of these teachers might have better qualifications too." But, like other Black Caribbean parents, he pointed to the presence of police in schools and the absence of "real uniforms" as signs of their ineffectiveness as learning environments.

"How you know seh [that] schools are better back home than over here?" I asked as we hopped out of the truck onto the street, with the clashing sounds of dancehall, calypso, hip-hop, and gospel ringing out from nearby stores. When he stepped into his restaurant, he said: "Breddrin', dem [they] have gun detectors an' police all over di school dem! It even deh pan TV inna di news [It's even on TV in the news]! Mi never see nuttin' [nothing] like dat [that] back home inna school."

"So that mean seh [that] school back home better? Just because of dem nuh have [they don't have] police? Dat nuh add up breddrin' [That doesn't add up, brethren]," I replied.

He sucked his teeth, chuckled, and then said "Come on," switching in an instant to an American accent. "A nuh dat nuh mo [It's not that alone]," he added in his undiluted Jamaican tongue. "These kids don't wear uniforms to school. Dese schools unorganized!" he exclaimed loudly. I realized that everyone in the restaurant had heard him when the women and men waiting in line for their servings of oxtail, patties, and other Caribbean culinary delights started chiming in. I got a focus group discussion I did not bargain for. Tony pointed to his patrons, calling my attention to their comments about why "these American schools ah nuh really di bes' [are not really the best]," as one woman put it. "You see," Tony asserted; "Ah nuh me one tink so [I'm not the only one who thinks so]." The views he expressed about school police, school uniforms, and school rules were widely shared. Clive, a Jamaican carpenter and father of four, said, "I was worried about all these police. That's not how schools run back home. The police only come to a school if something really serious happening."

When I met with Charmaine, a Jamaican nursing home aide and mother of two, she told me, "I didn't expect America and Jamaica to be the same. Of course, dem different. . . . But the high schools over here are doing things I have never seen a school do back home. Back home, uniforms meant something. That is how people got to know where you went to school and could look out for you. Students had to wear them. It taught them discipline. . . .

They say they have uniforms over here, but these kids still get to wear whatever they want. . . . If you can't get the basics right, why they expect that kids are going to listen to them? And then when things get bad they call the police. That's not how a school is supposed to be!" In response to my question about how schools should handle such matters, she replied that "what they are doing now is not working. . . . Back home, schools required discipline, respect, decency and order. Over here, anything goes. . . . It's just hard to really look forward to these kinds of schools for my children. Yuh know how many times mi plan fi [to] send them back home? They would get a better education out there!"

"You would send Tariq back home fi [for] real?" I asked.

"Yeah. He would be way ahead of where he is now. . . . The schools back home are harder. You have to take more classes. And the quality of the school environment is just better for kids like Tariq. He would learn to focus more because he would see more Black people achieving."

The perspectives Charmaine, Clive, and Tony shared about New York City public schools indicate a larger pattern of concern among immigrant Black Caribbean parents at Newlands. The presence of police as the coercive arm of the state, and the proliferation of surveillance technologies like metal detectors, struck them as "shocking," "scary," and either "signs of the times" or "unnecessary." Police officers had no place in schools in the Caribbean during these parents' years of schooling. These parents considered their experiences in the Caribbean "the good old days," "back when school was really school and everybody succeeded," "a time when teachers in the community really cared for us," and it was "hard because we didn't have money, but good because there was no racism." Their nostalgia was rooted in a peculiar golden vision of the Caribbean and its schools, and at a particular golden moment—though they often ignored the latter.

Much like their British counterparts, Black Caribbean parents in the United States summoned memories of Caribbean schooling to assert the value of Caribbean culture. Unlike their British counterparts, however, Black Caribbean parents in New York were not impressed by school buildings and material resources, which were often older and larger than schools like Londerville Secondary in London. They were centrally concerned with those who worked in the schools, and interpreted the presence of police as a key sign that US urban education was inferior to the schools they remembered attending in the Caribbean. In contrast to their children, they did not take the militarization of schools and the criminalization of pupils as a given.

Yet parents like Tony and Charmaine were aware that uniforms were used not only to classify students by school, but also to police their behavior and belonging in local communities in the Caribbean. Mandatory uniforms were a different way of "ensuring law and order," as Tony explained.

Black Caribbean parents like Tony and Charmaine came to think of schooling in New York City as problematic because of three main factors: media representations of urban public schools in the United States; memories of their own schooling in the Caribbean between the 1970s and the 1990s; and their own direct observations of schooling in New York City. These factors contributed to the collective and institutional distinctions, purportedly based on 'Caribbean culture', that Black Caribbean parents drew on to motivate their children to succeed.

Black Caribbean Parents in the United States and the Legacies of the US Empire

Throughout the Caribbean and the Caribbean diaspora, schooling is a practice of what Pierre Bourdieu called distinction.[75] The role of schools in reproducing economic, cultural, and symbolic boundaries in the Caribbean and its diaspora is an aspect of racial capitalism—or racial domination through structures and processes of economic (dis)investment and (dis)possession.[76] Commenting on these school-based distinctions in the post-independence Caribbean, Stuart Hall maintained that "people still ask, 'Where were you at school?', expecting the reply, 'I went to Jamaica College, or 'I'm a George's boy'; or in Barbados, 'from Harrison College'; or in Trinidad, 'Queen's Royal College'. Despite independence, these schools still function as a badge of social identification."[77]

This association is not simply an abstract quest for prestige and power; it is indicative of the lingering postcolonial habitus, ever-evolving, historically constituted dispositions and sensibilities rooted in (post)colonial legacies that live below consciousness.[78] The postcolonial habitus informs the habits of mind, emotions, and day-to-day actions of parents like Tony with regard to "good schools," "decent schools," and "bad schools."[79]

The schools 'back home' celebrated as 'good' by Black Caribbean parents like Charmaine are among the oldest on the islands, established by colonial authorities for the social uplift of the select few. Although parents are seldom aware of this history, they adhere to the logics of school-based distinctions to guide their expectations for their children's education, even in the diaspora. This lingering tendency is reinforced and reproduced across transnational migrant circuits in their evaluations of schools in New York City. Parents' positive descriptions of schooling in the Caribbean are part of the memories *and myths* that inform the postcolonial habitus. Schools in the Caribbean were hardly ever spaces in which "everybody succeeded." Indeed, the color-coded class hierarchies of Caribbean societies often mean that Caribbean configurations of race and racism are misrecognized or ignored in the context of US white supremacy.

The images of Caribbean schooling that parents like Tony and Tina conjure up are as partial and selective as the images of US public schools the media highlights. Both Black Caribbean parents' portraits of the Caribbean and its schools, and their preconceptions of urban schools based on US media, are skewed. Ideologies about urban spaces and schools inform meaning-making,[80] but so do the representational politics that shape what we think we know about people in urban settings, and who we regard as 'at-risk' or 'failing,' according to sociologist Ranita Ray.[81] Caribbean parents seldom account for the ongoing moral and economic disinvestment in US urban public schools in an era of privatization, high-stakes testing, and school 'choice' that shapes who is considered 'at-risk' or 'failing'.

The comparisons Black Caribbean parents like Tina and Troy make between schools in the Caribbean "back then" and schools in New York City "these days" often ignore the histories of power, prestige and international, colonial investment that shape *some* Caribbean schools in a regional political-economic context marked by debt and dependency on foreign aid. In this regard, Black Caribbean parents' perceptions of New York City public schools are complex formulations that negotiate the past in the present, and the present for the future.

Finding Schools, Finding Home

As I sat with Lorraine sipping ice-cold Malta drinks in New York and listened to Karlene over spicy brown stew chicken with rice and peas in London, I realized that home was more than the aesthetics of interior decoration and the culinary treats that signify Caribbean culture. For Karlene, Lorraine, and a host of other Black Caribbean parents in London and New York, home is both noun and verb. Home is an assemblage of mementos and memories from the Caribbean. But it also signifies power, creativity, and control. These parents' pursuit of 'good schools' and 'a good education' in London and New York City is an exercise in making new homes, spaces of belonging, and becoming for themselves and their second-generation children.

But home has its roots in the structures of power that mark the history of schooling in the homeland and the host society. British colonialism in Caribbean schools and society sustained an illusion of Britain as another home.[82] Parents like Karlene, Tiffany, and Clive entered Britain with high expectations that were often rooted in what Stuart Hall calls postcolonial nostalgia. Over time, however, they came to question the British state and reimagine education in the Caribbean when they recognized how badly British schools were failing their children. By contrast, American imperialist networks and media culture across the Caribbean broadcast a vision of urban life that made Black Caribbean immigrant parents enter the United States with comparatively low expectations of public schools. These differences shaped their reactive or proactive resistance to the schools their children attended in global cities.

I assert that we cannot fully understand Black Caribbean people's experiences of schooling in the diaspora unless we account for their perceptions of schooling in the homeland. This is what Mary Waters misses in her study, *Black Identities*, and US and British sociology of race, culture, education and immigration seldom explores. Colonialism and ongoing imperial ties facilitate Caribbean immigrant parents' perceptions and their positioning.

Historians, sociologists, and political economists have documented the social life of colonialism throughout the world—from its white supremacist investments in conquest, enslavement, and indentured servitude to its racial capitalist commitments to profit accumulation through the exploitation of land, labor, and people.[83] Despite the patterns of domination associated with colonialism globally, the character of colonialism differs across Empires and time periods.[84] British and US colonialism are distinct in their history, scale, expansion, contemporary significance, and the representations of English-speaking Black Caribbean people within them.[85]

Differences in cultural narratives about Black Caribbeans in Britain and the United States are not necessarily about who Caribbean people are, but *where* they are and how they are positioned. Black Caribbean people are *positioned differently* in US and British colonial projects. Black Caribbeans are *primary subjects* of British colonialism, and those who journey to the British Isles have been oriented by Caribbean schools and society to think of Britain as another home. In contrast, Black Caribbean people who have migrated to the United States are *secondary subjects* of ongoing settler colonialism, relative newcomers striving in the United States due, in no small part, to the advocacy and advancement of Native Americans and African Americans. These are some of the dynamics that Margaret Gibson, Signithia Fordham, and John Ogbu gestured toward as necessary for understanding the achievement and experiential differences in education of the same ethnic group across national contexts.[86]

The politics of colonial education in the Caribbean underscores the fact that the value of 'Caribbean identity' and Black Caribbean 'culture', as an asset or a liability, is not a given, but a historically situated social and political construct. 'Culture' and 'identity' acquire meaning in specific political-economic contexts. That is also true of colonial and imperial states. Britain's towering historical-political power is informed by the enduring structures of colonial life, including the structural similarities of British and Caribbean schools. The United States' imperial power and dominant cultural influence through the media are more recent, and constitute a pervasive set of social forces in the English-speaking Caribbean.

The image of urban public schools that is initially most salient to Black Caribbean immigrant parents is shaped, not by their own experiences or by realistic portrayals of the full range of US urban public schools, but by the invidious, racist caricatures of the disorder that allegedly characterizes educational institutions whose student bodies are predominantly Black, Latinx, and Asian, and are located in urban neighborhoods with concentrated poverty. That positions Black Caribbean students in New York differently than their counterparts in London, affording them modest and comparative structural advantage in an environment shaped by distinct, but pervasive, ethnic expectations. Failure to understand these historical nuances and structural factors can result in shoring up the culture trap.

The next chapter examines one of the principal institutional mechanisms that sustains ethnic expectations as a culture trap in schools: academic 'ability' grouping.

3

Tracking Structures and Cultures

The Role of Academic 'Ability' Grouping

Ethnic expectations are not only constructed through skewed perceptions of ethnic cultures' power to influence achievement. They are also produced and perpetuated through academic 'ability' grouping.[1] It is through institutional practices like academic 'ability' grouping that cultures are *made* to matter in schools.[2] This chapter points out that teachers at Londerville Secondary in London and at Newlands High in New York City too often focused on ethnic cultures, rather than on the organizational structures in their respective schools, as shaping Caribbean students' achievement.[3] Despite good intentions and deep commitments to supporting students, teachers were often caught in the culture trap. This misplaced preoccupation with culture as the motivating factor in Black Caribbean students' achievement reflects the limited attention paid to institutional mechanisms like 'ability' grouping that reproduce racial and ethnic inequalities in schools. Cross-national perspectives on "the structure, mobility and effects of tracking" and other forms of 'ability' grouping challenge the idea that culture is the primary cause of Caribbean students' success or failure.[4] Meetings of the English teachers at Londerville Secondary and Newlands High brought this home to me.

Setting in London

The staff meeting began at 1:35 p.m. with classic icebreakers for a chilly Tuesday afternoon in London: hot cups of tea, the ritual requests for milk and sugar, and the swift stirring of spoons. As English department staff sipped their teas and took their seats in the conference room, Ms. Tounsel, a veteran white teacher and department head at Londerville Secondary, distributed a six-page packet to everyone. Moments later, Mr. Thomas, the headteacher, called the meeting to order. Each page presented one of the six ranked classes for English Language in Year 10, which they referred to

The Culture Trap. Derron Wallace, Oxford University Press. © Oxford University Press 2023.
DOI: 10.1093/oso/9780197531464.003.0004

as 'sets.' The first page included students of Asian, Black African, and white British heritage in the 'top set,' the highest-ranking 'ability' group, all but one of whom had projected A* (A+) to B grades for their national GCSE exams.[5] The second page, which highlighted Set 2, noted the achievement of Asian, Black African, white, and mixed heritage students with projected A* to C grades. Strikingly, there was only one Black Caribbean student in the second set and none in the first.

Most of the discussion focused on the students in 'bottom sets.' I quickly realized that these students were disproportionately Black and disproportionately Caribbean. Unlike the Black Caribbean, Black African, Asian, white, and mixed heritage students in Sets 3 and 4, these 'bottom set kids' had projected C, D, and F grades for English GCSEs. They experienced more suspensions, detentions, and exclusions during the academic year than students in Sets 1–4. "As you can see," said Ms. Tounsel, "a number of these students have behavioral difficulties, more than half of them are boys, and about 10 of them joined us within the last two years as managed moves from other schools across the borough. . . . It's not easy to catch up all these students in a year."

Arranging students according to sets based on prior attainment and perceived abilities was a fundamental feature of Londerville's approach to teaching and learning. Sociologists Becky Francis and Louise Archer suggest that this is also the case in most London secondary schools.[6] 'Ability' grouping, which is often referred to as tracking in the United States and as setting in Britain, was practiced throughout Londerville Secondary in Years 8–11, particularly for national GCSE subjects. This practice had profound consequences for Black Caribbean students. For example, in September 2012, over 91 percent of Black Caribbean students at Londerville in Years 8–11 were allocated to the middle and bottom sets in English. The same was true for 90 percent of Black Caribbean students in September 2013. The disproportionate placement of Black Caribbean pupils in lower-ranked courses fortified widespread ethnic expectations of Black Caribbeans as underachievers.

Tracking in New York

Black Caribbean students were more evenly distributed across tracks in New York. But teachers framed the few high-achieving Black Caribbean students as exemplary models of what Caribbean students were capable of. An exchange between teachers in the English department at Newlands High in New York City made these differences especially vivid for me.

When Ms. Plummer rushed into the staff room, the oak door slammed shut behind her, and the chatter in the room stopped, as if on cue. "Good afternoon, everyone. Sorry I'm late," said Ms. Plummer, a white assistant principal and longtime member of the Newlands teaching staff. Teachers slowly took their seats around the staff room table. Mr. Green, a white, long-serving department head, welcomed Ms. Plummer, and presented a generally positive overview of the Grade 10 students' anticipated performance on the upcoming statewide English Language Regents exam.[7] "Okay, let us look at the data," Ms. Plummer said, as a stack of stapled sheets was distributed. For about five minutes all I could hear was the sharp rustling of turning pages and faint chatter from students in the classroom next door.

"Well," Mr. Green began, "the majority of the students got passing grades for the second marking period. Over 70 percent of all sophomores are passing, which is pretty good."[8] A number of teachers nodded in agreement.

"Our goal is to make sure that every kid passes," remarked Ms. Plummer calmly.

"Yes," Mr. Green replied. "But some kids are better prepared for this than others . . . Name any of the top students from the list and you'll see that they are from the islands or they are African."

"Or Asian," Ms. Forbes, a well-respected white English teacher, added casually.

Although the data we perused listed students in alphabetical order, the fact that there was an order of anticipated achievement became clear when teachers chimed in to comment on students' performance in their respective classes: first the two honors classes, followed by the three college prep classes, and finally the two special education classes. Given what I had experienced at the English department meeting at Londerville, this meeting at Newlands aroused a troubling sense of déjà vu.

In reviewing the data for their honors classes, Mr. Sterling and Ms. Forbes highlighted the highest achievers: two were recent immigrants from Jamaica, and another was a second-generation Black Caribbean student whose family hailed from Trinidad and Tobago. "All my students got 80 percent or above for the last marking period," Sterling said. "I think they'll do well on the Regents and be ready for AP next year."[9] Ms. Forbes nodded and offered a similar assessment. Like most of the classes at Londerville, the honors classes at Newlands were a rich mix of Black African, Black Caribbean, African American, Hispanic, white, and East Asian students. Black Caribbean students were not overrepresented in honors classes, but their achievement was overemphasized. Teachers like Mr. Sterling did not explain the measured successes of these few Black Caribbean students in terms of their immigrant status, prior fluency in English, or social class position. "It's in their culture," he opined. "They have discipline, manners and respect . . . they don't all live up to it, but they can."

Black Caribbean students at Newlands navigated a relatively flexible, subject-by-subject, school-specific tracking system, which allowed them regular access to more advanced material in a range of courses and years even if they were not in advanced classes. In London, by contrast, Black Caribbean students at Londerville negotiated a relatively regimented, subject-based, nationwide setting system, which often left them "stuck in their tracks," as one Black Caribbean teacher explained. The structure of academic 'ability' grouping, as noted in Table 3.1, shaped the nature of ethnic expectations at each school. 'Ability' grouping was one key strategy through which teachers inadvertently set up the culture trap in schools, despite their hard work on a day-to-day basis to support students. In what follows, I highlight how Black Caribbean students experience setting in London and tracking in New York. I point out how Black Caribbean students and their teachers make sense of such 'ability' grouping practices, and how these sorting practices facilitate ethnic expectations as a culture trap.

'Stuck in Their Tracks': Black Caribbean Pupils in London

"It all comes down to your marks," Mr. Andrews said with the crisp cadence that marked his London accent. This young, Black Caribbean Mathematics teacher with seven years of full-time teaching experience was a favorite among students. "How you do on your end-of-year assessments will determine which set you get into. That's what it comes down to, really." Mr. Andrews and I had been talking for an hour after his last class of the day when his comments on setting as an unequal process clarified the power of 'ability' grouping not only at Londerville, but in British schools and society.

Table 3.1 Academic 'Ability' Grouping Arrangements (2012–2015)

	Londerville	Newlands
Primary form of 'ability' grouping	Rigid, exam-based subject-by-subject setting	Flexible, interest-based subject-by-subject tracking
Academic tracks	• Top Sets (1 and 2) • Middle Sets (3 and 4) • Bottom Sets (5 and 6)	• Advanced placement • Honors • College Preparatory • Special Education
Primary criteria for assignment	• Test scores and prior attainment in subject at Londerville	• Test scores and prior attainment in subject at Newlands • Student's interest for Advanced Placement classes
Secondary criteria	• Disciplinary record • Behavioral reputation • Primary school grades • Initial assessments after secondary school enrollment	• Disciplinary record • Behavioral reputation • Teacher recommendations • Interviews • Work Samples • Middle school grades

When he emphasized the centrality of exam scores for set assignments, I pressed the question: "It really all comes down to grades and tests?"

"Well, when students come from primary school, yeah, we look at their record—grades, comments, disciplinary issues, etcetera. We also give them an exam or two when they start Year 7, and then setting begins. . . . But really, all the decisions are typically based on prior attainment data."

Teachers throughout Londerville corroborated Mr. Andrews's claim, pointing to test scores as the principal means through which students are assigned to sets. Ms. Tounsel offered a more complicated view: "Grades are very important, but we also think about how that student has done all year. If a student has been an A* student all year and then they get a C on the end-of-term exam, we will usually discuss that . . . to see which set we think the child should be placed in." But this was more the exception than the rule, and was often reserved for students in top sets. "It's usually for the odd student who slips on an exam," she said. When I shared these perspectives with Mr. Andrews, he agreed.

Despite teachers' efforts to support all students' academic success, the rigid, test-based set assignment mechanism at Londerville resulted in fundamentally different and unequal support for students, which was felt most acutely by those at the bottom of the hierarchy. "Setting don't really work for everybody, bruv," Mr. Andrews said, his baritone filled with an urgency uncharacteristic of this mild-mannered man.[10] "It works for students in top set, but it definitely doesn't work for us."

"What do you mean it doesn't work for us?" I asked.

He paused, searching my face as if to question my question.

"These Caribbean young people, man! It doesn't work for them lot, especially for these Black Caribbean boys . . . Looking at so many of them in my class, in the bottom sets or the bottom of the middle sets, is like watching a sad movie at the cinema I have watched too many times." Like a few recently hired Black and ethnic minority teachers at Londerville, Mr. Andrews was recruited with the hope that he would support "struggling students like Black Caribbean boys." At least, that is how he explained it. But, Mr. Andrews said later, setting as an institutional force at Londerville seemed more powerful than he was as an individual.

"Every year since I've been here, yeah, and even at the school where I was before, yeah, the middle and bottom sets have a lot of Caribbean boys and some girls . . . They come to secondary school bright and leave here at the bottom." Mr. Andrew's awareness of the institutional positioning of Black Caribbean students inspired his resistance: "I work hard, really hard bruv, to support them so that they can move up. But it's like once they're in bottom sets, it's like they can't get out. Once they're in the middle, it's easier for them to go down a set than go up a set. The sets are basically static . . . It's like they get stuck in their tracks."

For half an hour, Mr. Andrews spoke to me about how "setting in school causes setting in life." This time, I heard him with my heart as well as my ears. We both nodded slowly until silence joined us at the table. He dropped his eyes. He hung his head. I didn't understand Mr. Andrews's silence until I saw him wipe away tears. "Oh man, I'm sorry. You alright breddrin'?" I said. He raised his head. "These sets can impact the rest of your life, bruv . . . a lot of my brothers, my sister and even the man dem [young men] I grew up with lost opportunities in school and in general, yeah, and I think a lot of it started to happen through this set thing."

We paused again, before Mr. Andrews continued: "And it's tough, 'cause you can't say it's racism, 'cause if you do, management and even some of the teachers you're talking to, yeah, will just fob you off and say, 'Well, African students are doing alright, the Indian students are doing good, and white working-class students are doing worse . . . It can't be racism!' It's Caribbean culture, innit? How we act, innit?"

"Hhhhmmmm," I said, his statements reminding me of what Ms. Bell said at the beginning of this research project about the misuse of Caribbean culture to explain underachievement and misbehavior in British schools.

"But fam," Andrews said, fervor filling his voice, "I don't care what they want to say or what they want to call it! This set system, yeah, cause damage and disadvantage. It causes students at the bottom to suffer."

"I hear you bruv," I said, "but if you feel so strongly about setting, why do you teach in a school with it?" I cringed as soon as the last words left my lips.

He laughed. "Where else am I going to go where sets don't exist? It's all over the . . . school system. . . . You've just got to . . . study how it works in the school where you are and try to make a difference for these students."

Mr. Andrews's brief outburst of boisterous laughter to my awkwardly confrontational question was followed by what seemed like simmering fury about the power of setting as a system-wide institutional arrangement and the limits of his power to change it. "I fight the low expectations for Black Caribbean students that they get through sets all the time! I tell them they can do anything they want to. All the teachers here would say that . . . but where they fall in the set system is teaching them more, a whole lot more, about what we think of them and where they will go in life."

Many teachers agreed that setting adds disadvantage to already disadvantaged students, a burden that educational researcher Becky Francis and her colleagues refer to as "double disadvantage."[11]

Keeping Score: Teachers' Views of Setting

"Double disadvantage" contributes to inequalities in schools and society, and Mr. Andrews was not the only teacher at Londerville who knew it.[12] Mr. James, a white Mathematics teacher in his fourth year at Londerville who described himself as "a boy from the council estates," explained: "Setting sets up more students for failure than it sets them up for success . . . that's how we get the attainment gap."[13] Mr. Andrews's account focused on the advantages setting confers and whom it favors: "Setting helps out the students who are already getting help. A lot of them are middle-class students, white students,

Asian students, students that can pay for private tuition [tutoring], students who get help from their parents at home, kids who have parents who know a friend who can help their children think about uni and what it takes to get in."[14] For privileged pupils, placement in the top sets confers a double advantage. As I observed during my fieldwork, and other sociologists like Louise Archer and Karolyn Tyson suggest, privileged students are often rewarded with the most experienced teachers, more rigorous materials, and trips to cultural institutions.[15]

For teachers like Mr. James, Mr. Andrews, and their colleagues, setting informs students' experiences of distinction for those at the top and of disadvantage for those in the middle and at the bottom of the hierarchy. At schools like Londerville, top sets, which disproportionately serve the white and Asian middle classes, are sites of honor and prestige, recognizing and grooming high-achieving pupils for leadership in school and the workforce.[16] By contrast, those in the lower and bottom sets, who are disproportionately from Black, white, and South Asian working-class families, all too often experience these classes as sites of stigma—socially demoted spaces of punishment for controlling and redirecting low-performing students. They often have novice teachers, less rigorous course materials, and restricted access to co-curricular activities.[17] Set assignments are regarded as if they are 'objective' and 'fair,' but they inadvertently code achievement by ethnicity, race, and class.[18]

With only one exception, the teachers I observed at Londerville seemed acutely aware of the impact of setting on the reputation of Black Caribbean students. Mr. Thomas, the headteacher, explained, setting affects "all students in bottom sets, really. It's not about Caribbean people or Black people or minority ethnic people or working-class people." But to him and a number of department leaders, setting was not the problem. Using test results as the primary set assignment criterion was not the problem either. In fact, Mr. Thomas argued that "doing setting based on the same test makes it fair across the board." Leaders like Ms. Tounsel often rationalized students' outcomes as a consequence of their behavior, attitude, resources, and work ethic—or the lack thereof—rather than as the predictable result of the rigid set assignment system that in principle permits, but in practice restricts, mobility between sets. At least, that is how Black Caribbean students at Londerville experienced it. Although not a single student in Sets 5 and 6 moved to a higher set during the 2012–2013 academic year, Ms. Tounsel claimed, "it's not that setting doesn't work for students. I mean clearly it does . . . It's just that some students, including some Black Caribbean students, don't do their best in sets. That's why we have GCSE and BTEC options so that all our students can show what they are good at . . . Students can show their progress through projects, portfolios, etc. Exams don't work for everyone."[19]

"But Ms., isn't that just low expectations?" I asked.

"No, not at all. It's different high expectations," a phrase I heard frequently at Londerville.

Mr. Andrews disagreed. "BTEC is vocational and the students and teachers think it's not really intellectual. And that's where they want to place our Caribbean students, white working-class boys. . . . It's definitely preparing them for a different path in life and they are pretty much stuck on that path. . . . That's just a different kind of setting."

Ms. Tounsel's and Mr. Andrews's responses illustrate the sharp differences in teachers' perspectives on setting and other 'ability' grouping practices in Britain. In her defense of setting as a valuable tradition of teaching and learning, Ms. Tounsel did not recognize the rigid nature of set assignment criteria at Londerville and its consequences for disadvantaged Black Caribbean pupils. In principle, students from any background could move from the middle to the top sets based on their exams. In practice, however, students' opportunities for meaningful upward mobility between sets were limited. As Mr. Andrews understood it, and as I observed, setting at Londerville functioned as an organizational arrangement that systematizes and reinforces unequal perceptions, inequitable provisions, and different expectations of Black Caribbean young people.

The data from the 2012–2013 school year at Londeryille provide important evidence of ethnic differentials in set placement and mobility. While students who self-identified as Black Caribbean constituted 19 percent of students in Years 10 and 11, 47 percent of Black Caribbean students in Mathematics were assigned to the middle sets and 43 percent to the bottom sets. In English, 44 percent of Black Caribbean students were placed in the middle sets and 49 percent in the bottom sets. Furthermore, in Mathematics, while 91 percent of Black Caribbean students in the top and middle sets persisted or improved, only 4 percent of Year 10 Black Caribbean students in bottom sets moved up to the middle sets. The situation of Black Caribbean students in English was similar: 94 percent of Black Caribbean students in the top and middle sets maintained their rank, whereas only 3 percent moved from the bottom to the middle sets. The same was true in the two previous academic years, and it remained true when I visited Londerville again in 2014 and 2015.

Different and Divided in a British School

Black Caribbean pupils in the middle and bottom sets knew that they and their peers were often "stuck in their tracks." A meeting I had with four talkative Black Caribbean students in a brightly lit classroom at Londerville brought the issue into focus. When I asked them what they would like to change about their school and why, Daniel, a Year 10 student, asked, "How much time do you have?" Everyone chuckled. But what followed was a sobering exchange for us all.

"Well, first of all, yeah, this top set, middle set, bottom set thing is a problem that's got to go. It's a real problem still," said Odain, a Year 10 student of Grenadian and Jamaican heritage.

"Say more . . . How is it a problem?" I asked.

"The school is divided . . . the Caribbean lot dem are packed up in the middle and at the bottom in the lowest sets and only a couple of us are in top sets," Odain continued.

Without skipping a beat, Ted, who self-identified as British Trinidadian, added, "And the ones dem in the middle don't get pushed a lot. If we have a B or C, they're like, 'they are safe.' We're not safe, fam. Man's not safe!" Odain snapped his fingers in agreement.

"But placement in sets is based on grades and exam results, right?" I asked.

"Yeah, it's based on how hard you work and how you do on your exams," replied Joy, a Year 10 student. Her response seemed to be an affirmation of meritocracy.[20] Perhaps my question sounded like that too.

Odain sucked his teeth, and then looked straight at Joy. "Where you come from? That's rubbish, fam!" he said.

Laughter filled the room. After some hesitation, Joy stretched a smile across her face.

Odain continued: "Because we are in the bottom set so much, people think we don't work hard. Teachers look at us like we are not really good students even when we are in the middle sets . . . We stay in middle and bottom set, yeah, every year . . . You don't see it?"

Anthony, a Year 11 student, stood and clapped.

"Yeah, I see it," Daniel responded. "My mates dem run jokes that we [Black Caribbean young people] are cool but we're not clever."

"Hmmm . . . I've heard that before too. That's out of order!" said Joy.

Odain elaborated: "But, like, where do you think that kind of perspective about Black Caribbean people come from in this school? It's this top set bottom set foolishness bruv . . . People think that because we might be in the bottom set that we are at the bottom of the school. Teachers who don't know us meet us and just assume that we are not good students. That's disrespect for real."

Soft-spoken Joy seemed to be the contrarian in the room, with disconfirming cases at the ready. She said, "Well, it's not really like that exactly. Right? Ron is captain of the music band, Romel is captain of the football team. Monique is Deputy Head Girl and she is proper brilliant."

"Yeah," said Ted. "Akilah, who is always top in English in Year 10, yeah, got a 54 percent the other day and we were shocked 'cause she is really bright."

"But 'Kilah, Monique and Ron are different from the rest of us," Daniel responded. "I think that's how the teachers see it."

Ted elaborated: "And they look down on the rest of us and make us feel shame and say that we don't do good because we are . . . naughty and bad at the books . . . I've been seein' this since Year 8 still. I don't like it man."

"Yeah . . . and, like, none of that change the fact that so many of us are in the bottom set," Odain agreed. "The people at the top, yeah, get there because they get private tuition on the regular." Anthony found his feet again. Daniel and Ted joined him with loud claps. Joy rolled her eyes.

"Preach it!" Anthony exclaimed.

Odain had the final word. "Even the Caribbean students there have parents who went to uni and . . . who help them a lot . . . It's madness bruv . . . How is this fair? This is not right at all. People want us to believe that we [Caribbean students] are the problem. But I'm not with that still . . . Even the kids who need help the most don't get it. That's the problem." Odain spoke with a steely conviction I've yet to forget. Like other Black Caribbean students in this study, Odain possessed what sociologist Paul Willis referred to as "the penetrative gaze"—a capacity to see clearly and deeply the structures of inequality that shaped their cultural worlds.[21]

Among the wide range of focus group interviews I conducted with Black Caribbean pupils at Londerville, this discussion most poignantly typifies the multilayered meanings Black Caribbean youth associate with setting in school. Like Odain, Daniel, and Ted, although with varying degrees of conviction and passion, several students decried setting as a system that segregates and stigmatizes Black Caribbean students. They were acutely aware that setting is an institutionally legitimated arrangement that produces and reproduces deficit perceptions of Black Caribbean pupils, shores up meritocratic claims about ability, and misrepresents high achievement as a function of hard work, rather than as a result also shaped, at least in part, by teacher preferences and class advantages.

This discussion with Odain, Joy, Daniel, and Ted underscores the significance of ethnic expectations as a normative practice informed by institutional arrangements. The racial and ethnic achievement hierarchies in schools like Londerville are facilitated by the consistent placement of students in top, middle, and bottom sets. Black Caribbean students' low ranking was not regarded as an alarming sign of a flawed institutional strategy, but commonly interpreted as a signifier of aptitudes, attitudes, and achievement.[22] Black Caribbean pupils regularly contended with the misattribution of academic success to individual character and talents, given some educators' failure to recognize the everyday impact of setting at Londerville, just as they themselves contend with neoliberal market pressures of increased 'efficiency,' 'productivity,' 'assessments,' and 'targets' characteristic of high-stakes accountability in public schools imposed by local and national educational authorities.[23]

The negative perceptions of Black Caribbean young people at Londerville are not necessarily influenced by educators' individual racial animus or disdain for Black Caribbean culture and identity. Just as sociologists Amanda Lewis and John Diamond found in their study *Despite the Best Intentions*, teachers and administrators at Londerville were well-meaning and appreciative of racial and ethnic diversity.[24] The deficit narratives that students reported as associated with Black Caribbean young people, such as being 'naughty' and 'bad at the books,' are facilitated, at least in part, by the comparatively rigid sorting system that produces racialized and classed outcomes, and limits upward mobility between tracks for Black Caribbean students.

The 'Trickle Up' Effect

Black Caribbean students in the top and middle sets leveled critiques about setting as a segregating, stigmatizing practice similar to their peers in the bottom sets. The high concentration of Black Caribbean pupils in lower sets at Londerville shaped and reinforced popular deficit views of Black Caribbean pupils as underachievers. Black Caribbean students in the top and middle sets had to contend with this stubborn stereotype as well. Ethnic expectations 'trickle up' across sets and carry with them high costs for students' social-emotional health and well-being.

I first realized the significance of this problem when Akilah, a Year 10 student in the second set for English who usually got A's and B's, questioned Ms. James's remarks about her "already exceeding expectations," even though her mock exam grade was lower than many of her peers. When I spoke with Akilah a month later, her comments enriched and deepened my understanding of ethnic expectations as a culture trap and the affective consequences associated with them. She explained in a somber tone:

> When I got 54 percent on my English exam, I was shocked . . . To be honest, I was ashamed 'cause I usually do well on my exams. And I am one of three Black students in the top set for English and Maths. I felt like I let down my Caribbean friends who for whatever reason never make it to the top set . . . This is not happening out of the blue . . . Teachers who predict our grades have a lot to do with it.

As one of the only Black Caribbean students in the top set in English, Akilah said, "I just feel like, like I'm under a lot of pressure to show up for Caribbean people." Just as Black feminist sociologist Heidi Mirza suggests in *Young, Female and Black*, Black Caribbean girls like Akilah have strong desires to achieve but are often burdened by the politics of racial and ethnic representation in their schools.[25]

Akilah's Black Caribbean peers highlighted the emotional weight they carried as they pursued success. Roy, a precocious leader and gifted musician of Jamaican heritage who was also in top sets for English and Mathematics, expressed a sense of isolation and felt driven to succeed in order to puncture myths of Caribbean cultural identity as a signifier of academic failure at Londerville. He had been surprisingly terse during our chat that day, until I asked him about sets and their consequences. He responded:

> A lot of my Caribbean mates are in the bottom sets. Every year it's the same thing. I don't really like it, still, 'cause the Asian and white students, yeah, may think that Caribbean culture equal failure or struggle in school. I'm starting to see, yeah, that if you're Caribbean and even if you're not in the

bottom set, people just assume you'll be there sometime or they forget that you're Caribbean at all if you don't get there. It's like teachers and the other students, yeah, are just putting this burden on you one way or another . . . It's just how it is with this set thing.

Roy and Akilah understood setting as an organizational strategy that influences students' conception of their abilities, sense of self, and psycho-social well-being. Some Black Caribbean pupils, even those in the middle and top sets, are acutely aware of the emotional consequences of setting in their school. The shame, uneasiness, and frustration they express invite a re-consideration of setting as an institutional arrangement with affective as well as academic consequences. Sociologist Louise Archer and her colleagues found that young people across London schools respond in similar ways.[26] Popular narratives of Black Caribbean pupils as underachievers create what Roy called a 'burden' and serve as a yardstick against which their educational outcomes are assessed.

Peter and Peta-Gaye illuminated the multivalent nature of ethnic expectations for Black Caribbean students at Londerville Secondary. Peter, a jovial but studious artist who described himself as Black British Bajan [Barbadian], offered his perspective on setting and its discontents:

> People always talk about how Caribbean kids are this and that and whatnot and that we are not achieving . . . You are always fighting against this even if you're in the middle set . . . I have B's and a C in my subjects and I think I could get A's in some of them, but I don't really think our teachers push us up like that so you just get stuck . . . unless you can get private lessons or go to Saturday school or something.

Though Peter's fast-paced chatter and bellowing base were quintessentially his, the critiques of setting he articulated during our exchange echoed the views of many of his peers. Peta-Gaye voiced her perspectives with marked intensity while walking upstairs to the school library:

> You see, yeah, because lots of these teachers and students get these ideas about Caribbean students, you have to think about where it comes from . . . Dem have their perceptions yeah, but what is the source? . . . Tests and sets! It's so frustrating. When you're in top set yeah, you brag about it. You feel good, but you can't run away from the fact that most people

in top sets are not Caribbean and a lot of the rest are in middle and especially bottom set . . . The bad perspectives of Caribbean people in school just
trickle up to you, no matter which set you're in really.

All four students' comments signal their commitment to disrupting common
conceptions of Black Caribbean underachievement. Students question the
framing of Black Caribbean pupils as a group that, with a few remarkable
exceptions, is destined to fail. Instead, they regard the problem as the influence
of setting, which is a manifestation of institutional power. They refuse to be
complicit in the misrepresentation that distorts others' perceptions and stymies
the advancement of Black Caribbean pupils. Their trenchant critiques of setting are not a matter of principle alone. The concentration of Black Caribbean
pupils in lower sets at Londerville *and* the implications this disproportionate arrangement has for Black Caribbean young people across sets reveal that setting
reinforces racial, ethnic, and class domination.[27] As Peta-Gaye stated so clearly,
the distorted, negative narratives about Black Caribbean pupils in lower sets
"trickle up" to those in middle and top sets.

Black Caribbean young people must negotiate this set of preconceptions
every day. Placement in the middle and top sets does not insulate them from
the ramifications of low expectations. The pervasive stereotypes about Black
Caribbean young people in lower sets motivate academic progress for some
and undermine it for others. As Roy contended, these negative views encourage higher aspirations to avoid stigmatization, but they also ignore or de-
emphasize the achievement of Black Caribbean pupils in the top and middle
sets. At Londerville and other state (public) schools across Britain, setting
and other 'ability' grouping practices fuel ethnic expectations that damage
the self-confidence, ethnic group consciousness, and psychosocial well-
being of Black Caribbean youth, as well as perpetuate racial inequalities.[28]

Akilah, Paul, Roy, and Peta-Gaye maintained that teachers' perceptions
and expectations of this group inform students' placement in sets, their
predicted grades on exams, and the quality of the support they are offered.
Students I interviewed did not think that ethnic expectations are based on
disdain for Black Caribbean people per se. These prejudices are not enacted
in overtly racist, or violent attacks on individual students' cultural identities.[29] For educators, such blatantly discriminatory expressions would be in-
tolerable in an institution ostensibly committed to 'equality', 'diversity', and
'fairness'.[30] Instead, ethnic expectations are reproduced through a ranking
order in which race and ethnicity function as proxies for students' prospects
for academic success or failure.

* * *

At Londerville Secondary, ethnic expectations did not function as abrasive racist attacks on individual students' identities and belonging in the nation-state and its institutions, as was the case in the mid-to-late 20th century, with explicit expressions of cultural racism and violent assaults on Black students. Instead, ethnic expectations in the British context operate as the subtler repetition of negative perceptions and the projection of low achievement outcomes that are reinforced in the process of schooling. In this regard, ethnic expectations operate as a slow state of injury or unyielding misrepresentation for historically disadvantaged groups like Black Caribbean students in schools. In the remainder of this chapter, I examine the nature and influence of tracking on Black Caribbean students at Newlands High in New York. I explore how these students make sense of their cultural and political positioning facilitated by tracking in school. I highlight the intra-ethnic conflicts and collaborations that tracking inspired among second-generation Black Caribbean youth.

* * *

"They are in every program":
Black Caribbean Students in New York City

Ms. Forbes, a white tenured English teacher at Newlands High, declared in a tone that was both warm and matter-of-fact: "The Caribbean kids are in every program—regular college prep, honors, AP and everything in between. Caribbean kids are not really in honors or AP classes more than other students . . . Look in my classes, you'll see." Standing with me outside early one winter morning, letting off steam and blowing out smoke before her first class began, she questioned the claims about Black Caribbean students' high achievement that Mr. Sterling and other teachers insisted on.

"How do you know?" I asked. When Ms. Forbes sucked her teeth loudly, I realized that I probably should not have posed this searching question so casually.

"How you mean how I know? I've been here seven years and I've taught at all sort of levels. I know what I'm talking about," she replied.

"I didn't mean it that way," I said. "I meant, where's the evidence?"

Ms. Forbes responded: "We don't have concrete data on this because we don't track down scores for Africans separate from African Americans

and Caribbean kids like that, not in terms of statistics or numbers or whatever . . . maybe if they are just arriving in the country. . . but they all get listed
in the school database as Black." Administrators offered me the same explanation. Other teachers reinforced their claim about the relatively even distribution of Black Caribbean young people across academic tracks, despite the
lack of statistical data that identified Black students by ethnicity.

When we entered the building, Ms. Forbes sped up her pace as we
walked through the blue hallways under bright fluorescent lights reflected
on glossy gray floors. As we entered her classroom, with Spanish, Patois,
Pidgin, Kréyól, and English ringing out from all sides, Ms. Forbes articulated
teachers' common defense of ethnic expectations: "Some Caribbean students
stand out as top students, valedictorians, or scholarship winners." She then
ran through a shortlist of current and former students whose academic and
professional successes informed the high expectations many teachers have of
Black Caribbean students.

"Some of them do well, or really want to do well . . . they are motivated,
especially the ones straight from the islands, which is why they move up to
honors and AP so quick. . . . They're hungry for it . . . We want some of that
to rub off on the ones born over here," she said. As sociologist Mary Waters
noted in her study of Black Caribbeans in New York City, *Black Identities*,
public school teachers like Ms. Forbes noticed differences between immigrant and second-generation Black Caribbean young people.[31] But as I show
in this ethnography, the perceptions of ethnic culture and school structure
seemed to matter even more than Waters suggested.

Thinking of my experiences as a Jamaican who immigrated to New York
City in my mid-teens and attended a large public high school, I said to Ms.
Forbes, "All of the Caribbean kids from the islands are not like that."

"Well, not all of them," she conceded. "But a good number of them are
like that."

"Is that why Mr. Sterling talks like that about Caribbean kids in staff
meetings?" I asked.

"Well, . . . Sterling is taking the top or the best Caribbean students to mold
the rest . . . it don't matter to him if they are born here or not," Ms. Forbes
replied in a nonchalant manner. This effort to tokenize "the top or the best
Caribbean students" was central to the reproduction of cultural narratives
of Black Caribbean students as high achievers. The achievement of the top
Caribbean students was deemed so distinctive that it allowed teachers to
overlook the underachievement of others or attribute their poor performance

to what Ms. Forbes explained as "losing their culture" and "acting like Black Americans"—a framing that reinforces a cultural hierarchy between Black Caribbeans and African Americans.[32]

"Things Have Changed": Teachers' Views of Tracking

Mr. Green, the English department lead, offered me an orientation to tracking at Newlands as we sat in the corner of the staff room talking about what I had observed in his classes. He explained that, although tracking used to be based primarily on test scores, the criteria for placement had been changed. He was explicit about what was at stake for Black students, as well as for the school's reputation: "They are not grouped as the majority in one or another. That would be segregation . . . . Things are better now," he said, beaming with pride.

"But you still have a hierarchy of classes, from AP to honors . . ." I began. Before I could complete the sentence I had strung together in my mind, Mr. Green replied.

"Yes, but students have more opportunities now to get into top classes if they want to." The examples he offered were a snapshot of how tracking functioned at Newlands and other New York City public schools and its impact on, Black Caribbean students.

"A student like Janice who always gets 90 percent and above on her report card would be recommended to move up to AP or honors classes easily. But she could choose to stay in honors English or college prep English instead of taking the AP. . . . She can choose. . . . Not everybody can do that." Janice, a bright, easygoing 16-year-old in Grade 11 who had immigrated from Antigua three years earlier, had a reputation as a 'bookworm.' "They are not blocked in here like before," he reiterated. The ability to choose from all the track options seemed a privilege reserved for 'top students.'

"But not everyone is like Janice," I said, thinking of Black Caribbean students I observed occasionally skipping classes and publicly defending their lack of interest in school.

"Not everyone is like her, but there are more Janices out there," replied Green. He then listed a number of African, Asian, and Caribbean students. "Look at O'Neil. You know him, right?" I nodded, recalling the 11th-grade New Yorker of Jamaican heritage aspiring to attend an Ivy League institution. "Well, he's not the best English student in terms of grades, but he wanted to take AP English Language in his junior year and AP Literature in his senior year to help with his college applications.[33] So he got a letter from a former teacher, came and spoke with me about taking the course, like an interview, and then I asked him for a writing sample and he brought it to me. Now he's in AP English." Mr. Green was unable to hide the pride in his grin.

Mr. Green gave another example. Michael, an avid football player who self-identified as Jamaican and Caribbean American, "really struggled freshman year, especially in English . . . but when I saw he was ahead of his regular class last year, I started giving him and some other students honors work. . . . When he realized he could do the work, he moved up to honors English last year."

"In the same year?" I asked.

"In the middle of the school year," he replied with another grin.

"But that doesn't happen for Michael in every class," I said, trying to trouble Mr. Green's pride in the new approach to tracking at Newlands.

"No, but it can . . . it really comes down to the commitment the student shows in that subject. . . . A teacher can always give advanced work to help any student. . . . I support my teachers to do this."

Silence hung in the air, so I thought Mr. Green was done. I was wrong. He leaned across the table, his eyes half closed and his right index finger on his lips. "Ssssshhhh. It can make teaching hard," Mr. Green whispered. I watched his eyes scan the conference room to see if any of the other teachers over-heard him. "But it's what we have to do for the kids," he said.

Mr. Green's comments echoed sentiments expressed by other teachers and administrators at Newlands, who described the tracking system as "open" and "good for students now." A white Mathematics teacher, Ms. Kay, said it "empower[s] students," and Ms. Joyce, another white Mathematics teacher said it is "driven by students' talents and interests."[34]

Based on what Mr. Green suggested and what I observed, the flexibility of the tracking system at Newlands served at least two strategic purposes. First, subject-by-subject tracking actively accommodated students' aspirations even in the absence of high academic achievement, as O'Neil's case illustrates. Second, providing advanced work to selected students in lower-ranked courses introduced and prepared them for more rigorous courses for inter-ested students like Michael, boosting confidence and generating a pipeline to honors and advanced placement courses. Students were coached for suc-cess by teachers who encouraged their aspirations.[35] When Black Caribbean students emerged as 'top students,' teachers pointed to their example to mo-tivate other Black Caribbean students to do better. This process reproduced ethnic expectations and reinforced the claim that culture matters. Yet ethnic expectations functioned as a double-edged sword.

Divided by a Double-Edged Sword in an American School

The open secret about ethnic expectations is that they harm some Black Caribbean students, even as they uplift others. One exchange with five sophomores exemplified the mixture of pride and pain that figured prominently in my talks with Black Caribbean young people at Newlands. These cool, charismatic young men were all close friends. I had learned that hanging around them required not being unnerved by their jokes and disses, but hurling them back in fun as quickly as they came. When I sat with them in Newlands's spacious cafeteria one April afternoon, the smell of spaghetti Bolognese, hot dogs, beef patties, and curly fries wafted through the air. As they ate, they analyzed Black Caribbeans' academic success as a double-edged sword—often a point of pride for immigrant Black Caribbean students, but typically a source of pain for their second-generation counterparts.

Mark sparked the exchange when he asked fellow 10th graders Andre, Tom, Miguel, and Sean if they had heard about Tory's college acceptances. Ranked second in the senior class, Tory was regarded by her teachers and peers as a 'top student' and earned scholarships to all ten colleges and universities she applied to—a dream she had held since attending primary school in Jamaica. "I'm mad proud of her . . . that's up there for real. . . . It's a big deal," Mark said with more enthusiasm than I was used to from him. Andre's reply added spirit to the conversation: "Yo, Tory showin' them who run tings yaad man style."

"Yaad man? She's a girl," said Mark.

"I know, dumbass," Andre said to Mark, starting a tense to-and-fro between the two.

"So, what do you think Tory's accomplishments and other Caribbean students' accomplishments in school mean for you?" I asked, redirecting the conversation.

"Well, like, it's good for Tory and it's good for us . . . she is like on top. Like, at the end of the day, she's Jamaican. She's Caribbean. We rep that. She's one of us," Mark said.

"How do you rep that?" I asked.

Sean, a fast-talking, high-energy footballer, explained: "We shout her out . . . big her up . . . and we big up ourselves in class too . . . like, this one is for us as a team, as a group . . . we get to claim that 'cause we can do that . . . and now teachers are gonna shout us out in class . . . they know we can kill it." He gave Andre a quick fist bump.

I turned to Tom, who had been surprisingly quiet even during the banter between Mark and Andre—a match-up he hardly ever failed to referee. "What do you think, Tom?"

"I don't really care man. It don't matter," he said.

"Ah-haaa, dumbass," Mark replied. "He just mad cause he know Sterling comin' for him."

"Chill my nigga . . . what is you sayin' right now?" Andre remarked disapprovingly.

The heated exchange of insults between Mark and Andre reached a fever pitch. They did not stop until a school-based police officer intervened, and in so doing became their common target of disdain.

"So what'ch y'all think about Tory?" I asked again.

"Yo, this thing with Tory is not about us . . . this is not about Caribbean people," Tom said.

"Who is it about?" Mark asked. "You just hatin', man."

"Nah. I'm not. It's about Tory. We ain't like the kids from the islands," Tom contended.

"Sometimes these teachers act like these island kids are better than us . . . I'm like, nah. I kill it too," Mark said.

"But we still Caribbean. We eat Caribbean food, go to the same shops, live in the same place," Sean interjected. "We are one people."

"We might eat the same food and live in the same place, but we not like them," Tom insisted. "They come over here from school that be way harder than what we have here in America . . . that's what my moms and cousins be sayin' . . . and they not that smart . . . all of them are not good . . . but teachers like them. . . . Then stink Sterling grillin' me about a 70 'cause other Caribbean people from the islands get high grades."[36] Tom sucked his teeth, widened his eyes, raised his voice and said: "It's too much, man . . . I'm like, yo, I'm passin'. I'm good. We ain't all Tory."

"But most of the teachers don't be actin' like him," said Miguel. "Like, they will think what they want about us, but they ain't sayin' that in class like that."

Andre chimed in. "And it's not like people here don't think we out here smokin' weed, clockin' [punching] niggas, and cuttin' class." They all laughed.

"At least some of these teachers don't wanna see us fail like these Black American kids and Spanish kids and they try with us," Andre asserted.

"Man, some of these teachers think I'm Black American. They don't know the difference sometimes," objected Sean.

"But when some of them find out, like when my moms show up, it's a wrap," Tom said.

"Yeah, but still . . . you not gonna want someone to like, push you, and don't give up on you in class?" Miguel wondered.

This exchange between Tom, Miguel, Sean, Mark, and Andre encapsulates a central theme that emerged in discussions with all the second-generation Black Caribbean young people I spoke with at Newlands. These 10th-grade boys pointed out the tensions latent in the use of Black Caribbean cultural identity as a descriptive signifier of achievement and argued that its use as a prescriptive formula involved an unfair comparison. Their comments suggest that even if ethnic expectations aim to uplift and motivate some students, they undermine and marginalize others in the same school.

If we wade through the humor and banter, we find a salient political critique of the culture trap as a practice of cultural essentialism. When ethnicity is misused as a master code for interpreting students' achievement, irrespective of generational, class, and contextual differences, students experience ethnic expectations as a binding, obscuring force. Like other forms of the culture trap, ethnic expectations occlude a full view of Black Caribbean students and the varied structural and cultural reasons for their success and failure. The cultural essentialism that often undergirds ethnic expectations elides the significance of pre- and post-migration social class standing, gender distinctions, and immigrant generational differences, collapsing the variations among Black Caribbean students into a uniform 'culture.'

Mark, Andre, and Miguel found a discernable measure of pride in counting immigrant students like Tory as symbols of Caribbean culture, adding their support to the distinctiveness of Black Caribbeans as 'top students' and 'high achievers.' They celebrated these selective representations, even if these notions proved more limited and tokenistic than widespread and realistic. But to students like Tom, talk of 'Caribbean success' failed to recognize differences between immigrant and second-generation Black Caribbeans. These reductive claims treat culture "along ethnically absolute lines, not as something intrinsically fluid, changing, unstable, and dynamic, but as a fixed property of social groups," as historian and sociologist Paul Gilroy asserts.[37] For students like Tom, invidious comparisons between the individual and the group made by teachers like Mr. Sterling do not inspire emulation, but provoke anger and resentment, not only toward the teacher, but also toward immigrant co-ethnics whose successes are hoisted as evidence of others' underachievement.

The 'Trickle Down' Effect

The real and imagined positions of Black Caribbean students in the school's academic hierarchy shaped expectations of how they should perform. Teachers and students often assumed that even if Caribbean students were not ranked highly in their classes, "they could be at the top if they wanted to . . . especially the ones that have just come to America," as Mr. Green put it. Some teachers expressed these ethnic expectations in group or one-on-one meetings, rather than in front of students during class. Even in this milder, more measured form, though, these assumptions still had consequences for the opportunities and challenges Black Caribbean young people encountered.

Although teachers at Newlands held generally high expectations for what Black Caribbean young people were capable of achieving, praise from teachers proved more selective. The public celebration of Black Caribbean pupils was an earned reward distributed primarily to those perceived to be at 'the top of the top.' Tory and Janice won public praise from teachers and some of their peers for meeting or exceeding ethnic expectations. During staff meetings, Mr. Sterling, Ms. Forbes, and Mr. Green praised Caribbean students who received high scores. In sum, while performance expectations trickled down to Black Caribbean youth across tracks, teachers' effusive praise of Caribbean students was based primarily on performance distinctions, particularly exam grades and class rankings.[38] Curiously, students like Tory and Janice were not credits to their culture; their culture was a credit to them, making success, 'hard work,' 'discipline,' and 'drive' possible. By contrast, the 'failure' of students like Tom was not attributed to Caribbean culture. Mr. Sterling and Ms. Forbes perceived it as an individual shortcoming and a sign of cultural inauthenticity.

While conceiving of Caribbean culture as a significant contributing factor to students' success, teachers largely ignored the role of the school's institutional structures and programs. Newlands High's advanced work and tutoring programs facilitated the identification and development of top students across tracks. A series of exchanges with 10th Grade students

Kerry-Ann, Mark, and Miguel illuminated this fact. These three students had braved the blustery winds in the depths of winter to meet with their Mathematics teacher, Ms. Joyce, at 7:30 a.m. before school began. Like the two additional students in attendance, Kerry, Mark, and Miguel sat at their seats, as Ms. Joyce assisted them with problem sets they did not understand. After the tutoring session ended and Ms. Joyce left the room, I asked, "Do you think the teachers favor Black Caribbean students?"

"What?" Kerry-Ann remarked, her voice ice cold. She tensed up. Her eyes traveled to the two Asian and Hispanic students about to leave the room. When they closed the door, I continued: "I just wanted to know if you think the teachers prefer Caribbean students. Straight up."

"No," she mouthed slowly, "I don't think so."

Mark had a different opinion, and I knew this outspoken leader would tell me why. "I think they like some of us . . . it depends . . . Ms. Joyce likes the students who work hard and don't cause no trouble for her."

"But we [Caribbean students] get in trouble all the time!" Kerry-Ann insisted. I nodded in agreement, recalling recent fights in the hallway that resulted in the suspension of two Caribbean boys.

"I don't think it's every Caribbean kid . . . but some of us show up for lessons in the mornings or we ask for extra work, especially the island kids," Miguel responded.

"I'm mad surprised ain't none of them here," Kerry-Ann said, looking around her as if she saw people in the empty seats.

"For real," said Mark. "But I think teachers definitely prefer them [Caribbean immigrants]!"

"Yeah!!" Kerry-Ann and Miguel said. I could hear the tinge of excitement at the end of their voices. It was a eureka moment for them—and me.

"We, like, the ones that are born here, have to prove ourselves. Low key, the teachers don't think we're Caribbean unless we tell them," Miguel said. "Or unless they see we work hard a lot . . . like clubs, classes, extra help . . . then they be like, nah, he must have people from the islands."

"Or we're still, like, into the culture," Kerry-Ann added.

"So you think it's because you show them that you're smart? That's why they [teachers] support you?" I said.

"I dunno," Miguel said. "You gotta work hard. Get good grades."

Mark broke his silence. "When they give you extra work, it's not about getting the answer all right or whatever. You just gotta work hard. Try. Work at it. Come to tutoring. That's what they like."

" 'A' for effort," Kerry-Ann joked. "I got into honors because I kept doing the extra work."

"Yeah," Mark said, "'cause teachers only shout you out if you failin' or if you killin' it [excelling]."

"Or help you if you show up on the regular for tutoring," added Kerry-Ann.

At Newlands, ethnic expectations trickled down, and through the school's tutoring and advanced work programs some Caribbean students worked their way up to 'the top' of their track or were promoted to a higher one. Rather than possessing a superior culture, school-based mechanisms contributed to Black Caribbean students' pursuit of academic achievement. Combined with teachers' perceptions of Black Caribbean students' potential, these supports created a pathway to skewed representations of success.

Tracking Expectations

In both London and New York City, academic 'ability' grouping was a formative institutional practice that reproduced and reinforced ethnic expectations. Practices like setting in London and tracking in New York set the culture trap, *making* culture matter in schools. As Bernard Coard stated, setting shapes "how the West Indian child is made educationally subnormal."[39] More than fifty years after Coard's moving intervention, that is still true in Britain. At schools like Newlands High, in contrast, Black Caribbeans are made educationally 'superior.' But whether at Londerville Secondary or Newlands High, the position of Black Caribbean youth in the school's academic hierarchy shaped the ethnic expectations others had of them.

For Black Caribbean young people, tracking matters differently in London and New York City. Like Londerville, British secondary schools typically implement a regimented, score-based setting process that, although open to track mobility in principle, often restricts it in practice for historically disadvantaged groups. The criteria for set placement are generally uniform, in order to conform to national standards. By contrast, schools like Newlands in New York City practice a flexible, interest-based sorting process based on broad criteria that makes upward mobility within and across tracks feasible. The criteria for placement are multilayered and more subjective. These differences in 'ability' grouping structures and Black Caribbean students' positioning within them inform ethnic expectations. Ethnic expectations also reinforce 'ability' grouping structures and the paradoxical statuses of

Black Caribbean youth as high-achieving in the United States and under-achieving in Britain.

In Part II of this book, I examine how Black Caribbean young people make sense of ethnic expectations. I highlight the three dominant cultural strategies they use to recognize, reproduce, and resist the culture trap: distinctiveness, deference, and defiance. In the next three chapters, I explore each of these in turn.

PART II
NEGOTIATING
THE CULTURE TRAP

4

Distinctiveness and the Secret Life of Social Class in Representations of Culture

I rushed out of Ms. Forbes's honors English class at Newlands High and into the hallway at the invitation of a glorious soundscape. Dancehall, reggaetón, bachata, calypso, and hip-hop filled the air, one brief hit after another. One by one, final-year students filed through the hallway to cheers and applause. When Tory, a Jamaican immigrant ranked second in the graduating class, strolled through the corridor, shouts of 'Aaaayyyy!!!', 'Buup! Buup! Buup!', and 'Yeeaaaassss!' rang out. A group of students circled Tory near the end of the corridor, trading high fives, tight hugs, and bright smiles. Hearing students chanting, "Ah we do dat! [We did that!]" while Tory pumped her fist in the air, reminded me that to some Black Caribbean students, Tory's success was not just hers. A large swath of Black Caribbean students claimed her success as a reflection of Caribbean culture—as "one for the team," Mark, a witty Grade 10 student explained later as we walked to the train station. "It's like a football game," he said. "She got a touchdown. But, at the end of the day, we on the same team, so . . . they can't mess with us."

"Who's they?" I asked.

"Like these teachers who act like we ain't got kids in the hood that be mad smart or like Black people ain't that smart . . . or, like being Black means you failing."

To Mark, "they" also included "some of these kids like the Africans and Nigerians who, like, compete with us. . . . Spanish kids be copyin' us and Black Americans that try dis us."

"Okay. And when you say, 'they can't mess with us,' who's us?"

He widened his eyes and replied, "Us! Caribbean people!"

He paused and draped a disapproving look across his face, as if to question my cultural authenticity, then continued: "You know, my moms been telling me we come from high standards and good schools back home. . . . When

The Culture Trap. Derron Wallace, Oxford University Press. © Oxford University Press 2023.
DOI: 10.1093/oso/9780197531464.003.0005

I look at these kids fresh from Jamaica and whatnot, and they are like killin' it in school, I'm like, she right. We got that in us. We have a different culture. . . . How you think Tory learn to be so smart?"

Tory's academic success at Newlands High, and Mark's interpretation of culture's role in it, invite careful consideration of how some Black Caribbean students shored up ethnic expectations by defending their ethnic distinctiveness. They were caught in the culture trap, and when ethnic expectations elevated them above their peers, they reinforced these expectations to their advantage. In New York City, exceptional cases of individual students' success were deployed as both evidence of, and encouragement for, the high achievement of the group. Students like Mark emphasized 'we' and 'us' as part of a process of *collective distinctiveness* for Black Caribbean students to counter lingering impressions of Black underachievement and identify themselves as exceptions to those claims.

Call Mi a Yardie in London

In London, students expressed distinctiveness differently. But they, too, were stuck in the culture trap, and used distinctiveness as a strategy to escape it. They highlighted *individual distinctiveness* to rebut popular assertions of Black Caribbeans' collective underachievement. An encounter in a science class at Londerville Secondary made this especially plain to me.

From the back of Mr. Fuller's chemistry class, I could hear the faint sounds of alto voices carrying a melody I had heard before. When Kayla and two other Year 11 Caribbean girls in middle sets walked into the classroom, they did so singing the chorus of popular reggae tune, 'Call Mi a Yardie,' by Jamaican dancehall artist Stylo-G. Less than a minute later a group of white, Asian, Caribbean, and African students entered the class dancing to the same tune. Mr. Fuller rushed to the door, raised his voice above the swelling chorus, and exclaimed, "Come on! Leave that Caribbean street culture outside. This is not the place. This is a classroom." Kayla swung around in her seat, tilted her head to the side, stared at me and whispered: "You see what I mean?" To Kayla, this was an example of how markers of Caribbean culture are regularly pathologized at Londerville—repeatedly associated with "street," "ghetto," "lazy," and "the kind of culture they don't want inside class," Kayla said. I wasn't quite sure she was right.

"So, what did you think?" she asked me after class.

"I should ask you that," I replied.

"Chuh man!" she said in frustration. "I know he's going to say, yeah, that what he said was not bad, that it's not racist or prejudice or whatever, yeah, but sir, how are you going to put down Caribbean culture like that? What do you think that is showing people?"

"I hear you, Kay, but is Stylo-G Caribbean culture?" I asked.

"No, but kind of . . . The music is an example of it," she added.

"But teachers can say things about all kinds of music in their class, right?" I said.

"But they don't! They don't!! A lot of times they pick on Caribbean culture as bad. . . . It's like they want my body in the classroom but nothing else."

"Wheew!" I said. "Say more."

"Because of how Mr. Fuller and some of the other teachers react, some of us have to separate ourselves from Caribbean culture sometimes. . . . You have to be a different kind of person to show them you are not *that* kind of Caribbean person. . . . You have to show them you're not a yardie.[1] You have to stand out from the rest as an individual . . ."

Mr. Fuller's arguments, and Kayla's rebuttal of them, encapsulate the dominant and often convoluted representations of Caribbean expressive culture and ethnic identities as liabilities in London schools.[2] The frequent flattening of Caribbeanness to a default, derogatory "street" culture influences the ethnic expectations teachers develop and Caribbean students experience in classrooms. The individual distinctiveness that Kayla articulates requires strategic symbolic distancing from popular constructs of 'misbehaving' and 'underachieving' Black Caribbean pupils. But by separating themselves situationally as different from these others, some Black Caribbean pupils often reinforce stereotypes of Black Caribbean people and culture, even if they escape them momentarily.

Distinctiveness and Its Discontents

This chapter examines distinctiveness as a dominant cultural logic among Black Caribbean youth in London and New York City that unwittingly reinforces and reproduces ethnic expectations. Sociologist Pierre Bourdieu referred to this disposition as "inner sensibilities" of distinction.[3] Through ideologies of collective and individual distinctiveness, Black Caribbean pupils wrestle with the demands of ethnic expectations in and out of schools in the pursuit of positive recognition and higher status. These strategies by which Black Caribbean young people reframe their own identities in public schools and daily life are examples of what Stuart Hall called the politics of representation.[4] Collective and individual distinctiveness are different approaches to pursuing power and advantage because of the different constraints of the culture trap for Black Caribbean pupils in London and New York.

In the lived experiences of Black Caribbean young people like Mark and Kayla, distinctiveness is not only about the stories some Black Caribbean young people are told and tell themselves. It is also about the stories they wish to have told about them to counter racial stigmatization. Mark's use of collective distinctiveness at Newlands High is an attempt to thwart the racial stigmatization prevalent in the United States through ethnic distinction.[5] But for Kayla and other Black Caribbean pupils at Londerville Secondary, collective distinctiveness is a failed project, given the long-standing stigmatization of Caribbean ethnicity and the enduring influence of institutional racism in British schools.[6] Hence, some Black Caribbean young people invest in individual distinctiveness as a source of status elevation, an attempt to signify the kind of Black Caribbean person they are.

To be sure, Black Caribbean young people's expressions of collective and individual distinctiveness in response to ethnic expectations were not universal, but situational; not categorical, but conditional.[7] In New York, where Black Caribbean identities are deemed an asset, some Black Caribbean students deployed and defended claims of collective distinctiveness as an exercise in ethnic pride. Individual success, no matter how exceptional among Black Caribbean students, was deemed an expression of Caribbean cultural power. In London, where Black Caribbean culture is misrepresented as a liability, some Black Caribbean students recognize and reject negative appraisals of their cultural identities, countering them through claims of individual distinctiveness.

This chapter explores these differing formulations of distinctiveness and their consequences. While British and American sociologists of immigration and culture like Mary Waters, Natasha Warikoo, and Claire Alexander have assessed distinction and distancing practices among Black ethnic groups and other ethno-racial minorities, my findings complicate their arguments by noting how representations of ethnic distinctiveness used to counter racial stigma are also shaped by social class.[8] I show that for second-generation Black Caribbean young people in London and New York, the groups most consistently maligned are low-income Black people. I assert that these racialized class dynamics of ethnic distinctiveness are too frequently ignored, and constitute what I call the secret life of class in representations of culture.

Let me be abundantly clear: acknowledging the agency of these Black Caribbean young people in their practice of individual and collective distinctiveness and its classed dimensions should not result in blaming them or considering them personally responsible for ethnic expectations.[9] For these Black youth, individual and collective distinctiveness are mitigating strategies in institutional contexts shaped by gross racial inequality. These students are responding to the larger systems of meaning that overestimate the influence of ethnic culture in shaping individual Black Caribbean students' educational outcomes and underestimate institutional structures like academic 'ability' grouping that foment educational inequalities. I call this analytical orientation the culture trap. Individual and collective distinctiveness are strategies some second-generation Black Caribbean young people use to try to free themselves from the grip of the culture trap, but such efforts only loosen it momentarily.

Collective Distinctiveness in New York

We sat under bright fluorescent lights in spirited conversation about academic success at Newlands High, who attains it, and why. The loud chatter and excitement in the classroom might have suggested that there were more than a handful of us in the room. But there were only four students with me: Nadine, Ebony, Howie, and John, all of whom were 11th graders of Caribbean heritage. They knew each other from middle school, church, and community-based organizations prior to attending Newlands and called themselves "family." This family had its own dynamics, but the claims they made proved representative of second-generation Black Caribbean students' perspectives on collective distinctiveness.

After my first few questions during our focus group discussion, Ebony snapped her fingers and said, "This is the kind of stuff we talk about all the time." When I asked why, Howie replied, "Sometimes we just tryin' to figure out where we fit in our culture and whatnot, like especially because we were like born here and have Caribbean and American culture." Snaps and hhhmms quickly followed from John and Ebony before Nadine said, "Speak for yourself. I Trini. My blood Trini!" with a pronounced rhythmic syncopation characteristic of a Trinidadian accent. Ebony added, "I can be more Caribbean when I want to be and American when I need to be." Like a number of her second-generation Black Caribbean peers, Ebony signals her investment in cross-cultural flexibility to take on Caribbeanness when desired and to play up Americanness when preferred. In *Black Identities*, Mary Waters misses some of these situational and expressive nuances of second-generation Black Caribbean young people's cultural identities.[10]

In the United States, children of Caribbean immigrants often struggle with whether or not to identify as immigrants, Americans, or Caribbean Americans.[11] Despite variations in how Nadine, Ebony, Howie, and John labeled themselves, they all claimed collective ethnic distinctiveness at one point or another, making them "stand out as not really ordinary Americans," as Howie explained. "Or not American at all," John quipped. In our conversation that winter afternoon, it didn't take long for them to surface their investments in collective ethnic distinctiveness as a source of pride and power. "There are a lot of Black Americans in this school," Howie said. "And in this community," John interjected. "Yeah, so, basically, we blend in with them because we Black," Ebony chimed in. "We go to the same schools, take the same bus and trains, live near one another, go to the same corner stores and laundromats, and deal with the same racist cops," Howie continued. "And we kinda sound just like them sometimes." "That too," John agreed. Nadine elaborated: "We link up with Black Americans and they link with us, but, my moms been remindin' me I'm not like the Black Americans. . . . We're different because of our culture. Our family is not from here." I quickly realized that the term Black American, as Nadine used it in this instance, referred to African Americans.

In keeping with other second-generation Black Caribbean young people at Newlands, Nadine highlighted the simultaneous solidarity and distinction among Black youth across lines of ethnicity and national origin. Her acknowledgment that the racialized structures of schooling, transportation, housing, and policing generate the shared status of Black people and shape the lived experiences of Black individuals is what political scientist Michael Dawson refers to as "linked fate."[12] The linked fate of Black Caribbean, African, and African American young people is informed by different valences of enslavement, colonialism, and imperialism as features of historical and modern Empires.[13] As Black Caribbean feminist sociologist M. Jacqui Alexander asserts, "Neither of us as African Americans nor Caribbean people created those earlier conditions of colonialism and Atlantic slavery. Yet we continue to live through them in a state of selective forgetting, setting up an artificial antipathy between them in their earlier incarnation, behaving now as if they have ceased to be first cousins."[14] *The Culture Trap* suggests that this "artificial antipathy" is *not* produced solely or even primarily by Black Caribbeans, African Americans, and Africans—as if to suggest that there is something pathological about Black ethnic groups as inherently given to divisions, or as if white people in power and the racial and ethnic divisions they constructed are not features of white supremacy.

Not long after highlighting the shared structures of inequality that shape the lived experiences of Black Caribbeans and African Americans, Nadine commented on what she perceived to be the ethnic differences among Black students at Newlands, illustrating how some Black Caribbean young people slide between pan-ethnic solidarity and ethnic distinctiveness situationally. She argued: "We work really hard, and even harder than Black American and Spanish kids because for us, education is . . ." She paused. "The key!" they all shouted at the same time, as if they had rehearsed the line. Howie and Ebony jumped to their feet laughing. John sucked his teeth audibly. "How many times you hear that?" Howie asked. "My dad be sayin' that all day when he ain't got nothin' else to say," Ebony responded. "My moms too!!!" Howie added. "And my cousin, aunty, granny, great granny, and great granny's granny!" Nadine said before we all burst out into boisterous laughter. "You ain't never lie," John said as we settled down.

I pondered the familial circuits of expectations that Nadine humorously gestured toward before asking, "What do you mean by education is the key? Why does that matter?" "It's a saying a lot of Caribbean people say," Nadine replied. "My dad says it when he thinks I'm failing in school . . . like if I'm not studying enough or representing the family and Caribbean people good enough at school. It's like to remind me of what he expects from me in this country," Ebony said.

"What do you mean representing Caribbean people enough? What does education have to do with that?" I asked. "What kind of question is that?" Howie replied, perturbed. "It has a lot to do with it!" Ebony explained: "My pops [dad] and 'em [them] like to brag about Caribbean people who do good in school and go to college and achieve big things." "Like Tory," John said.

"Why?" I asked. After a period of silence and a series of I-don't-knows, Howie said, "It shows that we are different from Black Americans." "And it boosts up our pride, you know?" John said. "It makes us stand out," Ebony added.

This exchange underscores a central theme that emerged in focus group and one-on-one interviews with second-generation Black Caribbeans at Newlands: academic performance and educational pursuits functioned as programs of cultural distinction—not merely ways of differentiating one group from another, but strategies for deflecting the racial discrimination they anticipated in school and experienced in society. These young people's back-and-forth comments show that collective distinctiveness is a relational construct based on comparisons to more marginalized groups, as other researchers have also discovered.[15] The expressed ethnic expectations of Black Caribbeans are often contingent on the unstated ethnic expectations of African Americans.

Much like their teachers, parents, and peers, Ebony, Howie, John, and Nadine drew on representations, not of all African Americans, but of low-income and working-class African Americans in their school and neighborhood, to formulate perspectives on African Americans' work ethic and commitment to education that elide the role of social class and migration histories. This is due, at least in part, to the fact that class has a secret life in culture—and representations of it.

In *West Indian Immigrants: A Black Success Story?*, sociologist Suzanne Model suggests that there are no significant differences in the success rates of African Americans migrating from one part of the United States to another and Black Caribbean immigrants coming from the Anglophone Caribbean to cities across the United States.[16] What matters in predicting success is a willingness to migrate and the class resources to enable it. And yet, class differences are generally ignored in everyday comparisons of Black Caribbeans and African Americans, resulting in distorted representations of both groups. The dynamics of class privilege and disadvantage, along with the histories of migration and immigration, are marginalized by this sole focus on 'culture.' Class differences are disregarded and the ideology of collective distinctiveness is accentuated.

The Progress of Cultural Myths

The notion that Black Caribbeans work "even harder than Black American and Spanish kids," as Nadine put it, is a myth grounded in ideological biases and skewed comparisons that ultimately sustain investments in Caribbean ethnic distinctiveness in schools like Newlands. The same myth exists in the workforce, where, as sociologist Mary Waters argues in *Black Identities* and sociologist Milton Vickerman suggests in *Crosscurrents*, Black Caribbeans have long benefited from favoritism based on white Americans' belief that Black Caribbeans are more hard-working than African Americans.[17] As such, in New York City and other regions of the United States, whites have hired Black Caribbeans at higher rates than African Americans.[18] Assumptions about who is 'hard-working' and who is not reproduce ethnic expectations and reinforce symbolic boundaries between an in-group and an out-group among Black people.

During my discussion with Nadine, Ebony, Howie, and John, I responded to Ebony's declaration "It makes us stand out," by asking, "Who's us?" Howie and Nadine stared at each other, as if confused, until Ebony said, "All of us here. We are Caribbean."

"But hold up," I said. "Aren't you all Black Americans? You're Black and American." Nadine grimaced. John nodded. Others shrugged their shoulders.

"Nah, not like that," Ebony said.

"We're Black and American but we're not Black American," John said.

"What?" I asked.

"We were born here but our parents and family don't come from here," Ebony said. "We're different."

"How?" I continued.

"Our culture, our beliefs . . . like how we focus on education and school," Nadine added.

"Black Americans have that too," I said.

"Maybe, but not 'round here. Not like that." John quipped.

John's and Nadine's perspectives are based on class consciousness as a feature of cultural representation. What John gestured toward here is what I call the secret life of social class, in which class differences are misrepresented as wholly cultural distinctions. Though often unacknowledged by Black Caribbean young people like John and Nadine, the class composition of a school or neighborhood shapes the versions of cultures they encounter. What they regard as Black American culture is based on their experiences with largely low-income and working-class African Americans in racially segregated and economically disadvantaged neighborhoods who fare less well than they do in *their* school—at least, so they assumed. Low-income and working-class African Americans who excel are viewed as the exception to the rule. Both sides of that logic bear a telling resemblance to those applied to Black Caribbeans in Britain.

My time at Newlands taught me that immigrant and second-generation Black Caribbean students who failed academically were often chided by their teachers, parents, and peers for "becoming like the Black Americans," as John explained. But curiously, as I learned through classroom observations before and after my discussion with John, Nadine, Ebony, and Howie, the groups of low-income and working-class African American students who fared well at Newlands High were at times presumed to be partially of Caribbean background or not of African American heritage at all. As two high-achieving African American 10th graders told me in the cafeteria one cloudy spring day, "the teachers either act surprised to find out that I'm just Black or just Black American or just have Black American culture in me," "or they be like asking you like 'where's your family *really* from?' and like wanna know if we like hang out with African and Caribbean kids to see if like they're rubbin' off on us. They act like being Black American is bad!"

At Newlands High and in the surrounding neighborhood, the social construction of 'Black American culture' and the positioning of African Americans locally are based on symbolic and material class resources that are subject to racialized historical-structural forces.[19] In segregated and economically disadvantaged communities in New York City, where social services and public resources are increasingly subject to state austerity measures, the conditions of life for low-income and working-class African Americans are often treated with malign neglect, and the consequences of disinvestment are misrepresented as African Americans' cultural deficits. In this case, culture becomes the explanation for structure. But for the small groups of low-income and working-class African Americans at Newlands who distinguished themselves as gifted students, teachers and students at times assumed that they excelled due to their close connections with Caribbean students, or as Nadine explained, "not because of Black American culture." This, I contend, is a cultural myth worth disrupting.

Collective Distinctiveness and the Power of Culture

Collective distinctiveness was not only about 'ideal narratives' that Black Caribbeans promoted at Newlands High in contexts of racialized structural disadvantage. It was also about the use of educational accomplishments to demarcate ethnic boundaries between Black Caribbeans and African Americans.

"When we're in school, if the teachers see us pushing in class, like really working hard, they'll know that you're different and that you're probably Caribbean, straight from the islands, or African or somethin'," Howie said, revealing his own ethnic expectations. "We stand out round here 'cause we smart and we cool," John said. When I asked what he meant, Howie, Ebony, and John all pointed to Tory and three other Black Caribbean students who were at the top of their class as representatives of Caribbean culture and its commitment to education. These students included Janice, the 11th-grade Antiguan immigrant (discussed in Chapter 3), "set to be valedictorian next year," as assistant principal Ms. Plummer suggested. They also included Georgette and Jerome, both 11th-grade immigrants who attended elite high schools in Jamaica, and "are gonna be in the top five" students graduating next year, English department lead, Mr. Green explained. Yet Ebony concluded that "Caribbean kids are always at the top 'round here."

My analysis of the school archives indicates that this broad generalization was not quite true, and that Ebony's specific examples of successful Black Caribbean students underline a more accurate conclusion. *Immigrant*, rather than second-generation, Black Caribbean students ranked among the top three graduates of Newlands for all but one year between 2003 and 2013. Ongoing immigration from the Caribbean to New York City replenished Caribbean ethnicity and contributed to the maintenance of Caribbean collective distinctiveness that, at least at Newlands, reflected immigrant success more than ethnic distinction.[20] Young people de-emphasized the differences between immigrant and second-generation Black Caribbeans, not because tensions did not exist between them, but because of the power associated with Caribbean culture at Newlands and the social advantages it often afforded them—particularly if they selectively downplayed immigrant generational differences.

Time and again, second-generation Black Caribbean young people and their immigrant parents described education as a prized resource in Caribbean families. Even Tom, whom Mr. Sterling berated for his comparatively low academic performance (as recounted in the Introduction) insisted: "Education is not a joke in Caribbean families. Like, that's the main reason my moms came over to America." Mark, a 10th-grade student leader, argued: "This is the land of opportunity and the most important opportunity is not money; it's education. That's a big, big deal for my family and that's why we came to this country." Most Black Caribbean young people I spoke with, especially those from working-class backgrounds, described the pursuit of education as a key motivation for their parents' immigration—an aspiration and, perhaps, a debt that their parents reminded them of regularly.[21] For these and other second-generation Black Caribbean students, I realized, their investment in Black Caribbean immigrant students' academic success was not merely about the collective; it was also deeply personal. Nadine, Ebony, Howie, and John were not academic highfliers. Collective distinctiveness served as an impression management strategy used to signal that they were not "failing Black Americans," as Ebony put it. It helped them to deflect their individual shortcomings.

To the Caribbean young people at Newlands, the high value placed on education, along with the pursuit of it both at home and in the diaspora, made them "different from the rest." Ebony argued: "What makes Caribbean people stand out is not that all of us are smart like that, it's just that to us education is serious business, so we work hard for it. . . . that's what it's like back home." Much like her peers, Ebony's use of 'us' flattens the heterogeneity of Black Caribbean young people, casting all Black Caribbeans as committed to education, and using the Caribbean as a reference point for explaining Black Caribbeans' investment in education. In *Stigma and Culture*, cultural anthropologist J. Lorand Matory refers to this notion as "the mythical anthropology of the Caribbean," creating edited versions of the Caribbean homeland and overstating its influence in the diaspora.[22] As in Ebony's case, this 'mythical anthropology' is used to attribute educational distinctions to ethnic culture rather than social class or a combination of the two.

When I named other second-generation Black Caribbean students who did not fare well at school, Howie offered a prototypical response reflective of his peers' views: "They are not Caribbean like that. They're basically Black Americans." "They not like us and they definitely not like Tory!" Ebony added. "Or Janice, or Georgette and 'em [them]," Howie replied. Second-generation Black Caribbeans who fail to live up to ethnic expectations are at times cast off as Black Americans, or as ones outside the continuum of Caribbean cultural authenticity. To many second-generation Black Caribbean students at Newlands, Tory's academic success, and that of other Caribbean immigrants, was a "goal for the team," "a big-time win," and "a solid performance fi di whool ah wi [for all of us]!" But by normatively casting Tory, Janice, Georgette, and Jerome as exemplary through the logic of collective distinctiveness, Howie, Ebony, and their peers reinforced and reproduced ethnic expectations expressed by teachers, parents, and other students at Newlands. They reset the culture trap for African Americans and culturally assimilated Black Caribbean and African students in order to free themselves of it and pursue the elevated status that they see as open to them as "real Caribbean people," as Howie put it.

A Model of Black Minorities in New York?

Public recognition of the purported excellence of Black Caribbean immigrants was mistakenly ascribed to a culture shared by all "real Caribbean" students, reinforcing the presumption that ethnic culture is the principal source of distinction. The exceptional success of the few did not represent what *all* 'real' Black Caribbean children achieved individually, but was nevertheless considered representative of what they were *capable* of achieving. Students at Newlands used these inspirational few to reinforce a model minority myth about the success of Black Caribbean students. Indeed, Tory's story was told in 24 of the 25 focus group interviews I conducted with second-generation Black Caribbean students at Newlands. This public acclaim seemed like a local form of the national celebration of General Colin Powell, a second-generation Caribbean American raised in New York who became the first Black US Secretary of State at the turn of the 21st century, and the more recent fanfare about US Vice President Kamala Harris, the former US senator of Jamaican and Indian heritage who became the first female, first Black, and first South Asian to be elected to that office. Exceptional figures of first- and second-generation immigrants often shape ethnic expectations of the groups to which they belong.

Second-generation Black Caribbean pupils paid little attention to the fact that Tory, Janice, Georgette, and Jerome were from middle-class families. They seemed unaware that Tory's parents were university graduates, that her older siblings were at university, and that she had been a student at one of Jamaica's elite preparatory elementary schools. Additionally, they often downplayed the fact that Tory, Janice, Georgette, and Jerome were immigrants, while they were second-generation Black Caribbean Americans. They elided the class and immigrant generational differences among Black Caribbeans to promote an oversimplified rendition of Caribbean culture as *the* resource for success because at Newlands, Caribbean culture was associated with symbolic and political power.

Culture, then, was a cover-up for class distinctions. The secret life of class in culture results in a disfigured perception of what Caribbean culture is, what it does, and for whom. As Stuart Hall suggested, the meaning-making associated with 'Caribbean culture' and its distinctiveness "are not only 'in the head.'[23] They organize and regulate social practices, influence our conduct, and consequently have real, practical effects."[24]

Collective distinctiveness, as perceived and practiced by Black Caribbean young people at Newlands, is a key feature of what sociologist Vilna Bashi Treitler refers to as ethnic projects—cultural strategies and ideologies used to deflect or diminish racial discrimination or to pursue and promote status elevation.[25] As articulated and experienced by Black Caribbean young people in New York City, collective distinctiveness was an exercise in ethnic uplift in contexts of anti-Black racism and resurgent xenophobia, when Black immigrants and their children thought it prudent to prove themselves to be worthy newcomers. This phenomenon has been observed among other ethno-racial groups as well.[26] Treitler states: "In specific historical moments, various outsider groups undertook concerted social action (namely, an 'ethnic project') to foster a perception of themselves as 'different' from the bottom and 'similar' to the top of that racial hierarchy."[27] Distinctiveness involves claiming or bestowing honor and power *relative to* a more marginalized group, which historically in the United States has included economically disadvantaged African Americans.

* * *

As an orienting belief, distinctiveness is fraught with troubles because the elevation of an individual or group necessarily depends on the demotion of another.[28] A tricky frame associated with the culture trap, distinctiveness allows some to escape momentarily while holding the other groups captive. In the next sections of this chapter, I examine *individual distinctiveness* as a powerful cultural ideology among Black Caribbean pupils in London. I explain why second-generation Black Caribbean pupils draw on this strategy and show that it reproduces negative ethnic expectations of themselves and their peers—even as they seek to differentiate themselves from economically disadvantaged Black Caribbean immigrants, whom students positioned as 'yardies,' regularly stigmatized and criminalized in the British public, and positioned as cultural outsiders in the nation.

* * *

Individual Distinctiveness in London

On a wet autumn day, five Black Caribbean students trickled into a class-room to discuss key features of their educational experiences at Londerville Secondary. They were an awkward bunch, drawn from different sets (tracks), class years, and extracurricular groups at school. Romel and Rachel were Year 10 students from different 'ability' groups who had never taken a class together; Kadeem and Shanice were Year 11 students whose 'friendship' had ended a year before; and Jalani of Year 10 was Shanice's new 'ting' and source of affection—personal details I only learned about during and after our gathering. Despite the group's unusually strained dynamics, the striking perspectives of these students were representative of their second-generation Black Caribbean peers' claims of individual distinctiveness and Britishness.[29]

When I asked them if they were British, Kadeem nodded enthusiastically. Jalani sucked his teeth and shuffled in his seat. Romel expressed ambiva-lence: "I was born here and I live here, so, I guess I'm British." Jalani sucked his teeth even louder before muttering, "You havin' a laugh fam! Man's not stupid. British?!"

"Well, I'm British and I care about this country," Rachel said with the bold-ness she was known for in her mostly middle set classes.

"I care, but you can care about this country all you want, but you think, yeah, that this country care about you?" Jalani retorted.

"I'm British! Of course it does!" Rachel replied. "I'm not going to not be British because some people think I shouldn't be in this country. I'm from here. They can't throw me out."

"British is for white people! I'm Black CA-RI-BBE-AN!" Jalani said firmly.

"And British," a cheeky Kadeem quipped.

With that, the strained awkwardness of our initial meeting was replaced by pouting, finger-pointing, eye-rolling, sighing and, at times, loud silence. A charged and lengthy exchange ensued between Jalani and Rachel about the meaning of British citizenship and national belonging—talk that was characteristic of decades-long debates about the limits of multiculturalism, immigrant exclusion and inclusion, and the profound feelings of displace-ment held by those who see themselves as born in the nation, but still not of it.[30] Rachel and Jalani reached no resolution. Neither has the British state, a situation which sociologist and historian Paul Gilroy ascribes to "postcolo-nial melancholia"—Britain's "inability to mourn its loss of Empire and ac-commodate the Empire's consequences."[31] The affirmation of being British that Rachel expressed, the ambivalence Romel articulated, and the resistance Jalani voiced are representative of the range of relationships with Britishness that scholars have identified among Black Caribbeans and other ethno-racial minorities in British society.[32] The heterogeneity of these second-generation Black Caribbeans' perspectives reveals that the meanings associated with British national identity and belonging are not fixed, but made and modified situationally from one generation to the next.[33]

Rachel, Jalani, Kadeem, Shanice, and Romel shared the view that Black Caribbeans are disadvantaged in British schools. "They stereotype us as failing, rude, and just bad," Rachel said. The sounds of "hhhmm" and "yeah" followed from the other four. One by one, they explained that widespread preconceptions of Black Caribbean underachievement and misbehavior tinted the lenses through which they were understood. But they were by no means passive victims of this prejudice; individual distinctiveness proved to be their cultural strategy of choice. "You have to separate yourself from that," Jalani said. "You see me, yeah, I'm not going to let them stereotype me like a yardie and ray-tay-tay.[34] I'm different." Rachel, Kareem, Shanice, and Romel also said they were different. When I asked for examples of how they proved that they were different from others, they shared stories of encounters with teachers at Londerville.

Shanice recounted her first day at Londerville after leaving primary school: "When my teacher started to explain what's different and what's hard about secondary school, he was like, 'If you don't work hard and respect your teachers, you won't really be successful here,' yeah. He said that to the whole class, with a lot of white students, yeah, but I think he kind of was looking at me when he said that, so I put my hand up and was like, 'Sir, I'm not like these other Caribbean young people. I'm not from the streets or whatever. I'm hardworking.'"

"And what did the other Caribbean students in the class say?" I inquired. Shanice replied: "I don't really remember what everybody said, but I know there was this Caribbean girl next to me, yeah . . . who basically agreed with me. . . . Like, she wasn't one of these Caribbean kids with bad behavior either."

Romel had a similar story about his defense of individual distinctiveness in school, although the circumstances that shaped his expression of this view differed from Shanice's. In a moment when he found himself in trouble, he tried to distance himself from the stereotypical cast of misbehaving Black Caribbean boys, even though teachers like English department head Ms. Tounsel identified him to me as one of them. Romel explained: "Last year, yeah, I got in a bit of trouble for some things I did and I had to go to the Headteacher.... When I talked to him, yeah, I basically just told him, yeah, that I'm not one of these yardies. I'm not like one of the bad man dem from the Caribbean or the streets. Like, my dad lives at home with me and my mom, and we work hard."

Here, Romel summons the image of a hard-working, two-parent Black Caribbean family as a prop in a performance of individual distinctiveness.[35] He confronts and counters the controlling images of Black Caribbean men as 'bad' absentee fathers to free himself of the racialized gender stereotypes that frame perceptions of Black Caribbean boys at Londerville.[36] Like a number of his ethnic peers, Romel marshals deficit cultural representations to elevate himself, if only momentarily, above them. His story highlights a central theme in my 25 focus group discussions with Black Caribbean young people at Londerville: distinctiveness requires the demotion or stigmatization of an ethnic group *and* a class of people, even the very group to which they belong. The Black Caribbean people demoted for the momentary rhetorical elevation of the speaker are working-class or low income. Repeated references to 'yardies' and 'the street,' which regularly surfaced in one-on-one and focus group interviews with students, indicate how class is implicated in contestations over racial and ethnic differences in schools. Representations of Black Caribbean young people that are regarded as wholly cultural are, in fact, articulated in class terms and shaped by class relations.

The Myths of Cultural Progress

I realized that individual distinctiveness was neither a universal logic nor an undifferentiated practice for Black Caribbean young people when Kadeem followed Romel's remarks with a confession of his love for Caribbean people and his effort to distinguish himself from them "sometimes when I have to defend myself." He explained: "For me, yeah, it was when my teacher gave me a compliment when I didn't even pass. He was like talking down to me like he talks down to the other students. I had to defend myself. So, I was like, 'I'm a good student. I'm not bad. I'm not like what you think these Caribbean boys are like 'round here. I'm not like that. I'm a good student.'"

Kadeem's account points to a key feature of the complex development and deployment of individual distinctiveness. It is not based on selfish pride or a complete lack of regard for the collective. Rather, it emerges situationally in response to *perceived threat* (as in Shanice's case), *trouble* (as in Romel's case), and *low expectations* (as in Kadeem's case)—all situations in which Black Caribbean students regularly found themselves at Londerville.

What struck me most as Kadeem, Shanice, and Rachel told their stories was how unmoved they were by each other's claims of individual distinctiveness. None took offense at the stinging stereotypes of Black Caribbean people and families the others cited. This response was common, not simply because individual distinctiveness was widespread, but because Black Caribbean students at Londerville believed it to be among the most effective strategies for racial and ethnic uplift for a group at the bottom of the ethno-racial hierarchy in Britain. Students suggested that such perspectives were seeded in how Black History is taught in Britain: the biographies of exceptional Black individuals are heralded as worthy of emulation.[37] These curricular contributions are reinforced by ideological investments in an "aspiration nation," as former Prime Minister David Cameron put it, coupled with neoliberal market logics that overemphasize the role of the individual in promoting social uplift through personal responsibility in a context of economic austerity.[38]

Strategic declarations of individual distinctiveness are expressed in opposition to the looming specter of the underachieving and misbehaving Black Caribbean pupil. None of the second-generation Black Caribbean students I spoke with at Londerville identified with this stereotype. Instead, they regularly insisted that these views were invidious misrepresentations of Black Caribbean youth. Nevertheless, they drew on what they perceived to be cultural misrepresentations to stage their own self-representation. In plain terms, Black Caribbean young people like Kadeem and Shanice were willing to accept the idea that some Caribbean individuals conformed to the stereotype. They just refused to be counted among them.

Individual distinctiveness is a strategy for asserting and obtaining power in hostile circumstances. Individual distinctiveness is a way of making cultural progress despite structural constraints. While it enables young people like Jalani and Rachel to control their own narratives in a context where negative and low ethnic expectations govern day-to-day interactions, as they do at Londerville, individual distinctiveness does not transform the wider public narrative and political structures that limit what is expected of all Black Caribbean young people. Individual distinctiveness at once rejects *and* reinforces dominant deficit representations of Black Caribbean young people in schools. Individual distinctiveness is seen as a way out of the culture trap, but to the extent that such a strategy works, it keeps the trap in place for other groups of Black Caribbeans.

Individual Distinctiveness and the Power of Culture Outside of School

Individual distinctiveness is about more than the pursuit of status in school; it is also about the pursuit of protection outside of school. It serves as a strategic attempt by students to distance themselves from popular misconceptions of Black youth generally, and Black Caribbean youth particularly, as "suspicious," "unruly," "thieves," and "walking problems after school," as Jalani described the preconceptions he thought bus drivers, store clerks, and police officers held. Commenting on how officials outside of school treat Black Caribbean young people, Odain, a Year 10 student, said: "A lot of times, yeah, they treat us like we are guilty before we even do anything! . . . The only place man's safe is chicken shop 'cause they are glad for us to be there and they show man respect for my one pound."

In my observations of life after school for students at Londerville, I realized that this disrespect and suspicion were not confined to Black Caribbean youth. On the streets, in stores, and even at bus stops across London, teenagers of all racial and ethnic backgrounds, particularly in economically disadvantaged sections of the city, were seen as potential troublemakers, especially when traveling in a group.[39] According to participants, however, Black Caribbeans and other young people were often misperceived "as bad behaving yardies," as Rachel put it. They sought to distance themselves from those stereotypes in situations where Black Caribbean young people needed protection, especially from the police and security guards in stores and malls.

Cory, a Year 10 student, explained an encounter when he was harassed by the police, commonly known as the FEDs, at a bus stop for what the officers called "anti-social behavior."[40]

I was proper vex that the FEDs stop and searched me . . . in my uniform, bruv. . . . I had a hoodie on, but that's not a crime. The whole time, yeah, I kept trying to tell them, like, look, I'm not like these Black Caribbean boys in gangs or whatever. You know, they think Caribbean people are bad, so I was just trying to make sure, yeah, that they know I'm not one of the bad ones. I'm a different yute [youth].

Rachel offered an equally gripping account of summoning individual distinctiveness to "manage the police and security" outside of school. "I went
into a store with two of my Caribbean friends," she began, "'cause they don't
allow more than three young people from school in the store." I recalled the
signs I saw at the entrance of shops and stores across South London limiting
the number of school youth entering at a time.

> So, we were looking at some magazines and laughing . . . just having fun.
> Two-twos, yeah, they asked us to leave the store.[41] So, I started asking if
> they don't want us to read and learn as young people. When I got out-
> side, the security for the mall was waiting for me and started asking me
> questions. I kept telling them, me and my friends are good girls. I'm not like
> one of these skets or yardie girls.[42] I'm different still. I'm a good girl from a
> very good home with very good grades. . . . Do you know they still called the
> FEDs [police]?

Jalani deployed individual distinctiveness to defend his friendship with
African youth whose parents disapproved of Caribbean boys.

> I was supposed to meet two of my Ghanaian and Nigerian [male] friends
> on the weekend and they didn't show up. They just changed their plans. . . .
> They told me that their parents were like, they didn't want them hanging
> out with no Black Caribbean boy. And I was like, for real? I'm not even like
> that. I'm not bad. I don't hang around with the Black Caribbean man dem
> that not going anywhere either.

Like many of their Black Caribbean peers, Jalani, Cory, and Rachel
highlighted the significance of individual distinctiveness relative to other
Black Caribbean people. Describing themselves as "different," "not bad," and
"not like yardie girls" hardly disrupts the pervasive ethnic expectations of
Black Caribbean people, but instead fortifies them. They unwittingly collude
with the dominant power structures while seeking to escape them. These
Black Caribbean young people do not wish to distance themselves from Black
Caribbean people as a whole, but to separate themselves from the stereotypical representations associated with Black Caribbean identities. The figure of
the yardie is most objectionable: loud, crass, criminalized, low-income and
working-class immigrants from the Caribbean.

Jalani, Cory, and Rachel's articulations of the 'other' Black Caribbean young people confirm their participation in symbolic violence—what sociologist Pierre Bourdieu regarded as an expression of power produced through language in which subordinated groups internalize and normalize the logics of their domination and in so doing legitimize the system.[43] Bourdieu maintained that as powerful social groups and individuals impose their ideals, norms, and expectations on the less powerful, the less powerful participate in this domination by accepting its prevalence.[44] In turn, this internalization contributes to the cultural reproduction of negative ethnic expectations for Black Caribbean young people in and outside of schools. Beyond the internalization of these logics, what matters most, or perhaps just as much, are the institutional structures of cultural inequalities in schools that shape setting, suspensions, exclusions, and ultimately achievement.

A Model for Black Minorities in London?

It would be a mistake to think of individual distinctiveness as merely an expression of Black Caribbean young people's imaginations or as a strategy they made up based on their own erroneous logics, independent beliefs, and personal preferences. Individual distinctiveness was practiced and promoted at Londerville and proved to be a cardinal feature of ethnic expectations that Black Caribbean students witnessed, experienced, and learned from their teachers. All teachers were cognizant of the White British–Black Caribbean attainment gap (see Figure 4.1), and some teachers were aware of the extent to which low expectations for Black Caribbean young people contributed to the underachievement of these pupils relative to their white British counterparts. These teachers often emphasized the academic accomplishments of individual Black Caribbeans—especially those considered "promising and particularly hardworking," as Year 10 English teacher Ms. James suggested.

Teachers like Ms. Tounsel marshaled the success of individual Black Caribbean students as "evidence that a student's class, race, culture or background are not barriers to success," as she so plainly put it. Akilah was one student Ms. Tounsel thought deserved to be highlighted for her academic performance.

"She's quite a different child, isn't she?" Ms. Tounsel suggested.

"How do you think she's different?" I asked.

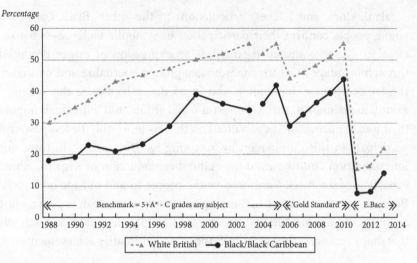

Figure 4.1   Black Caribbean/White British Educational Attainment Gap in Britain (Gillborn et al. 2008).

"Well, that's easy really. She's rather different from the other Black Caribbean students. She's different from a lot of other students. She works very hard.... She's a real star, really."

Teachers often deployed individual distinctiveness to counter unspoken claims of the universality of Black Caribbean underachievement. They sought to prove to others in and outside their schools that they had "some good Caribbean students," as Ms. James said, and to challenge what Mr. Thomas, the headteacher, called "the prejudice and low expectations many people have of Black Caribbean students." Individual distinctiveness allowed some teachers to identify, recognize, and perhaps tokenize select high-achieving Black Caribbean students to motivate other Black and ethno-racial minority students. Some teachers often tried to fight the stereotypes of Black Caribbean students, but inadvertently reinforced them. Exchanges with Ms. James and Akilah added richness and depth to what Black Caribbean pupils told me about the power of individual distinctiveness in school. To Ms. James, "Akilah is a great example for other Black Caribbean students to follow." But Akilah perceived the situation differently.

Akilah told me that she found Ms. James's praise of her curiously ambiguous, given the comments Ms. James made to her in my presence (recounted in the Introduction) in an effort to assuage this top student's concern about an unusually low mark she received on an exam. To Akilah and me, Ms. James's response—telling Akilah that she was "already exceeding expectations"—seemed to communicate low expectations of Akilah and other Black Caribbean young people.

"I know she will single me out for something positive in class, and that feels good when we're under so much pressure to achieve. But sometimes, I don't know if it's really positive, do you know what I mean?" Akilah said.

"I think I do," I replied. "But say more."

"Well, she'll make me seem like I stand out as a person because of my grades, and all the other students will see and they'll talk about how I stand out or whatever. But I don't know if that's 'cause of me or because she is looking at me against the other Black Caribbean young people or Black Caribbean culture. I don't know if that's about me or if that's about her."

"What do you mean? How do you think it could be about her?"

"Like, I don't know, like maybe if I'm good in her class it's like she's better than other teachers. Like, she can help a Caribbean girl like me succeed."

"Oh snap!" I said.

"It's kind of true though. And that means that she doesn't have to pay attention to other Caribbean kids. It's not like a lot of us are in top sets any way."

"I hear you," I replied.

"I know I stand out and that she likes to use me as the example when she's like dealing with Black students outside of my class, which is fine, but my situation is different from my friends. Like, I have loads of support for my GCSE exams . . . like from my church, Saturday school, family and that. You can't just compare me to them. That's not fair."

Akilah's observations accord with the perspectives of several Black Caribbean young people I spoke with at Londerville. As the only Year 10 Black Caribbean girl in a top track (Set 2) for English Language and as the only Year 10 student frequently referenced by the Black Caribbean students I interviewed as "proof of what Black Caribbean young people can do," as Ms. Tounsel explained, Akilah offers a unique vantage point from which to understand some of the points Black Caribbean students frequently made about the power and pitfalls of individual distinctiveness.

First, individual distinctiveness is an acquired sensibility that Black Caribbean students learn at schools like Londerville. Young people are observant participants attuned to the nature of power in schools.[45] Even when they are not being praised by comparison to their collectively underachieving peers, they are mindful of the selective celebration of Black

Caribbean individuals among them and the status elevation afforded them. Individual distinctiveness, then, becomes a personalized political project worth investing in to offset ethnic marginalization and racial stigmatization, if only for a short while.

Second, Akilah suggests that efforts to render individual students like her distinctive might not be about lifting her up, but about teachers like Ms. James claiming they were "better teachers" than their peers, closing the attainment gap one Black Caribbean student at a time.[46] In Akilah's view, teachers like Ms. James may be invested in identifying and rewarding talented Black Caribbean students in their classes because it also distinguishes them as individual teachers.

Third, Akilah expressed measured skepticism about the praise she receives at Londerville because she sees these compliments not as solely informed by her performance, but as contingent on invidious comparisons to other Black Caribbean students. To Akilah, such comparisons are "not fair." She points to the secret life of social class by noting the material, relational, and institutional resources that enable her success. Those resources often go unacknowledged and unappreciated by teachers like Ms. James, who perceive Akilah's success through a cultural lens. As teachers sought to elevate Akilah above her Black Caribbean peers based on her grades, Black Caribbean students like Jalani, Rachel, Kadeem, and Shanice learned that there is power in distancing themselves from low-performing, poor-behaving students—even their own Black Caribbean peers.

Just as Akilah opened my eyes to the complexities of what she called "singling me out as good or, like, better than other Caribbean students," Ms. James deepened my understanding of how teachers rationalize individual distinctiveness. Reflecting on what she had told Akilah in the stairwell about her "exceeding expectations," Ms. James told me, eyes dim and cheeks flushed red, that expressing low expectations of Black Caribbean students was neither her perception nor her intention. "I think Akilah is a star," she confessed. "She is clever and hardworking. I call on her a lot in class because I think she can motivate other students. She's a model for the rest of them in class, and especially other Caribbean students in our school." I realized that Ms. James and other teachers rationalized the low ethnic expectations they held of Black Caribbeans as acceptable, at least in part, because they praised individual Black Caribbean students like Akilah—absolving them from any claims of anti-Blackness or anti-Caribbeanness. A small group of higher-achieving students functioned as disconfirming cases that made having lower expectations generally more acceptable because it did not look like prejudice against all Black Caribbean students. As individual distinctiveness was enacted and witnessed at Londerville, ethnic expectations appeared as if they were situational and provisional, not totalizing and permanent, and as if they were informed only by achievement data rather than personal and institutional biases. In other words, individual distinctiveness practiced by teachers made their collective ethnic expectations *seem* less suspicious.

Distinctiveness in Two Cities

Collective distinctiveness in New York and individual distinctiveness in London functioned as what Stuart Hall called "frameworks of intelligibility"—cognitive schemas used to make sense of the social world and pursue action within it.[47] These frameworks have profound implications for the lived experiences of Black Caribbean young people in schools, shaping what others say about them, and what they say about themselves. In this regard, collective and individual distinctiveness are not abstract ideological formulations independent of history and opportunity structures. Instead, they are *situational responses* to social structures and to the contextually specific historical, political, and economic forces that shape them.

In New York, where Black Caribbean culture and identities are counted as 'ethnic credits' relative to African Americans, some Black Caribbean students promote collective distinctiveness in order to access symbolic power in schools and pursue elevated status in a highly racialized and intensely segregated society.[48] In London, where Caribbean culture and collective identities are marginalized and stigmatized as 'ethnic penalties' in comparison to other ethno-racial minorities, some Black Caribbean students summon individual distinctiveness as a mitigating strategy.[49] These differing formulations of distinctiveness remind us that expressions and experiences of ethnic culture shift depending on where and how Black Caribbean people are *positioned*.

As this chapter shows, collective and individual distinctiveness are baits around the culture trap that still ensnare many, even if it loosens its grip on a few. What seems like solely a response to Black Caribbeans' cultural positioning in schools and society conceals the power of social class in shaping the day-to-day representation of Caribbean culture as 'good culture' in New York and 'bad culture' in London.

In both London and New York City, social class has a secret life in representations of Caribbean culture. The students who were repeatedly singled out as model students were middle-class Black Caribbean youth who had access to educational resources beyond their public schools. In New York, Tory is framed as a model *of* Black Caribbean students' academic capacity, while in London, Akilah is represented as a model *for* Black Caribbean students. Tory's history of elite private school education in Jamaica and Akilah's long-standing experiences with fee-paying Saturday school programs are altogether ignored by teachers and students. Furthermore, the unacknowledged dominant social and cultural capital they access in families with university-educated parents and siblings contributes to their academic achievement. In the public recognition of their success, we see how claims of ethnic distinctiveness and representations of Caribbean culture conceal the significance of class distinctions.

But the promotion of pupils like Akilah and Tory as model Black Caribbean students is not only about the class resources they have access to that often go unacknowledged. To be clear, the positive recognition students like Akilah and Tory experienced is not because Black Caribbean middle-class students are somehow better than working-class and low-income students by virtue of their class status. It is about the fact that Black middle-class students often have access to dominant social, cultural, and economic capital that teachers recognize and reward. Additionally, and perhaps more significantly, it is fundamentally about the fact that schools are middle-class institutions that reward middle-class students with praise, prestige, and power, as sociologist Pierre Bourdieu suggested.

The hidden power of social class in claims of collective and individual distinctiveness also shapes who gets demoted as examples of failure. At Newlands High in New York, Black Caribbean young people distanced themselves from low-income and working-class African Americans in their neighborhood, as second-generation Black Caribbean and their immigrant parents have been socialized to think of these native-born others as steeped in a 'culture of poverty' (as noted in the Introduction and Chapters 1 and 2). At Londerville Secondary in London, in contrast, Black Caribbean young people strategically separated themselves from 'yardies'—low-income and working-class Black Caribbean immigrants who are represented in British media and popular discourses as 'uncouth', 'uncultured' and even 'unworthy' members of British society.[50] Moreover, on both sides of the Atlantic, Black Caribbean young people position themselves against representations of the

Black working-classes and the economically disadvantaged to free themselves from, or lessen the impact of, the culture trap. This is the secret life of class in culture and associated claims of distinctiveness.

With these findings, this chapter highlights the class dynamics of ethnic distinctions used to counter racial stigmatization—subtle perspectives too frequently overlooked in British, American, and comparative sociology of culture, race, and education. While popular and academic discourses, including Mary Waters's *Black Identities*, note tensions between Black Caribbeans and African Americans as expressions of cultural differences in racialized contexts, this is only part of the story. This chapter points out that particular groups of African Americans in New York and specific groups of Black Caribbeans in London are the ones from which others seek to distance themselves. In both cases, these groups are economically disadvantaged Black people. The cross-national analysis advanced in *The Culture Trap*, therefore, suggests that what is at stake socially and politically is not only the marginalization of African Americans in New York and the stigmatization of Black Caribbeans in London, but the degradation of low-income and working-class Black people.

The next chapter explores another secret embedded in ethnic expectations: the racialized gender politics of 'good' behavior.

5

Deference and the Gendered Rewards of 'Good' Behavior

"Get out!"

Ms. Davis's sharp words and rhythmic Birmingham cadence hung in the air, as she pointed her finger to the door at the front of the classroom at Londerville Secondary. Anthony remained seated—his usual deference deferred, it seemed. Ms. Davis stitched a frown across her forehead and stared at him. "Anthony, I said get out!" she added louder. Anthony raised his head, squinted his eyes, and replied: "What? What am I leaving for? What did I do, Ms.?"

"I saw you hitting Khelechi and making trouble with Raymond," Ms. Davis responded.

"Them lot was hitting people too, Ms.," another student claimed, pointing to the white, Black Caribbean, and Black African boys at the back of the room. A chorus of yeahs and mm-hmms reinforced the point. Still, Anthony remained seated, this time holding Ms. Davis's stare.

"Go to isolation right now, young man!!" Ms. Davis shouted, face flushed red, as she walked toward Anthony's desk.[1] Anthony sighed, tossed his belongings in his backpack, and walked out, as the sounds of sucking teeth and faint chatter swelled, then faded.

"Excuse me, Ms.," Imogen, a Black Caribbean girl in the Set 5 English class said sweetly. "What do you want me to do now? I'm ready for more work." Ms. Davis ignored Imogen despite her repeated polite inquiries and said, "You all need to learn how to behave yourselves, especially you, Kingston, Mario and Mike"—all Black Caribbean boys.

"Excuse me, Ms. Did you hear me?" Imogen asked with a tender, tentative tone. "I'm like, proper talking to you and trying to do my work." Ms. Davis ignored Imogen once more. Imogen shrugged her shoulders, sighed loudly, then rested her head on her desk.

Imogen's display of 'good' behavior did not garner her the support she hoped it would that day; it seldom did for Black Caribbean girls. Deference

The Culture Trap. Derron Wallace, Oxford University Press. © Oxford University Press 2023.
DOI: 10.1093/oso/9780197531464.003.0006

came with unequal rewards at Londerville Secondary, where teachers were quick to punish Black Caribbean boys for misbehavior but slow to praise Black Caribbean girls for good behavior. Teachers often expected "Black Caribbean boys to be troublesome or get in trouble at some point" but expected "Black Caribbean girls to know better and do better in general," as Ms. Davis later explained to me. This pattern reveals *gendered* ethnic expectations at work. Despite the different behavioral expectations teachers like Ms. Davis held of Caribbean girls and boys, students like Imogen frequently drew on deference—defined here as a strategic regard for authority—as part of a range of approaches to counter negative ethnic expectations in London. Most often, deference manifested as a stated commitment to and public practice of "good behavior," "having manners," and "respecting elders." Crucially, for Black Caribbean girls and boys in London, deference was one in a series of exercises in *damage reduction*—attempts to redeem their stigmatized ethnic identities through 'good' behavior.

Gendered Behavioral Expectations in New York City

At Newlands High, by contrast, Black Caribbean students marshaled deference as a strategy for *damage prevention*, to limit the spoiling of their positive reputation and to shore up positive ethnic expectations.[2] But, just as in London, deference was profoundly gendered. The differing rewards of deference for Black Caribbean boys and girls dawned on me on one particularly windy winter day in New York.

"Sit down!" Ms. Johns told Andre after he strolled into her English class ten minutes late with an easy smile on his face. "Yo, my fault, Ms.," the Grade 10 student replied.

"Answer the question on the board," Ms. Johns said. "You all should know the answer." After exchanging pleasantries with those next to him and scribbling down a response, Andre displayed marked deference toward Ms. Johns in her College Prep English class.[3] He was the first student to raise his hand and he proudly beat his chest when Ms. Johns corrected his answer but announced that she was proud of him "for giving it a shot."

When a small group of African, African American, Black Caribbean, and Latino boys began interrupting Ms. Johns, Andre stood up and implored his peers to "show some respect!" And when a Jamaican immigrant among them continued to interrupt the lesson, all while speaking Jamaican patois, which

Ms. Johns did not understand, Andre came to Ms. Johns's defense: "Yo Shrek, fix them crooked-ass teeth and shut up!" Laughter filled the room. Andre continued with an American-sounding Jamaican patois twang: "You know you couldn't talk to your teachers or your moms like that back in the islands. You nuh hav' no manners [don't you have any manners]? You makin' the rest of Caribbean people dem look bad." Ms. Johns interrupted and reminded Andre that managing the classroom was her responsibility.

"I gotchu, Ms. You right," Andre replied. "Imma [I'm going to] chill . . . but I'm not gettin' in no trouble 'cause ah [of] this dumbass."[4]

"Thank you, Mr. Brown," Ms. Johns said, her voice suddenly cool and calming.

"Awwiiight! You welcome, Ms." Andre replied.

"So Ms., how you so nice with him today and you're like tough on me all the time?" Shelly-Ann, a second-generation Black Caribbean girl, asked in a frank, near-furious tone.

"Keep talking," Ms. Johns warned, "and you might find out why in the Dean's office." Shelly-Ann rolled her eyes and turned her head away.

This exchange brought into view the gendered inequalities latent in ethnic expectations in the classroom—inequalities enacted in disparate routines of punishment and praise. Andre's deployment of deference in the presence of authority is representative of numerous such moments for him and several of his second-generation Black Caribbean peers at Newlands. But the rewards were unequal for Black Caribbean girls and boys. At Newlands, teachers were quick to praise Black Caribbean boys for good behavior, and slow to praise Black Caribbean girls for the same conduct. Yet they were quick to punish Black Caribbean girls if they deviated from dominant gender scripts, or challenged the belief that girls *should* behave properly.

Deference and the Gendered Reproduction of Ethnic Expectations

This chapter examines the purpose *and* practice of deference as a strategic situational tactic deployed by Black Caribbean students in London and New York City. For Imogen in London and Andre in New York, deference is not naïve reverence or unyielding acquiescence to school officials. Rather, these students articulate significant regard for authority in pursuit of enhanced social status in school. When understood from the perspectives of

Black Caribbean young people like Imogen and Andre, deference is a strategic response to how schools reward what is considered good behavior with
social, cultural, relational, and material advantages, and discipline those who
do not display culturally appropriate behaviors in institutions governed by
white middle-class values.[5]

For Black Caribbean young people at Londerville negotiating negative
ethnic expectations, deference was a common tactic for promoting damage
reduction—limiting anticipated punishment and cultural misrepresentation, or what cultural sociologist Alford Young Jr. calls "incomplete representation."[6] For Black Caribbean youth in New York City benefiting from
positive ethnic expectations, in contrast, deference was an investment in
damage prevention, evident, for example, in Andre's insistence on avoiding
"trouble," and others' efforts to avert attempts to spoil the positive reputation
Black Caribbean youth enjoyed. Deference was a means of resisting ethnic
expectations in London and reinforcing them in New York, where they
proved advantageous. But Black Caribbean young people's ways of deploying
deference were unmistakably gendered. I came to learn that ethnic expectations as a culture trap was also a gendered entanglement.

Deference was practiced differently based on racialized gender norms.[7]
On both sides of the Atlantic, Black Caribbean boys who practiced deference
were often publicly praised as "boys with potential, with a proper outlook on
life," as Londerville Secondary headteacher Mr. Thomas put it, or as "boys
with the right attitude for success," as Newlands High assistant principal Ms.
Plummer explained. This is what I call *complimentary deference*—or deference for the sake of receiving praise. When Black Caribbean girls practiced deference, their good behavior was often taken for granted: they were
"just being girls." This is what I refer to as *compulsory deference*—or deference by 'nature.' This disparity is based not only on gender norms across the
Caribbean diaspora—as Black Caribbean feminists Sylvia Wynter and Rhoda
Reddock have noted[8]—but also on a transnational regime of gendered power
that predetermines the extent to which Black boys' and girls' (mis)behavior is
punished, praised, or publicly ignored in schools and society.

Despite the gender inequalities that shape their educational experiences
in London and New York City, Black Caribbean girls continue to invest in
deference as a cultural strategy because of the socialization they experience
in school and at home about what it means to be "good" Black Caribbean
girls. The result is what sociologist Nancy López refers to as the "cumula-
tive race-gender 'lessons'" that leave "significant but contrasting imprints

on men and women's outlooks toward education."[9] In what follows, I note the shared ethnic purpose yet different gendered practice of deference as a cultural strategy. To that end, I structure this chapter to advance a two-way comparison. In addition to highlighting the contrasting purposes of deference in London and New York, I show that Black Caribbean girls and boys are unequally rewarded for it. This sort of gendered difference is too often ignored in day-to-day representations of culture that ultimately shore up the culture trap.

Complimentary Deference and the Rules of the Game for Boys in London

"There are rules to this thing, bruv," Rashawn said, leaning back in his chair as he, Charles, Garnett, Toby, Aaron, and I discussed the promises and consequences of 'good behavior' at Londerville Secondary. Two of these Year 10 and Year 11 boys played football together. Three regularly played video games with each other after school and on the weekends. Two were in the same middle set class for English Language Arts. The others were in separate classes in lower-ranked sets. Toby called the meeting of the five of us "a big man ting." I called it an all-male focus group. Their perceptive comments on the causes and consequences of deference are representative of Black Caribbean boys' understandings of deference at Londerville Secondary.

"What are the rules?" I asked Rashawn.

"First of all, yeah, you have to try to listen to the teachers. Show respect," Rashawn replied. "It's like they don't really expect it from you still, but like shock them anyway."

"Why don't they expect it?" I asked.

"They expect that a lot Black Caribbean boys to, like, be boys . . . and get into trouble sometimes. . . . It's like normal to them 'cause we are boys. . . . Sometimes, they see us like we're different from Black African boys, but at the end of the day, it's like, we're still boys," Rashawn replied. They all nodded in agreement.

"Like, don't kiss up to them or whatever," Garnett added. "But, don't, like, be rude or nothin' for no reason. Act polite. Be cool. Be decent. Nawh mean? [Do you know what I mean]?"

"Show them you're focused, that you're not trouble," Rashawn continued.

"Why?" I asked.

"'Cause a lot of times, yeah, they don't expect you to be really, *really* good. They expect you to give trouble sometimes . . . like, all the boys give trouble sometimes," Toby said.

"Man dem like me, yeah, that like come from a Caribbean family and have my kind of background, yeah, they don't really expect a lot of good from us . . . in terms of how we act," Aaron stated.

"Who's they? Who are you talking about?" I inquired.

"Like a lot of these teachers," Aaron replied.

"Sometimes, they don't think we're *bad* bad, but they don't think we're good either," Garnett chimed in.

"Being a decent Caribbean bredrin [man] is like a good thing 'cause they like show you respect and it change some of the negative things they think about Caribbean people—especially di [the] man dem," Aaron added. In this and subsequent discussions with Black Caribbean boys in London, I learned that complimentary deference was intended to change low expectations and reduce the damage associated with their ethno-racial identities in school.

"Do you think good behavior matters if you're a Caribbean boy or Caribbean girl?" I asked the boys. I thought the question would quiet them or perhaps provoke defensiveness. But without skipping a beat, Garnett replied: "It's the same."

"Nah, it's different," said Rashawn. "The girls are better than us. They do better on exams and they act better as well. . . . They have to be nice and girly, but, you know, big man ah big man," Rashawn continued, chuckling. Aaron and Toby smiled and nodded in agreement. But Garnett insisted that school life was harder for Black Caribbean boys than Black Caribbean girls, because "we don't usually get top marks . . . and the teachers send us to exclusion a lot."

Complicating this point, Charles said: "But the girls get in trouble sometimes and they're not getting all the top marks either. You know any Caribbean girls in top sets?" Toby and Aaron began shouting out names, including Akilah's. But, in fact, not one of those girls was in the highest-ranking sets for Mathematics or English. Black Caribbean girls had their struggles too, but few people recognized them, except for the girls themselves.

Eventually, we got to the second rule and its meaning in the lives of these boys.

"The second one, yeah, is know where you are," Rashawn said, gesturing to the contextual conditions under which complimentary deference is practiced. "Like, know who's around you and who you're talking to all proper and good to so man don't take you for no clown, still. Gal dem [girls] can't think man's soft, still," he said, rocking from side to side with his unmistakable bravado. The head nodding that followed was even more vigorous than before. For boys like Rashawn, it seemed that practicing complimentary deference required not only contextual awareness, but performing a "hard" masculinity that they perceived as garnering approval from their female counterparts, as well as respect from their male peers. This compensatory masculinity illuminates the complex gender politics of deference in response to ethnic expectations.

Highlighting the third rule of deference, Garnett emphatically claimed, "The next one is, yeah, do your work!" Rashawn and Toby agreed, one after another in quick succession. Charles sighed. When I asked Garnett what he meant, he explained that "they see Caribbean boys like us as trouble, like we are not doing good, like we just here failing." When I asked "Who's they?" the boys replied in chorus, "teachers dem," "bare [lots of] young people," "people in the community," "a lot of white people." "Yeah, like, even if they don't see you as trouble, they see Caribbean boys as trouble. That's the expectation."

"Not all of us," Charles suggested. A perennial skeptic, Charles reminded his peers and me of the conditions and nuances of complimentary deference in school for other Black Caribbean boys. "Yeah, obviously, not all of us," Garnett explained, "but worse if you're Caribbean and you par wid [with] the man dem pan di ends [hang out with other boys on the streets]," Garnett explained. "That's it!" Charles replied, reminding us that certain performances of masculinity by Black Caribbean boys in public spaces have negative consequences for their reputations.

"For me, it's like, a lot of us Caribbean boys don't go really far," Toby explained. "It's a little better if you're Nigerian or Ghanaian and you have some change [money], but like, you don't see loads of Caribbean man dem as like proper doing good for themselves. . . . They talk about us on tele [TV] for sports and shottin' [drug dealing]."[10]

"And shankin'," Garnett added, immediately conjuring up for me the scores of Black Caribbean and African boys killed or injured as a result of knife crime on South London streets.[11]

Rashawn, Toby and their peers reinforced popular claims of what some pundits call "the crisis of Black boys" in Britain. Scholars have documented aspects of this crisis ranging from educational disadvantage in schools,[12] and misrepresentation in the media,[13] to marginalization in the economic marketplace,[14] and aggressive policing on the streets by state authorities.[15] During the 1970s, Stuart Hall wrote about the interplay of structural and cultural factors in England, and his perspectives still resonate in the 21st century. In *Policing the Crisis: Mugging, the State and Law and Order*, Hall and his colleagues suggested that the perceived problem of Black men in Britain and the resulting attempts to police them are a consequence of long-standing economic, racial, and structural inequalities.[16] He argued that the sense of crisis is, in fact, a moral panic represented as a gendered cultural pathology rather than a state-sanctioned structural condition that stymies the economic and educational progress of Black men and women. Like Hall, Black Caribbean boys like Rashawn and Charles were deciphering the nature of power in school and society. Unlike Hall, however, they were not engaged in decoding the crisis of the state; rather, they were deciphering the rules of the game at school for damage reduction and the role of complimentary deference within it.

The Returns on Boys' Investments in Complimentary Deference in London

After a period of witty banter about the English Premier League, followed by strange, searching silence, Charles asked, "So, what's the next rule? 'Cause I didn't realize we had rules." He grinned, as if to poke fun at the sequence Rashawn began. "Don't go to no isolation [exclusion room]," Toby replied.[17] Garnett flashed his fingers rapidly in agreement. "A lot of Caribbean man dem in there," Aaron commented. At Londerville, being sent to the isolation room, where Black Caribbeans were often overrepresented, reinforced the damage to Black Caribbean identities.

When I pressed for an explanation, they all suggested that they were acutely aware of the negative academic consequences of isolation. Rashawn shouted, "It's like prison"—the most common descriptor students used for exclusion rooms.[18] They explained that the "real punishment" associated with exclusion rooms was the enduring educational disadvantage that came with it. Charles maintained, "If you're in isolation a lot, yeah, it's like you're below bottom sets really. You're not really learning anything." This perspective complemented the view held by teachers like Mr. Andrews, who told me that "students who need the most help get the least help in isolation." Students in isolation were not "stuck in their tracks"; they were spiraling down the academic ladder, unable to access a robust curriculum, grade-appropriate teaching, or creative class instruction as consistently as they needed to. What they experienced in isolation was a system of monitoring in which school officials seemed more concerned with comportment than curriculum, more invested in good behavior than deep learning. This pedagogy of surveillance offers more memorable punishment than meaningful academic instruction.[19] Furthermore, the overrepresentation of Black Caribbean boys in exclusion rooms as an exercise of punitive discipline reinforces gendered ethnic expectations.

Eventually, after another period of silence, Toby said, "man, dis is a long ting. Man's tiyad [tired]." I knew I had time for only one more question: "How do you know good behavior works for you boys?" "That's easy," Toby said, yawning. "They respect us. They actually, like, treat us proper." "They definitely treat you different," Charles agreed. "They act like we are special, sort of in a good way for once," Aaron added. When I asked for examples, the boys took turns telling me stories about how teachers gave them second chances they did not always think they deserved. Teachers complimented them "a lot," Aaron claimed. Some teachers were willing to help them out after class as they prepared for their GCSEs because they were considered "the good lads." It was clear to me and to these Black Caribbean boys I spoke with that their complimentary deference was a politically calculated investment in receiving praise that not only mitigated the damaging effects of negative ethnic expectations, but brought relational and academic advantages as well.

Some Black Caribbean boys were aware that their commitment to complimentary deference often came with conditions. I realized this when Rashawn said, "My big rule, yeah, is that I don't respect no teacher who don't respect me." The boys slapped the table loudly. "Man's not stupid!" Rashawn declared. Toby objected: "Hold on breddrin', you don't think we should show respect to teachers first? . . . They don't have to respect us. What if they said, they don't respect students who don't respect them?" Rashawn sucked his teeth, then said: "They would be right. We should respect them and they should respect us. . . . But I'm not going to respect you just 'cause you're a teacher if you are like mean and rude to me and my mates and don't show man no respect. I respect you 'cause you get to know us, and you treat us right, and like you help us and that. . . . Like, you done know a lot of these teachers not treatin' Caribbean young people right."[20]

Since these Black Caribbean boys were cognizant of how good behavior enhanced their status in classrooms and reduced the damage they often experienced from negative gendered ethnic expectations, their display of

deference was conditional in at least two ways. First, they signal complimentary deference not because of teachers' titles or roles, but because of the
respect engendered in their relationships with teachers. Unlike their immigrant parents who sometimes respected teachers based on their general appreciation for trained teachers in the (post)colonial Caribbean and the piety
prescribed in public schools sponsored by religious orders, Black Caribbean
young people like Rashawn do not regard teachers with uncritical reverence.
Some Black Caribbean boys selectively draw on complimentary deference as
a set of techniques for seeking praise and navigating schools as disciplinary
institutions.

The second condition of Black Caribbean boys' complimentary deference involved other people's perceptions of the boys' performance and
masculinity.[21] Rashawn's admonition to "know . . . who you're talking to
all proper and good" and not to appear "soft" in the eyes of girls reveals the
relational structures of heteronormative masculinity—the socially hegemonic representation of masculinity it defined through its power over other
forms of masculinity and over narrow but normative perceptions of fem-
ininity.[22] To Bourdieu, this is how masculine domination works.[23] Black
Caribbean pupils like Rashawn must balance their performance of complimentary deference and the pursuit of academic success with the gendered
ethnic expectations of what it means for them to be one of the "man dem."
According to sociologist Natasha Warikoo, these multiple demands require
a "balancing act" in the cultural and political lives of Black youth in global
cities.[24]

For Rashawn and Toby, as well as other Black Caribbean boys I spoke
with, complimentary deference is a strategic and situational action, not
what others regard as a fixed characteristic of their ethnic culture. In a
context of gendered ethnic expectations, Black Caribbean boys were
attuned to the role of teachers as political actors with subjective power
to punish and demote, or to praise and promote. In settings where the
default master narrative of Black male underachievement shapes the perception and reception of Black Caribbean boys in schools, complimentary
deference becomes a way to write an alternative gendered social script for
social and educational advantages. What Black Caribbean boys did not realize is that while complimentary deference loosened the culture trap for
them, if only symbolically and situationally, this approach did not yield
the same rewards for Black Caribbean girls in London for whom 'good'
behavior was deemed compulsory.

Girls' Views on the Unequal Rewards of Compulsory Deference in London

Black Caribbean girls were often keenly aware of the unequal rewards associated with deference at Londerville, even as they worked to challenge negative ethnic expectations for the purposes of damage reduction. Black Caribbean boys were less aware of Black Caribbean girls' struggles, and some of these girls knew it. As Imogen reasoned:

> The boys see their side, like how the teachers are like ready a lot of times to send them out of class, get them in trouble quick and send them to internal [isolation] or whatever, but they don't really see what we go through. . . . They see things one way, but we see what they go through and what we go through.

In a toasty classroom on a gloomy autumn day, surrounded by four of her Black Caribbean female peers from Years 10 and 11 at Londerville, Imogen shared her own version of what could be described as "a race-gender double consciousness"—informed by sociologist W. E. B. Du Bois and developed by Black feminists including Evelyn Brooks Higginbotham, Farah Jasmine Griffin, and Gail Lewis.[25] This cadre of girls included athletes, band members, performing artists, and student leaders with a vested interest in attending 'uni,' as they called university. When I asked Imogen to describe the expectations she thought teachers held of Black Caribbean girls at Londerville, her peers responded before she could string her words together.

"Well, first of all," Brenda replied, "I feel like these teachers are watching us when we don't do good, but they don't like recognize us when we do good. . . . It's like you're bad if you're bad, but you're really not good if you're good. Does that make sense?" "What do you mean by that?" I asked, as the girls nodded and smirked.

"It's like, it's just what they expect from us . . . it's like they are not going to celebrate us because we behave. . . . They think we're supposed to act right 'cause we're girls." Everyone seemed convinced—except Tanisha, my quick critic, who asked "Sir, you don't get it?" When I responded "I think I do, but I want to know what you think," Tanisha said: "Riiiight" in a doubting tone, turning to the girls sitting in a circle.

Lisa, a shy Year 10 student, said, "We try to do what the teachers want, and I definitely represent my family by like behaving, being polite, being helpful, just being a nice person. But when the boys do that, the teachers give them attention. I don't get any attention for that." This disparity occurs because deference was deemed compulsory for Black Caribbean girls—as a normative and supposedly natural way of being girls.[26] Imogen, Tanisha, Shelice, and Petra all clapped for Lisa. The applause and cheers made Lisa's eyes smile. Pointing to Lisa, Tanisha said, "What she said is true, still."

"Mr. Wallace," Imogen soon added. "You remember when I was in Ms. Davis's class and she was all angry and upset and she sent Anthony out of the class? I was being polite, right?" After I agreed, she continued: "I tried not to give a lot of talking. I did my work and I was nice to her the whole time, but she wasn't polite to me really." I nodded again and said, "Yeah. I think she didn't respond to you or something like that." Imogen then stated, "But she responded to the boys when they act nice. It's really odd. 'Cause, I'm like, we're doing the same thing. . . . We are there trying to act the right way." Imogen and her peers were aware that Black Caribbean girls and boys in London shared a commitment to damage reduction, but their responses highlight the fact that their efforts to be deferential produced starkly different outcomes.

When I asked, "Why do you think it's different?" Shelice explained: "I think they expect Black Caribbean boys to be bad, so when they are nice it's like, 'Oh my days! Let's listen to them.'" Petra and Lisa chuckled. Tanisha chimed in, "Trrrruuuueeee!" and continued, "But when we're nice. It's nothing. It's what they think we should be anyway." "Why?" I asked. "'Cause we girls, fam! Wi ah di gyal dem [We are the girls]!" Tanisha shouted, emphasizing the gendered ethnic expectations of Black Caribbean girls' behavior and the compulsory deference required of them. The group chuckled some more.

"Can I finish what I was saying?" Imogen asked. "Can you let me talk?" A series of "sorry" followed from the girls, and she went on:

> Like in Ms. Davis's class, I'm polite. But I don't get extra help 'cause of it. But when Anthony came back to class after isolation and was acting all nice and what-what, Ms. Davis was there listening to him, helping him. . . . And I'm like, I understand 'cause things have been rough for him. But I'm like, what about me? I'm polite with my teachers and sometimes I get help, but not a lot. . . . My Mum and sisters always say, yeah, that when you're a Black girl in this country, you have to be polite 'cause you have a big price to pay if you're not. . . . They'll think you're an angry Black woman and then you don't get opportunities or whatever.

"Can't tell me dem tings [those things]," Tanisha asserted. "What am I? A dolly? My Mum don't tell me that!"

"I get it at church and in my yard [home]," Petra said sheepishly. Then Shelice, Lisa, and Imogen recounted the lessons on Black Caribbean girlhood they regularly received. "Have manners, gyal [girl]!" "Be a good girl!" "Sit properly!" "Don't be rude!" "Act like a lady!" "Be pure like the Virgin Mary!" The last one had us in stitches laughing. These messages, shaped by Caribbean cultural mores and religious norms regarding what it means to be a "good girl," provide insight into how cultural expressions are mediated by gender politics. These racialized, cultural, and religious dynamics shape what historian Evelyn Brooks Higginbotham refers to as "the politics of respectability."[27] For Black Caribbean girls, the politics of respectability they experience is an integral part of what Stuart Hall called the "politics of cultural differences."[28] Like class, gender is often hidden under the guise of culture. These girls described circuits of gendered ethnic expectations and compulsory deference that flowed through their homes, churches, supplementary schools, and community-based organizations that complicated their lived experiences, socializing them into regular acceptance of the gender inequalities concealed in ethnic expectations, even though they were not always compliant.

The lessons on girlhood that students like Imogen and Petra received in and out of school constitute a racialized gender program of (dis)orientation. As the girls experienced it, this informal gender curriculum is steeped in commitments to respectability, which involves coded patterns of comportment, communication, and control, and it grooms them for particular forms of womanhood and cultural belonging. Girls like Imogen who subscribe to these logics and internalize them experience what Pierre Bourdieu regarded as symbolic violence[29]—"violence which is exercised upon a social agent with his or her complicity" who "collude in the conditions from which they suffer."[30] And yet, others like Tanisha both resisted respectable gender scripts and reinforced what they deem more conventional expectations of Black Caribbean girls in everyday social life.

Differences in Tanisha's and Imogen's comments offer glimpses into the variation in Black Caribbean girls' responses to lessons on being 'good' Caribbean girls across a range of social institutions. Their viewpoints illustrate that there is no singular gendered cultural representation of Caribbean girlhood at Londerville, despite attempts to cast an often negative narrative about how Black Caribbean girls act and achieve in British society. In *Young,*

Female and Black and *Race, Gender and Educational Desire*, Black feminist sociologist Heidi Mirza suggests that the complexities of Black Caribbean girls' educational experiences and academic achievement in Britain are frequently ignored based on a national narrative of Black Caribbean underachievement broadly, and increasing attention to the "crisis" of Black boys in education specifically.[31] Despite Black Caribbean girls' efforts, their compulsory deference did not earn them positive recognition like it did for the boys. They find themselves caught in a more complicated culture trap than their Black Caribbean male peers.

The Hidden Returns on Girls' Investment in Compulsory Deference in London

Given Imogen's and other Black Caribbean girls' clear-eyed view of the comparatively limited returns on compulsory deference in the presence of school officials, I sought to understand how they made sense of these inequalities and why they continued to practice compulsory deference. Their responses revealed that although compulsory deference did not afford them praise in classrooms that their Black Caribbean male colleagues regularly received, it proved consequential in avoiding excessive punishment in schools, and in promoting 'damage reduction' in school and other institutional settings where their ethnic identities were stigmatized. My journey to this awareness was slow because of my own positionality as a Black Caribbean man, and because, as Imogen explained, "this is the kind of thing we don't really talk about like that."

I hurried into the school canteen one breezy November afternoon. The sun had already said goodbye for the day, having only said hello an hour before. "I was looking for you, sir," a tall, athletic Year 11 student named Michelle said, her voice echoing in the large space. "I was thinking about what you asked me in the interview, and I think I know the answer for sure now." I wasn't quite sure what she was referring to, but I sat down at one of the long tables across from her to find out.

"You asked me why I still behave properly if it only helps the boys." Her description did not match mine, but the framing of the question was relevant enough.

"Yeah, why?" I probed.

"I've been thinking about it. I even talk to some of my friends about it. . . . And the truth is, yeah, I think I am proper and polite in class because that's what I'm supposed to do as a Caribbean girl. . . . That is what they expect from girls in general. . . . But a big reason, yeah, is that it helps to keep me out of trouble with the teachers in class."

"What do you mean?" I asked. "How?"

"Like, if I do something wrong, my teacher might not punish me right away, like if I'm like polite or whatever. My teacher might just talk to me angry or whatever, but I'm not going to get kicked out. . . . You have to know how to play this thing and deal with it so that you can win."

Long after I spoke with Michelle, I found her response at once curious and critical. She signaled an awareness of compulsory deference as a strategy for deterring punishment in schools. It was not the first or even the tenth time that a Black Caribbean girl told me one-on-one that deference was useful for avoiding or diminishing punishment—perspectives on the politics of Black girlhood underscored by feminist sociologists Nikki Jones and Ranita Ray.[32] But Michelle sharpened my perceptions of compulsory deference as a strategy and the quiet political work it does in teacher-student relations for some Black Caribbean girls.

Trudy, a Year 10 singer-songwriter, explained her strategic use of deference as more about protecting herself than protecting the logic about "how Black Caribbean girls should behave as girls," as Trudy put it. With a rousing voice, Trudy shared her sobering truth: "I don't act *proper* proper because I want to do what my Mum or anybody says. . . . I act proper 'cause the key to this whole thing, yeah, is that you have to do it a lot so that the teachers realize that's who you are, that you're not just doing it to like sweet them up. . . . That's what a lot of boys do." Here, Trudy signals the lived differences between compulsory deference for Black Caribbean girls and complimentary deference for Black Caribbean boys. Trudy reminded me, as did other Black Caribbean girls, that the power of deference is not necessarily in compliance but in consistency, cumulatively shaping how teachers perceive Black Caribbean students' character.

I wanted to hear more of Trudy's analysis, so I asked her again, "Why do you behave?"

"Deep down, yeah, these teachers expect that you should not give as much trouble as boys because we are girls. . . . They expect us to be talkative, but not big, big trouble."

"Is that your final answer?" I said, picking up on an inside joke among some of the Black students at Londerville, a reference to the game show *Who Wants to be a Millionaire*. She smiled.

"No, it's not," she replied. "I do it 'cause, to be honest yeah, I don't want to go to isolation. . . .That's how you get a bad reputation." Trudy pointed out that if a Caribbean boy goes to the isolation room regularly, he receives some praise from his male peers for "being tough," "a rude boy," or "being one of the man dem." If a Black Caribbean girl is sent to the isolation room repeatedly, "something must be wrong with her 'cause that's not really normal for a girl. Like that girl is a problem and people don't really rate her, like especially if you're like Caribbean."

"Why is it like that?" I asked.

" 'Cause how people expect boys to act is different from what they expect from girls."

"But why did you say 'especially if you're Caribbean'?"

" 'Cause, like, teachers expect more from us [Caribbean girls] than the Caribbean boys behavior-wise and academic-wise, but I kind of think they expect less from us than other people."

"Yeah? Like who?"

"Definitely less than white girls, like especially the ones dem with bare [a lot of] money or whatever."

Like some of her Black Caribbean female peers, Trudy noted important differences in expectations across racial, ethnic, and class lines. Not only did Trudy illuminate how gendered ethnic expectations inform compulsory deference, but she also suggested that in peer networks, the stigmatization of Black Caribbean girls sent to isolation was more intense than what Black Caribbean boys experienced. A reputation for being "bad" is more often a credit to Black Caribbean boys in peer networks than it is for Black Caribbean girls. Feminist educational researchers such as Venus Evans-Winter, Connie Wun, and Ann Ferguson have advanced similar views about the racialized gender politics of behavior and comportment in schools.[33] But Akilah, a Year 10 student-leader, put it plainly: "It's not an equal world for Caribbean girls and Caribbean boys, but for me and girls who, like, want to avoid a bad reputation or like stay away from exclusion, being good and polite is helpful. We just have to use our good work to get positive attention from teachers, which sometimes they don't expect from us because we're Caribbean." With that, Akilah brings into focus the complicated returns on deference: more often than not, the route to praise for Black Caribbean girls is their unexpected "good work" rather than their displays of good behavior. In so doing, Akilah echoes the research findings of Black feminist scholars on both sides of the Atlantic—from Ann Phoenix, Nicola Rollock, and April-Louise Pennant in

Britain to Kimberlé Crenshaw, Patricia Hill Collins, and Bettina Love in the United States[34]—who highlight the unequal racialized gender inequalities that shape Black girls' lives and schooling.

Imogen's, Akilah's, and Trudy's responses typify how Black Caribbean girls rationalize compulsory deference as a worthwhile investment despite unequal gendered rewards. While Black Caribbean boys knew complimentary deference worked because it garnered them praise from their teachers, Black Caribbean girls counted compulsory deference as beneficial because, through its performance, they often avoided punishment, and sought to 'redeem' their often-stigmatized ethnic identity, much like the boys. As a method of negotiating power in punitive school settings, compulsory deference reveals a set of co-constituted gender hegemonies rooted in the differing expectations of Black Caribbean girls and boys. These complexities are often unstated or understated when ethnic expectations are presented as culturally uniform. In fact, ethnic expectations are gendered formulations with predetermined behavioral scripts for Black Caribbean boys and girls in London—and even in New York.

* * *

Deference is not a character trait intrinsic to the ethnic culture of Black Caribbean young people. Furthermore, compulsory deference is not a strategy exclusive to Black Caribbean girls in London—or New York City, for that matter. Nor is complimentary deference practiced only by Black Caribbean boys. As savvy and often underestimated political actors, young people from a host of ethno-racial backgrounds practice deference to develop and sustain positive teacher-student relationships. Black Caribbean girls and boys in London deploy deference strategically to challenge stubborn beliefs about their possible 'bad' behavior as a feature of ethnic expectations.

In the remainder of this chapter, I illustrate how deference is also an integral part of *gendered* ethnic expectations at work in New York City. However, Black Caribbean girls and boys in New York rationalized deference as one approach to 'damage prevention'—as an attempt to maintain a positive reputation and avoid 'spoiling' it. Despite the differences that arise from low expectations in London and high expectations in New York City, the experiences of Black Caribbean boys and girls at Newlands High in New York City are shaped by a shared orientation and rigid behavioral norms that are similar to those in London, and reinforced and reproduced across familial, educational, religious, and cultural institutions as an acceptable way of living and doing gender.[35]

* * *

Boys' Investments in and Returns on Complimentary Deference in New York

"This behavior thing is tricky," Ricky said, as he threw his bags, cleats, and shank guards on the floor. "You gotta know when to turn it on and when to turn it off. . . . You gotta know when and how to switch it up." Ricky and three other 10th and 11th Grade students walked into the weight room to meet me, leaning and limping after football practice, but sure-footed about the value of regard for school authority and its everyday rewards.[36] Like other Black Caribbean boys at Newlands, Ricky never used the word 'deference' during our discussions. Instead, he spoke of "good behavior," "having manners," and "being decent in class" as successful strategies for shaping positive teacher-student relationships. Other Black Caribbean boys in New York underlined "showing respect," "respecting your elders," and "listening to teachers" as significant strategies, which seemed quite similar to those espoused by their Black Caribbean counterparts in London.

As the boys sat down on worn-out benches, Ricky said to his peers, "Two-left-foot-Wally wanna know why we behave in class sometimes," continuing the conversation he and I began on the football field. "Talk to the bredda [brother]," he emphasized. I did not like the framing of the point. I did not like the nickname he and the football players gave me either. Nevertheless, I went along with it.

"I mean, it's like, good behavior is a good thing, right? You just don't overdo it. . . . The teachers like it," Ronny said.

His reply piqued my curiosity. "How do you know teachers like it?" I asked.

"Because they like tell me. . . . They like give me a shout-out and say good things about me in class," Ronny replied.

'"They show me respect and like support me," Ernie explained. "For me, they call on me, and like, encourage me on the side to think about college and honors. . . . These teachers are not gonna do that if you're a problem in their class. Period."

"Yeah. For real." Ricky said.

"You know they like it 'cause they use you as an example to the other kids in the class," Howie chimed in.

"And that's because of how you behave? That's it?" I said, sounding unconvinced.

"It's not just because of that, but it helps," Ricky said.

"Acting right and being decent in class is a big deal, especially like when we have fights in this school, and people gettin' detention and suspension from school, and people out here wildin' [acting out]," Ronny said, signaling how 'good' behavior in social contexts shapes the public praise some students receive at Newlands. Commenting on the relationship between 'good' behavior and academic achievement, Ernie said that "good behavior is like icing on the cake. The cake is the cake, but the icing make it look goooood!" shimmying from the seat to the floor. We laughed at his antics—well, everyone except Howie.

When I asked Howie why he thought good behavior in class mattered, he replied, "Man, my parents be all up on me about school. My pops [father] be like, 'listen to yuh teacher!' 'Have manners!' 'Yuh do yuh homework [Did you do your homework]? 'Tun [Turn] off Facebook and pick up yuh [your] book!'" he said, frustration clear in his voice and on his face.

"You mad tight, breddrin' [very upset, brother]," I said to Howie.

"It's mad annoying, son," he said.

"Word," Ernie replied.

Each of the boys affirmed Howie's experience, some with head nods and one with a fist bump.

For Black Caribbean boys like Howie, Ricky, Ernie, and Romel, complimentary deference was an investment in rewards, which they understood as praise and added support from teachers at Newlands. They also understood complimentary deference as a means of doing damage prevention—a way of sustaining the positive reputation often associated with Caribbean ethnic identity in school. Deferential behavior facilitated the development of what Pierre Bourdieu conceptualized as social capital: networks, relationships, and resources that aid students in their struggles for power, and enable them to pursue their interests for long-term educational and economic returns.[37] Unlike the boys in London, who used complimentary deference to help counteract the negative ethnic expectations that they faced, the Black Caribbean boys at Newlands in New York used complimentary deference to reinforce positive ethnic expectations.

Not all Black Caribbean boys at Newlands were committed to representing 'Caribbean culture' based on family and teacher expectations. Some, like

Howie, found ethnic expectations constraining and frustrating, routinely inducing pressure to perform. In this context, complimentary deference was not a universal practice; it was situationally deployed in institutional contexts that rewarded it—in the moments Black Caribbean boys desired those rewards to increase their status among their teachers and peers.

Complimentary Deference and Boys Gaming the Rules in New York

Ricky circled back to the measured rewards teachers bestowed when Black Caribbean boys were deferential to them, and the debate resumed. "You know, Howie, it really depends on where you are, 'cause, I don't know, I think if you want to get more help or like move up to a higher class, to like AP or whatever, I definitely think how you act makes a big difference." Ernie agreed: "Oh, that's true. I can see that." But Howie asked, "What you mean?" Ernie responded: "Like, if these teachers think you just out here wildin' [acting out], they not gonna waste time helping you 'cause you messin' with their class." "Yeah, that make sense," Howie responded, "but what if you act normal, like Spanish kids and some of the yaad man dem [immigrant young men from Jamaica]? You still get help." Ronny commented: "Normal is still respect though 'cause you not disrespectful. You don't have to do a lot. I'm normal sometimes." "Yeah, but like actin' right, *and*," Ricky emphasized, "havin' manners can take you far. It's a big ting if you are a Black male, 'cause you stand out."

Howie shrugged his shoulders, blew out his cheeks, and shuffled in his seat. I could feel the tension thickening in the air. "How?" I asked. "What do you mean how?" Howie said, his tone curt. Ronny interjected: "The bredda mean that you must explain yourself." "You lyin'!" Howie responded sarcastically. I laughed before saying, "How do you know that's true? How do you know that having manners gets you far? Give me an example." Howie responded: "Alright, like with AP classes, if you want to get in you can just get in, but you need teachers to recommend you, right?" "Yeah," Ernie and Ronny agreed. Then Ronny elaborated: "And teachers are not gon' [going to] recommend niggas for AP if you're crazy and ain't got no respect, like, even if you got good grades. And if you're just normal, yeah, then whatever, but if you're decent in class and show respect and you respect your elders, you're the kind of student they will promote fast, as long as you working hard."

Ricky, Howie, and Ernie tilted their heads and eyes to the side, pondering Ronny's point.

"How you think you're in AP World History?" Ronny said, looking at Howie.

I widened my eyes.

"You think it's just cause you're smart? It's 'cause Ms. Francis like you 'cause you show her respect, you do your work and don't give no trouble. It's not because of your grades."

Howie gave Ronny a choice selection of expletives of the Caribbean and American variety—perhaps furious about Ronny questioning his intelligence. Ronny sprung to his feet, stepped toward Howie and doubled down on his claims.

"Yo, chill fam," I said standing between the two.

"Wally, sit down," Ricky said. "They not gon' do nothin'." Ernie shook his head from side to side in agreement.

"Howie," Ronny said, "You didn't talk to me last year about wanting to get into that AP class and how you wanted a letter from Ms. Francis? You wasn't actin' mad nice? You wasn't tryna convince Francis?"

"So what?" Howie replied.

"So why you actin' like you don't know? You were workin' the system mi bredda [my brother]," Ronny said conclusively.

Ricky broadened Ronny's assertion: "Everybody does that."

But Howie added, "Nah. I work hard. That's what it comes down to."

"Yo, this fool!" Ricky said.

Long after the meeting ended, this provocative exchange between Ronny and Howie sparked critical reflections on the social function of complimentary deference in school and the institutional mechanisms at Newlands that facilitate it. Furthermore, Ronnie stated plainly what other Black Caribbean students suggested and what I observed among teachers: deference mattered because it informed teachers' positive perception of Black Caribbean students who practiced it, helping them pursue damage prevention. However, in some cases, complimentary deference aided in the promotion of Black Caribbean boys like Howie to higher tracks. We already know from sociologists such as Karolyn Tyson, Bedelia Richards, Gilda Ochoa, and Adam Gamoran that educational expectations can influence track placements.[38] However, this ethnography indicates that deference is one of the mechanisms through which teachers' positive perceptions of students can influence tracking. In his response to Howie, Ronny suggested that deference was a way of gaming the rules on track placement in order to access higher-ranked classes. In the absence of rigid academic tracking structures determined by statewide eligibility requirements, school-based assessments, and statewide Regents exams, teachers had more subjective power to promote students based on perceptions of intelligence, diligence, *and* deference.

In my observation of English and Mathematics teachers in course placement meetings for students interested in Advanced Placement classes, some Black Caribbean boys on the cusp of getting in were granted access because "this one is a good kid. He's always polite. I'd definitely have him in my AP class," as Ms. Forbes said. Or, as Mr. Green explained, "he is well behaved. . . . He doesn't have the grades necessarily, but he won't cause any trouble and he will work hard." Boys like Ronny and Ricky consistently earned praise in class because of positive ethnic expectations *and* low gender expectations in a school that worries "about the Black boys failing," as assistant principal Ms. Plummer explained. As the head of the English department, Mr. Green, argued, "We have a big issue with the boys. They don't have the same kind of grades as the girls so we search for ways to encourage them." Caribbean boys benefited from teachers' subjective behavioral screening, even if they, like Howie, regarded their position in higher-level classes as the result of their own hard work. Meritocracy, the myth that the most talented in society achieve success based largely on their individual hard work,[39] informed Howie's response to Ricky. But it also motivated complimentary deference as a resource for improving the educational experiences and academic achievement of some Black Caribbean boys.

Girls' Awareness of the Unequal Returns of Compulsory Deference in New York

Like Black Caribbean girls in London, Black Caribbean girls in New York were conscious and critical of the gender inequalities that shaped their experiences of ethnic expectations and the comparatively limited rewards for compulsory deference. When they observed that teachers were quick to praise Black Caribbean boys for good behavior and slow to praise them for the same, they accepted such inequalities as "just the way it is." Melissa, an 11th Grade cheerleader, told me: "That ain't nothin' new. They be clapping for these Caribbean boys for the basics since middle school and we gotta work twice as hard to get the same attention." Melissa regarded the gender dynamics in the classroom that led to such disparities in praise and support as disrespectful to her male peers, not as an insult to herself and other girls: "I'm not mad about it. All that hype around these boys because they do better and act better than Black American boys sometimes is like a diss if you think about it for real.... It's cause these teachers don't expect a lot from Black boys in this school.... I ain't mad. The boys should be."

Black Caribbean girls I spoke with in New York often explained that, both in and out of school, the behavioral expectations for boys were lower than for them. Caribbean boys could be loud in class because "boys will be boys," Stacey said. "Caribbean girls can be loud too, but there is a price to pay," she continued. I asked, "What's the price?" "Your reputation," Stacey immediately replied. "Caribbean bad boys get respect and support, but Caribbean bad girls get a bad reputation, no support in school and pure disrespect at home. The world is not leveled for us."

Initially, Stacey's narrative about the gendered ethnic expectations of Caribbean boys and girls left the searching skeptic in me feeling uncertain. But when I heard her core claims repeated with equal conviction by other Black Caribbean girls at Newlands, I recognized a pattern in their perception of gender inequalities in New York. They suggested that, as Caribbean girls, their lives were organized by "a set of principles," which Mona promptly articulated: "Dress properly!" "Be nice!" "Learn fi [to] cook good!" "Sit properly!" "Don't sit on the stoop!" These are classed and gendered "principles that nobody never ever tell these boys to follow," said Melissa. These notions are mediated through ethnic expectations. Good behavior marked Black Caribbean boys as "exceptional boys," according to Ms. Plummer. In Melissa's view, however, good behavior marked the Black Caribbean girls as "ordinary girls"—ones from whom teachers expected compulsory deference.

"But, I'm not mad about that," Melissa insisted. "What I'm mad about is that some of these boys out here talking about it's 'cause they work hard why teachers call on 'em and support them. I'm like where? When? In which world?... I work very hard and I don't get half as much support." Stacey and Jenny sucked their teeth. Lisa rolled her eyes. Mona sighed and said, "I'm sick of these idiots!" These Black Caribbean girls took issue with Black Caribbean boys' use of meritocracy as justification for their elevation, not because they held critical views of meritocracy in its own right, but because of what Black Caribbean boys' meritocratic claims implied about them as Black Caribbean girls. "This is not about hard work," Jenny declared, "This is about who gets their work seen on a regular basis. Right now, it's the boys, 'cause in general, they don't expect them to do much work." Stacey chimed in: "It's always been the boys—Caribbean, African, Black American, Asian, white. Don't matter."

"Hold on," I said. "I see some Black Caribbean girls being celebrated by their teachers. What about them?" "Here he go!" Stacey said with a one-of-a-kind neck and eyeroll. Instantly, I felt ashamed. "I never said Black Caribbean girls don't get no shine," Melissa responded. "I'm just saying we don't get shine for our behavior. That's just normal to them. But good behavior for the boys is abnormal to them. You don't get it?" I nodded, and said: "Mmhhhhmm." Melissa continued: "If we are responsible and respectful, we don't get nothin' for that." Jenny mentioned the recognition Tory received for her achievements, and Lisa agreed. "But I'm not Tory," Melissa objected. "None of us can be like Tory, and we shouldn't have to be to get support. None of the boys are bright like Tory, and still the teachers are like falling over these boys. I'm like, yo, whatever!"

"Why do you think teachers are falling over the boys?" I inquired, wondering if a different rationale would surface. Mona replied, " 'Cause in general, the boys are not doing good." Lisa took up the theme: "We come to class, do our work, we are respectful to the teachers. We try to sit at the front or the middle to show them that we mean business. Like, I'm tryna do something with my life. . . . Sometimes, I definitely don't back-answer (talk back), and sometimes I help out the teacher. Sometimes I even do the 'Yes, Ms., No, Sir' thing so that they can know that I respect them and they respect me." "But it don't work," Melissa said, her voice and passion soaring with each syllable. "Nope!" Mona said. When I asked what they meant, Mona continued: "Breddrin, we don't get no extra clap or compliments from teachers for this. . . . But the boys? These boys are getting that for basic things like sitting still in class and not fighting and turning in home work on time. I'm like, really?" Melissa added: "We gotta get into a lot of colleges and get a 4.0. GPA like Tory to get any sort of shout-out in class."

Like other Black Caribbean girls at Newlands, Melissa and her peers suggested that praise was reserved for the exceptional academic achievement of Black Caribbean girls like Tory, not for their everyday 'good behavior.' By contrast, Black Caribbean boys were celebrated for their "basic" behavior, not their academic achievement. This exchange and others like it suggest that the social construction of gender informs, and at times facilitates, ethnic expectations. The differential regulation of boys' and girls' behavior, coupled with the intensive gender socialization Black Caribbean girls experience in and outside of school, inform how ethnic expectations are reproduced and enforced in schools.

Girls' Perceptions of Pride and Punishment in New York

Despite unequal rewards, why do Black Caribbean girls in New York continue to invest in compulsory deference as a cultural strategy? I learned that their rationale was not dissimilar to Black Caribbean girls in London, but their reactions to gender inequalities were. Black Caribbean girls at Newlands expressed opposition to the punishment they received for behaviors their teachers excused from boys. "I don't understand why they have two different set of rules for us when it comes down to who does something wrong," Shelly-Ann said. "Actually, nah. I know what it is. . . . I am not taking it!"

"What is it, Shelly-Ann?" I asked her in the company of four girls on a balmy afternoon in May. According to Terese, these girls "know *of* one another, but we don't *know* one another." After pondering my question, Shelly-Ann leaned·forward to the edge of her seat and said: "The reality is that they don't expect the same from us and the boys. They can be bad, we gotta be good. They can be stupid and careless, we have to be smart and responsible."

"Giiirrrrllll!! Say that again!" Kedesha chimed in. "Did you write that down Wallace? 'Cause you stay writin' down stuff." I nodded.

"And they don't tell you or talk to you about it," Shelly-Ann continued. "You just experience it. It just happens."

These logics of gender inequality were significant for a host of ethno-racial groups, but what differed in this case was that Caribbean girls like Shelly-Ann experienced them and understood them through the prism of ethnic expectations.

"Who's they?" I queried.

"I mean the teachers," Shelly-Ann replied. "I don't even know if they realize it."

"How do you experience the differences in expectations?" I asked.

"That's easy," Terese said. "Show up for class late. Set these teachers straight when they talk to you stupid. Talk back to them when they say something bad to you."

"Act like you're going to step to somebody or charge them in class or something like that," Kedesha added. "You will see that they allow the boys to get away with that, but not us."

"But hang on a minute. Do you think this is acceptable?" I asked.

"No, I don't think so," Tamara said. "That's wrong."

"Definitely not. . . . if you are a Jamaican boy or a Trini girl, you can't afford to mash-up [destroy] our good reputation," Kedesha added, reaffirming the common commitment to damage prevention among Black Caribbean girls and boys in New York.

"But it ain't wrong for everybody 'cause a lot of times the boys do the same thing and they get away with it," Shelly-Ann said. Tamara, Kedesha, and Terese snapped their fingers repeatedly, signaling their agreement.

According to these girls, the gendered inequalities in punishment are not always extreme measures or significant sanctions. These inequalities also include mundane measures such as whose dress code is policed. "The boys can sag [their pants/trousers] and nobody is out here telling them that if they don't pull they pants up, they're gonna go to the Dean's office," Shelly-Ann said. "But let me lose my mind and decide to wear tight leather pants, or a really fitted shirt, and before you know it, I get sent to the Dean's office," Kedesha responded. "They send a lot of girls down there!" Mona added. When I asked who sent Caribbean girls to the Dean's office, the consensus was that female teachers policed the girls' dress code. But, based on my observations, male teachers were not uninvolved. They simply reported the "poor dress code" to a female teacher, dean, or school resource officer to address the matter with the students.

"I think it's hard to have that experience in a class because you might act up one time, when everyday you are mad nice and honest and good to everybody," Tamara said.

"But if you don't really show good behavior, these teachers don't have leeway for you like that," Kedesha added. "They have way more for the boys. . . ."

"I'm like, look at that. I been mad good for months and then I wild out 'cause of something you do or say, and then they send me to the Dean's office and I get detention, but you try to calm down these boys and keep them in class?" Terese explained, exposing the gendered inequalities associated with compulsory deference.

"It's 'cause they're 'fraid of them," Shelly-Ann said. Snaps followed.

"And they don't really respect us," Kedesha added. More snaps.

"But not all teachers are like this, right?" I said.

"No," Tamara replied.

"Too many of them!" Kedesha answered.

"So why don't you complain about this?" I asked.

" 'Cause it's not gonna change. School, home, work, church, party. It's the same thing in a different place," Kedesha replied.

"Plus, at the end of the day, I know I want to hold up a good reputation as a Caribbean girl. . . . The Caribbean boys do as well, but the rules are different for them," Shelly-Ann explained. In London and New York City, Black Caribbean girls practice compulsory deference similarly, but with different purposes in mind. Black Caribbean girls in London practice compulsory deference to reduce the stigma associated with negative ethnic expectations, whereas those in New York practice compulsory deference to prevent them from losing any advantages they might be getting from positive ethnic expectations.

The Difference Deference Makes

As we have seen, deference is a consequential strategy shaping the educational experiences of some Black Caribbean girls and boys in London and New York City. At Londerville Secondary in London, where behavioral expectations were low and the punishment of Black Caribbean boys and girls was frequent and disproportionate, deference emerged as one of several strategies for damage reduction used to challenge common perceptions of Black Caribbean boys and girls as misbehaving students. At Newlands High in New York City, where academic expectations were high for Black Caribbeans, deference supported Black Caribbean pupils' attempts to sustain a positive ethnic reputation and promote damage prevention in schools. Noticing the institutional context ensures that we do not misperceive deference as a reflection of ethnic culture when it is a strategic performance in response to school structures. In both London and New York, deference functioned as a key response to ethnic expectations as a culture trap.

Despite shared commitments to damage prevention among Black Caribbean students in New York and damage reduction among those in London, girls on both sides of the Atlantic used a strikingly similar approach to ethnic expectations—what I call compulsory deference, used to avoid punishment. Black Caribbean boys in London and New York draw on what I refer to as complimentary deference—used to earn praise, attention, and rewards. Gender inequalities constitute a quiet orthodoxy as part of ethnic expectations, an un(der)stated but consequential social script illuminated by the unequal rewards accorded Black Caribbean boys and girls.

Despite the situational utility of compulsory and complimentary deference as gendered cultural strategies, deference reproduces claims of good or bad conduct as representations of culture, and fortifies the culture trap. As Stuart Hall argued, "institutional racism has clearly taken the argument that *culture* regulates *conduct*. These behavioral norms are carried within the occupational culture of an organization, and transmitted by informal and implicit ways through its routine, everyday practices as an indestructible part of the institutional habitus."[40] The gendered ethnic expectations teachers message to students about their behavior, and how teachers monitor students' day-to-day actions in classrooms, detention halls, and isolation rooms based on perceptions of students' ethnic culture, are all indicative of the culture trap in schools.

Although compulsory and complimentary deference are practiced by Black Caribbean youth in local state institutions like Londerville Secondary and Newlands High, these strategies are shaped by wider beliefs about how Black boys and girls behave and why. Increasing attention to the "crisis of Black boys" in schools and society,[41] along with the quiet elision of the challenges Black girls face, prolongs what Pierre Bourdieu calls misrecognition.[42] For Black Caribbean pupils in both London and New York, the cultural framing of behavioral expectations often obscures the reality that these expectations are gendered. This arbitrary gendered curriculum extends far beyond Londerville Secondary and Newlands High. Common sayings such as "boys will be boys" and "you don't need to worry about the girls" foster a discursive and political context in which Black Caribbean boys' complimentary deference yields rewards and Black Caribbean girls' compulsory deference goes unrewarded, even while these young people seek to escape the culture trap.

In the next chapter, I explore the strategy that emerges when deference fails to yield the power Black Caribbean young people anticipated: defiance.

6

Defiance and Black Students' Resistance to Cultural Racism

I stood at a crowded bus stop near Londerville Secondary one chilly autumn afternoon in South London, hoping the bus would arrive before the rain did. As I tilted my head toward the dark gray clouds sleeping over the city, I felt three quick taps on my shoulder.

"My Mum and Dad just told Mr. Thomas [the headteacher] that I'm leaving this school at the end of the year!" Akilah said.

"For real?" I asked in wide-eyed surprise. Akilah nodded slowly.

"I'm tired of what's going on at this school," she continued, her face vexed, her arms crossed, and her voice steaming with fury.

"Are you serious?" I asked.

"Yeah. I'm like a mascot to them, Mr. Wallace," she said.

"What?!" I exclaimed. "What are you talking about? You're not a mascot."

"That's how they treat me, like I'm a mascot," she replied.

"How?"

"They bring me up, show me off and then put down the rest of Caribbean students and Black students," she said.

Akilah became critical of teachers when she received a "practically failing" grade on a mock exam and her English teacher, Ms. James, praised her for "exceeding expectations" of Black Caribbean students. "They like to use me if I'm doing better than other Black students, especially the Caribbean lot," she pointed out. Akilah's searing comments and soaring tone invited a larger audience at the bus stop.

"How does the school use you?" I asked in a half-whisper.

"They use top Black students like me, and especially the African students dem, yeah, to say this place is not racist, like Caribbean students failing is completely our fault, like we're the problem." Her loud reply was endorsed with applause from Black students.

"How can you say this place is racist?" a white girl in the midst of the crowd shouted. "Like, nobody in this school hates Black people. Nobody's going to

The Culture Trap. Derron Wallace, Oxford University Press. © Oxford University Press 2023.
DOI: 10.1093/oso/9780197531464.003.0007

hit a Black student because they're Black. Like, yous lot are all my friends."
Silence washed over the group until a few Black and Asian students lost their
battle against laughter. Others rolled their eyes.

Akilah turned to look at the white student and replied: "I'm not saying
that . . . But basically, yeah, white students get a lot more support than Black
students, especially the lot in the top sets. . . . And some of us get put down
because of our culture, and a lot of times, yeah, it's the Caribbean lot that it's
happening to, still. . . . I need to leave this place, man!"

Akilah and her parents' decision to leave Londerville was an act of *institutional defiance*, one among many resistance strategies Black Caribbean
students and parents deployed to challenge ethnic expectations—
dominant assumptions about students' academic performance and
behavior based on their race and ethnicity. Akilah felt tokenized at
Londerville Secondary. The selection of 'ethnic picks' was a strategy for
deflecting claims of racism, and Akilah knew it. Her success, along with
the accomplishments of a few African students, was used as an alibi,
suggesting that Black Caribbean students' academic 'failure' was not about
race and racism. These quiet claims shore up the culture trap, reinforcing
culturalist arguments that Caribbean culture and Caribbean people are
"the problem," as Akilah asserted. Her remarks indicate her awareness of
how race and ethnicity function as synonyms in a political grammar of
cultural difference.

Demonstrating Defiance in New York

Defying ethnic expectations and the racial logics that undergird them was
a powerful response among Black Caribbean young people both in London
and in New York City. A discussion with Howie at Newlands High underlined
the power of defiance for me.

"Nah. We tired of this!" Howie said to Mr. Sterling, his voice brimming
with unmistakable seriousness. "That ain't right!" He challenged Mr. Sterling
near the end of English class for "using our culture against us." The previous
day, Mr. Sterling had chided Tom for "not doing a good job like the other
Caribbean kids" on exams. This time, Howie did not ignore Mr. Sterling; instead, his response was markedly defiant. "Ay yo, Mister!" he yelled, "You
messin' with the wrong one . . . 'cause we're Caribbean and you know a little
about our culture or whatever, don't mean you can just say whatever."

"Sit down!" said Sterling.

"Yo, let the man talk!" a Black African boy shouted from the back.

"It's all good." Howie said. "We goin' to [assistant principal] Plummer after this."

"We?" Mr. Sterling responded in surprise.

"Yeah, we," Howie said firmly, just before the bell rang signaling the end of class. "We gonna go see Plummer about you!" Shouts of "Yeah!" and "That's wassup [what's up]" came from different corners of the room.

I followed Howie as he left the classroom, curious to see how he would explain his turn from deference the day before to defiance today. "I can do it 'cause he [Sterling] knows I normally listen to him," Howie said. "But right now, he needs to listen to me. . . . He thinks that what he's doin' is innocent, but it's not. . . . It's not really 'cause of my skin. It's 'cause of my culture. It's like culture racism. . . . or culture prejudice, or whatever you wanna call it."

"But you heard this before and you didn't say nothin'," I replied. "So why you sayin' something now?"

" 'Cause Sterling be talkin' like this to a lot of us now, 'cause Regents [state exams] is coming up. It's too much pressure."

"What did he say to you?" I probed.

"He was like, the Caribbean kids and the African kids, like even the kids like me born over here, are becoming like the Black American kids because we're not doing good."

"What do you think about that?" I asked.

"Sometimes, it's just like a competition for the Black students," Howie replied.

He paused, lowered his eyes, then momentarily raised his head and voice: "All I'm saying, yeah, is that Sterling can't really celebrate Caribbean culture . . . and then use our culture against us in class. Nah, nah, nah!"

The deliberate resistance Howie expressed that cool spring afternoon was an act of *interpersonal defiance*, an approach to resistance that opposes teachers like Mr. Sterling as an individual, not Newlands as an institution. Howie took issue with the teacher's expectations for Black Caribbean students as a group. In the process, he illuminated the racialized assumptions hidden behind ethnic expectations: Black Caribbean, Black African, and African American students are evaluated in comparison to one another, not in relation to white and Asian students. Race and ethnicity operate as related signifiers of difference, and Black Caribbean and African students enjoy elevated minority status relative to African Americans, who are thereby further demoted.

Defiance and Degrees of Resistance

This chapter examines defiance as a complex strategy for resisting ethnic expectations in schools. Defiance emerged as a rejection of ethnic expectations that induce a sense of shame and disadvantage. The predominant types of defiance I encountered in London and New York were different. Black Caribbean students at Londerville practiced what I call *institutional defiance*, targeting the school rather than the individuals within it. In contrast, Black Caribbean students at Newlands practiced what I call *interpersonal defiance*, identifying specific teachers, rather than the school, as problematic.[1] Their strategies were shaped, not by ethnic culture, but by the different school contexts. In a school where Black Caribbeans were advantaged but individual teachers consciously or unconsciously constrained their identities, like Newlands in New York, interpersonal defiance predominated. Where Black Caribbeans were disadvantaged by structures of power, not necessarily individual teachers, as in Londerville in London, institutional defiance developed as a common form of resistance. In both cases, however, defiance emerged when the burden of cultural (mis)representation proved too much to bear.

At the heart of Black Caribbean students' defiance of ethnic expectations in London and New York is their perception of cultural racism, which Howie called "using our culture against us" and Akilah identified as "putting people down because of our culture." Cultural racism often escapes criticism because this form of racism does not refer to people's physical characteristics, but draws on explanations of their "culture" as a seemingly race-neutral formulation to reproduce racial difference.[2] Confusingly but significantly, it does this by making invidious distinctions *within* the racial group. While sociologist Paul Willis's framing of Black Caribbeans in *Learning to Labor* reproduces cultural racism, the complexities of cultural racism I highlight in this chapter, and Black youth's resistance to it, are not explored in his ethnography, Mary Waters's *Black Identities*, Natasha Warikoo's *Balancing Acts*, or Claire Alexander's *The Art of Being Black*. I show that while Black Caribbean students in London and New York were rarely as precise as Howie and Akilah in identifying these dynamics, they expressed acute awareness of the misuses of ethnic culture in constructing their experiences of racial inequality in school. In what follows, I explore the two dominant forms of defiance used to subvert the negative effects of ethnic expectations.

"I'm Leaving!": Talk of School Departure as Institutional Defiance in London

Akilah was the first of eight Black Caribbean students in Year 10 who told school leaders that they planned to leave Londerville "because the expectations for Black Caribbean students are low," as Jimmy, a gregarious Black Caribbean student-athlete, explained. Trudy, another Year 10 student, put the point this way: "It just don't seem like this school is supporting all of us as students for real." Four days after Akilah's announcement at the bus stop, when I finally got a chance to speak with her in depth, I realized that threatening to leave was an act of institutional defiance that demonstrated the degree of Black Caribbean students' shared discontent. As Akilah and I stood with Jimmy and Trudy in a cafeteria line during lunch, we discussed why all three of them told administrators they planned to leave Londerville.

"They can't afford to lose us," Akilah explained. "There are a lot of students at this school, and there should be more. They need us. All of us."

"What you mean by that?" Trudy inquired.

"If any of us, yeah, decide to leave, it's like, it's not something light," Jimmy replied.

"I get that," I said. "But how is your decision to leave a big deal for the school, really?" "They are used to moving students from other schools to fill up this school," Akilah said. "So if we as students, and our parents, decide we want to leave one by one, that's different.... We're controlling the moves this time," Akilah concluded, as the others agreed.

This political calculus was based on the funding formula for public (state) schools in London. Their budgets are determined mainly by the number of students enrolled, with additional funding for the number of economically disadvantaged students. When I asked Akilah how she knew all this, she said with a deeply dimpled smile: "My Mum and my Dad are teachers ... and they know lots of teachers all over London and in this borough." Her parents knew teachers from church, Saturday supplementary school, community-based organizations, and the neighborhood. Akilah's family used its broad social networks, which Pierre Bourdieu called social capital, to share information and seek advancement in middle-class institutions. Akilah continued: "Like, I know they don't want to lose their good students, especially right before GCSEs."[3] "When I started telling my parents what was going on at this school again, my Dad was like, 'That keeps happening to you? It's time for you to leave.' My Mum was like, 'Londerville is going to feel it in their overall marks.'" Aware that students' grades on national GCSE exams influence the ranking and reputation of schools, she realized that gave high-achieving students like her a degree of power.

But Akilah did not consider the 'underachieving' and 'poorly behaved' Caribbean students whom the Londerville staff did not mind getting rid of but could not *afford* to lose. The economics of school funding constrained school leaders' desires to pursue permanent student expulsion, making in-school exclusion more cost-effective. Her peers in the middle sets were aware that, while they were retained, they were not pushed to excel in their classes, which promoted some to want to change schools as well.

"My Mum said it's time to leave too," Trudy said, "because I'm just doing alright, and college and uni are coming up soon. I need top marks on my GCSEs. . . . My Mum knows I can do a lot more and I know I can do more if they just pushed me and gave me support. . . . A lot of us Caribbean students have to deal with teachers not pushing us." "Or they push us too late," Jimmy added. Trudy agreed: "A lot of times it's subtle. It's not, like, in your face or nothin'. . . as long as we are getting B's and C's, it's like, we don't need any help and they don't help us." The nuances of ethnic expectations were not manifest in direct commentary or malicious disregard, but in the neglect of those deemed 'passing' even if they were not excelling or reaching their potential.

"At least your teacher didn't, like, tell you that it's 'cause you're 'already exceeding expectations,'" Akilah said, curling her index fingers in air quotes as she repeated what Ms. James told her. "That's mad [crazy]," Trudy replied; "what did you say?" "I was like in shock," Akilah responded. "Mr. Wallace was there too, you know?" I nodded somberly. "But at least they told you and they are not acting like nothin' is going on," Jimmy commented. "Innit [Isn't it]?" Trudy interjected. Akilah agreed: "She [Mrs. James] *was* acting like nothing was going on . . . like she didn't say anything wrong." "You know that's how things work," Trudy explained. "They keep us in bottom sets and middle sets with a smile and a 'you alright?' Like no, fam! I'm not alright. They think we don't know what's going on?" She looked at Jimmy, who nodded, and continued: "They don't push us every day . . . and when they really push us, it's for some big exam when it's too late."

Here, Trudy highlighted the slow injury of low expectations, which are reproduced in the positioning of Black Caribbean students mainly in the bottom and middle sets. Moreover, upcoming exams often shape the intensity and quality of teachers' support. Sociologist Stephen Ball suggests that the culture of achievement shaping British schools is test driven;[4] examinations and exam results often motivate teachers' support of students. But like students, teachers and school administrators are also subject to this exam-based achievement pressure, whether they recognize, resist, or reproduce it.

The Reasons for Institutional Defiance

"Do you think they don't push you because you're Black Caribbean?" I asked as we sat down with our meals in the cafeteria. Jimmy nodded in affirmation, while Akilah shook her head in disagreement. Trudy said: "Not really. It's kind of subtle. . . . Like who the teacher picks for extra support . . . and who they tell to take BTEC[5] classes and who they put in isolation. It's a lot of Caribbean students that don't get pushed." "Yeah, that's it for real," Akilah agreed.

Jimmy and Akilah endorsed Trudy's analysis that the institutional positioning of Black Caribbean students contributes to their limited access to sets marked by high expectations. Black Caribbean students in Britain are often demoted through academic and disciplinary practices that schools control, yet their underachievement is often misrepresented as the result of their individual problems, rather than institutional issues. Given the success of a few Caribbean and Black African students, this pattern is not consistently, or even often, recognized as a result of institutional practices, but takes the form of cultural racism.

"My dad, yeah, says all the time that racism is smart. It changes. . . ." Trudy explained. "You can't have all the Black students at the bottom and the white students at the top. That looks bad, fam! That looks racist! They need a few Black students at the top so people can't say they are racist. . . . They can still have you in a top set, yeah, but only some of us make it there as Black students even though there's bare [a lot of] Black people here." Jimmy stated, "The big problem, yeah, is that they are not trying to get more Black students to the top, especially Caribbean students." "Exactly!" Akilah and Trudy shouted. "They just want to try and make us pass," Jimmy continued.

"That's why I'm leaving," said Trudy. "People need to see what's really going on here for Black Caribbean students." Akilah elaborated: "Like, at the end of the day, they don't want to lose us. . . . These teachers might act like what we think about this school don't really matter, but it will if we leave and find another school . . ." Her voice trailed off, her implication lingering in the air. After a pause, Trudy posed a rhetorical question: "What you think other students are going to think when they hear that Black students are leaving this school?" Jimmy replied, "They are going to think this is a rubbish school. I'm definitely not going to sixth form here, but I know they'd want me here."[6]

These three students' comments on the nuances of ethnic expectations at Londerville as a motivating factor for leaving the school reminded me of what David, a Year 11 Black Caribbean student, had explained about his intention to leave Londerville just days before. He contended: "When Black Caribbean students fail, they say it's our behavior, how we act, and things like we don't work hard. . . . But what about the behavior of this school? . . . What about racism in the school?" "But isn't that true at other schools?" I queried, curious to hear his reply. "Yeah," he said. "That's true, but you can stay at this school and take it in silence, or you can find another school where they will listen to you. Like my Mum said, yeah, the best thing for me is to leave and go find another school."

I realized that these students' threats to leave the school were expressions of their power to challenge the status quo. Institutional defiance affirmed their desire for rigorous, high-quality education, despite some teachers' belief that Black Caribbean students and their families are not as invested in academic success as white and Asian parents.

The Politics of Institutional Defiance

Black Caribbean students were aware of the low educational expectations they encountered in public schools, and some resisted them by seeking other, more culturally affirming educational institutions. They saw their departure as a consequential political action that could give Londerville a spoiled reputation as a "rubbish school" and thus enable Black Caribbean pupils and their parents to influence the institution. Their collective defiance builds upon a long tradition of resistance to structural and cultural racism in British schools.[7]

The incisive exchange between Akilah, Trudy, and Jimmy underscores the fact that some Black Caribbean students possessed an acute awareness of just how racism works and of the discursive fallacies that reinforce racism in everyday life. They were, as sociologist Stephen Ball argues, alert to the "deep structures of institutionalized racial disadvantage, operative in . . . education," from academic tracking to school exclusion.[8] They address four key fallacies that often emerge when discussing racism in British society. The first is what sociologists Matthew Desmond and Mustafa Emirbayer refer to as the *individualistic fallacy*,[9] the notion that racism can be attributed solely to individuals' prejudicial ideas and acts. When a white student at the bus stop challenged Akilah's claims about racism at Londerville by pointing out that "nobody in this school hates Black people," she articulated the individualistic fallacy. A more capacious understanding of racism acknowledges that, even when exchanging pleasantries and building friendships, the effects of racism as an institutional and cultural phenomenon are embedded in the structures of schools and society.

Akilah also challenged the *tokenistic fallacy*, the assumption that having a few Black and ethnic minority people in positions of power and influence confirms the absence of racism.[10] She regarded the rare success of Black Caribbean students like her as evidence of institutional racism, not an excuse for it. The strategic use of her exceptional story, and those of other high-achieving Black students at Londerville, was part of the everyday cultural production of racism. Akilah explained this fallacy bluntly: "The teachers are like, 'Look, look, we have Akilah. She's great, innit? We're not racist, innit [isn't it]?'" "Not here! Not at this school," Jimmy said with a smirk. "Innnnnniiiiiitttt?" Trudy said, chuckling. Akilah rolled her eyes.

The tokenistic fallacy elevates and idealizes a few Blacks while demoting and stigmatizing the Black population as a whole.[11] Moreover, it is frequently marshaled to blame Black and ethnic minority people for their own social and educational failures, as outsiders wonder why the others have not all done as well. In plain terms, the tokenistic fallacy is used as evidence of the declining significance of racism in contemporary society.[12]

When Trudy reiterated what her father told her, that "racism is smart" and "it changes," she challenged another prominent fallacy about racism: the *fixed fallacy*. The fixed fallacy does not attend to racism's changing character, but presumes that its form does not shift over time and space and regards it as deliberate discrimination driven by hate. Popular perceptions of spectacular violence as the only real evidence of racism can preclude understandings of the subtle, structural, and systemic forms of racism that shape teaching and learning in schools. The fixed fallacy fails to perceive racism in the everyday processes and practices in schools and society that produce unequal outcomes for Black and ethnic minority people.[13] Standing at the bus stop and later in the queue waiting for lunch, Akilah pointed out how racism shapeshifts—this time, by using culture as a guise for racism.

When Akilah commented that teachers at Londerville use her success as evidence that racism is nonexistent and Jimmy mockingly said, "Not here! Not at this school," he called attention to what I call the *contextual fallacy*. In organizations that pride themselves on being diverse, white people often fallaciously contend that racism exists somewhere else, but "not here." This fallacy that exists at Londerville is also found in the British nation, which has historically treated racism as a real problem in the Empire, but not at home.[14] Such perceptions shore up racism as relevant only to certain geographies and far-off fields, but not one's immediate location.

Like many of their Black Caribbean peers, Akilah, Trudy, and Jimmy connected personal problems to public issues.[15] Yet, even as the Black Caribbean young people who wanted to leave Londerville were critical of racial and ethnic inequalities at the institutional level, they were seldom as attentive to the inequalities in the wider British educational system. Despite their racial and political consciousness and their efforts to find other schools, their aspirations were often thwarted by the limited opportunities to transfer to other public schools. As Trudy explained: "I didn't have a choice, really. It's like you have to take what you get. There is not much options really if you want to go to another comprehensive."

When I visited these students a year later, only Akilah had actually moved to another school. This high-achieving, Black Caribbean girl had unusual advantages because her parents were primary and secondary school teachers. When I sat down with Akilah and her parents in their home, her father maintained, "We had to go private 'cause that school [Londerville] wasn't fair or good for my daughter really. I don't think it was good for Caribbean students." This choice cost the family over £15,000 ($20,000 USD) per year. Akilah's mother explained that they "had to scrimp and save to send her" to a private school "because we don't get big salaries.... It's been hard 'cause we teach in state [public] schools, but they didn't have a lot of options in the state system." Class privileges afforded Akilah an alternative to the public school system, which some of her working-class peers desired but could not afford.

Enrollment in Black Supplementary Schools
as Institutional Defiance

For those who remained in public schools, Black supplementary schools provided a way to move beyond the low expectations they encountered there.
Trudy and Jimmy each explained to me that they developed a critical orientation to schooling through regular discussions of race and racism with their
families over a meal, in the car heading to church and sports arenas, or on
the bus to the shopping center. But Black supplementary schools helped to
sharpen their critique of racism and develop their sense of pride. Attending
Black supplementary schools was the most significant way that defiant
students attempted to escape and combat the systematic, institutional racism
of public schools like Londerville. Black supplementary schools proved to
be one meaningful way to resist the culture trap. As sociologists Heidi Mirza
and Diane Reay suggest, these "organic, grassroots organizations" constitute
"a covert social movement for educational change,"[16] offering Black students
the opportunity to obtain a culturally sustaining, antiracist education.[17]

"I learned long time, yeah, that I can't really trust Londerville or any of
these schools with my education as a Black Caribbean boy," Kareem said
to me during a one-on-one interview. "My mum had to find a place where
you can get extra help, where the teachers believe in me and push me." "You
couldn't find that at Londerville?" I asked. "Probably not," Kareem replied.
"I've been here for five years and I still can't find that. . . . And even if you get
that in one class, you're not really going to get that in every class all the time
at this school." I asked, "But do you get that outside of Londerville for real?"
"At my Saturday school? Definitely!" he exclaimed. "They're not going to
really push you here. But at my Saturday school, you get support and there's
bare [a lot of] people to motivate you . . . young people from other schools,
Black teachers, and even a couple of white teachers that really, really care.
Sometimes, parents pop by and help out or bring food or they come to talk
to the teachers. . . . The people there really want you to succeed. It made me
feel like I was part of a big family, and like I really mattered to them as a
person."

Kareem and many of his Black Caribbean peers practiced what he
called "proper fighting the school for my education," and what I call institutional defiance, by participating in this alternative learning environment.
Enrollment in Black supplementary schools was a means of resisting the culture trap and finding fairer, more equitable alternatives to it. Black Caribbean

young people told me stories about the educational benefits of supplementary schools; the affective bonds they facilitated across racial, class, and generational lines; and the choices these informal schools afforded them that the public school system did not. When I asked students if attending supplementary schools was really about helping themselves, the typical reply was, "Yes, but when you are Black and Caribbean in this country, you have to fight the system *and* help yourself," as Odain, a Year 10 student, put it.

For these students, supplementary schools were creative, emancipatory educational environments that held high expectations for all. Unlike the culture trap, supplementary schools offered Black Caribbean students a chance to be seen more clearly as individuals. I heard more about the value of supplementary schools when I visited siblings Kayla and Cory, ages 16 and 14 respectively, at home one wet, windy autumn evening. We sat with cups of hot tea in the living room as I scanned framed photographs on the wall. One with scores of children smiling brightly stood out to me. "What's that one about?" I asked. "Oh," Kayla replied. "That's our Saturday school and they are our friends from primary [school] days." "I'm glad I'm able to go to a Saturday school," Cory said. "Me too," Kayla added. "It's so important 'cause I think I'd be in bottom set if I didn't go to CEC" [Community Empowerment Center]. "How come?" I asked. Kayla explained, "The students in top sets are getting a lot of help. Some of my white friends, and posh friends, yeah, have private tutors to help them for their GCSEs. A lot of us can't afford that."

"I cannot afford that!" Kayla and Cory's mother, Jennifer, a mental health counselor, shouted from the kitchen.

"But I think so many students could benefit from a Saturday school, like students that are new to the country, kids that come from families that are struggling with money," Cory said.

"And Black students too," Kayla chimed in.

"Caribbean students, African students, Asian students, Muslim students," Cory added.

"And girls!" Kayla said loudly.

"You're not going to stop interrupting me?" Cory shouted.

"No!" Kayla grinned.

"Behave, man. Chuh!" Cory yelled. Jennifer walked in from the kitchen and asked, "What's going on out here? Are you two arguing in front of Mr. Wallace?" She took their silence as a resounding yes. "What are you arguing about now?"

"CEC," Kayla said softly.

"You can't argue about CEC! It's so good for both of you. It's where real learning happens for you two. You just can't trust these mainstream schools with your Black children."

Praise of supplementary schools was common among the Black Caribbean young people I spoke with at Londerville. Kareem, Kayla, and Cory described them as "my real school," "the kind of school where they expected us to be smart and wanted us to be smarter than before," "a community ting," "a group where it was alright to be brilliant," "a place where teachers care about who we are and who we are going to be." Black supplementary schools in Britain are highlighted in "Education," the fifth episode of Steve McQueen's internationally acclaimed series, *Small Axe*.[18]

Sociologists Heidi Mirza and Diane Reay argue that what began as a grassroots development in opposition to exclusionary practices and a lack of cultural affirmation in schools has become a social movement for educational change and community building.[19] In addition to providing support for students across the ability spectrum, supplementary schools enable parents to exercise some control over their children's education, counter low expectations, and redefine pupils' identities. For Black Caribbean and other ethnic minority parents, supplementary schooling remains a reliable strategy of defying public schools and a source of self-help necessary to counter prevailing myths about Black intellectual and behavioral inferiority.[20] As Luke, a Black Caribbean musician in Year 11, put it, "Saturday schools taught us how to study and how to proper fight what these teachers believed about us at Londerville. . . . I don't believe what that school believes about me."

Black Caribbean pupils' and parents' support for supplementary schools was a rebuke of mainstream public schooling. I must admit, though, that their uniformly positive descriptions occasionally seemed too good to be true. I had spent time volunteering at Ms. Bell's supplementary school and recalled moments when students seemed distinctly uninterested. I saw Black Caribbean and other ethnic minority students roll their eyes, and blow out their cheeks when teachers asked them to complete assignments they deemed too challenging. I witnessed veteran Black teachers and long-term volunteers like Pastor Williams give tough talks to students and summon British schools' history of low ethnic expectations, particularly for Black Caribbean students, as a reason to "work hard at your studies and prove them wrong." There seemed to be no escaping ethnic expectations as a culture trap, even in the alternative educational spaces that aimed to counter them.

I shared my skepticism with a group of Year 11 Black Caribbean students at Londerville, perhaps too bluntly. "So, let me ask you something." I began. "If so many of you go to supplementary schools, and they are really good, like you said, why are so many Black Caribbean students in middle and bottom sets?" I could tell by the expressions on their faces that I'd hit a nerve.

"Was that rude?" I asked Michelle, who was sitting next to me.

"No, it's not," said Luke before anyone else could.

"It's not rude," Michelle replied. "I just can't believe you asked that question. It's like proper [really] in your face."

"No, no, it's a tough question. It's not rude. Let's just answer it," Kayla said.

"Yeah," Joseph said. They paused for a moment.

"I don't know," Michelle began.

"Look," Kayla interrupted. "I don't think it's fair to expect us to go to a school that really helps us one day a week, where we get to learn from each other, yeah, and then we have to deal with normal school for five days and expect a big change."

"It's true," Akilah added. "Like, we are not the problem. We just don't have the kind of school that's going to help us all the time."

Kayla elaborated: "You know, what I like a lot about my Saturday school is that I get to study with students from top sets. Like, I'm not just in middle sets or with students in middle sets like at Londerville. . . . The separation is not good overall."

"When I see what some of the top set students do, I'm like, I can do that! They're not smarter than me," Michelle said.

"Exactly!" Kayla agreed.

"Like, Londerville always makes me feel like I'm not smart, like the lot in middle sets are just not working hard or we're just not really smart. We are average; but they are not doing anything really to make us brilliant," Michelle continued, tears welling up in her eyes. Kayla leaned toward Michelle and hugged her. "It's alright," Michelle said, wiping her eyes with the sleeve of her blouse. She continued: "And if you think about it, yeah, like, if I do something wrong at my Saturday program, they are not going to send me [to] no isolation room." Akilah clapped and said, "If Londerville and these schools 'round here can't do good for us, we have to do good for ourselves and go for Saturday schools on the weekends."

Like a number of their Black Caribbean peers, Kayla, Akilah, Michelle, and Luke emphasized that supplementary schools supported institutional defiance. Although their participation may not result in many Black students being moved to higher-ranked sets or achieving higher test scores, these alternative learning environments were less punitive and more egalitarian than public schools. They were viable alternatives to the culture trap. The education and support Black Caribbean students received there provided them with the political imagination to practice institutional defiance while pursuing their own education as a liberatory project.

* * *

For a host of Black Caribbean young people in London and their counterparts in New York, defiance was a salient strategy for challenging what Stuart Hall referred to as "the spectacle of ethnicity"[21]—the day-to-day representations of ethnic cultures to signify awareness and acceptance of cultural diversity. Despite the positive intentions that may motivate the dominant group to emphasize ethnicity, it devolves into cultural racism when culture is proffered as the cause of the differential achievement *and* when culture is used to justify the mistreatment of ethno-racial minority groups.[22] The culture trap reflects and reproduces cultural racism.

In schools like Londerville and Newlands, the recognition of ethnic diversity is used to rank and subordinate specific groups of Black students based on preconceptions of their academic aptitude.[23] Ethnic expectations appear to escape the dominant Black-white racial binary and, instead, draw on ethnic culture as a rationale for justifying differing social behavior, academic achievement, and student attitudes.[24] When mobilized by educators, ethnic expectations facilitate casual, ordinary suffering among Black students. But as this chapter reveals, some Black Caribbean students defy this imposition, whether at the institutional level in London or at the interpersonal level in New York. The examples in the remainder of this chapter illustrate that defiance is not a single, discrete act. Instead, it is a dynamic set of organized practices to resist what students and their parents regard as unjust power relations. Interpersonal defiance as practiced by Black Caribbean young people in New York highlights what they regarded as socially and culturally unacceptable words and actions by individual teachers and leaders at Newlands High.

* * *

"This Ain't Right!": Challenging Teachers' Views as Interpersonal Defiance in New York

"You rollin' with me or nah?" Howie shouted to me, striding cool on the right side of the corridor. "I'mma [I'm going to] talk to Plummer 'bout Sterling now," he continued. I stood on the side of the hallway feverishly jotting down all I had observed.

"Yo, Wally where you at?" he yelled. It seemed more of a command than a question.

This invitation to witness interpersonal defiance in action at Newlands in New York was priceless. I slipped my phone into my back pocket and joined him. As Howie and I walked through the corridor toward the stairwell, both of us trading daps,[25] fist bumps, and head nods with passersby, Howie invited some of his "boys" to join him. Two agreed.

"Just let me talk to Plummer [the assistant principal]," Howie said when we got to the top of the stairs.

"Alright," Tom said.

"I'mma say somethin' right quick 'cause this ain't right," Dwayne added.

"Why don't y'all let Tom talk as well?" I queried. "Sterling said a lot of stuff to him."

"Nah, we gon' talk," Howie said, pointing to himself and Dwayne.

Over shouts of "Out of the halls!" from deans of discipline and "keep it moving!" from security guards, Howie explained that Ms. Plummer would be more likely to listen to him and Dwayne than to Tom because both of them were known for their deference, while Tom was known for his disrespect in the classroom. These boys had calculated the role of deference in making their interpersonal defiance excusable.

"Yo, Wally, don't say nothin' neither!" Dwayne stopped abruptly and said to me.

I snapped my head back and agreed, "Nah. I'm just gonna listen."

When we got to the end of the corridor and turned toward Ms. Plummer's office, we saw Mr. Sterling talking to Ms. Plummer. Howie, Dwayne, and Tom hastened their pace, hurrying to tell their side of the story. Ms. Plummer smiled widely and said, "Mr. Sterling told me you were coming. Let me finish talking with him first." She encouraged the boys to go to class and speak with her at the end of the school day. Mr. Sterling smirked. Tom hurled expletives. Two security guards walked toward the group. Dwayne yanked Tom by his sleeve and pulled him away, and at the top of his voice bid Tom to "chill." As we stood in the hallway, Howie pleaded to Ms. Plummer that the matter was urgent. It worked.

"Alright. Go ahead," Ms. Plummer said. Howie waved his two boys over, while Mr. Sterling stepped into the English department staff room.

"Ms. Plummer," Howie began. "You need to do somethin' about Sterling and what he's saying to us in class. You gotta do something about him."

"What did he say?" Ms. Plummer asked.

"He's saying that the Caribbean kids and the African kids are like becoming like Black American kids because our grades are going down," Dwayne said.

"Boys," Ms. Plummer said firmly, "Regents [exams] and college are right around the corner. Are your grades going down?"

"Ms., that's not why we came to talk. It's something more serious than that," Howie continued, intending to explain the negative consequences of Mr. Sterling's cultural comparisons.

"What's wrong with being like Black American kids?" Ms. Plummer interjected.

"Nothin'" Howie said. "We're Black and American."

"So, what's the problem?" Ms. Plummer reiterated.

"He tryna diss us, Ms.!" Tom yelled.

Howie shushed him: "He's using our culture against us. He's saying our Caribbean culture is good when we have good grades or whatever, but our culture is bad when we don't do good."

"But did he say your culture was bad or that you're becoming like Black Americans?"

"He did!" Tom shouted. "Like, if my grades are bad, he's like, 'you're not actin' like a real Caribbean person.' He's judgin' me. He's puttin' me down in front of everybody, in front of the whole class. He thinks it's a joke. . . . I told Mr. Robinson [the dean of discipline] the last time."

Here, Tom reminded me that when he walked out of class following Mr. Sterling's crass comments, he reported Mr. Sterling to a school administrator. Interpersonal defiance did not always take the form of orchestrated public action. But when Black Caribbean students confronted educators about their racially inflected comments about ethnicity by themselves, it was much less effective than when they did so as part of a group. The power of defiance was not in the resistance itself, but in the teamwork that shaped it. At least, that is what seemed to have caught Ms. Plummer's attention.

"It's good that you boys came to talk to me about your teacher," Ms. Plummer began. But then she insisted that Mr. Sterling "loved Caribbean culture and Caribbean people" and claimed that "his heart is in a good place, even though he's got a smart mouth," comments I also heard from other teachers about Mr. Sterling. Dwayne somberly nodded. I paused and wondered whether Mr. Sterling's comparison of Black Caribbean and Black American youth reinforced what some Black Caribbean immigrant students and parents practiced: discouraging cultural assimilation, which for Black immigrants often meant losing touch with their ethnic identities. In that process of cultural assimilation, Caribbean immigrants and their children "fade to Black," as sociologist Philip Kasinitz and his colleagues have argued.[26]

The Results of Interpersonal Defiance

"I can definitely talk to him about not saying these things in class," Ms. Plummer said to Tom. "But it's like you're really upset about him making you feel bad in front of the class," she added with a caring, calming tone as she looked Howie in his eyes. "Did it make you feel sad? Did it hurt your feelings?" I couldn't tell whether she meant the questions to be sobering or silly. I searched her face for signs until Dwayne said: "No, no, no, Ms." He explained that his objection was not about his hurt feelings, but about a problem in the way some teachers treated students.

"This should not happen to any of us in school, Ms. Like, for real," Howie said. "Like, I thought this was a free country with the American dream, and liberty and justice for all?" I raised my eyebrows, startled by Howie's piercingly shrewd remarks.

"Every time my friends hear what Sterling and other people say, they are like, "What's going on at your school, my G?" Dwayne said.[27]

"Yeah, but what's the real issue here?" Ms. Plummer prodded.

"He's using our culture against us!" Howie insisted. "You don't see it?"

Ms. Plummer paused, as if trying to ascertain the full meaning of Howie's assertion.

"It's like culture racism," Howie said loudly. "What he is saying is like culture racism." Howie had told me before that he thought he was "making up" this phrase to describe what he experienced; he did not know that cultural racism is a recognized form of racial bias. "I just knew that this was like some sort of prejudice or discrimination," he said.

Mr. Sterling suddenly stormed out of the staff room, slamming the oak door against the wall, and protested: "That is not racism! I'm talking about culture, not about your skin color. I would never judge you by the color of your skin. I'm just talking about your culture and the difference between Caribbean students and African students, African American students. . . . That's not racism. . . . What happened a hundred years ago does not really affect Caribbean students. . . . We have better laws in this country now." His pale skin turned red then purple with rage. Ms. Plummer widened her eyes. Dwayne dropped his jaw. Tom smiled. Howie stood with a blank look on his face, his eyes dim. It seemed that Mr. Sterling was ignorant of the many faces of racism, perhaps subscribing to its old, Black-versus-white form, as opposed to its related iterations that use ethnic culture as an alibi for racism to say, "See, this is not about race and racism!" all the while reinforcing racial hierarchies.

At this point, although I was itching to clarify the shapeshifting nature of racism across time and space, I pursed my lips instead.

Mr. Sterling explained that he had been teaching at Newlands for over two decades and "worked with hundreds of Caribbean students, African students, African American students, and ones from all sorts of backgrounds." He boasted that he had remained at Newlands despite offers to move to specialized high schools in Manhattan, Brooklyn, and the Bronx because "I really love the diversity of our school. . . . I decided to live in Crown Heights [Brooklyn] when lots of other white people were moving out." He later told me that he had chosen to stay in New York City when his white family and friends moved to the suburbs of New York and the US South in search of "better homes" and "better schools."

"You can't call me racist!" he declared to Tom in a tone that tried to assert his authority.

"Why not? Why the hell not?!" Tom shouted. I'd never seen him so angry. The class clown had become the teacher's chief critic.

Three teachers hurried out of the staff room, with one asking, "Is everything alright?" After Ms. Plummer reassured them and the teachers left, Dwayne shared his views.

"Look," Dwayne said with a quiet voice and calming tone. "I don't know if it's racist, but I know it ain't right."

"Right," Howie added.

"I said what I said to motivate you a little bit more to focus on your Regents [exams]," Mr. Sterling replied. "I did this before and you all just laughed. Nobody said anything, but now it's bothering you?" The tone that accompanied his question made it seem like a jab or a jeer. "At the end of the day," he continued, "I want you boys to go to college. Your parents want you to go to college. And you need good grades to get there." Mr. Sterling then turned to Ms. Plummer and said, "and let's face it, we need all our students to do well before the DOE [New York City Department of Education] starts talking about closing us down or putting charter schools in our building."

Ms. Plummer turned abruptly to Howie, Dwayne, and Tom as she said, "I think this was just a misunderstanding. We'll make sure Mr. Sterling doesn't do this again."

Mr. Sterling grimaced, grunted, and walked away.

This public confrontation was the most intense exchange I witnessed during my time at Newlands. Yet Howie, Tom, and Dwayne's strategy of challenging an individual teacher's ethnic expectations was followed by other Black Caribbean students. Their defiance did not include threatening to leave the school, as in London, but strategically confronting school leaders to report specific teachers who misrepresented, disrespected, or disadvantaged Black Caribbean students.

After the tense exchange between Sterling and a few Black Caribbean boys, it occurred to me that Howie and Tom did not take issue with Mr. Sterling's expression of ethnic expectations per se. Nor was the problem primarily one of misnaming Black Caribbean people as "Black Americans," which Caribbean students like Howie often understood to mean African Americans. To them, ethnic expectations warranted defiance, not when used as a form of praise, but when deployed as a correction strategy for getting them in line. The issue at hand was not simply public understandings of Caribbean culture, but teachers' attempts to use Black Caribbean students' positive representation and comparatively high status at Newlands to humiliate and punish individuals who did not meet that standard.

Political Calculations of Race and Culture

The tense exchange between Howie, Tom, Dwayne, Ms. Plummer, and Mr. Sterling calls attention to the fact that some Black Caribbean students had an acute awareness of racism as a system of power used to classify them and organize their world. The emotionally charged to-and-fro underscored ethnicity's role as race's surrogate, its twin playing hide-and-seek in a game of cultural difference.[28] Black Caribbean young people like Howie, Tom, and Dwayne spoke to three central fallacies that figure in public discussions of racism in American and British society. The first is the *ahistorical fallacy*, the view that the past has little influence over contemporary affairs.[29] When Mr. Sterling said that "what happened a hundred years ago does not really affect Caribbean students," he invoked the ahistorical fallacy. This view is steeped in a perception that Black Caribbean immigration to the United States is a mid-to-late 20th-century phenomenon and ignores the centuries-long, entangled history of interethnic relations among Black people in the hemisphere.

Furthermore, Mr. Sterling ignored the staying power of structures that generate inequality, from residential segregation and policing in the local community to academic tracking and disciplinary practices throughout New York City public schools. Mr. Sterling was correct to assert that Black Caribbean young people do not have the intimate familial connection with enslavement in the United States that African Americans do; Black Caribbean immigrants and their children are secondary subjects of settler colonialism in the United States, as I noted in Chapter 2. Nevertheless, the history of Black Caribbeans in the United States is more deeply marked by structural and cultural racism than Mr. Sterling admits.

Another key fallacy that surfaced in Mr. Sterling's response is the *legalistic fallacy*, which conflates legal changes with societal transformation.[30] Mr. Sterling's assertion that the existence of "better laws" disproves Howie's claims of racism fails to account for the persistence of racialized structures that reproduce inequality. The legalistic fallacy fails to account for the ways in which racialized structures and unequal outcomes persist despite legislative advances.

But there is a third racial fallacy that animates Mr. Sterling's comments— what I call the *diversity fallacy*. This fallacy claims that choosing to live and work in a racially diverse environment disproves investments in interpersonal racism. In keeping with Tom's indignant reply, I maintain that living among Black people and ethno-racial minorities is not synonymous with treating everyone equitably, or sharing power fairly. In some cases, diversity can be used to decorate the cultural lives of white people, all while deflecting the structural power white people hold in urban schools and neighborhoods.

Black Caribbean youth like Howie are sensitive to the use of culture as a code for ranking and sorting groups at Newlands in a way that supports, rather than disrupts, prevailing racial hierarchies. While they are critical of cultural racism when ethnic expectations come with negative consequences for their status in school, they minimize or ignore cultural racism when it does not disadvantage them. When Black Caribbean students who excel are celebrated, that praise is often based on comparison with African Americans, a group that is stereotypically framed as underachieving at Newlands. Just as the 'success' of Black Caribbeans is regarded as a consequence of Caribbean culture despite being conditioned by class and context, so, too, the 'failure' of African Americans that is deemed to result from African American culture is a woeful misrepresentation of African Americans locally and nationally. Such misrepresentations are, in fact, culturally racist.

This kind of taken-for-granted folk racism—often called 'new racism' that is grounded in essentialist perceptions of culture rather than biology yet is still used to determine inferior and superior groups and predict group success or failure—underlines cultural conceptions of race, motivates differential treatment of groups, and evokes judgment of groups as having 'good cultures' and 'bad cultures'. But the ideologies and practices associated with cultural racism in schools and society often affect Black youth differently based on their ethnicity—and dominant representations of them in their *situated contexts*. For Black youth at Newlands High, cultural racism reinforced the culture of poverty thesis, bolstered the Black model minority myth, undermined the complexities of African American and Caribbean identities, and ultimately marginalized one group for the elevation of another. At Newlands High, cultural racism was not necessarily a manifestation of cultural intolerance, but an expression of serial cultural misrepresentation.

Status beliefs about African Americans reinforce and reproduce historical and structural inequalities that are unmistakably shaped by racism.[31] Only on rare occasions during the course of my fieldwork did Black Caribbean students object to the skewed, culturally racist representations of African Americans. Black Caribbean students at Newlands aligned with African Americans and African students to decry stop-and-frisk policing practices and racial profiling they experienced en route to and from school.[32] But they often did not acknowledge the cultural valence of racism when it targeted African Americans. At Newlands High, the casual and everyday silences, elisions, and misrepresentations that shape the role of 'culture' in sustaining racial hierarchies are experienced most acutely by those disadvantaged by virtue of their race *and* their ethnicity—those held most tightly in the culture trap.

Whether in ignorance, inconsistency, or indifference, Black Caribbean students in New York City, like a host of people of varied racial and ethnic backgrounds, colluded with the power structure that disadvantages African Americans. These Black Caribbean young people at Newlands are complex social actors, who, like many of us, challenge institutional practices when they disadvantage us, but seldom do so when they benefit us. In this regard, these young people are a reflection of us, and highlight the complex and at times contradictory nature of the human condition.

A Quiet Protest: Selective Class Participation as Interpersonal Defiance

Interpersonal defiance was fueled by anger, although not necessarily the expressions of rage that can get Black Caribbean students disciplined or cause some Black Caribbean parents to "cuss out som' ah dem teecha deh [curse out some of those teachers]," as one parent threatened to do. Class participation was a key, albeit deliberately quiet, strategy of interpersonal defiance that students used to challenge specific teachers and protect themselves. In a school like Newlands where 10 to 15 percent of students' grades were based on their attendance and class participation, Black Caribbean students like Stacey, a straight-A student, were strategic about the frequency of their participation. A rich exchange with 11th graders Stacey, Sam and Camille after their AP English class revealed this subtle strategy to me.

The three friends strolled out of class into a corridor teeming with students speaking more languages than I could recognize. I tapped Sam on his shoulder, hoping to pose a question or two. "Meet us in the lunchroom," he shouted over the din. When I arrived, I sat down with them and asked, "How come you all were so quiet today?"

They stared at one another, then shrugged their shoulders. They were normally a talkative, opinionated bunch, leading discussions among their peers on literary criticism. Mr. Thomas described them as "the kinds of students who pushed the class to think." During the last few classes, however, I had noticed the group's relative disengagement. It puzzled me.

"So how come you all were so quiet today?" I asked again.

"I don't really like how Mr. Thomas be going on in class with us, so I decided to just do my work and not, like, do extra work or nothin'," Stacey said. "What she said," Sam agreed. "I'm not dumb," Stacey continued. "Thomas can't be out here talkin' to me and Caribbean kids any old way and still expect me to just come to class smiling and with my hand up on a regular. . . . We don't have to argue about it."

"We can keep the fight quiet," Camille said.

"You can't disrespect me and expect me to just act normal. Like, nah," Stacey said.

I asked, "Do you think Mr. Thomas knows what's going on? I didn't know what was going on for sure until you just told me."

"I think he knows that something is different," Stacey replied. "Yeah, he know wassup [what's up]," Sam stated. When, as is my wont, I asked for examples, Stacey said: "Like today, he was calling on me and Camille to answer questions, show the class like we usually do. We just did our work." Stacey chuckled, and Camille continued: "Yeah. At the end of the day, you can't force me to help your discussion in class or use me to explain a good thesis, but you're talking down to me, or tell me you know I can do better 'cause my family is from the islands."

Sam sucked his teeth loudly.

"He can't force us. It's my choice to participate and how much," Camille added.

"But won't that impact your grades?" I asked.

"No, not really," Camille replied. "I still participate, but I just hold back. I don't participate too much."

Stacey added, "I still try to give the right answer, but I don't talk out loud a lot."

Stacey, Camille, and Sam suggested that they deliberately limit the frequency and intensity of their class participation as a quiet form of interpersonal defiance. Their responses were typical; other second-generation Black Caribbean pupils regarded participation as a choice they made when they felt fully affirmed. By being selective about their participation in class, they withheld some power that teachers often draw on to improve class discussions.

Strikingly, this quiet, calculated refusal was more frequently practiced by Black Caribbean girls than Black Caribbean boys. Owing to the gendered behavioral scripts and a disciplinary context in which Caribbean girls were punished for infractions that boys were excused from, girls learned how to stage interpersonal defiance without incurring disproportionate consequences. Boys, on the other hand, had the flexibility to be as calm and collected as Sam, or as loud and angry as Tom. Even as Black Caribbean girls practiced interpersonal defiance, they did so with an acute awareness that their expressions were constrained by gender norms.

The Power of Defiance

This chapter demonstrates the power of defiance for resisting the negative consequences of ethnic expectations for Black Caribbean young people in London and New York City. Students did not perceive defiance to be self-defeating. Instead, it was a calculated refusal of the perspectives, practices, and processes that create public shame and intensify achievement anxieties. Defiance is not simply an oppositional stance when engaging with individual teachers and institutions at points of disagreement. Rather, this peculiar *kind* of resistance is pro-school but anti-oppression. At Londerville Secondary in London and Newlands High in New York, defiance, like distinctiveness and deference, emerges situationally. Participants deploy defiance that is both public and private, noisy and quiet, respectful and disrespectful, singular and coalitional, institutional and interpersonal, all to challenge the conditions that generate and perpetuate racial and ethnic inequality. Irrespective of the type of defiance Black Caribbean students deploy, defiance is born out of a deep commitment to education and a desire for high-quality, equitable schooling in which race and ethnicity are not grounds for unequal expectations.

Crucially, institutional defiance in London and interpersonal defiance in New York City are not what anthropologists John Ogbu and Signithia Fordham referred to as oppositional cultures, Black youth's peer cultures of resistance to academic achievement based on a fear of "acting white."[33] I found no evidence of this phenomenon among Black youth on either side of the Atlantic. To Akilah, Howie, and their peers, defiance was a reasoned response to oppositional structures—institutional practices and relations of power that undermine the educational experiences of Black Caribbean youth. These oppositional structures contribute to the cultural reproduction of race and ethnicity as "signifiers of difference."[34] Setting, isolation, and exclusion in London and tracking, in-school and out-of-school suspensions in New York, as well as expulsion and compulsory transfers in both cities, remake the significance of Blackness, Caribbean-ness, African-ness, and African American-ness in the lived experiences of young people. But the meanings of 'Caribbean-ness' are entirely contingent and historically situated, even though they are frequently misrepresented as wholly cultural. Failure to recognize this fact leaves us all stuck in the culture trap.

Conclusion

Dismantling the Culture Trap in Schools

The sun shone brightly in the clear London skies the last time I met Ms. Bell. This veteran Black teacher greeted me with her signature warm embrace on a cool, autumn afternoon. From the moment I decided to pursue this comparative ethnography, Ms. Bell insisted that I meet with her to tell her all that I had learned. Four years later, we sat down in an empty classroom at her Saturday school with hot cups of tea warming our hands and hearts, as we reflected on her former students I had worked with as a community organizer, and her concerns about the achievement of Black Caribbean students at her new school in North London. In time, she leaned forward in her chair and said:

"So, what did you find out about Caribbean students in this country and in America?"

"'Ole eep [a whole heap]!" I chuckled.

She waved her right hand forward in a circular motion, bidding me to share what I had uncovered. "Ah long time mi ah wait fi hear dis. [I've been waiting a long time to hear this]," she said.

I pulled out a 30-page paper from my bag and leafed through it, hoping to share the most compelling, polished prose and moving quotes from participants that answered her question. Ms. Bell rested her hand on mine and said, "Just talk, Mr. Wallace."

I breathed a sigh of relief and said, "Alright."

"I just really want to know why our Caribbean young people fail here and succeed in the schools over there," she continued. "This was what I kept thinking about all these years."

I explained to Ms. Bell that the educational experiences and achievement outcomes of Black Caribbeans in London and New York are complicated cultural phenomena with deep structural roots. Given ongoing commitments to racial equity in British and American public schools, paying careful attention to the hidden, taken-for-granted ways in which 'culture' is strategically

The Culture Trap. Derron Wallace, Oxford University Press. © Oxford University Press 2023.
DOI: 10.1093/oso/9780197531464.003.0008

used to make sense of students' academic achievement and behavior is essential. Failure to do so may result in school leaders, teachers, parents, and young people falling into the culture trap—a reductive, interpretive frame that centers ethnic culture as the explanation for students' achievement, but ultimately constrains students' identities and foments racial inequalities in education. But simply acknowledging the influence of stated and unstated ethnic expectations is insufficient for dismantling the culture trap and pursuing equity in schools. When I reflected on my talk with Ms. Bell years later, I was reminded of the need to transform the beliefs and practices that sustain the culture trap in schools.[1]

Ethnic Expectations and the Pursuit of Equity

"So, tell mi what yuh find out nuh [no]?!" Ms. Bell insisted.

"Well, it's really a number of things that shape the education of Black Caribbean young people in London and New York," I replied. She waved her right hand forward repeatedly, as if to say, 'Go on!' She had a pen in her left hand and a notepad at the ready.

"What's the big issue for Caribbean students in England and America?" she asked.

Years later, I realized that I should have told Ms. Bell that what I found out about Black Caribbeans in the US was more about New York than the United States, whereas what I learned about Black Caribbeans in London was emblematic of Black Caribbean education in England. But in the moment, I said:

"It's complicated, Ms. Bell. I learned so much about education, race, ethnicity, culture, gender, class, context, immigration, immigrant and second-generation identity, history, politics, public policy, religion. . . ." I raced on. By her raised eyebrows, I could tell this was perhaps more than she expected. It certainly was more than I ever expected before I began this cross-national research.

"Alright," she said softly and slowly. "Put it this way. What did you see in the schools, or what did you learn from all of this?" I told her about the main theme that emerged in my research: ethnic expectations.

"Woooiii!!" Ms. Bell shouted in a distinct Jamaican drawl as she slapped the desk and spilled some of her tea. "Ethnic expectations! Dat mek [that makes] so much sense to mi already. Tell mi more 'bout dat [that]!" Ms. Bell said.

"Ethnic expectations are beliefs teachers, students and parents have about what Caribbean students will likely achieve in school," I said quickly. "People don't always share those expectations out loud . . . It's sometimes in the back of our minds, but it shapes how we are seen as Caribbean people, and even how we see ourselves and what we think we can achieve. . . . It's about what people expect from us in schools, and sometimes, what we even expect from ourselves."

Ms. Bell leaned back in her chair, crossed her arms, tilted her head to the side, squinted her eyes, and bobbed them from side to side. Eventually, she looked down and stared at the notes she wrote down about ethnic expectations. I had a feeling that she was about to question me some more, but I was ready. In my mind, I knew that the differing ethnic expectations Black Caribbean young people experienced in London and New York City schools demonstrate that cultures are understood and experienced differently based on the context of reception and the opportunities within it. I had become convinced more than ever before that ethnic cultures do not hold a fixed position across national contexts and local organizations, nor remain immutable over time. I realized, in the words of Stuart Hall, that "what we have here, then, is an emergent field of racial, cultural and ethnic difference and contestation . . . that is articulated in different ways in different places."[2] I knew I should have explained more of this to Ms. Bell when she replied:

"But it's not just Caribbean students! What about Chinese, Indian and even some of the African students? . . . People just expect them to be smart or hard workers, like it's in their culture. . . . like it's in their genes. I've seen a lot of that over the years."

Her response caught me off guard, but affirmed important questions raised by sociologists and anthropologists such as Stacey Lee, Antonia Randolph, Natasha Warikoo, Louise Archer, David Gillborn, and Sally Tomlinson.[3] I thought Black Caribbean students were the ones she was concerned about. Her response forced me to look beyond the Black Caribbean case and remember the wider goal: educational equity for all ethno-racial groups. Perhaps this is not what she intended, but once again, her probing question pushed me to think further. So, after a moment of silence, I said to her:

"Yeah. Caribbean people are not the only ones that deal with ethnic expectations. Lots of ethnic groups do."

In my analysis of my discussion with Ms. Bell, I've come to realize that over the past decade, sociologists such as Jennifer Lee, Min Zhou, Jamie Lew, Louise Archer and Kalwant Bhopal have examined how Chinese, Indian, and

Korean students are often constrained by imposed and internalized expectations regarding their performance.[4] Research by Onoso Imoagene, Mercy Agyepong, Pere Ayling, and Steve Strand calls attention to the behavioral and achievement expectations others hold of Nigerian and Ghanaian students, even as racism constrains their social mobility.[5] It became clearer to me over time than when I last spoke with Ms. Bell that ethnic expectations shape the educational experiences of other ethno-racial minorities.

But truth be told, Ms. Bell's comments also forced me to think more deeply about the specificity of the Black Caribbean case. So, I continued: "But what makes the example of Caribbean people so powerful is that you get to see how ethnic expectations are really different for the same ethnic groups across two national contexts." In this regard, Black Caribbeans in London and New York City provide an important comparison that troubles essentialist claims about culture as a single, uniform essence, and continues the unfinished examination of inequalities and identities.[6]

"Hhhhhmmm," Ms. Bell said, scribbling down portions of my explanation. Future research may help us understand how ethnic expectations function similarly and differently for other ethnic groups across national contexts.

I glanced at the 30-page paper I placed on the desk and realized that what I wrote was illuminating but incomplete because it only considered Black Caribbean young people. I needed to explain in broader terms that ethnic expectations operate as a conscious and unconscious method of categorizing students of various ethnic backgrounds, and function as a key lens through which individual and group distinctions are reproduced. In US and British schools, we often use symbolic markers of race, ethnicity, and gender at an unconscious and at times conscious level to guide understandings of students' potential for achievement even while acknowledging that such judgments are limiting and perhaps socially unacceptable. The model minority myth matters for students not simply because of the stereotypical logics of cultural distinction that shape it and the practices of stratification it produces, but also because it informs the educational expectations teachers and students mobilize in classrooms in pursuit of academic achievement.[7]

But there is another side of ethnic expectations that is commonly accepted and often unspoken in schools. Consider the surprise expressed when students from Roma, Indigenous, African American, and other historically disadvantaged ethno-racial groups excel academically. Such celebrations often emerge when *individuals* in these groups defy long-standing societal assumptions of underachievement, or when they rise above ethnic expectations.[8] In cases where groups are either celebrated or degraded based on high or low expectations, ethnic expectations constitute a quiet orthodoxy shaped by perceptions of culture used to predict (under)achievement, and in some cases even (mis)behavior. Though I didn't realize it until Ms. Bell questioned me, ethnic expectations are relevant, implicitly and explicitly, to a host of ethno-racial groups.[9]

Ethnic Expectations as Strategic and Casual Expressions of Power

Ms. Bell waved her right hand forward when she was ready for me to continue. "Give me some examples," she said.

None were at the tip of my tongue. I told her I needed to get a drink of water, but what I needed even more was time to think. When I returned moments later, I told Ms. Bell that "when teachers and students believe that Indian and Chinese students are going to be high-achieving, that's because of ethnic expectations."

Ms. Bell nodded.

"When people on the streets and in the community just assume Caribbean kids in London and African American kids in New York are underachievers or troublemakers after school, that's an example of ethnic expectations."

Ms. Bell nodded again and wrote quickly.

"And when teachers or anybody act really shocked when Caribbean kids get into Oxford or Cambridge, that might be because of ethnic expectations."

"Sounds about right," she commented.

I replied: "You know, like when you didn't believe that I could be at Cambridge as a Black Caribbean man, and you said, 'Africans maybe, but not Black Caribbean people'? Maybe that's ethnic expectations."[10]

Ms. Bell gasped. "A me yuh a talk 'bout [You're talking about me]?" she said. We laughed hysterically. "I never meant anything by that," she said. "I was just surprised because a lot of Caribbean people don't get into those universities."

I understood that the nature and history of admission to elite British and American universities can shape our perceptions of the groups we think are likely to be admitted—or not.[11] As I told Ms. Bell, "Even our well-meaning comments can reflect and reinforce ethnic expectations about specific groups of people."

"I understand," she said, and then reassured me that she "didn't mean to offend" me.

"Other teachers use ethnic expectations, you know, Ms. Bell," I added. "Sometimes, it's even worse."

"I know," she replied. "My children, my niece and nephews dem tell me all sort of things dem [they] hear or that teachers say to them inna [in] school."

I told Ms. Bell about Mr. Sterling in New York, and how, in an attempt to push Tom to earn a grade higher than C, he said to Tom: "You are capable of more. . . . The other West Indian children are smart and you are too. . . . You know how to work harder."

She widened her eyes and shook her head. I told her that, like other teachers, Mr. Sterling thought his intentions were good; he aimed to motivate Caribbean students to achieve academically. Nevertheless, his expressions had negative consequences—shaming, annoying, and even undermining students based on their cultural heritage. She asked if Mr. Sterling was white. I nodded. She replied: "But at least his expectations were high fi dem [for them]. A nuh so it work inna Englan' [That's not how it works it England]."

I also told her what Ms. James in London said to Akilah after she almost failed the mock exam, even though she usually received top marks. When I pointed out that Ms. James, a very experienced white teacher, told Akilah to "remember this is just one exam. You are already exceeding expectations. . . . Most students don't do as well as you," Ms. Bell shook her head from side to side, this time more vigorously.

"Oh my God!" she exclaimed. "You know I can believe that! That's a microaggression!" I nodded in agreement—but I really wish I hadn't without explaining more. I realized years later that identifying microaggressions is only part of the story. Ethnic expectations have power not simply because of what is said about Black Caribbeans and other minoritized ethno-racial groups, but because of the organized structures such as setting/tracking and routine practices such as in-school exclusion and out-of-school suspension that reinforce prevailing myths about the educational performance of ethno-racial groups. Reflecting on Ms. Bell's reaction and my own, I've come to realize that we are often shocked, displeased, and even infuriated by what teachers like Mr. Sterling and Ms. James say to students, but less moved by the entrenched mechanisms of inequality that reproduce racialized power differentials in schools. We are more angered by statements than by structures of schooling that increase inequality. I wish I had told Ms. Bell that simply calling out microaggressions, while important, does not produce sustainable racial equity in schools. Changing the institutional structures and organizational cultures does.

I should have told Ms. Bell that ethnic expectations in schools are not simply the result of cultural ideologies, but are also unconsciously reproduced by entrenched organizational practices. Through their 'ability' grouping mechanisms, behavior management techniques, and disciplinary processes, schools socialize Black Caribbean youth and their peers in London and New York City into racial and ethnic hierarchies—stratified arrangements that reinforce dominant discursive claims about group performance and the role of ethnic culture in predicting it. Schools bolster status differentiation, reinforce patterns of social exclusion in peer networks, and constrain students' identities to a set of anticipated achievement and behavioral outcomes.[12] In the remainder of our conversation with Ms. Bell, I signaled the limits of cultural awareness for changing schools and society.

Understanding the Roles of Culture, Class, and Context

After Ms. Bell and I spoke about different expressions of ethnic expectations—from the stated to the unstated, the conscious to the unconscious—I told her of my most surprising finding.

"You know how I told you that culture didn't have anything to do with the experiences of Black Caribbean young people in London and New York schools?" I said to Ms. Bell.

"Mi nuh memba dat [I don't remember that]," she said. I recounted details from the notes I took that day.

"That was four or five years ago," she replied, "and I don't walk around with [note]books or doing one-to-ones like you."[13]

"Well," I continued, "what I wanted to tell you is that I thought culture didn't matter, but I was wrong."

"What?! Ah wah yuh a seh to mi [what are you saying to me]?" Ms. Bell replied. "Owah [our] culturah is di reason fi [for] all of this?"

"No, no," I hastened to say.

I told Ms. Bell that despite my strong, long-held opposition to claims that culture explains group experiences and outcomes, my interviews and observations with second-generation Black Caribbean young people, their teachers, parents, and peers suggest that culture plays an important role, at least at Londerville Secondary in London and Newlands High in New York.

I never imagined discovering that culture matters. But, I learned that there is a significant difference between acknowledging culture and overemphasizing its significance. Culturalist explanations that posit culture as *the* key factor shaping the divergent representations and experiences of Black Caribbean people on both sides of the Atlantic are flawed not only because they exaggerate culture's influence, but also because they do not account for the structural and historical factors that inform ethnic groups' success. Nevertheless, culture *still* plays a critical role in shaping the day-to-day lived experiences of Black Caribbean people, informing the everyday meaning-making, ritual representations, and situational strategies used to address ethnic expectations.[14]

I pointed out to Ms. Bell that culture is mobilized as a set of strategies to reproduce ethnic expectations, but also to resist them. Dominant beliefs about Caribbean culture held by teachers, parents, and students *socialized* Caribbean students into ethnic expectations. From observing and listening to Black Caribbean young people, I learned that culture, broadly understood, is a way of making sense of the norms, practices, and processes that govern the social world.

When I saw the look of confusion on Ms. Bell's face, I told her, "There is more to culture than ethnic culture. . . . Plus, culture is not the only factor to consider." She waved her right hand forward again, telling me to say more. I glanced at my paper full of quotations and key points before I explained that culture alone does not determine success. The confluence of culture, class, and context informs the differing outcomes, expectations, and *positioning* of Black Caribbeans in London and New York. Cultural representations of Black Caribbean young people as 'underachieving' in London and 'high achieving' in New York are not shaped by Caribbean culture per se, but by the contexts of opportunity Black Caribbean immigrants and their second-generation children experience in the two national contexts.

In the United States, Caribbean identity has historically functioned as an ethnic credit, as Antonia Randolph suggests,[15] and is highlighted in an attempt to displace racial stereotypes and delineate ethnic distinctions among Black people. As Natasha Warikoo acknowledges in *Balancing Acts*, and Mary Waters notes in *Black Identities*, Black Caribbeans in the United States have been deemed a Black model minority for decades based on their levels of educational attainment, home ownership, and cultural prominence.[16] Additionally, Black Caribbeans are disproportionately represented at Ivy League institutions.[17] In public discourse, Black Caribbeans have garnered positive recognition for their industriousness, immigrant 'grit,' and investment in education.[18] But the celebration of Black Caribbeans' elevated minority status in the United States is relational and often contingent on the negative stereotyping of African Americans in under-resourced urban neighborhoods and schools.[19] The role of such perspectives is not fully captured in Mary Waters's *Black Identities*, but are ones I illuminate in detail in *The Culture Trap*.

In Britain, by contrast, Black Caribbeans are often stereotyped negatively, and they are the group from whom other Blacks, ethno-racial minorities, and in the case of Paul Willis's *Learning to Labor*, even the white working classes, often seek to distance themselves in select situations when such groups are seeking elevation in a hierarchy of belonging.[20] Black Caribbeans in Britain have been deemed a persistently underachieving minority over the past seven decades, most notably in education. Black Caribbean young people experience low levels of educational attainment and disproportionate school exclusion and detention.[21] In *The Art of Being Black*, and subsequent works on race and culture, Claire Alexander observes that Black Caribbeans in Britain "remain concentrated in deprived urban areas, are concentrated in the rental housing sector and demonstrate poorer health outcomes."[22] These striking differences in the experiences and representations of Black Caribbean young people underscore the significance of historical, national and school contexts in shaping perceptions of Caribbean ethnic culture.

I explained to Ms. Bell that for Black Caribbean young people in London and New York City public schools, national *and* school contexts facilitate the function and reproduction of culture. While the dynamics of ethnic expectations I uncovered at Londerville Secondary in London and Newlands High in New York represent those specific schools and cities, the institutional mechanisms that sustain ethnic expectations—such as academic 'ability' grouping, school exclusion and suspension, and gendered patterns of praise and punishment—are representative of common formal and informal approaches to teaching and learning in schools in Britain, the United States, and around the world.

With a look of confusion or perhaps displeasure on her face, Ms. Bell asked for "a concrete example."

"Ms. Bell, you know seh [that] setting [tracking] work[s] differently in the two countries?" I said. She shook her head and replied, "mi neva know that."

"Yeah, and it's different in these two schools too," I added.

Britain has a national curriculum and a nationwide setting system at the secondary level. This rigid structure constrains mobility across sets and allocates students to sets in key subjects based on test scores and academic performance. The United States, in contrast, has tracking systems with considerable variations across regions. In some regions, test scores are not the only criteria for accessing top tracks. I told Ms. Bell that in New York, particularly in recent years, public schools had a flexible subject-by-subject tracking process that sorted students based on their interests as well as their abilities. Tracking systems like the one I observed at Newlands High in New York afforded teachers greater autonomy to scout and mentor students for higher-track placement. These different 'ability' grouping structures in different educational contexts influence the different experiences of Black Caribbean students. In both London and New York, 'ability' grouping practices stratify students by race and ethnicity, inform the segregation or integration of students through day-to-day socialization, and facilitate the status beliefs associated with ethno-racial groups.

Ms. Bell nodded slowly, seemingly deep in thought. I got a sense of what she was thinking when she stood up from her desk and said, "Bredda [Brother], all of this is news to me."

I had more news to share with Ms. Bell, particularly about social class, but in the moment, I completely forgot. This is exactly why I wanted to read my findings to her from my 30-page paper in the first place. If I did, I would have told Ms. Bell that while national and school contexts inform the positioning of Black Caribbean young people in schools, social class shapes the dominant representations of these youth. As culture is elevated in schools and public discourse, the role of class in shaping representations of culture is elided.[23] By forgetting to account for the power of social class in representations of culture during my conversation with Ms. Bell, I had done precisely what I critiqued teachers and researchers of doing. I found this at once deeply unsettling and profoundly humbling.

In specific situations that proved advantageous for them, Black Caribbean students in New York sought to distinguish themselves from low-income and working-class African Americans in their neighborhoods. In London, by contrast, I noticed that some Black Caribbean students distanced themselves from 'yardies'—low-income and working-class Black Caribbean immigrants. In both cases, second-generation Black Caribbean young people's responses were not simply about their cultural preferences or intraracial ethnic tensions; they were also about the politics of social class in identifying authentic and acceptable *public* representations of Caribbean culture in schools. In fact, middle-class Black Caribbean students were frequently regarded as model students, even though ethnic culture was consistently deemed the secret of their success. This is what I call the secret life of class in representations of culture. Class politics is masked in what is often described as purely a matter of culture.

Eventually, Ms. Bell said matter-of-factly, "So, Mr. Wallace, what does all of this mean for our Caribbean kids, especially our boys?" I explained to Ms. Bell that the punitive disciplinary measures in secondary schools affect Black Caribbean boys and girls differently; Black Caribbean boys and girls have distinct vulnerabilities in schools, and that they are all worth addressing. At Newlands High and Londerville Secondary, Black Caribbean boys who displayed 'good behavior' were often praised—more quickly and frequently than Black Caribbean girls. This disparity was due, in part, to the low expectations teachers often held for boys' behavior. Yet Black Caribbean girls on both sides of the Atlantic were seldom praised for 'good behavior' because as girls they were expected to be well-behaved.

"Is true enuh [you know]!" Ms. Bell retorted. "But our Caribbean boys are struggling. I mean really struggling," she continued. She told me about four of the Black Caribbean boys from her class I had worked with as a community organizer who were now struggling in secondary school. "You have to do something about it, Mr. Wallace," she insisted.

"*We* have to do something about this," I said emphatically.[24] I told Ms. Bell that "Black Caribbean boys need support, but Black Caribbean girls need support too. They have different struggles and strengths we have to recognize." For instance, while Black Caribbean boys fare less well than Black Caribbean girls on Britain's national GCSE exams, Black Caribbean girls do not fare as well as white and Asian girls.[25] While Black Caribbean boys experience the highest rates of school exclusion in London comprehensive schools, Black Caribbean girls are more than two times as likely to be excluded from schools than their white and Asian female counterparts.[26] Given this pattern, I told Ms. Bell that "we do not and should not have to choose between supporting Black Caribbean boys over supporting Black Caribbean girls in schools." Black Caribbean boys *and* girls need our attention, though sometimes with different approaches. It became even clearer to me years later after talking to Ms. Bell that we must resist policy and discursive investments that position Black Caribbean boys and their needs over and against those of Black Caribbean girls. The social and political context necessitates a clear-eyed focus on the gendered particularities of institutional racism as they are experienced by Black Caribbean boys and girls.

Ms. Bell stood up from her desk, walked around it toward me, and gave me a firm, fast, and unexpected high-five. "That's really important, Mr. Wallace," she said. As she sat down next to me, she told me stories of Black Caribbean girls we both knew who struggled similarly and differently from Black Caribbean boys and were considered "just sort of odd," as she put it. "They are treated as though something is wrong with them as individuals, but for the Caribbean boys, we almost talk about them like something is wrong with them as a group," she explained.

"And both of those frames or both those lenses or perspectives limit what we see *in* Black Caribbean girls and boys and what we can understand about them," I replied.

I extended Ms. Bell's astute assessment by pointing out that it is the alignment of gendered behavioral expectations for Black Caribbean boys and girls across academic, familial, and community-based institutions that make them so casually forceful and so culturally effective. Accordingly, support for Black Caribbean boys and girls should be developed across these institutions.[27] To begin, we must understand that the problem is grounded in the politics of culture, class, and context.

In retrospect, I should have reminded Ms. Bell, and perhaps myself, that Black girls like Akilah in London, Black Caribbean boys like Tom in New York, and their peers at Londerville Secondary and Newlands High are *young people*—teenagers making meaning of the power of culture and the culture of power in schools. They are dynamic social actors whose wide-ranging understandings and experiences of inequality should not be discounted or underestimated. Some young people like Trudy, Howie, and several of their peers (noted in Chapter 6) may point out with stunning precision the racism they encounter in schools. Some like John in New York and Rachel in London (highlighted in Chapter 4) may express uncertainty about class inequalities along with their own national identities as participants in schools and society. Still other young people, like several of the Black Caribbean boys at Londerville and Newlands (discussed in Chapter 5) may only be able to point out the racial and ethnic disadvantages they encounter, not the gender privileges and class advantages that shape their everyday experiences. In this regard, they are arguably no different from us—complex, varied, and at times contradictory.

As this ethnography shows, Black young people like Akilah and Tom can be remarkably insightful. But like all of us, they have blind spots worth seeing, if only to enable us to recognize our own. And despite their blind spots, the perspectives and stories of young people are worth listening to and learning from in order to improve processes of teaching and learning in schools, particularly when promoting racial equity for historically disadvantaged Black youth.

Ethnic Expectations: Implications for Education Politics and Practice

After we refilled our cups with hot tea, and Ms. Bell took a sip, she pulled her chair closer to mine, leaned forward in her seat and asked, "So Mr. Wallace, tell mi now, wah we ago do 'bout alla dis [What are we going to do about all of this]?" The fiery passion in her voice warmed my heart. "We need solutions," she insisted.

I told Ms. Bell that I had no easy, quick-fix solutions. Instead, I suggested that identifying solutions was not necessarily the key to ending the enduring racial, ethnic, economic, and gender inequities shaping the educational experiences of Black Caribbean and ethnic minority students in schools. We already know some of the solutions. I said to her, "The biggest issue here in England and even inna di [in the] States is not solutions. It's political will."

"Backside! See it deh [Look at that]!" she replied, and clapped her hands. "Now yuh talkin', Mr. Wallace!"

"It's not like government and school leaders don't know what to do," I said. "We know we need to fund our state [public] schools better to improve students' educational experiences and outcomes. We know we need to recruit and train a more diverse teacher workforce for an increasingly diverse student body to improve racial equity. We know we need to recruit and retain a more diverse teaching force that is well prepared to engage issues of race, culture, and equity. We know that in-school exclusion, suspension, and expulsion negatively impact Black students, especially working-class and low-income students, all over the United States and England, and that we need to change those patterns. We know setting [tracking] creates inequality and needs to stop to improve equity. But we continue because we lack the political will to imagine new possibilities and to act on them," I said to Ms. Bell. "We also do not devote resources to sustain effective policy and practices like mixed 'ability' grouping."

"Wait deh," she interrupted. "You are saying we should get rid of setting [tracking]."

"If we truly care about equity for Black, minority ethnic and even white working-class students," I responded, "we need to prioritize mixed 'ability' groupings in classrooms. That's what you have at your supplementary school. . . . This hasn't happened in a lot of state [public] schools because we lack the political will."

"But Mr. Wallace," Ms. Bell said, "sometimes we just don't know what else we can do. It's not like *nobody* cares to make it better."

"Of course not. A lot of people in education care. Teachers like you definitely care. But we often lack the collective will to act for equity and justice in schools." This is perhaps why our school practices contradict our public commitments to equity and inclusion.

"Hhhmmmm . . ." she murmured as she thought it over. "Is true," she eventually said.

In Britain and the United States, a host of policy and programmatic solutions have been proposed at the school, district, and national levels about how to enhance the educational experiences of Black and ethnic minority students. Several policy reports and government white papers have been published with targeted recommendations for improving the educational experiences of Black youth.[28] And yet, these recommendations have seldom garnered significant or sustainable traction over time. In Britain, solutions proposed over 50 years ago have just received widespread support. In 1971, Bernard Coard made valuable suggestions for addressing racism in the British educational system in *How the West Indian Child Is Made Educationally Sub-normal.*[29] He called for the sustained recruitment and retention of Black and ethnic minority teachers in schools, the eradication of in-school and between-school 'ability' grouping, and strategic engagement with immigrant parents beyond interests in policing and disciplining in order to improve the conditions of schooling for all children. Yet, only recently, during the Black Lives Matter movement and the rise in antiracist consciousness, did the recruitment and retention of Black and ethnic minority teachers become a concerted policy priority in London and across Britain. Despite studies documenting the positive impact and academic gains of students in mixed 'ability' groups, setting remains entrenched among school leaders in Britain.[30] One reason for this, I told Ms. Bell, is the constraint on our political will to pursue alternative educational practices that promote racial equity in education.

Center Race and Culture in Teacher Preparation

I told Ms. Bell that there are specific educational strategies and programmatic solutions that can be further developed to advance racial equity in
public schools at the national, district, and local levels, which I will expand
upon in more detail here. A key strategy for challenging ethnic expectations
is to transform teacher education in London and New York by broadening
the curriculum to include repeated, critical examinations of racial and cultural inequalities in schools and their relevance for subject-matter courses, as
well as academic and disciplinary outcomes. As part of ongoing professional
development, such sessions would further develop preservice teachers',
teacher-leaders', and current and aspiring leaders' capacities to be culturally
and structurally competent to lead the increasingly diverse student population in Britain and the United States.[31] While the teacher certification process in Britain involves an intensive, yearlong postgraduate program with
mandatory coursework and classroom experiences, it seldom engages race,
ethnicity, and culture in deep and meaningful ways. In fact, in most British
teacher training programs, discussions about race, ethnicity, and culture are
relegated to a week-long module or two.[32] Preservice and in-service teachers
are ill-equipped to engage cultural differences through an equity lens, or
to view ethnic and youth cultures as pedagogical resources for reshaping
teaching and learning.[33] When they enter classrooms, too many teachers are
unprepared to identify their own conscious and unconscious biases.

Teacher education programs in the United States face comparable
challenges to British programs, albeit for different reasons. While there is
one, national credentialing degree standard for teachers in Britain, the postgraduate certificate in education (PGCE), there are multiple routes to teacher
certification and licensure in the United States, which depend on the state
and type of school prospective teachers wish to work in. In fact, some schools
require neither certification nor licensure. With the wide range of teacher
preparation options, teachers can lead classes of students from diverse, mul-
tilingual backgrounds without having any meaningful engagement with race,
culture, and equity as part of their preparation for teaching. And programs
that include introductory or immersive training on race, culture, and equity
rarely focus on Black ethnic diversity. Teacher training programs have paid
insufficient attention to the educational trajectories of African American,

African, and Black Caribbean students and the cultural differences among them. And, to the extent that they do, these distinctions are often treated as either exotic or exceptional. The limited exposure preservice teachers and school leaders have to sustained training on race, culture, and Black ethnic diversity severely limits their capacities to regularly identify the stereotypes, and proactively address the biases, that inform their teaching.

University teacher preparatory programs and school-based professional development should be redesigned on both sides of the Atlantic to underscore race, culture, and equity as central, rather than peripheral, to effective 21st-century teacher education. Robust antiracist education is urgently necessary if teachers are to create affirming, culturally, and linguistically sustaining modes of teaching and learning for all young people in schools. Centering race and culture in teacher education matters for teachers because they cannot teach what they have not learned. In both Britain and the United States, the vast majority of preservice teachers are white and come from middle-class families.[34] Like many of us with good intentions, these teachers often do not recognize racism when veiled as 'culture.' We cannot be antiracist unless we can effectively identify the expressions, effects, and structures of racism—including less well-known forms such as cultural racism, and the insidious ways in which class is elided and culture is conflated with class. Moreover, effective antiracist education for teachers can afford students a well-rounded and creative education that promotes critical consciousness of race, culture, and equity so that students are prepared to effectively participate in racially and culturally diverse democracies.

Implement and Monitor Mixed 'Ability' Grouping as a District-Wide Practice

A second strategy for promoting equity in schools that I discussed with Ms. Bell is to promote mixed 'ability' grouping as a district-wide practice so that all students can have access to higher levels of rigor, risk-taking, creativity, and achievement. The flexible tracking I observed at Newlands High in New York between 2012 and 2015, which enabled mobility between tracks based on students' scores and interests, is markedly different from the very rigid tracking I experienced as a high school student in New York City from 2000 to 2003, which produced minimal mobility across tracks. Changes were made in New York's tracking practices because of local activism to promote equity by providing access to advanced classes for students irrespective of their prior academic achievement and assumed capacity. These efforts led to New York City's Advanced Placement for All initiative, which grants all New York City public school students "access to at least five Advanced Placement classes, thereby increasing college and career readiness for all students."[35]

Despite the promise of this innovative policy, the popular and unpopular practices associated with it in New York City public schools require careful monitoring. My research indicates that while all students have access to advanced classes, they don't all pursue them equally. In fact, some teachers can use uncommon criteria such as good behavior, discipline, and compliance to select and recommend some students for Advanced Placement courses and related opportunities. Such actions recreate old patterns of inequity through new mechanisms, even as the policy garners praise for providing access for all. Innovative equity policies are insufficient for sustaining equity if not effectively implemented, consistently practiced, and continually monitored.

While the vast majority of secondary schools in Britain draw on some form of 'ability' grouping, my research adds to the growing body of evidence that indicates that setting and other 'ability' grouping practices reproduce racial and ethnic inequalities in schools. Black Caribbean and certain other ethnic minority students in London comprehensive schools are frequently misassigned and disproportionately confined to lower sets, and as a result, they develop low levels of confidence, which ultimately limits their academic attainment and long-term career paths.[36] Furthermore, students in low 'ability' groups are likely to come from working-class and low-income backgrounds, and thus experience a "double disadvantage" in schools.[37]

Mixed 'ability' grouping remains a strong and viable alternative, particularly if implemented more effectively than in New York. Countries such as Norway and Sweden, for instance, have long prohibited academic 'ability' grouping and emphasized heterogeneous schools and classrooms for all. This structure limits ethnic stereotypes and gendered status beliefs about specific groups. In this context, mixed 'ability' groups work because they communicate high expectations for everyone and encourage students to support one another without relying on high-achieving students as informal instructors.[38] London schools committed to racial equity should promote, evaluate, and monitor mixed 'ability' grouping, not as an antidote or silver bullet to inequalities, but as a promising set of practices that supports equality of opportunity.

Recent research by sociologists Becky Francis, Louise Archer, Becky Taylor, and their colleagues underscores the need to monitor mixed 'ability' grouping so teachers can avoid practices that reinforce and reproduce un-intended inequalities.[39] Based on an assessment of over 120 primary and secondary schools in London, these researchers advise teachers to hold high expectations of all students and refrain from teaching to the middle; avoid developing fixed 'ability' groups in classes; and resist providing different lessons for high-, middle-, and low-achieving groups, even within mixed 'ability' classes. These findings and recommendations reinforce the impor-tance of not simply implementing mixed 'ability' groupings in secondary school classes, but of evaluating them for the subtle practices of differenti-ation that foment the very inequalities that mixed 'ability' groupings aim to disrupt.

Examine Expectations Institutionally and Introspectively

For much of my discussion, Ms. Bell listened, smiled, and nodded. But as our conversation was coming to a close, Ms. Bell had more to say than before. She started with a piercing comment that once again took me down an unantic-ipated path.

"Mr. Wallace," she began, "it looks like nobody have bias these days. It's all unconscious." She couldn't hide her sarcasm. "I know teachers and parents and students mean well, but if we want to fix what's going on in our schools, we have to admit what we are doing and pay attention to what we are doing."

"Yes, Ms. Bell, we have to acknowledge our role in all of this." Ms. Bell reminded me of the reflexive work we all must do as school leaders, teachers, parents, and students to examine biases and ultimately eliminate ethnic expectations.

"It's very hard to find teachers and parents who are willing to just admit what they are doing . . . the students are willing sometimes, but it's hard."

Ms. Bell was right. Years after my conversation with her, and years after talking with teachers and parents in London and New York City about ethnic expectations in schools, it dawned on me that we often use deflection strat-egies when confronted by critiques of our participation in, or promotion of, ethnic expectations. Some of us espouse *distinctiveness*—a belief that we are well-intentioned and well-educated individuals who do not harbor ra-cial, ethnic, or gender biases. Such mistaken ideas are found in *other people*, not in ourselves. They pertain to other members of staff, not us. Some of us reject claims that we espouse ethnic expectations for other ethno-racial groups because we practice *deference*—a view that our 'good behavior' toward others is evidence of a lack of bias. We are polite to minorities. We take an interest in their language, food, and customs. Ethnic expectations are found among those who make nasty comments, not among people like ourselves. Additionally, some of us may defend our *defiance*—a commitment to resisting any discussions of ethnic expectations, racism, or bias as "woke work." We may view these activities as an attempt to infuse critical race theory in schools, or think that if we are "colorblind" it is unnecessary to include discussions of race, culture, and equity as part of teaching and learning. We may even misrepresent talk of race and culture as attempts to promote racism or social divisiveness. Or we may not wish to participate in such conversations. We may refuse to talk but opt to listen as a form of quiet protest. These defense mechanisms keep ethnic expectations intact.

What I now realize is that distinctiveness, deference, and defiance are not simply cultural strategies the Black Caribbean students I spoke with used. Many of us use modified versions of them in everyday life to challenge claims of racism, sexism, and cultural bias leveled against us. But if we are to promote fairer, more just, and equitable education systems in which all students can thrive—not only those with racial privilege or class advantages, along with the tokenized few from marginalized backgrounds—we must commit to the regular examination of ethnic expectations that emerge from our ideologies and in our practices. This deep, soul-searching work, as part of what education scholar and poet Yolanda Sealey-Ruiz refers to as "the archaeology of the self," is necessary for us to move from the constraints of ethnic expectations for some to the promise of great expectations for all.[40] The consistent investment in this work to change ideologies and institutions, beliefs and behaviors, and attitudes and actions is how we eliminate ethnic expectations and dismantle the culture trap.

Organizing Methods
for Ethnographic Fieldwork

Before I became an ethnographer, I was a community organizer. I traversed the streets and schools of South London listening to people's stories about local problems, building relationships between young people and civil society officials, and developing campaigns with neighborhood leaders based on pressing needs. Community organizing sharpened my ethnographic skills and sensibilities in ways I never imagined. Throughout my time as an organizer, I hosted scores of listening campaigns, organized dozens of public actions, and conducted hundreds of what organizers referred to as 1-2-1s: one-to-one meetings in which two people discover each other's key motivations, recognize each other's self-interests, and identify possibilities for working together on issues of the common good.

Although I didn't realize it then, broad-based community organizing was meaningful (though unorthodox) training for ethnographic fieldwork. Conducting one-to-ones made me a skilled listener, an attentive observer, and a seasoned interviewer. Hosting small group listening campaigns prepared me to conduct focus group interviews. Collaborating with leaders of different political affiliations forced me to contend with conflicting arguments and counter-evidence that must be acknowledged in order to build consensus or to understand underlying tensions. Community organizing trained me to ask probing questions, sustain public relationships, collate personal notes and local news commentary, host focus group discussions, develop an acute awareness of individuals' problems as community issues, and understand history as context for the future. In sum, community organizing methods enhanced my ethnographic fieldwork.

Negotiating Access

From the beginning of my time as a community organizer, I was taught never to enter institutions 'cold,' without relationships with the people who are at home there. It is through relationships that we gain meaningful access to the institutions that shape local communities. I brought this logic to bear on my ethnographic fieldwork when negotiating access to schools for my research. It was sweet serendipity when I learned that Londerville Secondary, a school I visited and collaborated with several times before during my time as an organizer, was among the South London schools with the highest intake of Black Caribbean pupils. Long before I identified it as a site for my cross-national ethnography, I had worked with some of its teachers in nonprofit organizations serving local youth. I led leadership workshops for Londerville students for two consecutive summers, including three who later participated in this study. School administrators invited me to participate in the school's annual Career Fair. I met with a handful of Londerville parents regarding immigration, safer streets, and living wage campaigns through their churches, mosques, and community groups. I even attended church with a few of the Black Caribbean students at Londerville. My work as a community organizer in and around Londerville Secondary meant that when I began ethnographic fieldwork, I already had meaningful relationships with some students, parents, teachers, and school leaders.

Gaining access to Newlands High in New York City was not as easy. I did not have the same kinds of relationships as I did in London. Nevertheless, I used what I learned through community organizing and started with the relationships I had. Friends from high school and college in the United States liaised with school leaders on my behalf as I searched for a public school with a large Black Caribbean population of comparable size to Londerville Secondary. Teachers I knew from church and community-based organizations made similar connections.

What proved most helpful was reconnecting with the teachers and administrators from my high school. The assistant principal who had interviewed and admitted me to the school less than a month after I arrived in the United States from Jamaica took me under her wing and connected me with principals and assistant principals of large high schools in Caribbean enclaves in Brooklyn, the Bronx, and Queens. With her guidance, I ultimately gained access to Newlands High. She spoke to the school leaders and vouched for me. The maxim 'your relationships will take you places' took on new significance. When I visited Newlands to talk with school leaders, I realized that I already knew some of the teachers from the community. They allowed me to follow them to class and introduced me to other staff members. Some Newlands students knew me and my family well through churches we attended and sports teams my brother had played on. I later discovered that two students' fathers knew me, my brothers, and my parents. These meaningful connections meant I did not begin fieldwork 'cold,' which immeasurably enhanced the quality of access I had in both schools.

Entry as an Ethnographer

Although I had been to Londerville Secondary in London as a community organizer and had a thick web of personal relationships with people at Newlands High in New York, where I had lived and attended high school, I was not automatically given access as an ethnographer. I secured formal support from the headteacher at Londerville Secondary in London and the principal at Newlands High in New York in the early spring of 2012. I then sought and received Institutional Review Board Approval through the University of Cambridge in Britain and the New York City Department of Education with support from the City University of New York. But approval at the top was not enough. My years of organizing taught me that formal access to schools was not the same as meaningful inclusion in them. I had to appeal to the self-interests of the institutions and build relationships with leaders if I wanted to become an insider of sorts, at least temporarily.

Before beginning my fieldwork, I asked the principals how I could be of use to their schools. The teachers at Newlands insisted that I work directly with students if I really cared about the education of Black students. The headteacher at Londerville told me time and again that he was pleased to have a 'Cambridge student' at the school and wanted me to help students interested in applying to university, just as efforts to widen participation in British universities were gaining traction in secondary schools. I had experience coaching students through the undergraduate and graduate school admission processes in both the United States and the United Kingdom, so I served as a university advisor throughout the spring and summer helping students interested in applying in the following year to sixth form programs, British universities, apprenticeships, and even

American colleges and universities. My meetings with Londerville students allowed me to build more relationships with some Year 11 and Year 12 students.

Although none of these students became part of the study, they gave me great advice on how to interest others. They spread the word among Black Caribbean students and personally introduced me to them, which amounted to an implicit endorsement. They encouraged me to have 'good food' at my focus group meetings. When I explained that I would need the consent of students and their parents to participate in this research, two students told me I had to send home those forms early in the school year, when parents are enthusiastic about starting the year off right and completing all required forms. The headteacher sent copies of my letter to families of all Black Caribbean students from Years 7–11 to notify them of the study. Many parents called me, questioned my intentions, asked what I planned on asking their children, and invited me to meet with them in person. Black Caribbean mothers in particular insisted that I could not fully understand what was happening to Black Caribbean children in Britain if I did not speak with parents. I adjusted the design of my study based on the feedback I received from Black Caribbean parents and young people.

When I spoke with the principal at Newlands High in New York, she was flexible about what I could do for the school, but a few teachers quickly asked me to help students applying for scholarships to college. In May 2012, I met with seven 11th Grade students interested in applying to college, and I worked with them over the summer via phone and Skype on writing and revising their college essays and preparing for interviews. One of those students became my chief connector with Black Caribbean students at Newlands. Two of them invited me to their homes to meet their more traditional parents in hopes of convincing their parents to let them apply to colleges and universities outside the city and state. One invited me to a birthday bash his mother hosted for him every summer, where she introduced me to other Black Caribbean mothers and fathers. As in London, these parents had their own gendered ethnic expectations of me and were excited about my working with their sons and supporting their daughters in applying to colleges and universities. I met a number of the popular Black Caribbean students from the track team and football (soccer) team. It was clear to me that, like community organizing, effective ethnographic fieldwork included hanging out, listening to people, asking questions, accepting invitations, finding leaders, and having a sense of humor. It was by serving the students at Newlands and Londerville that I eventually built trust with students and developed relationships with students and their families where they knew me as more than just an ethnographer.

In preparation for fieldwork, I spent June in New York and July in London walking around the neighborhood of each school. My time as an organizer taught me that if I wanted to understand an institution in all its complexities, I had to find out its relevance to the local community and what those in the neighborhood thought of it. On Mondays and Tuesdays, I strolled through the streets, visited corner shops, restaurants and stores, documented the housing and public transportation in the neighborhood, listened to the loud music and soft sounds in the air, examined where young people hung out, and spoke with local residents about the schools' histories and reputations. I witnessed students' interactions with the police, teachers, and adults in the neighborhood toward the end of term. These observations sensitized me to the cultural worlds of students just outside Londerville Secondary and Newlands High. I spent Wednesdays and Thursdays building an archive of news articles, reports from clerks in corner stores and shops, and publicly available information about each school. My efforts to study the neighborhood and learn the schools' histories from multiple sources and perspectives enabled me to pose well-informed questions about the schools' accomplishments and long-standing challenges.

Learning to Labor in the Field

During my time as an organizer, I was accustomed to conducting between 40 and 50 one-to-ones each week. I learned that no small group should have more than five people if the aim was for them to *listen* to one another. I wrote notes after most one-to-one and focus group meetings to record what participants had told me. I learned the importance of tea or cold drinks and a meal in breaking the ice for a conversation and sustaining warmth throughout it. During my ethnographic fieldwork, I took the time to build relationships, not just to extract and collect what I was looking for. All my interviews focused on listening deeply to what young people said and encouraging them to listen to one another. They were the authorities on their own experience, and I was privileged to learn from them. All my focus group interviews had food students liked, whether pizzas, patties with coco bread, or chicken tenders with fries. The moments eating together before our meeting added levity to what could have otherwise been a stressful exchange. I never left the room when the interview was over, but lingered. We continued the conversation even if there were only a few people mulling over a point. I welcomed pushback in words or body language, asked about what I sensed, and accepted correction (sometimes even scolding and name-calling) when I got a point wrong. I responded to their questions any time, before, during, and after interviews. My relational approach to interviewing often yielded interesting exchanges among students, particularly when we met in the places they chose—in the gym, cafeteria, and local restaurants.

The quotations and notes highlighted in this ethnography are based on 184 interviews, 16 months of school-based observations, 500 hours of classroom observations, and archival analysis of school- and community-based sources. The aim throughout the study was to understand the cultural logics and everyday practices that shape Black Caribbean young people's educational experiences in schools and society. I conducted 50 focus group interviews with Black Caribbean students, 25 in London and 25 in New York. In both cities, I interviewed Black Caribbean students who were members of the second generation. In this study and in keeping with immigration research, second-generation Black Caribbeans are ones who were born in Britain or the United States to at least one parent who was born in the Caribbean but later emigrated to Britain or the United States. My focus on second-generation Black Caribbean young people, which is rather atypical in British sociological and educational research, allowed me to provide a more fine-grained analysis of Black Caribbeans in cultural institutions like schools. While academic and popular discourses in Britain often focus on the post-1948 wave of Black Caribbean immigrants, and their second-generation children of the 1960s and 1970s, the experiences of more recent Caribbean immigrants of the 1980s and 1990s, like the parents in this study, along with their second-generation children, have often been overlooked, especially given a large wave of third-generation Black Caribbeans and an emerging wave of fourth-generation children.

In addition to the 50 focus group interviews with second-generation students, I also conducted 134 one-to-one, in-depth interviews: 60 with students, 40 with parents, 16 with teachers, and 18 with school administrators. See Table A.1 below.

Table A.1 One-on-One Interview Data

	Students	Parents	Teachers	Administrators	Totals
Londerville Secondary in London	30	20	8	10	68
Newlands High in New York	30	20	8	8	66
Totals	60	40	16	18	134

The 134 in-depth interviews and 50 focus group interviews were carefully transcribed professionally, and eventually translated from patois to English. Although some nuance and subtlety may have faded or been lost in translation, what remains is vital, given the paucity of relevant ethnographic scholarship on Black Caribbean youth and their understandings of the cultural and structural conditions of schooling.

Beginning Institutional Fieldwork

Between August 2012 and December 2013, I spent eight months in Newlands High and another eight in Londerville Secondary engaging Caribbean young people in classrooms and sports fields, gymnasiums and auditoriums, guidance counseling offices and detention rooms. Once formal fieldwork began, I focused my observations on classroom interactions between students and teachers. I spent a total of 250 hours observing classes in each school, 25 hours per week for two and a half months. As I built a network of interested students, focus group interviews began with those second-generation Black Caribbean pupils who returned their consent forms first and completed a short screening questionnaire to check that they were born in Britain or the United States, self-identified as the child of a Black Caribbean immigrant, and that at least one of their parents was born in the Anglophone Caribbean. This interview process continued with the help of a snowball approach; as more students completed the consent forms and screening questionnaire, focus group interviews multiplied. I also gave students opportunities to have focus group interviews with their friends. Some of the most exciting, hilarious, and moving exchanges took place in these friendship groups because they allowed students to feel more comfortable and, in some cases, come to terms with the differences between what they said and what they did. Friends are able to challenge one another in ways strangers cannot.

At each school, 120 second-generation Black Caribbean students indicated interest in participating in focus group interviews, returned consent forms, and completed screening questionnaires. (Additional consent forms trickled in throughout the process, but 120 was a sufficient number and I ceased to recruit new participants.) The relatively high response rate was influenced by the relationships I had built in each school; the fact that students could participate in focus group interviews with their friends; and I offered them what they considered 'good food,' as well as brief talks with parents over the phone and in person to address their questions. Each of the 50 focus groups had between 4 and 6 participants who were aged 14–16, although most sessions had 5 students. A total of 25 focus group interviews took place in each school, with each recorded session ranging between 40 and 65 minutes. We often spent at least 15 minutes before the interviews eating, listening to music, and engaging in informal conversation, and spent as much as an hour together after I stopped the recording. Though I wish I had known of sociologist Annette Lareau's sage advice in her book, *Listening to People*, to keep the recorder on after the interview ends, I took copious notes throughout to capture key points and took detailed fieldnotes afterward to begin making sense of it all.[1]

At the end of each focus group interview, student participants were asked if they would be willing to have a one-on-one interview. A total of 85 agreed, 40 in London and 45 in New York, although many said they would not have the time or later changed their minds. I followed up with those who agreed, checked that they were available after school for interviews, and made sure their parents consented to another round of interviewing. A cardinal rule for me during fieldwork is that students should never, ever be pulled from class for an interview. When I struggled with scheduling and a few teachers offered to have students leave a class session, I always declined. I was accustomed to students being pulled from class for community organizing meetings and local actions, but the ethics of school ethnography with racially minoritized youth required stricter guidelines. Of those 85 second-generation Black Caribbean young people, 61 completed one-on-one interviews. One interview was discarded, as during the interview the participant expressed her desire to discontinue participation in the study.

When I contacted the parents of the interviewees to seek additional permission to interview their children, the research design changed unexpectedly. During my initial courtesy calls, parents expressed their opinions about the factors shaping the educational experiences of their children and offered recommendations for future studies. Much to my surprise, the focus group interview questions shared with pupils generated some debates in their homes, with parents sometimes having perspectives that differed from those of their children. I was elated by parents' desires to have their voices included in the study. Some demanded that I include them—and so I did. Donna, a hairdresser whose son, David, played on Newlands's football (soccer) team in New York, argued, "if you talk to David and don't talk to me, you only getting half the story." Parents in London made similar assertions. Jennifer, a mental health professional with two pupils at Londerville, claimed that parents could offer fresh insights into the social status of Black Caribbean young people in schools.

Although I had not initially planned to incorporate parents' perspectives into the study, I quickly realized that students consistently referenced their immigrant parents as sources of considerable influence in celebrating or resisting popular claims about Black Caribbean identities. I became convinced that insights from parents would add richness and depth to claims and critiques of education in London and New York. So I held open-ended interviews with 40 parent participants, 20 in London and 20 in New York, using a purposive sampling approach. I met with most parents on the weekends whenever they were available and, as one parent put it, "when mi less stress out" [when I am less stressed out]. It was as true for her as it was for me. Like the semi-structured interviews with pupils, the interviews with parents were friendly conversations, and in some instances, spirited debates. As I probed for details, evidence, and examples to justify their claims about their children's educational experiences I made strong efforts to be empathetic and friendly, with nods, smiles, and gestures, deliberately avoiding a 'neutral' demeanor that some erroneously assume is necessary for 'objectivity.' To my mind, this kind of relational engagement builds trust and pulls the outsider inside the cultural worlds of participants.

Students reported that teachers play an influential role in their educational experiences, whether for good or for ill. To better understand *how* teachers engage in the selective promotion or demotion of Black Caribbean youth, I observed 16 English, Mathematics, History, and Science teachers, eight at each case site. I sought and got access to English department meetings. I also sat in on key senior leadership meetings at both schools, particularly those focused on students' performance. All this allowed me to understand how ethnic expectations were mobilized and deployed by teachers, not necessarily the frequency with which they did so. I also observed class sessions with teachers, which often included several of the study's student participants and allowed me to see whether what students said about themselves and their teachers matched what they did. These observations allowed me to recognize the specific *situations* in which ethnic expectations emerged.

The study draws on documentary analysis in order to get a better sense of the history of the schools and how they have changed recently. Primary sources such as data on track/set placement and allocation, school newspapers, and yearbooks were useful not only for contextualizing the contemporary experiences of Black Caribbean young people, but for sensitizing me to the historical experiences of senior teachers and long-time administrators. Documentary materials were interpreted as 'situated resources' and analyzed to produce textured, layered understandings of young people's lived experiences as they challenged erroneous representations of culture.

Trials and Turmoil in the Field

I encountered a number of challenges during fieldwork. I discuss the most important of them here, lest this account seem like a tidy, nostalgic narrative. At both Londerville and Newlands, some white teachers began shunning me when I did not sit with them for lunch and sat with students instead. One teacher at Londerville refused to grant me access to his classroom after I asked him about his comments about what he called "Caribbean street culture." I knocked and waited outside the door for over 10 minutes. One of the students asked to go to the bathroom and then told me, "he's being kind of mean today 'cause he thinks you're going to tell the headteacher about him and whatnot." Beyond short greetings and salutations, this teacher did not talk to me for three weeks. I had to learn that building and sustaining relationships with teachers and other participants was even more important than interviewing them.

In the course of my fieldwork, I came to realize that standing outside in the cold while teachers smoked and others drank coffee or tea, was *key* to building relationships with many of them, whether they were participants in the study or not. At both schools, teachers often spoke among themselves about students, the administration, me, and each other. Teachers had their own focus group discussions outside on a regular basis. I learned that they want to talk *and* they want someone to listen. Teachers vouched for me, and often made jaw-dropping comments they might not have made to me in another setting. They encouraged other teachers to trust me. Still, I found the ongoing effort to win the trust of teachers, students, and administrators deeply stressful. Most of all, I worried day and night that I was letting down Black youth by not calling out exactly what I was seeing about ethnic expectations and structural forms of racism in these schools.

In order to reduce the stress, I began weightlifting seriously for the first time in my life when I started preparing for my fieldwork in 2012. I moved from 170 lbs. to 205 lbs. in approximately six months. I packed on a lot of muscle, so much so that my own brother could hardly recognize me when I returned to New York in preparation for fieldwork. A number of the Caribbean boys in New York called me a linebacker when I tried to play the global sport of football (soccer) with them, as football players are expected to be lean. One white male student in London who played American football asked me if I played football because "you look like you play," but I have never played the sport.

Black Caribbean boys in London asked me for workout tips. Their counterparts in New York asked me to help them in the weight room at school. It was through weight-lifting and playing football (despite being teased for my poor skills) that I connected with Black Caribbean boys in New York. The moments chatting after we took off our cleats, or just listening to music and walking to the bus stop, were profound bonding moments. They called me 'General,' 'Breddrin,' and 'Wally.' They meant these as terms of endear-ment. Although I hated nicknames at that point in my life and told them so, most con-tinued to use them anyway.

Hanging out with the boys was not always smooth sailing. I had a run-in with one Black Caribbean boy when I reprimanded him publicly about catcalling girls and explained why he should not do it. He was so furious that he swore at me and told me to "stop acting like you dah damn police." Those words hit me very hard. Swearing was a key source of pain for me in my childhood, so for a long time, I would quail when people swore at me. All my close friends from college knew this. That Black Caribbean boy didn't know that—and he didn't care. I left Newlands early that day and had to take a day off after. Not even long sessions at the gym or listening to my favorite tunes could help me. Fieldwork created lots of inner struggles—forcing me to wrestle with my past, my own gender politics, and my sense of belonging.

One of the striking similarities in my fieldwork experiences in London and New York was realizing that, despite talks about Black male endangerment and underachievement, Black Caribbean boys often controlled social relationships in their schools. They were dominant powerbrokers. On both sides of the Atlantic, several Black Caribbean girls were critical of my presumed unwillingness to "stop letting the man dem get away with fool-ishness." "You're one of them, so you can't really get it," another girl said. I did not shy away from such comments. I knew they were right and consistently welcomed the girls' critiques of my positionality as a cisgender Black Caribbean man. Some were surprised by my position; others seemed suspicious. A few asked if I could talk to their fathers and brothers "about how Caribbean man dem flex [behave] and how we have to manage that as girls."

Throughout the course of my fieldwork, I also noticed that the girls often did not show any deference to me, especially in informal spaces. Although I knew some of the girls at Londerville through community organizing, they often critiqued what seemed like an undue focus on Black Caribbean boys. I did not shy away from their criticisms, but that was not enough. I bonded with some of them by helping them prepare to apply for college. I met with several of them in club meetings and local organizations. But I often worried that this was not enough. I searched for books and articles about Black male gender poli-tics during ethnographic fieldwork. Although I struggled to find relevant works, I found sociologist L'Heureux Lewis-McCoy's paper on "Confronting Black Male Privilege" sobering.[2] Building strong connections with Black Caribbean girls on both sides of the Atlantic was not as straightforward for me. It was part of the unresolved challenges of the fieldwork experience.

Revelations in the Field

Toward the end of my fieldwork, as I began analyzing the one-on-one and focus group interviews, fieldnotes, and school documents through the coding process using NVivo software, two crucial aspects of my fieldwork became especially clear. First, my role as a community organizer with meaningful ties to people connected to Londerville Secondary and Newlands High gave me privileged access to spaces and situations I probably would not have been privy to otherwise. At department meetings and in classrooms, students and teachers leveled strong, and sometimes shockingly frank, critiques of ethnic cultures and school structures not only because I asked, but because some of them, particularly in London, were accustomed to me *listening* to them. Some found being *heard* uplifting. Mr. Andrews, the Black teacher discussed in Chapter 3, remarked that "talking with you about what's going on and what I see 'round here is like therapy, fam." There were few Black men in his school to talk to. Furthermore, talking with me was not like talking with colleagues because he did not have to worry that my opinion might affect his salary. I realized I could not chalk this up to Mr. Andrews and I both being Black men when white teachers and some female teachers made similar remarks about the high price they might end up paying for talking frankly to their colleagues at school.

When I discussed this dilemma with my life partner Danya, who had been a youth worker in London schools for over a decade, she pointed out that students often do not have help in making sense of what's happening to them in schools. Most young people lack regular access to adults in and outside their homes who will "just listen." At the end of my fieldwork in New York, I realized just how right Danya was. Working in schools taught me that listening is a political exercise worth pursuing.

The second and equally significant discovery I made about my fieldwork was that while community organizing eased me into ethnography in creative and unexpected ways, a community-oriented approach to ethnographic fieldwork was practiced by others. Sociologists in the Black ethnographic tradition have done this kind of immersive relational work for decades, particularly in contexts where research questions emerged during community work. W. E .B. Du Bois's engrossing study, *The Philadelphia Negro*, included years of fieldwork in Philadelphia's disadvantaged Seventh Ward, during which Du Bois connected with Black people in their homes and community-based organizations.[3] Similarly, Stuart Hall's and his colleagues' study, *Policing the Crisis*, drew on collaborations with Black and Asian people in highly surveilled regions of Birmingham to analyze how the state created social problems through aggressive neglect and then presented policing as a solution to them.[4] Sociologists such as Claire Alexander, Joyce Ladner, Prudence Carter, Orly Clergé, Waverly Duck, Saida Grundy, Marcus Hunter, Nikki Jones, Marcelle Medford, Heidi Mirza, Nicola Rollock, Tracey Reynolds, and Zandria Robinson have brought a decidedly feminist orientation to this Black ethnographic tradition. When I completed fieldwork for *The Culture Trap*, I became consciously committed to this inclusive, yet critical approach.

Notes

Preface

1. Located in the borough of Lambeth, Brixton has been the cultural and political heart of the Black Caribbean community in Britain throughout much of the 20th century.
2. In this and subsequent chapters, I refer to US colleges like the one I attended as universities, just as Bachelor's degree-granting institutions would be considered in Britain.
3. In Britain, Oxbridge refers to Oxford and Cambridge universities.
4. David Lammy continued: "Merton College, Oxford, has not admitted a single black student for five years. At Robinson College, Cambridge, a white applicant is four times more likely to be successful than a black applicant. Last year, 292 black students achieved three A grades at A-level and 475 black students applied to Oxbridge. Applications are being made but places are not being awarded." David Lammy, "The Oxbridge Whitewash," *The Guardian*, December 6, 2010. https://www.theguardian.com/commentisfree/2010/dec/06/the-oxbridge-whitewash-black-students. David Lammy's findings were corroborated by other government officials and explored in research by Arday and Mirza 2018; Bhopal 2018; Warikoo 2016, and others.
5. Sara Rimer and Karen W. Arenson, "Top Colleges Take More Blacks, but Which Ones?" *New York Times*, June 24, 2004: https://www.nytimes.com/2004/06/24/us/top-colleges-take-more-blacks-but-which-ones.html?searchResultPosition=1
6. Massey et al. 2007.
7. In fact, sociologists Douglas Massey, Camille Charles, and their collaborators (2007) found that one in four Black students matriculating at elite universities were immigrants or the children of immigrants.
8. Charles et al. 2009.
9. Black supplementary schools are weekend and after-school programs historically run by Black teachers and parents for Black and ethnic minority students to remedy the limitations of public schools (or what are called state schools in Britain). They are hosted in private and government-run community centers, churches of multiple denominations, schools, and other anchor institutions in localities throughout Britain. On the history of Black supplementary schools, see Reay and Mirza 1997 and Andrews 2013.
10. See Foner 2018, 2005; Imoagene 2012.
11. Throughout my fieldwork, participants on both sides of the Atlantic spoke in Standard English, Caribbean Vernacular English, Mother-tongues like patois and various iterations of Caribbean creole, or some combination of these. These linguistic

nuances are not elided or diluted in this ethnography, but translations into US and British Standard English are provided in square brackets.

12. Culture is arguably the proverbial 'black box' of social science research, as cultural sociologists Mario Small, David Harding and Michèle Lamont suggest. It accounts for what cannot be explained and serves as the default causal factor when all other explanatory variables are controlled for. In this book, I suggest that despite its potential pitfalls, culture must be considered alongside structure in order to discern new and evolving formations of inequality. For an extended explication, see Alexander 2016, 1996; Small, Harding and Lamont 2010.

13. Stuart Hall 1996b, 1994; Alexander 1996.

14. Lee and Zhou 2015; Carter 2012; Warikoo 2011; Clergé 2019; Lee 2005.

15. Gibson and Ogbu 1991; Foner 2005, 1979; Treitler 2007.

16. Stuart Hall 1994.

17. Patterson 2005; Modood 1992; Imoagene 2012.

Introduction

1. Pseudonyms are used for the schools, educators, and students throughout this book.

2. Although 'West Indian' and, to a lesser extent, 'Afro-Caribbean' remain popular in US scholarship as descriptors for people of African descent from the Anglophone Caribbean, these terms sound outdated to British ears. Throughout the course of my fieldwork, I noticed that in London, participants self-identified as Black Caribbean, while in New York City, they often introduced themselves as Caribbean. I have opted for the consistent use of Black Caribbean as the primary ethno-racial descriptor for participants throughout this book because this term honors their representations of themselves. To be clear, the term Black Caribbean as used here and throughout this book refers to immigrant and second-generation people from the Anglophone Caribbean, not those from the Francophone Caribbean (e.g., Haitians) and the Hispanophone Caribbean (e.g., Dominicans and Puerto Ricans).

3. I refer to all government-run schools maintained at the public's expense to support the tuition-free education of children and young people in both Britain and the United States as public schools. While the term public school is the common phrase for government-managed schools in the United States, such schools are called state schools in Britain, whereas 'public schools' in Britain are private institutions with little or no government involvement.

4. Sucking teeth, now popularized in the United Kingdom, United States, the Caribbean, and other regions of the African diaspora as 'kissing my teeth' or 'kiss-teeth,' is an oral gesture that signifies irritation, annoyance, or dissatisfaction. 'Kiss-teeth' is a sign of the cultural continuities between Caribbean Creoles, African American Vernacular English, and Indigenous African communication systems (Figueroa and Patrick 2002, 4). It can also be understood as one of the "Africanisms in the New World" that shape contemporary Black linguistic expressions (Rickford and Rickford 1999, 170).

5. In Britain, a mock exam refers to a practice test, usually taken as a pre-test assessment.

6. In British and American sociology of education, there are important differences between educational aspirations and educational expectations. Put simply, aspirations are broad hopes and general desires for education, while expectations are more concrete goals that reflect the likelihood of reaching a specific level of educational attainment. While both are important mechanisms that inform educational attainment and social reproduction, the two are not always aligned and can result in an 'aspiration-expectation mismatch' based on discordant interpersonal and institutional messaging to students. See Kao and Tienda 1998, Ingram 2011, Mickelson 1990, Museus et al. 2010, Diamond et al. 2004.

7. Treitler 2013; Gans 2012; Gilroy 2004; Lee and Zhou 2015.

8. Stuart Hall 1990, 2017a.

9. Race is not a biological category, as popularly assumed, but a social fabrication and modern cultural development. Race functions as a symbolic category in everyday life based on appearance, ancestry, and sociopolitical context. See Stuart Hall 1990; Solomos 2003; and Treitler 2007.

10. Claire Alexander 2016, 1427.

11. Solomon 1992.

12. Patterson and Fosse 2015.

13. Hall 1990.

14. Bourdieu 1973.

15. Simko and Olick 2021.

16. Pierre 2004, 141.

17. Stacey Lee 2009; Ifantunji 2016; Model 2008.

18. Alexander 2002; Small et al. 2010.

19. Ethnicity is understood as a symbolic category related to race. As Desmond and Emirbayer (2009, 21) assert, "ethnicity refers to a shared lifestyle informed by cultural, historical, religious and/national affiliations." Throughout this work, references to ethnicity are not synonymous with nationality. I use 'Caribbean' as a pan-ethnic identity based on participants' self-identification and Anglophone Caribbean heritage. On the significance of national identities in the Caribbean diaspora, see Clergé 2019; Richards 2017; and Medford 2019.

20. In this book, I examine race and ethnicity as distinct but related signifiers. While North American sociology and public policy discourses often deploy "race and ethnicity," "race-ethnicity" or "race/ethnicity" as a catch-all category or analytical shorthand in an attempt to be inclusive of all demographic groups, the empirical and theoretical significance of race *and* ethnicity are too often flattened or ignored. In an attempt to see the social world as Black Caribbean participants on both sides of the Atlantic see it, I explore the meanings associated with race *and* ethnicity.

21. Model 2008; James 2002; Waters 1990.

22. Demie 2021; Tomlinson 1977; Gillborn and Mirza 2000; Coard 1971.

23. Steele and Aronson 1995.

24. Jennifer Lee and Min Zhou 2015.

25. Lewis and Diamond 2015; Ridgeway and Correll 2006.

26. Ridgeway 1982.
27. Lewis and Diamond 2015.
28. For more on performance expectations, see Ridgeway 2011, 2019.
29. Lewis and Diamond's *Despite the Best Intentions* (2015) provides an in-depth analysis of structural racism as maintained through academic tracking and disciplinary practices despite symbolic and stated commitments to equity and diversity in schools. They draw on interviews with students, teachers, administrators and parents, school-based ethnographic observations, and administrative data to show how entrenched institutional practices thwart educational equity.
30. I define culture broadly, in the tradition of Stuart Hall, the Jamaican-born British sociologist and cultural theorist, as "a system of representation . . . the way we make sense of, and give meaning to, the world." Hall suggested that "cultures consist of the maps of meaning, the frameworks of intelligibility, which allow us to make sense of the world" (Hall 1994, 32). He conceived of culture not as an 'essence' fixed across time and space, but as a complex process subject to both continuity and change based on historical structural forces and contemporary meaning-making. Culture, in Hall's view, is always 'in production' and cannot be understood separately from the social, economic, and political structures that shape it. This complex conception of culture "negates the either/or seesawing between structural and cultural sociology and the 'in the last instance' wrangling which seeks to privilege either structure or culture" (Alexander 2016, 1432).
31. Ethnic expectations are especially significant in a context of educational policy discourses on the achievement gap. On both sides of the Atlantic, dominant narratives have long framed Black students as underperforming (Carey 2014). Explanations for some Black youth's low academic have varied from pseudo-scientific claims that people of African descent have limited intelligence to culturalist concerns about waning commitments to hard work (Tyson 2012; Strand 2012). Although both biological and cultural claims have been debunked repeatedly in educational research, they continue to function in public discourse as durable bio-logics and persistent myths that posit group-level differences in inherent abilities, values, and merit (Strand 2010; Tyson et al. 2005). On both sides of the Atlantic, 'achievement-gap talk' shores up assumptions of Black intellectual and cultural inferiority, which are seldom openly stated but often underlie discussions of Black educational underachievement. For more, see Gillborn 2005; and Carter and Welner 2013.
32. Reay 2017.
33. Ochoa 2013; Tomlinson 2019.
34. Imoagene 2017.
35. Ogbu 1974, 1978; Sewell and Majors 2001.
36. Swidler 1986.
37. Warikoo and Carter 2009.
38. Stuart Hall 1990; Alexander 2016; Gans 2012; William Julius Wilson 2010; Carter 2012; Hunter and Robinson 2018.
39. Ochoa 2013; Neckerman et al. 1999; Jennifer Lee and Min Zhou 2015; Valenzuela 1999.

40. Warikoo 2010b; Solomon 1992; Rollock et al. 2015; Coleman-King 2014; Conchas 2006; Dillabough and Kennelly 2010; Paulle 2013; O'Connor et al. 2011; Gibson and Ogbu 1991.
41. Small et al. 2010.
42. Modood 1992; Gilroy 1993, 1992.
43. Patterson and Fosse 2015.
44. Alexander 2016.
45. Benson 1996.
46. Jennifer Lee and Min Zhou 2015, 2016.
47. Stacey Lee 2009; Lew 2006; Kao 1995.
48. Randolph 2015, 42. For more on cultural explanations of the achievement gap, see Carey 2014; Warikoo and Carter 2009.
49. Kao 1995; Stacey Lee 2005; Carey 2014.
50. Solomon 1992; Harris 2011; Mirza 1992.
51. This theory suggests that Black and other racialized groups resist assimilation into the white middle classes and develop an oppositional orientation to school authorities, usually resulting in low academic achievement. Proponents argue that Black youth develop an adversarial stance toward schooling because they doubt that education is a remedy for unequal opportunities in society. For more on this, see Ogbu 1978; Fordham and Ogbu 1986.
52. Despite the valid critiques of John Ogbu's and Signithia Fordham's oppositional culture theory, which I address briefly in Chapters 1 and 6, their understanding of context's role and influence in shaping representations of Black ethnic groups and cultures seems correct. John Ogbu and Margaret Gibson's *Minority Status and Schooling* (1991) and R. Patrick Solomon's *Black Resistance in High School* (1992) provide original insights into how Black ethnic identities and cultures are framed and differently positioned across national contexts. *The Culture Trap* builds on Gibson and Ogbu's comparative analysis of schooling in the Caribbean and the United States, and on Solomon's comparative study of Black youth in Canada and the United States, to deepen scholarly and public understandings of Black ethnic cultures in national contexts in large public schools.
53. In fact, ethnic expectations can reinforce anti-Blackness and reproduce white supremacy by selecting a few Black students for elevation and support at the expense of the majority; see Wallace 2018b.
54. Throughout this book, context refers not only to social space, but also to the historical, cultural, and political dynamics that give such settings their complex and varied meanings. As this ethnography reveals, context influences—and is influenced by—cultural identification, class ideologies, and associated sense-making strategies of Black Caribbean young people. Beyond acknowledging that context matters, I illuminate *how* context matters differently for Black Caribbean students in London and New York City by calling attention to institutional mechanisms like academic 'ability' grouping that differ in their formulation and function across contexts.
55. Randolph 2015; Model 2008.

56. The celebration of Black Caribbeans' elevated minority status in the United States is often contingent on the demotion of African Americans, particularly those in under-resourced urban neighborhoods. See Greer 2013 and Rong and Brown 2001.

57. On the other hand, Caribbean culture in Britain and African American culture in the United States (and around the world) are deemed 'cool' expressive and aesthetic cultures worthy of consumption.

58. Willis 1977.

59. Gilroy 2013.

60. Willis 1977, 153–54.

61. In keeping with immigration research, I refer to the US- and British-born children of Black Caribbean immigrants as second-generation Black Caribbeans. Like their Black Caribbean immigrant peers who often spoke with a distinctively rhythmic cadence and occasionally with clear British or American accents, these second-generation Black Caribbean youth proudly self-identified as Caribbean—though not without the occasional side-eye or firm rebuttal from Caribbean immigrant youth who questioned their cultural authenticity.

62. Waters 1999. For a critique of *Black Identities*, see Matory's *Stigma and Culture* 2015.

63. Pierre 2004, 153.

64. Willis 1977; Waters 1999; Alexander 1996; Warikoo 2011.

65. While select works in comparative youth studies offer nuanced insights into youth surveillance and insecurity (Shedd 2015; Dillabough and Kennelly 2010; Paulle 2013); taste profiles and expressive cultures (Warikoo 2011; Carter 2005; Alexander 1996); the role of social and symbolic boundaries in reproducing educational ine-quality (Carter 2012; Warikoo 2010a; Calarco 2014; Feliciano 2018); and subcultural identity development and political belonging (Paulle 2013; Nayak 2003; Law and Swann 2011; Hall and Jefferson 1993), in-depth cross-national explorations of Black youth's educational experiences are seldom advanced in contemporary sociological scholarship.

66. Blume Oeur 2018; Apple et al. 2010.

67. Stuart Hall 1990.

68. Bourdieu 1993.

69. Office of National Statistics, 2011. https://www.ons.gov.uk/peoplepopulationandco mmunity/populationandmigration/populationestimates/bulletins/keystatisticsandq uickstatisticsforlocalauthoritiesintheunitedkingdom/2013-10-11.

70. The 2020 American Community Survey results indicate that 44.35 percent of Black Caribbean immigrants lived in New York City in 2020. It also suggests that Black Caribbean immigrants accounted for 0.73 percent of the total US population, and 5.88 percent of the immigrant population in 2020. The 2018 Current Population Survey results suggest that 35.50 percent of immigrant and second-generation Black Caribbeans from the English-speaking Caribbean lived in New York City in 2018. For more, see Ruggles et al. 2022 and Flood et al. 2021. Tod Hamilton's *Immigration and the Remaking of Black America* indicates that the vast majority of Black Caribbean immigrants from the English-speaking Caribbean in the United States and New York

City hail from Jamaica, Trinidad and Tobago, Guyana, Barbados, Grenada, the Bahamas, and St. Vincent.

71. Here and throughout this ethnography, Year refers to class year in the United Kingdom; this is similar to grade in the United States. In keeping with the labels used in each national context, I use Year to refer to class year in London, and grade to refer to class year in New York.

72. GCSE refers to General Certificate of Secondary Education, national exams whose results affect students' post-secondary educational and employment opportunities.

73. Anderson 2021, 3.

74. The attention to context throughout this ethnography accords with Stuart Hall's and Pierre Bourdieu's understandings of culture and class. While Hall's scholarship gave credence to 'conjuncture' and 'positioning' and Bourdieu's analyses focused on 'social space' and 'field,' both Hall and Bourdieu articulated the importance of investigating culture and class in their *situated* contexts, which were shaped by past and present public policies and political ideologies. For both theorists, careful consideration of contexts proved necessary for understanding how culture and class functioned, and to what ends. See Hall 1993a and Bourdieu 1979 for more on this.

75. Wallace 2017b, 2018a.

76. Berger and Quinney 2005.

77. Hall 2017a.

78. Bourdieu et al. 1999.

79. Scott 2017, 5.

80. Deborah A. Thomas 2019, xii.

81. See Babbie 2004; Huberman and Miles 2002; and Silverman 2010 for more information.

82. Hall 2017a.

Chapter 1

1. Here and elsewhere in this ethnography, the term West Indian, which is now less frequently used in Britain and the United States than in the 20th century, refers to people from the English-speaking Caribbean, including Antigua, Barbados, the Bahamas, Grenada, Guyana, Jamaica, Trinidad and Tobago, St. Lucia, among others.

2. Gilroy 1992; Rodgers 2000.

3. As Stuart Hall (1986, 20) suggests, "commonsense represents itself as the 'traditional wisdom or truth of the ages,' but, in fact, it is deeply a product of history." For analyses of how the historical representations of Black Caribbeans shape the contemporary racial socialization, cultural identity development, and political incorporation of Black Caribbeans in the United States and Britain today, see Alexander 1996; Greer 2013; Rogers 2006; Vickerman 1999; and Foner 1979, 2018.

4. Clergé 2019; Tikly 2022.

5. Kasinitz 1992.

6. Model 2008.

7. The comparisons between these Black Caribbean newcomers as high achievers and their native ethnic peers as underachievers inspired questions about the salience of racism in limiting the educational experiences of Black Caribbeans, but did not assess the significance of generational and social class positions of Montserratian movers. See Gillborn 2005.

8. Historically, the accounts in the United States promoting positive ethnic reputation focus on Black Caribbeans' social, athletic, musical, cultural, and educational achievements (Waters 1999; Kasinitz 1992; Vickerman 1999), while the pathological reviews in Britain often center on their behavioral, political, and educational shortcomings (Gillborn and Mirza 2000; Mirza 1992; Tomlinson 1981; Troyna 1984). There are elements of both in the United States and Britain, but these mixed reviews do not feature as strongly as long-standing stereotypes and reputations about Black Caribbeans in each national context.

9. Greer 2013.

10. Ifantunji 2016; Model 2008.

11. Kasinitz et al. 2008; Waters 1999; Hamilton 2019.

12. Bashi 2001; Pierre 2004.

13. In Bourdieu's formulation of distinction, he accounts for taste profiles and class practices (of dressing, speaking, and reading) that reinforce economic inequality and class stratification. But as I have argued elsewhere, class distinctions are not race-neutral. Racial and ethnic identities complicate expressions of class distinctions. For more, see Wallace 2017b, 2018a, 2019b. Also see Bourdieu 1993.

14. Matory 2015; Treitler 2007; Hinzten 2001.

15. U.S. Census 1918.

16. Greene 1987; Horton 1993.

17. James 1998, 11.

18. Walter 1981, 18.

19. The Reconstruction era (1865–1877) is the period after the American Civil War and the legal abolition of slavery. See Phillips 1981 and Lamson 1973 for more on Black Caribbeans' political leadership during the 19th century.

20. Matory 2015.

21. The number of foreign-born Black Caribbeans entering the United States rose from 412 in 1899 to 12,243 in 1924.

22. Wendell Malliet 1938, 9.

23. Clergé 2019; Treitler 2007; Watkins-Owens 1996.

24. Other sociopolitical reasons shaped the rise of Black Caribbeans in Harlem. As Watkins-Owens (1996) points out, Black Caribbeans were not seen simply as foreign-born Blacks; their connection to Britain distinguished them from African Americans. Second, a sizable proportion of the nearly 30,000 Black Caribbeans in Harlem in the early 20th century was of middle-class origin (Model 2008). Many became part of New York City's Black middle class, leading key political, cultural, and religious organizations and owning successful businesses. See LaBennett 2011; Daniels 1914; Watkins-Owens 1996; James 1998; Maddox 2018.

25. Fenton Johnson 1919, 210.

26. Kasinitz 1992, 47.
27. Aptheker 1973, 263.
28. Du Bois 1920, 214.
29. Watkins-Owens 1996, 3.
30. Economic, social, and cultural capital are signature concepts of Pierre Bourdieu's theoretical program. Put plainly here, economic capital refers to material wealth (income, money, assets, etc.); social capital refers to social relationships and networks; and cultural capital refers to the social and at times nonmaterial assets (including education, along with speech and dress styles), all of which can be converted for the reproduction of wealth and power in dominant society, and all of which yield market returns. For more on the history of the Black Caribbean middle classes in the US, see Clergé 2019; Watkins-Owens 1996; Foner 1979.
31. Parascandola 2005.
32. Clergé 2019.
33. Johnson 1930.
34. Johnson 1930, 130.
35. Johnson 1930, 153.
36. James 2002, 232.
37. James 2002, 242.
38. Woodson 1933, 83.
39. Clergé 2019.
40. Kasinitz 1992; Watkins-Owens 1996.
41. Anderson 1988; Walker 1996; Givens 2021.
42. Ridgeway 1982; Ridgeway 2019.
43. This "much smaller and somewhat more middle class group" entered the United States from the early stages of the Great Depression until the implementation of the 1952 McCarran-Walter Act (Kasinitz 1992, 24), which strengthened the immigration restrictions established in 1924. Before 1952, Jamaicans and people from other British colonies and Commonwealth countries had been admitted to the United States as subjects of the British Empire.
44. In addition to assessing the social and cultural contributions of Black Caribbeans to American society, Reid (1939) highlighted the bidirectional migration patterns among Black Caribbeans, pointing out that between 1932 and 1937 more Black Caribbeans returned to their island homes than came to the United States. A high rate of return migration was common during the Great Depression.
45. Reid 1939, 416.
46. For historical accounts of the deployment of Caribbean immigrant identities and achievements in public discourse, see Watkins-Owens 1996 and James 2002.
47. Patillo-McCoy 1999; Lacy 2007; Matory 2015.
48. With the 1965 Hart-Celler Immigration Reform Act, Black Caribbeans regained access to the United States. Waters (1999, 35) suggests that "the volume of immigration to Great Britain" from the Anglophone Caribbean and other former British colonies was heaviest in the 1950s and diminished in the 1960s. When Britain passed restrictive immigration laws limiting the arrival of Commonwealth residents, the

United States loosened its immigration rules. For more, see Owens Smith 1985; Coombs 1970; Forsythe 1976; and Bryce-Laporte 1972.

49. Glazer and Moynihan 1963.

50. Glazer and Moynihan 1963, 52.

51. Treitler 2007.

52. Sowell 1978.

53. Sowell 1978; Sowell 1975.

54. Sowell 1975, 130–31. For a critique of Sowell's arguments on Black Caribbeans, see Pierre 2004, and Model 2008.

55. Sowell 1978, 42.

56. Treitler (2007) and Kasinitz (1992) point out that Sowell's culturalist arguments supported white Americans' fascination with Black Caribbeans as former British subjects, including their distinctive accents, attitudes, athleticism, international acclaim, and use of the Queen's English.

57. Wilson 2010; Small et al. 2010.

58. Systemic racism is here defined as multi-institutional discriminatory action that disadvantages minoritized racial and ethnic groups. Achievement, opportunity and wealth gaps, for instance, are not based on culture but state policies, programs, and practices that reproduce disparities in health, housing, employment, education, the media, and more. For more on systemic racism, see Desmond and Emirbayer 2009.

59. Young, Jr. 2004; Small et al. 2010; Patterson and Fosse 2015.

60. Model 2008; Ifantunji 2016, 2017; Waters 1999.

61. Matory 2015, 459.

62. Treitler 2007.

63. Hamilton et al. 2018, 60.

64. Ivan Light's *Ethnic Enterprise in America* highlights the overrepresentation of Black Caribbeans (along with Chinese and Japanese immigrants) among entrepreneurs. Light suggests that Black Caribbeans are more entrepreneurial than African Americans because of the microlending practices in rotating credit associations. Model's (2008) analysis of the 1970 US census, however, reveals that Black Caribbeans and African Americans had similar rates of self-employment. Model (2008), Bryce-Laporte (1972), and Chiswick (1979) argue that factors such as immigrant selectivity were at play. For an elaboration on the influence of immigrant selectivity bias and human capital differences, not between African Americans and Black Caribbeans but between movers and non-movers, see Model 2008, Ifantunji 2016, and James 2002.

65. US educational authorities at the national, state, and district levels very rarely account for ethnicity when measuring the attainment of Black students. Failure to control for race *and* ethnicity limits our understanding of the achievement differentials between African Americans, Black Africans, and Black Caribbeans, if these disparities exist at all. See Waters 1999 and Warikoo 2011 for more.

66. Greer 2013.

67. Rogers 2006; Vickerman 1999; Dawson 1994, 2001.

68. Model 2008, 544.

69. Model (2008) emphasizes that Black Caribbean movers represented some of the most educated of the Caribbean population. Like Kasinitz (1992) and Waters (1999), Model (2008) also argues that earlier Caribbean immigrants had a more significant 'educational edge' than those arriving after 1990.

70. The National Survey of American Life is one of the most recent surveys with an oversample of Black Caribbeans. Other surveys are either region-specific (i.e., Kasinitz et al.'s (2009) New York-based study) or not specific to the Black Caribbean community. See Ifantunji 2016.

71. Ifantunji 2017.

72. Maddox 2018; Vickerman 1999; Kasinitz and Vickerman 2001; Treitler 2007.

73. Stacey Lee 2009; Jennifer Lee and Min Zhou 2015.

74. Treitler 2013.

75. Ransby 2003; Kelley 2002; Robinson 2000.

76. Wallace and Joseph-Salisbury 2022; Tomlinson 2019.

77. Strand 2014.

78. Gillborn 2011.

79. Ward 2008; Tomlinson 1978.

80. British Cabinet Office 2018.

81. Carby 2019; Perry 2016.

82. McKay 1912, 63.

83. Gilroy 1992.

84. Phillips and Phillips 1998; Nubia 2019; Kaufman 2017.

85. Cohen 2010.

86. Brown 2005; Gerrard 2013.

87. Walvin 1973; Shyllon 1977.

88. Dabydeen et al. 2008, 218.

89. Bressey 2009; Buckley 1979.

90. Gilroy 1992.

91. Reports at the George Padmore Institute and the Black Cultural Archives in London point to the education of specific individuals like Francis Barber, a formerly enslaved Jamaican brought to England, who served Samuel Johnson and was sponsored to study at an elite grammar school in Yorkshire when he was in his early twenties. Archival materials also highlight the education of specific groups of students from African and Caribbean countries who came to England to enroll in medical school throughout the 19th and 20th centuries. Specific examples from the London Metropolitan Archives include: "African Prince awarded Ph.D. (Oxon)," LCP News Letter, May, 1940; "Dr. W. Arthur Lewis," LCP News Letter, Oct. 1940: 3–4; Moody, Youth and Race, 7–12; "Standards for Blacks," LCP News Notes, Dec. 1939, 3; "Education for better under-standing," The Keys, Jan.–March 1935, 57, 64. See also Rich 1987.

92. Rich 1987, 152.

93. Andrews 2014; Perry 2016.

94. Whittall 2012, 157.

95. Carby 2019; Catherine Hall 2008.

96. Dhondy 1982.

97. Carrington 2019.
98. Histories of Black Caribbeans' contributions during the first and second World Wars point out that while early arrivals often enjoyed considerable class privileges in their homeland, working-class Caribbean women and men were also enlisted in the service of the Empire. Irrespective of their class positions in their homeland, however, the racial politics and constrained opportunity structures of Britain caused some Black Caribbeans and Black Africans to experience downward social mobility, strengthening a formidable Black working-class community with a tradition of resistance. See Tomlinson 2019; File and Power 1981.
99. Hickman (2005) suggests that before the 20th century, the Irish were considered an 'ill-bred' group and were despised by white working-class and middle-class Britons. After the Irish became white, they were considered the 'worst whites'. Germans and Jews also experienced differing degrees of inferiorization in the hierarchy of Britishness. See Fryer 1984; Jones 2016.
100. Troyna 1984, 89.
101. Winder 2004.
102. Peach 1995; Phillips and Phillips 1998.
103. Fryer 1984.
104. Phillips and Phillips 1998.
105. Given the entry restrictions the United States imposed on Black Caribbeans in 1952, the much revered 'Mother Country' seemed the next best option. See M. Phillips and Phillips 1998 and Fryer 1984 for more on this.
106. For specific examples from the Black Cultural Archives in London, see Edward Pilkington; *Kensington News*, Aug. 2 and 7, 1959; *Daily Worker*, May 18, 1959. See also M. Phillips and Phillips (1998).
107. Dabydeen et al. 2008; Winder 2004.
108. Fryer 1984, 347.
109. Grosvenor 1997.
110. The Commonwealth Immigrants Act proved effective in limiting access to England, but a voucher system allowed dependents to be reunited with their relatives, and allowed qualified Black Caribbeans seeking jobs to be sponsored by friends and family already in England. In the years that followed, more Black Caribbeans came as family dependents than as job-seekers (Olusoga 2016). They settled into existing Black communities in London, Liverpool, Nottingham, and Manchester and turned sections of these cities into new ethnic enclaves and symbolic cultural sites, such as Brixton.
111. Perry 2016.
112. Mirza 2009; Tomlinson 1977.
113. Troyna 1984; Coard 1971.
114. Troyna and Williams 1986, 19.
115. Newham Monitoring Project 1991, 24. While the Black model minority narrative of Black Caribbeans in the United States was arguably more of a New York story than a national one, representations of Black Caribbeans as a failing minority are not only a London story, but a national one. The historically significant, positive representation of Black Caribbeans in New York, as opposed to all of the US, might suggest that there

is a difference between being Black Caribbean in the US and being Black Caribbean in an ethnic enclave, like in various parts of New York. In this case, too, we see that context matters.

116. Coard 1971.
117. Coard 1971, 2.
118. Tomlinson 1977.
119. Wallace and Joseph-Salisbury 2022.
120. Mirza and Reay 2000; Andrews 2014.
121. Gerrard 2013.
122. Black supplementary schools have been in existence since the late 1950s. Their reach and reputation increased throughout the 1970s and 1980s in response to Black parents' concerns that assimilationist British schools were sites of suffering for their children. Black supplementary schools were hosted in private and government-run community centers; churches of multiple theological persuasions; educational institutions at the primary, secondary, and tertiary levels; and a host of other anchor institutions in local boroughs throughout major cities. For more on the genealogy of supplementary schools, see Mirza and Reay 2000.
123. Fraser 1992, 123.
124. Rampton 1981, 3.
125. Rampton 1981, 13.
126. Grosvenor 1997.
127. Swann 1985, 36.
128. Richardson 2007.
129. Swann 1985, 86.
130. Benson 1996.
131. Grosvenor 1997, 72.
132. Mirza and Meetoo 2012; Gilroy 2012.
133. Matory 2015, 26.
134. Tikly 2022; Tikly et al. 2006; Demie 2022; Wallace and Joseph-Salisbury 2022.
135. Sivanandan 2008; Troyna 1993; Gillborn 2005.
136. Ward 2008, 11.
137. Ward 2008, 11.
138. Mirza 2006.
139. Commission on Race and Ethnic Disparity 2021, 55.
140. Commission on Race and Ethnic Disparity 2021, 55.
141. Tikly 2022; Wallace and Joseph-Salisbury 2022.
142. Hall and Jefferson; Mirza 2006; Back 1996; Goulbourne and Solomos 2004.
143. Wallace and Joseph-Salisbury 2022.
144. Alexander 2016; Reynolds 2010a.
145. Gibson and Ogbu 1991; Ogbu 1978; Fordham and Ogbu 1986; Fordham 1996.
146. Cantres 2020.
147. Olusoga 2016; Gilroy 1992.
148. Patterson 1982; Fordham 1996.
149. Gibson and Ogbu 1991; Solomon 1992.
150. Imoagene 2012; Warikoo 2011, 2007; Treitler 2007.

151. Whether in the first wave of migration in the 19th century or during subsequent migration flows from the 1960s to present, Black Caribbean immigrants have arrived in US gateway cities where large groups of African Americans are their neighbors and proximal hosts in racially segregated residential and school settings. See Greer 2013; Rogers 2006; Mittelberg and Waters 1992.
152. Hamilton 2019; Dawson 1994.
153. Ifantunji 2017; Model 2008.
154. Foner 2018.
155. Perry 2016; Coard 1971.
156. Andrews 2016; Sivanandan 2008.
157. Kasinitz 1992; Greer 2013; Vickerman; Rogers 2006.
158. Phillips and Phillips 1998; Winder 2004; Perry 2016.
159. Gilroy 1992; Hall 1993a.
160. Perry 2016; Sivanandan 2008.
161. Brown 2005.
162. Foner 2018.
163. Feliciano 2005.
164. Thomas 2012; LaBennett 2011.
165. In *Replenished Ethnicity*, Jiménez argues that the consistent immigration of Mexicans to the United States often has negative consequences for the dominant representation of Mexican Americans. He suggests that second- and third-generation Mexican Americans experience discrimination, not necessarily because they are Mexican Americans, but due to the fact that they are associated with new, usually undocumented, Mexican immigrants in US society. I extend Jiménez's formulation, noting that replenished ethnicity can have *positive* effects on Caribbean community formation and second-generation Black Caribbean young people's ethnic identity development.
166. Treitler 2007; Greer 2013; Thomas 2021.
167. Butterfield 2014.
168. Foner 2018; Loury et al. 2005.
169. Gillborn 1997.
170. Hall 1990, 392.

Chapter 2

1. Like a few of the Black Caribbean participants in London and New York, Odain attributed his critical awareness to growing up in a Rastafari or politically conscious household, participating in supplementary schools over a number of years, and contributing to local politics in their respective boroughs through community-based organizations focused on young people. These endeavors provided a political socialization that enabled what Paul Willis (1977) referred to as "the penetrative gaze."
2. As British filmmaker Steve McQueen's award-winning documentary series, *Small Axe* (2020), shows, immigrant Black Caribbean parents who came as part of the

post-1948 wave of Caribbean immigration to Britain challenged the state's disproportionate labeling of Black Caribbean children as 'subnormal' and organized politically to limit between-school and in-school 'ability' grouping processes that placed
Black Caribbean children in lower-ranking classes and lower-ranking schools than
their white British counterparts.

3. Here, I marshal Stuart Hall's reflexive analyses in his intellectual memoir *Familiar
Stranger* (2017), a formulation that denotes his positioning between Britain and
Jamaica, nation-states caught in a web of colonial entanglement. Hall counts each
national context "a familiar stranger" to the other, and considers himself "a familiar
stranger" within each of them. I extend Hall's explications here, thinking not only
about national contexts, but also institutions within them; not only space, but also
place; not only the relationship between the macro and micro, but between the meso
and micro as well.

4. Carter 2012.

5. This chapter focuses on the Anglophone Caribbean that was formerly part of the
British Empire. These countries include Antigua and Barbuda, Jamaica, Trinidad and
Tobago, St. Lucia, Nevis, Grenada, Guyana, Barbados, and Montserrat, among others.

6. Contemporary postcolonial relations are asymmetrical networks of power marked
by uneven development across the metropole/colony, center/periphery, and West/
rest divides (Snyder 1983; Maurer 2001; Dunn 1994). Such "inter-national domination, at once material and symbolic," shapes Caribbean parents' perceptions of US
and British schooling (Giroux 2002, 245). These historical and structural differences
inform Black Caribbean parents' postcolonial habitus—durable dispositions
based on history, social structure, and memories of the colonial 'past' that inform
Caribbean parents' perceptions in the postcolonial present. For more on the postcolonial habitus, see Ayling 2019. To learn more about habitus, see Reay 2004b.

7. Sociologists Stuart Hall and Pierre Bourdieu recognized colonialism not simply as
a modality of power that influenced geographical, political, institutional, and cultural arrangements in the Caribbean, but a global *networked* arrangement—a material, geopolitical, and symbolic system of relations that informs both historical
conditions *and* the contemporary social order. See Go 2011, 72 for more.

8. Fanon 1959; Stuart Hall 2012; Wynter 2003.

9. Stuart Hall 2017a; Gilroy 1987.

10. Cantres 2020.

11. de Noronha 2020; Solomos 2003.

12. Gail Kelly 1979; Steinbock-Pratt 2019.

13. Blouet 1990; Hudson 1994.

14. Shirley Gordon 1958; Campbell 1997.

15. Rooke 1978, 1980; Bartle 1983.

16. Beckles and Shepherd 1990; Sharpe 2003; Jensz 2012.

17. Beckles and Shepherd 2007; Shepherd and Payne 2003.

18. Catherine Hall 2008; Hickling-Hudson 2006.

19. For comparisons of the structure of British schools in the Caribbean and those in
the United Kingdom, see Kelly 1979 and Barrow and Reddock 2001.

20. Barrow and Reddock 2001, 643.

21. In advancing this claim, I do not intend to suggest that free and enslaved Black people in the English-speaking Caribbean did not access education before 1834. Free Blacks found other fugitive ways to access reading and learning in the pre-emancipation Anglophone Caribbean outside of formal, state-sponsored schooling. See Brereton 1981, 2002 for more on this. Missionaries came from England with the express purpose of teaching poor and working-class Blacks to read the Bible. Literate freed and enslaved Blacks taught others. Adults even paid literate children to teach them reading as a valuable skill. These practices were often strategically covert and small-scale. See Dornan 2019; Turner 1977; and Catherine Hall 2008 for more on this.

22. Dornan 2019, 113.

23. Dornan 2019, 113.

24. Beckles and Shepherd 1999; Jensz (2012).

25. Campbell 1967; Bacchus 1994; Beckles and Shepherd 1999.

26. Rooke 1980; Turner 1982.

27. In this regard, schools were what Pierre Bourdieu would regard as colonial fields. See Lougheed 2021; Ayling 2019; Colonial Office Circular Despatch, 26 January 1847, quoted in Gordon 1963, 5.

28. For instance, when Jamaica and Trinidad and Tobago received independence in 1962, over one-third of adult Jamaicans and over one-fifth of adults in Trinidad and Tobago were illiterate. See Barrow and Reddock 2001; Gordon 1963.

29. Stuart Hall 2017a; Gordon 1963.

30. Kelly 1979, 211.

31. Gordon 1958; Campbell 1967.

32. Blouet 1990; Stuart Hall 2017a.

33. Turner 1977, 1982.

34. Barrow and Reddock 2001.

35. Gordon 1963.

36. Ayling 2019.

37. Stuart Hall 2017a; Gordon 1958.

38. Willis 1977; Waters 1999; Warikoo 2011; Alexander 1996.

39. Stuart Hall 2017a, 113.

40. While three of the Caribbean parents in London that I interviewed expressed some reservation about their own capacity to achieve educational success, they, like all the other Black Caribbean parents I interviewed, expressed enthusiasm about education for their children.

41. Carter 2012, 5.

42. On Black Caribbean parents' and pupils' experiences with state, private, and parochial schools, see Crozier 2006; Gillborn 2005; Tomlinson 1991; Mirza 1992; Rollock et al. 2015; Demie 2019; Joseph-Salisbury 2020; Wallace 2017b, 2018a, 2019b.

43. Joseph-Salisbury 2020.

44. Joseph-Salisbury 2020; Wallace 2018b; Dumas 2014

45. Back 1996.

46. The mythical anthropology of the diaspora is a riff on J. Lorand Matory's "mythical anthropology of the Caribbean," which I explain and engage in Chapter 4. Matory (2015) identifies the symbolic distinctions drawn by Black Caribbeans in the United States as at times based on myths of a 'good life' in the Caribbean. With the mythical anthropology of the diaspora, I note the ways in which Black Caribbean parents develop their views of life in British and US schools based on stereotypical media representations. In extending Matory's concept, I show that this 'mythical anthropology' is relevant to both the homeland and host society. For greater context on the relationship between myths about the diaspora and homeland, see Stuart Hall 2017a; Gordon 1963.

47. Kincaid 1991, 32.

48. Wallace 2019a.

49. Joseph-Salisbury 2020; Wallace 2018b.

50. Mirza and Reay 2005; Tomlinson 1977; Reynolds 2010b; Rollock et al. 2015.

51. Coard 1971; Smith 2011; Gilroy 1992.

52. Stuart Hall 2017a, 204.

53. Waters 1999.

54. Born out of resistance to British imperialism, the United States expanded the settler colonial project inaugurated by British forces, which resulted in the domination and displacement of Indigenous people and the transportation and enslavement of millions of Africans to labor on plantations. The United States' investment in the slave trade extended to the Caribbean and played a key role in global trade between the American, British, French, Portuguese, and Spanish Empires. See James 2005; Patterson 2005.

55. Barrow and Reddock 2001.

56. Patterson 2005; Beckles and Shepherd 1999.

57. Steinbock-Pratt 2019.

58. Barrow and Reddock 2001; Smith 2002.

59. Scott 2004) Thomas 2007, 2019.

60. Boyce Davies and Jardine 2003.

61. Nigel Bollano 1987.

62. The influence of British media is of declining significance in the Anglophone Caribbean. In my interviews with Black Caribbean parents in London, only once was a British show or movie mentioned as influencing their perception of schooling. This movie was *To Sir, with Love* (1967). In this piece, Sidney Poitier stars as Mark Thackerey, an immigrant Black Guyanese man who becomes a teacher in a largely white working-class school in East London. As the parent who mentioned it put it, "the show just show seh [that] white children have a bag ah [of] issues." For more on the politics of media culture, see Giroux, 2002.

63. Fanon 1959; Stuart Hall 1996c.

64. Simon 2002.

65. Avildsen 1989.

66. Snyder 1983; Maurer 2011; Dunn 1994.

67. Reay 2017; Woodson 1993.

68. Giroux 2002, 245.

69. The critiques of these movies often focus on the white savior complex they engender. Baldridge (2019) and Blume Oeur (2018) challenge the cinematic promotion of white *and* racially minoritized protagonists who seek to rescue, redeem, and ultimately 'save' Black, Latinx, Asian, and low-income youth. In this chapter, I offer complementary transnational perspectives based on what Black Caribbean parents told me. Owing to the stigmatization of urban life for low-income African Americans in these films, Black Caribbean parents became determined to distinguish themselves and their children from *othered* Black identities. For a cultural analysis of US media production and its impact on public education, see Giroux 2008.

70. Atkinson and Bridge 2013; Stuart Hall 2016.

71. Carter and Welner 2013.

72. Carey 2014; Kirkland 2010; Lyiscott et al. 2018.

73. Clergé 2019; Paulle 2013.

74. Anderson 1988; Walker 1996.

75. Schooling was not only a practice of distinction in 1960s France when sociologist Pierre Bourdieu developed his cultural critique of class relations. Nor was it exclusive to the late 20th century, when sociologist Stuart Hall articulated his cultural and political-economic analysis of Britain's racialized inequalities. For more see Bourdieu 1993; and Hall 2017a.

76. Though critiques of the relationship between racism, classism and the state are evident in the work of W. E. B. Du Bois, Oliver Cromwell Cox, and Anna Julia Cooper, and critically articulated in the work of South African activist intellectuals like Neville Alexander who wrote under the alias No Sizwe, decrying the apartheid regime, Cedric Robinson's global historical analysis of racial capitalism emerged as the most dominant rendition in US and British sociology. In *Black Marxism: The Making of a Black Radical Tradition* (2000 [1983]), Robinson issued a trenchant critique to dominant provincial Marxist analyses that considered capitalism as a rejection of feudalism, rather than a peculiar racialized evolution of it in Western societies. Robinson maintained that when understood in historical and political economic terms, capitalism is, in fact, racial capitalism. As Ruth Wilson Gilmore (2020, 2:06) asserts in "Geographies of Racial Capitalism," racial capitalism is "all of capitalism." In the context of the contemporary capitalist world system, the acquisition, accumulation, and production of capital have long been part of an unmistakable racial project. For more on racial capitalism, see Jenkins and Leroy's *Histories of Racial Capitalism* 2021.

77. Stuart Hall 2017a, 113.

78. Bourdieu 1993; Ayling 2019.

79. Ayling 2019; Reay 2004c.

80. Stuart Hall 1997a.

81. Ray 2017.

82. Stuart Hall 2017a.

83. Mayblin 2017; Reddock 2014; Bhambra 2014; Wynter 2003; Shilliam 2010.

84. Go 2011.

85. Hall 2017a; Stuart Hall 1994.

86. Gibson and Ogbu 1991; Fordham and Ogbu 1986; and Ogbu 1978.

Chapter 3

1. Although grouping by 'ability' or attainment is typically referred to as tracking in the United States and setting or streaming in Britain, I use the term academic 'ability' grouping for this practice in both countries in keeping with international educational research. See OECD 2014.
2. Stuart Hall 1993; Bourdieu 1993.
3. Despite the dearth of evidence supporting 'ability' grouping as an effective or equitable pedagogical strategy and the critiques highlighting its negative academic and psychosocial consequences for Black, ethnic minority, and economically disadvantaged pupils, setting remains a default educational strategy throughout the British educational system and tracking persists as a dominant approach to teaching and learning in American schools. 'Ability' grouping persists because it is a tradition of teaching and learning and because it is believed to match learning with students' skill sets. Although 'ability' grouping structures vary across national contexts, as this chapter shows, the impact of tracking and setting on students' experiences of segregation, stigmatization and subordination is especially significant for minoritized groups like Black Caribbean students. To learn more about setting and tracking, see Francis et al. 2020; Connolly et al. 2019; Tyson 2012; Gamoran 2009.
4. Lucas 1999, 121.
5. In the British school system, GCSE refers to General Certificate of Secondary Education, national exams whose results affect students' post-secondary educational and employment opportunities.
6. Francis et al. 2020; Archer et al. 2018.
7. Regents examinations are statewide assessments in New York that public school students must pass in order to graduate with a high school diploma. Like GCSEs, Regents exams test in a variety of academic subjects, from English Literature to Physics and World Languages. Unlike GCSE exams, which are typically administered to students in Years 10 and 11, students in New York City can take Regents exams at the end of grades 9–12.
8. Sophomore, an American term, refers to second-year students, typically in secondary school and university. Relatedly, freshman refers to first-year students.
9. In New York state, public school students must pass Regents exams in order to graduate with a state-endorsed high school diploma.
10. Like 'bro,' 'bruh,' and 'breddrin,' 'bruv' means brother.
11. Setting not only facilitates achievement gaps at the national level, but also exacerbates the opportunity gaps through the unequal distribution of resources accorded to sets at the local level. For more, see Francis et al. 2020, 3.
12. Archer et al. 2018; Carter and Welner 2013; Oakes 1985.
13. In Britain, 'council estates' are similar to what Americans call public housing projects.
14. One-on-one tutoring is paid for by parents. Companies offering private tutoring have recently proliferated in the United Kingdom.
15. Archer et al. 2018; Tyson 2012.
16. Anyon 1997.

17. Gamoran 2009; Francis et al. 2020.
18. Youdell 2004.
19. BTEC is an acronym for Business and Technology Education Council, which offers vocational, work-related qualifications.
20. Meritocracy is a social system that holds academic and economic advancement in society as based on individual merits and hard work, rather than institutional advantage through families, for instance. For more on meritocracy, see Warikoo 2016.
21. Willis 1977.
22. Mickelson 1990; Reay 2001.
23. Archer et al. 2018.
24. Lewis and Diamond 2015.
25. Mirza 1992.
26. Archer et al. 2018.
27. Researchers have noted elsewhere that setting reinforces structural and cultural inequalities in education. For more, see Archer et al. 2018; Connolly et al. 2019.
28. Francis et al. 2020.
29. Stuart Hall 2017c; Gilroy 1992.
30. Lewis and Diamond 2015; Lewis 2003; Vincent et al. 2013.
31. Waters 1999.
32. In this case and others, Black Caribbean students used 'Black American' to refer to both African Americans *and* culturally assimilated Black immigrant and second-generation youth.
33. Regardless of students' marks on the AP exams, US colleges and universities look favorably on this demanding course of study as preparing students for higher education.
34. By the end of 2015, with the endorsement of the newly elected Mayor, Bill de Blasio, formal tracking was eliminated in New York City's public schools, and new programs like Advanced Placement for All were introduced. From then on, the criteria for and process of admission to advanced classes mirrored Newlands High's approach during my fieldwork—requiring grades, samples of work, recommendations, interviews, and students' expressions of interest.
35. Calarco 2014; Anyon 2005.
36. It should be noted that in New York City public schools, 65 percent is a passing grade.
37. Gilroy 1990, 266.
38. Ridgeway 1982; Lewis and Diamond 2015.
39. Coard 1971, 16.

Chapter 4

1. The term 'yardie' (pronounced yaahdie) is used informally throughout Britain to typically refer to 'uncouth' Black Caribbean immigrants, often from rural, township and 'inner-city' contexts in the Caribbean. Yardies are consistently stigmatized and often

criminalized in Britain. Though originally used to refer to recent Jamaican immigrants, the term is applied to other Black Caribbeans, especially those from low-income and working-class backgrounds. That yardie is utilized as a racialized, pan-ethnic class code is evidence of how Jamaican culture is often mobilized to symbolically represent Black Caribbean people. See Richards 2013 and Medford 2019 for more.

2. Wallace 2017b; Mirza 2006.

3. Bourdieu's theory of practice is now dominant in European and North American sociology of culture and education Rooted in a tradition critical of social inequality, Bourdieu's theoretical scheme is a multilayered, relational view of the role of social class in shaping cultures and the trajectories of those who bear them. It holds that schools, like other social institutions, are cultural and political sites for separating social classes and dividing social resources, and thus "are more likely to reproduce, rather than challenge, social inequality in the state" (Dillabough 2004, 790). Bourdieu suggested that culture is not a consequence of social origin, but at least in part is fostered by class systems. This study engages Bourdieu's social theory to critique forces that dominate, disempower, and ultimately disadvantage Black Caribbean and other ethno-racial minority youth, and to reveal the extent to which class-based differences are concealed under the cover of culture.

4. Stuart Hall 1993b.

5. For more on racial stigmatization and ethnic distinctions, see Treitler 2013.

6. Solomos 2003; Wallace and Joseph-Salisbury 2022.

7. As Stuart Hall suggests, repertoires of cultural meaning are strategic and positional. For more, see Hall 1996b.

8. Waters 1999; Warikoo 2011; Alexander 1996.

9. I credit and salute sociologists Amanda Lewis and Karolyn Tyson, whose in-depth qualitative studies of Black youth in schools have called attention to the agency of Black young people without mispresenting Black youth's agency to respond to social problems as synonymous with their responsibility to fix them. For more, see Lewis 2003; Tyson 2012.

10. Waters 1999.

11. Butterfield 2004; Richards 2013; Clergé 2012.

12. Dawson 1994.

13. Stuart Hall 1997b; Gilroy 1993.

14. Alexander 2005.

15. Treitler 2007, 2013; Matory 2015.

16. Model 2008.

17. Ifantunji 2017; Waters 1999; Model 2008.

18. Hamilton et al., 2018; Model 1991, 1997, 2018; Ifantunji 2017.

19. Hamilton 2019; Clergé 2019; Mose 2011.

20. For more on replenished ethnicity, see Jiménez 2010.

21. See Olwig (1993) and Foner (2009) for more on immigrant generational differences between Caribbean parents and their second-generation children.

22. Matory 2015, 307.

23. Stuart Hall 1997b, 3.

24. Caribbean culture is not a singular or static formulation, but an ever-evolving range of expressions and identifications informed by history, contexts and social structures. See Stuart Hall 1994, 2017a, 1993a.

25. Treitler 2013.

26. Matory 2015; Lamont et al. 2016; Baker 2010.

27. See Treitler 2013, 4. This perspective draws on US ethnic history to point out that intra-racial distinctions are not exclusive to Black people. Furthermore, intra-racial distinctions are not necessarily forms of self-hatred or internalized racism. Rather, they are strategic responses to a global racial project of white supremacy with particular national characteristics. Some minoritized groups pursue the aesthetic, cultural, and political dimensions of power by distinguishing themselves from historically stigmatized groups (Omi and Winant 1994). However, Black immigrants' efforts to differentiate themselves from poor and working-class African Americans in pursuit of marginal advantages is a problematic, prejudicial formula I take issue with in this book. Sociologists such as Vilna Bashi Treitler (2013) are critical of such distancing practices, whether deployed by Black immigrants or other minoritized groups. To Treitler's arguments, I point out that these distancing practices are not simply ethnic projects, but also class projects; see Wallace 2019a.

28. There is a powerful reciprocal relationship between distinction and stigma. To Bourdieu, class distinction, and to Hall, racial stigma, are expressions of structural and cultural power and constitute "a way of organizing and meaningfully classifying the world" (Hall 2017b, 49).

29. As Stuart Hall (2017a), Paul Gilroy (1992), John Solomos (2019), and Claire Alexander (2002; 1996) have argued, 'British' is a fraught category of identification for Black and Asian people in Britain. Owing to the nature of institutional racism in Britain, Black and Asian immigrants and their children have often been treated as 'forever foreigners'—locked outside the bounds of authentic British nationality. To challenge the racist limits placed on the category 'British' in the 1950s, '60s, '70s and '80s, and to engender solidarity across racial, ethnic, class, and gender lines, Caribbean, African, and Asian communities self-identified as 'Black.' In this instance, 'Black' can be understood as a strategic political signifier—or as what Stuart Hall (2017b) calls, "a political color." This particular use of Black as a coalitional symbol in service of anti-racism was later deemed problematic in Britain in the 1990s and beyond. For more on this see Alexander 2002; Andrews 2016.

30. Their responses contrast sharply with the typical rejection of British identities by Black and ethnic minority populations in the 1980s and 1990s. For more on these debates, see Alexander 1996, 2016 and Byrne et al. 2020.

31. Gilroy 2004, 111.

32. Britain's legacies of slavery, colonialism, and imperial policing, along with its persistent white supremacy, xenophobia, and economic inequality inform the degrees of disassociation and identification Black Caribbean and other ethnic minority youth express. See Elliott-Cooper 2021; de Noronha 2020; Byrne et al. 2020b; Virdee 2014.

33. Solomos 2003.

34. "Ray-tay-tay" is a popular expression in Jamaica and the Caribbean diaspora. It is a verbal filler, perhaps synonymous with "blah, blah, blah" or "and what not."

35. For more on representations of Black Caribbean families in Britain, see Reynolds 2009, 2010b.

36. To learn more about 'controlling images,' a term coined by Black feminist sociologist Patricia Hill Collins, see Collins 2004, 2000.

37. Doharty 2019, 2015.

38. Stuart Hall 2011; Roberts and Mahtani 2010.

39. Wallace 2018b

40. The police are called the FEDs because their professional union is the City of London Police Federation.

41. "Two-twos" is a Jamaican expression, now more widely adopted in Britain by Caribbean people, that refers to the quick passing of time. It is perhaps akin to 'all of a sudden.'

42. "Skets" refers to promiscuous girls in Britain, particularly Black girls; the term is perhaps analogous with 'sluts.' Skets is arguably a derivative of 'sketel,' a popular 1990s label from Jamaican dancehall that identified and pathologized sexually expressive girls, often from low-income and working-class backgrounds.

43. Bourdieu 1999.

44. Bourdieu 1989.

45. Wallace 2018a; Bourdieu 1989.

46. Demie 2019.

47. Stuart Hall 1996a.

48. For more on ethnic credits and ethnic penalties, see Randolph 2015. To learn more about distinction practices among Black ethnics see Clergé 2019; Wallace 2018a.

49. Wallace 2018b.

50. African Americans in the United States and Black Caribbeans in Britain occupy similar structural and cultural positions as *signifying minorities*—serially stigmatized Black ethnics with differing migration and national histories but comparable symbolic and political representation in education. See Anim-Addo 2009 for more on signifying minorities in Britain.

Chapter 5

1. The "isolation room" and Londerville students' experiences in it are similar to "in-school detention" or "in-school suspension" common in select US schools. Students' duration in isolation depended on the nature of the offense.

2. In drawing distinctions between how Black Caribbean young people practice deference and the conditions under which they do so, I do not wish to dichotomize Black Caribbean young people on either side of the Atlantic, or to suggest that no Black Caribbean students in London drew on deference to stay out

of trouble. Two London-based Black Caribbean students' perspectives represent disconfirming cases; they spoke of deference as an aid for accessing relational power in classrooms, particularly with authority figures. But they were outliers. My claims about deference for damage reduction in London and deference for damage prevention in New York are based on the predominant cultural strategies and patterns of practice that were described in focus-group interviews and one-on-one interviews and witnessed during school-based ethnographic observations. The results point to how different ethnic expectations shape patterns of behavior in school.

3. Newland's College Prep classes are generally equivalent to middle sets at Londerville in Britain.

4. In New York City, deans are school officials, often former teachers, whose task it is to monitor students and enforce discipline in schools. They are formally referred to as Deans of Discipline. They are often part of the school's security team, serving as a link between School Resource Officers and classroom teachers.

5. Although not all Black Caribbean students practiced deference, it was one of the strategies some used to combat the impact of ethnic expectations. More than half of the Black Caribbean young people I spoke with one-on-one in both London and New York City performed deference.

6. Young, Jr. 2004.

7. While recent studies of Black Caribbean boyhood and girlhood highlight the political conditions that shape Black Caribbean youth's identity development, few cross-national analyses attend to gendered cultural logics and institutional processes. For related studies of gender politics among Black Caribbeans, see LaBennett 2011; Mirza 2009; Alexander 1996.

8. Wynter 2003; Reddock 2007.

9. López 2002, 41.

10. In this instance, it means selling or trading drugs. In other cases, however, shottin' refers to students who have access to free lunch selling their lunch to paying students at a lower price than the school charged.

11. Younge 2017; Wallace 2018b.

12. Demie 2019; Strand 2014.

13. Stuart Hall 1996b; Alexander 1996.

14. Byrne et al. 2020.

15. Tyler et al. 2014; Elliott-Cooper 2011.

16. Stuart Hall et al. 1978.

17. "Isolation" refers to a large room in which groups of students from all class years were removed from class sessions—some for a single class period, some for several consecutive periods, and others for days at a time. "Isolation" was, in fact, an exclusion room. Teachers at Londerville and other secondary schools across South London also referred to these exclusion rooms as "inclusion rooms," or as "internal," arguably a less stigmatizing euphemism for school-based exclusion. The irony involved in these word games was noticed by perceptive students like Year 11 pupil Kayla, who in

reference to school staff changing terms for exclusion rooms said to me, "dem tek wi fi fool [They think we're fools]!"

18. When in the isolation room right after Anthony was sent there, I documented the demographics of the room on my phone: 33 boys, 10 girls; 15 white, 5 Asian, and 23 Black students. Of the 23 Black students, 16 were Black Caribbean, and 12 of the 16 were Black Caribbean boys. In its management and make-up, this isolation room seemed eerily similar to the separate classrooms and schools for "educationally sub-normal" students that Black parents protested against throughout North and South London in the 1960s and 1970s (Coard 1971; Wallace and Joseph-Salisbury 2021). Now, however, the criteria for exclusion were not scores on IQ tests, English language proficiency, or other skills perceived as markers of intelligence. At Londerville, these rooms were designated for disruptive students, often with emotional and behavioral difficulties, who failed at one point or another to display deference or denied its power.

19. It is easy to frame the overrepresentation of Black Caribbean pupils in isolation at Londerville as an issue of "a lot of rude boys," as another teacher, Mr. Scott, suggested. But the patterns of exclusion are deeply layered, affecting Black Caribbean boys *and* Black Caribbean girls to different degrees, in ways that are frequently ignored. My visits to the isolation room revealed that there were more Black Caribbean girls than girls of any other ethno-racial group. But because Black Caribbean girls are frequently compared to Black Caribbean boys, the gendered, racialized layers of exclusion that trap Black Caribbean girls are frequently elided at Londerville, as in wider public and educational policy discourses throughout Britain. In popular discourses on the public crisis of Black boys, the private or less pronounced challenges of Black girls are ignored, perhaps in ways symbolically similar to how Ms. Davis ignored Imogen before she chided the class.

20. For Rashawn and Toby, as well as other Black Caribbean young people I spoke with, deference is a strategic and situational action, not a universal cultural trait. It can enable those who often experience powerlessness in schools to reposition themselves as powerful. For more on the racialized gender politics of behavior, particularly among school-age boys, see Wallace 2019a; Ferguson 2000; Mac an Ghaill 1988.

21. Dumas and Nelson 2016; Noguera 2008.

22. Grundy 2021; Connell 1995; Wallace 2017a.

23. Bourdieu 1977.

24. Warikoo 2011.

25. Du Bois 1903; Higginbotham 1993; Griffin 2011; Lewis 2013.

26. In the United States and Britain, feminist sociological and educational research on Black women and girls in schools has long indicated that Black female subjects are often viewed outside the prism of normative womanhood by virtue of their race. Scholars such as Heidi Mirza (1992; 2009); Akwugo Emejulu (2011); Uvanney Maylor (2009); Victoria Showunmi (2017); April-Louise Pennant (2022); Patricia Hill Collins (2000, 2004); Kimberlé Crenshaw (1991, 1993); Oyèrónke Oyewùmí (2003); Whitney

Pirtle (2021), Zakiya Luna (2021), Saida Grundy (2021), among many others, detail the overlapping history and politics of racism and sexism, or what Moya Bailey (2021) more precisely calls misogynoir, experienced by Black women and girls in public institutions like schools. Recent ethnographic research indicates that Black girls are often held to stricter gender norms than their Black male peers and their white and non-Black female peers, and are more often punished when they deviate from such norms. See Ray 2017, 2022; and Cox 2015 for examples. The relational analysis deployed in this chapter contributes to sociological and educational research that illuminates the frequently ignored, casual marginalization of Black girls in schools relative to Black boys.

27. In *Righteous Discontent: The Women's Movement in the Black Baptist Church, 1880–1920*, feminist historian Evelyn Brooks Higginbotham coined "the politics of respectability" to highlight the long-ignored political work of the Women's Convention of the Black Baptist Church. Higginbotham examined African American Baptist women's politeness, sexual purity, and cleanliness strategically deployed as part of cultural 'uplift politics' to encourage Black people to be respectable through individual behavioral reform and to demonstrate to white people, given white people's increasing investments in discussing Black cultural pathology, that Black people could be respectable citizens, culturally and politically. The Black Baptist women in Higginbotham's analysis symbolized and embodied 'the politics of respectability.' Critics of the politics of respectability have also noted that this strategy proved more useful for women who sought power to relate to men within a certain class stratum of the Black community than in securing respect and regard for all Black people from whites. Critics also note that the investments in the politics of respectability often included the demotion and disrespect of low-income and working class Black women.

28. Stuart Hall 2017b, 97.

29. Bourdieu and Wacquant 1992, 167.

30. Desmond and Emirbayer 2009, 347.

31. Mirza 1992, 2009.

32. Jones 2009; Ray 2007.

33. Evans-Winters 2005; Evans-Winters and Esposito 2010; Wun 2016; Ferguson 2000.

34. Phoenix 2009; Rollock 2007; Pennant 2022; Crenshaw et al. 2015; Crenshaw 1991; Collins 2011, 2004; Love 2012.

35. In New York, as in London, Black Caribbean girls and boys experience a common way of being, perceiving, and understanding the social world, which Pierre Bourdieu *and* Stuart Hall referred to as habitus, though Bourdieu elaborated on habitus much more than Hall. Bourdieu defined habitus as "a system of disposition" that shapes the perceptions and practices of social actors depending on the social field. I draw on the work of feminist sociologists to extend Bourdieu's formulation of habitus to consider the gendered logics of behavior that sustain hierarchies of power and privilege in schools and society. The gendered habitus of Black Caribbean young people is a shared orientation reinforced and reproduced across familial, educational, religious, and cultural institutions as an acceptable way of living and doing gender. For feminist analyses of habitus and gender relations, see Reay 2005; Mirza 2009; Ingram 2011; Wilson et al. 2021.

36. Most of my references to football in this book are about the global sport, which US players and enthusiasts refer to as soccer. For more on the sociology of race and sports, see the work of Ben Carrington (1998, 2010, 2019), perhaps the most ardent and vocal supporter of Stuart Hall's work in North American sociology.
37. Bourdieu 1986.
38. Tyson 2012; Richards 2017; Ochoa 2013; Gamoran 2009.
39. Warikoo 2016; Mirza 2006,
40. Hall 1999, 195.
41. Young, Jr. 2004; Blume Oeur 2018; Reddock 2007.
42. Misrecognition is "an arbitrary curriculum that is 'naturalized' so that social classifications are transformed into academic ones. The result is that instead of being experienced for what they are (i.e., partial and technical hierarchies), such social classifications become 'total' hierarchies, experienced as if they were grounded in nature" (Grenfell 2008, 23–24).

Chapter 6

1. In discussing these two forms of defiance among Black Caribbean pupils in London and interpersonal defiance among Black Caribbeans in New York, I do not wish to propose a fixed dichotomy. Incidents of institutional defiance occurred in New York and interpersonal defiance in London, but they were atypical. Black Caribbean students, and students from any ethno-racial group for that matter, can practice institutional and/or interpersonal defiance—depending on the institutional context or social situation. These nuances are important to note in order to avoid stereotyping Black Caribbean people and other ethno-racial groups.
2. Sociologist Eduardo Bonilla-Silva (2012) suggests that such explanations are not simply biased, but racist, because they subtly and strategically misrepresent structural and institutional factors as personal problems. Cultural racism attributes the outcomes of ethno-racial groups to the lack of appropriate skills, tastes, values, attitudes, and behavior, as opposed to the historical and contemporary differences in representation and the distribution of resources.
3. GCSE stands for General Certificate of Secondary Education. GCSEs are national exams required for college and university admission.
4. Ball 2009.
5. BTEC stands for Business and Technology Education Council—specialist, often practice-based and work-related qualifications in areas such as art and design, childcare, construction, hospitality, performing arts, and sports.
6. In Britain and the British Commonwealth, sixth form refers to Years 12 and 13—an important preparatory stage for university.
7. Reay et al. 2005.
8. Ball 2012, 52.
9. Desmond and Emirbayer 2009.
10. Desmond and Emirbayer 2009.
11. Treitler 2013; Pierre 2004.

12. Byrne et al. 2020; Archer and Mendick 2010.
13. Bonilla-Silva 2012.
14. Perry 2016.
15. Mills 2000.
16. Mirza and Reay 2000, 521.
17. Paris and Alim 2017.
18. McQueen 2020; Wallace and Joseph-Salisbury 2022.
19. Reay and Mirza 1997; Mirza and Reay 2000.
20. Mirza 2006; Delpit 2012.
21. Hall 2017b.
22. Bonilla-Silva 2006; Mirza 2006.
23. Lewis and Diamond 2015; Warikoo 2011, 2016.
24. Hall 2017b; Bonilla-Silva 2012.
25. A "dap" is a handshake common among Black people throughout the United States. Cultural critics and historians suggest that the dap was developed among African American soldiers during the Vietnam war and "expresses unity, strength, defiance, or resistance" (Hamilton 2014, 28). In a war where white military officers often disrespected and mistreated Black soldiers, the gesture emerged as a greeting affirming racial solidarity. D.A.P was sometimes understood as an acronym for Dignity And Pride.
26. Kasinitz et al. 2001.
27. Here, "my G," short for "my General," is a sign of respect and comradery.
28. Hall 2017b.
29. Desmond and Emirbayer 2009.
30. Holt 2000.
31. Ridgeway 2019; Lewis and Diamond 2015.
32. Wallace 2018b.
33. Fordham and Ogbu 1986; Tyson 2012; O'Connor et al. 2011.
34. Hall 2017b, 39.

Conclusion

1. I must confess that when I met with Ms. Bell, I had not yet identified or theorized the culture trap. When I finished my doctoral dissertation, I thought the central story was about ethnic expectations and ethnic exceptionalism. My dialogue with Ms. Bell that guides this chapter highlights my investments in examining ethnic expectations. However, my analysis of this discussion with Ms. Bell and my repeated exploration of interview and observation data at the heart of this ethnography revealed ethnic expectations as an iteration of the culture trap—and the culture trap as the bigger story.
2. Stuart Hall 2017b, 98.
3. Stacey Lee 2009; Randolph 2015; Archer and Francis 2007; Gillborn 2008; Tomlinson 2019.

4. Lee and Zhou 2015; Lew 2011; Bhopal 2018.

5. Imoagene 2017; Agyepong 2017; Ayling 2019.

6. Despite their largely contrasting status positions as celebrated and demoted minorities in American and British societies, Black Caribbeans in London and New York City share a common experience of negotiating a Black ethnic imaginary. The myth undergirding the Black ethnic imaginary is not that ethnicity trumps race, but that ethnicity has the capacity to temper racism—to shape public perceptions of what type of Black person you are. Such narratives aid in the development of distinctions among Black people and the assertion of rigid ethnic hierarchies among Blacks largely ignored in sociological research on race, culture, and education. In contexts where 'diversity' and 'inclusion' are now normative "slogan systems," and where the explicit dismissal of all Blacks will yield unwelcome public claims of anti-Black racism, the alternate cultural strategies that are not explicitly about race and enable preference for some Blacks by virtue of culture or class is but a different take on an old problem in a putatively post-racial age. For more on what I call the Black ethnic imaginary, see Wallace 2018b.

7. This is perhaps a different iteration of *collective distinctiveness*, discussed in Chapter 4.

8. This, it seems, is a different but related articulation of *individual distinctiveness* noted in Chapter 4.

9. Other minority groups experience divergent outcomes in various parts of the world when subjected to differing degrees of racial and ethnic discrimination, and complex incorporation trajectories in contexts of reception. Consider, for instance, the case of Koreans, who since the latter half of the 20th century have been framed as a model minority in the United States based on their academic and economic attainment (Braxton 1999; Lew 2006). However, the recent positive racialization of Koreans in the United States is not universal across contexts. In Japan, Koreans endure persistent discrimination in the employment, education, and housing arenas. Additionally, they have lower levels of educational attainment relative to their Japanese counterparts (Ahn 2012; C. Lee and DeVos 1981; Y. Lee 1991). Ahn (2012, 250) asserts, "many Koreans adopt Japanese names, known as 'tsumei,' in order to hide their ethnicity while others choose to become naturalized as 'new Japanese' in order to avoid the negative consequences of being Korean." Chinese immigrants and their progeny living in Indonesia have also resorted to changing their names to popular Indonesian-sounding ones in order to hide their ethnic identities and limit discrimination. For over a century, people of Chinese heritage in Indonesia have experienced structural discrimination and the negative racialization of their ethnicity—first under Dutch colonial rule followed by subsequent retaliations by native Indonesians. Such experiences differ greatly from the positive appraisals of Chinese immigrants and their children in Australia, where they are recruited and celebrated for their intelligence, market investments, and creative ingenuity.

10. Upon reflection, I realized that when individuals meet African American students and professionals in the United States and ask them "where are you really from?" as an African American student at Newlands recalled, or directly ask them if they are Caribbean or African immigrants, that is often because of ethnic expectations.

248 NOTES

11. Warikoo 2016; Bhopal 2018.
12. Bourdieu 1993; Stuart Hall 2017c.
13. One-to-ones is a key method in community organizing. It is through these semi-structured, face-to-face meetings between two individuals that leaders and organizers build relationships. For more, see Appendix.
14. Swidler 1986.
15. Randolph 2015.
16. Foner 1979, 2005; Model 2008; Treitler 2007, 2013.
17. Massey et al. 2007.
18. Rong and Brown 2001.
19. Greer 2013; Ifantunji 2016.
20. Alexander 1996; Gilroy 2013.
21. Gillborn and Mirza 2012.
22. Furthermore, the ongoing denial of legal citizenship experienced by Black Caribbeans of the Windrush generation who immigrated legally to England as members of the British Empire emblematizes the prolonged precarity of Black Caribbeans in British society. See Alexander 2016 for more.
23. Matory 2015.
24. On one hand, I said this to deflect the gendered ethnic expectations teachers and parents had of me as a Black Caribbean man—a lingering belief they often expressed that I would be able to reach the boys and address the issues affecting them. Black male teachers and youth workers often encounter that assumption (Maylor 2009; Brockenbrough 2012; Bristol and Mentor 2018). On the other hand, I wanted to emphasize that any sustainable solution to the social and academic challenges Black Caribbean boys face in British schools would require meaningful, organized partnerships.
25. Mirza 1992, 2006; Rollock 2007; Demie 2021.
26. Demie 2019.
27. I did not hold these perspectives prior to this cross-national research project. I, too, had bought into discourses regarding the 'crisis' of Black males in education inadvertently used to justify a lack of focus on the experiences of Black girls (Blume Oeur 2018; Morris 2016; Evans-Winter and Esposito 2010). I came to fully appreciate these racialized gender dynamics when I spent time listening to Black Caribbean boys and girls in order to understand their different but related challenges in school.
28. Weekes and Wright 1998; Doharty 2015; Modood 1992; Haque 2017; Joseph-Salisbury 2020; Reay 2009; Demuth 1978.
29. Coard 1971.
30. Francis et al. 2020; Archer et al. 2018.
31. Maylor 2009b; Howard 2010.
32. Korthagen et al. 2001; Mirza and Meetoo 2012.
33. Hollins and Guzman 2005.
34. Bristol 2018; Bristol and Shirrell 2019.
35. Office of Equity and Access 2021, 3.
36. Connolly et al. 2019; Francis et al. 2020.

37. Archer et al. 2018.
38. Francis et al. 2020.
39. Francis et al. 2020.
40. Sealey-Ruiz 2022.

Appendix

1. Lareau 2021.
2. Lewis-McCoy 2016, 2010.
3. Du Bois 1899.
4. Hall et al. 1978.

About the Author

Derron Wallace is Assistant Professor of Sociology and Education at Brandeis University, and Research Fellow at the Centre on the Dynamics of Ethnicity at the University of Manchester. He is a cultural sociologist of race, ethnicity, and education. His research and teaching interests are concerned with the analysis and amelioration of structural and cultural inequalities that shape schooling in the United States, Britain, the Caribbean, and around the world.

References

Agyepong, Mercy. 2017. "The Struggles of Invisibility: Perception and Treatment of African Students in the United States." In *Erasing Invisibility, Inequity and Social Injustice of Africans in the Diaspora and the Continent*, edited by O. N. Ukpokodu and P. O. Ojiambo, 56–75. Newcastle upon Tyne, UK: Cambridge Scholars Publishing.

Ahn, Ruth. 2012. "Korean Students' Minority Schooling Experience in Japan." *Intercultural Education* 23 (3): 249–63.

Alexander, Claire. 1996. *The Art of Being Black: The Creation of Black British Youth Identities.* Oxford: Oxford University Press.

Alexander, Claire. 2002. "Beyond Black: Re-thinking the Colour/Culture Divide." *Ethnic and Racial Studies* 25 (4): 522–71.

Alexander, Claire. 2016. "The Culture Question: A View from the UK." *Ethnic and Racial Studies* 39 (8): 1426–35.

Alexander, M. Jacqui. 2005. *Pedagogies of Crossing: Meditations on Feminism, Sexual Politics, Memory and the Sacred.* Durham, NC: Duke University Press.

Anderson, James. 1988. *The Education of Blacks in the South, 1860–1935.* Chapel Hill: University of North Carolina Press.

Anderson, Jon. 2021. *Understanding Cultural Geography: Places and Traces.* London: Routledge.

Andrew, Smith. 2011. "'Concrete Freedom': C.L.R. James on Culture and Black Politics." *Cultural Sociology* 4 (2): 479–99.

Andrews, Kehinde. 2013. *Resisting Racism: Race, Inequality and the Black Supplementary School Movement.* London: Institute of Education Press.

Andrews, Kehinde. 2014. "Toward a Black Radical Independent Education: Black Radicalism, Independence and the Supplementary School Movement." *The Journal of Negro Education* 83 (1): 5–14.

Andrews, Kehinde. 2016. "The Problem of Political Blackness: Lessons from the Black Supplementary School Movement." *Ethnic and Racial Studies* 39 (11): 2060–78.

Anim-Addo, Joan. 2009. "Tracing Knowledge, Culture and Power: Towards an Intercultural Approach to Literary Studies." In *Interculturality and Gender*, edited by Joan Anim-Addo, Giovanna Covi, and Mina Karavanta, 115–45. London: Mango Publishing.

Anyon, Jean. 1997. *Ghetto Schooling.* New York: Teachers College Press.

Anyon, Jean. 2005. *Radical Possibilties: Public Policy, Urban Education and a New Social Movement.* New York: Routledge.

Apple, Michael W., Stephen J. Ball, and Luis Armando Gandin. 2010. *The Routledge International Handbook of the Sociology of Education.* London: Routledge.

April-Louise, Pennant. 2022. "'Who's Checkin' for Black Girls and Women in the "Pandemic within a Pandemic'? COVID-19, Black Lives Matter and Educational Implications." *Educational Review* 74 (3): 534–57.

Aptheker, Herbert. 1973. *The Correspondence of W.E.B. Du Bois, Selections 1877–1934*. Vol. 1. Amherst: University of Massachusetts Press.

Archer, Louise. 2010. "'We Raised It with the Head': The Educational Practices of Minority Ethnic, Middle-Class Families." *British Journal of Sociology of Education* 31 (4): 449–69.

Archer, Louise, and Becky Francis. 2007. *Understanding Minority Ethnic Achievement: Race, Gender, Class and "Success."* London: Routledge.

Archer, Louise, Becky Francis, Sarah Miller, Becky Taylor, Antonia Tereshchenko, Anna Mazenod, David Pepper, and Mary-Claire Travers. 2018. "The Symbolic Violence of Setting: A Bourdieusian Analysis of Mixed Methods Data on Secondary Students' Views about Setting." *British Education Research Journal* 44 (1): 119–40.

Archer, Louise, and Semi Mendick. 2010. *Urban Youth and Schooling*. Berkshire: Open University Press.

Arday, Jason, and Heidi Safia Mirza. 2018. *Dismantling Race in Higher Education: Racism, Whiteness and Decolonising the Academy*. London: Palgrave Macmillan.

Atkinson, Rowland, and Gary Bridge. 2013. "Globalization and the New Urban Colonialism." In *The Gentrification Debates: A Reader*, edited by Japonica Brown-Saracino, 51–70. London: Routledge.

Avildsen, John. 1989. *Lean on Me*. Hollywood, California: Warner Brothers Studios.

Ayling, Pere. 2019. *Distinction, Exclusivity and Whiteness: Elite Nigerian Parents and the International Education Market*. London: Springer.

Babbie, Earl. 2004. *The Practice of Social Research*. 10th ed. Belmont, CA: Wadsworth/ Thomson Learning.

Bacchus, M. Kazim. 1994. *Education as and for Legitimacy: Developments in West Indian Education between 1846 and 1895*. Ontario: Wilfred Laurier University Press.

Back, Les. 1996. *New Ethnicities and Urban Culture: Racisms and Multiculture in Young Lives*. London: UCL Press.

Bailey, Moya. 2021. *Misogynoir Transformed: Black Women's Digital Resistance*. New York: New York University Press.

Baker, Lee. 2010. *Anthropology and the Racial Politics of Culture*. Durham, NC: Duke University Press.

Baldridge, Bianca. 2019. *Reclaiming Community: Race and the Uncertain Future of Youth Work*. Stanford, CA: Stanford University Press.

Ball, Stephen. 2009. "Privatizing Education, Privatizing Education Policy, Privatizing Educational Research: Network Governance and the 'Competition State.'" *Journal of Education Policy* 24 (1): 83–100.

Ball, Stephen. 2012. *Global Education Inc.: New Policy Networks and the Neo-Liberal Imaginary*. London: Routledge.

Barrow, Christine, and Rhoda Reddock. 2001. "Education." In *Caribbean Sociology: Introductory Readings*, edited by Christine Barrow and Rhoda Reddock, 643–44. Kingston: Ian Randle Publishers.

Bartle, George. 1983. "The Role of the British and Foreign School Society in the Education of the Emancipated Negro, 1814–75." *Journal of Educational Administration and History* xv (1): 1–9.

Bashi, Vilna. 2001. "Neither Ignorance or Bliss: Race, Racism, and the West Indian Immigrant Experience." In *Migration, Transnationalization & Race in a Changing New York*, edited by H. Cordero-Guzman, R. Smith, and R Grosfoguel, 212–38. Philadelphia: Temple University Press.

Beckles, Hilary, and Verene Shepherd. 1999. *Caribbean Slavery in the Atlantic World: A Student Reader*. New York: M. Weiner Publishers.

Beckles, Hilary, and Verene Shepherd. 2007. *Trading Souls: Europe's Transatlantic Trade in Africans*. Jamaica: Ian Randle Publishers.

Benson, Susan. 1996. "Asians Have Culture, West Indians Have Problems: Discourses of Race and Ethnicity in and out of Anthropology." In *Culture, Identity and Politics: Ethnic Minorities in Britain*, edited by Terrance Ranger, Yunas Samas, and Ossie Stuart, 47–56. Aldershot: Avebury Press.

Berger, Ronald, and Richard Quinney. 2005. *Storytelling Sociology: Narrative as Social Inquiry*. Boulder, CO: Lynne Rienner Publishers.

Bhambra, Gurminder K. 2014. "Postcolonial and Decolonial Dialogues." *Postcolonial Studies* 17 (2): 115–21.

Bhopal, Kalwant. 2018. *White Privilege: The Myth of a Post-Racial Society*. Bristol: Policy Press.

Blouet, Olwyn Mary. 1990. "Slavery and Freedom in the British West Indies, 1823–33: The Role of Education." *History of Education Quarterly* 30 (4): 625–43.

Blume Oeur, Freeden. 2018. *Black Boys Apart: Racial Uplift and Respectability in All-Male Public Schools*. Minneapolis: University of Minnesota Press.

Bonilla-Silva, Eduardo. 1997. "Rethinking Racism: Toward a Structural Interpretation." *American Sociological Review* 62 (3): 465–480.

Bonilla-Silva, Eduardo. 2006. *Racism without Racists: Color-Blind Racism and the Persistence of Racial Inequality in the United States*. Lanham, MD: Rowman & Littlefield Publishers.

Bonilla-Silva, Eduardo. 2012. "The Invisible Weight of Whiteness: The Racial Grammar of Everyday Life in Contemporary America." *Ethnic and Racial Studies* 35 (2): 173–94.

Bourdieu, Pierre. 1973. "Cultural Reproduction and Social Reproduction." In *Knowledge, Education and Cultural Change*, edited by R. Brown, 71–112. London: Tavistock Press.

Bourdieu, Pierre. 1977. *Outline of a Theory of Practice*. Cambridge: Cambridge University Press.

Bourdieu, Pierre. 1979. *Algeria 1960: The Disenchantment of the World, the Sense of Honour, the Kabyle House or the World Reversed*. Cambridge: Cambridge University Press.

Bourdieu, Pierre. 1986. "The Forms of Capital." In *Handbook of Theory and Research for the Sociology of Education*, edited by John C. Richardson, 241–58. London: Greenwood Press.

Bourdieu, Pierre. 1989. "Social Space and Symbolic Power." *Sociological Theory* 7 (1): 14–25.

Bourdieu, Pierre. 1993. *Distinction: A Social Critique of the Judgement of Taste*. London: Routledge.

Bourdieu, Pierre. 1998. *Practical Reason: On the Theory of Action*. Cambridge: Polity Press.

Bourdieu, Pierre, et al. 1999. *Weight of the World: Social Suffering in Contemporary Society*. Cambridge: Polity Press.

Bourdieu, Pierre. 2006. "The Forms of Capital." In *Education, Globalisation and Social Change*, edited by H. Lauder, P. Brown, J. Dillabough, and A Halsey, 105–18. Oxford: Oxford University Press.

Bourdieu, Pierre, and Loïc Wacquant. 1992. *An Invitation to Reflexive Sociology*. Chicago: Chicago University Press.

Boyce Davies, Carole, and Monica Jardine. 2003. "Imperial Geographies and Caribbean Nationalism: At the Border between 'A Dying Colonialism' and U.S. Hegemony." *The New Centennial Review* 3 (3): 151–74.

Brah, Avtar, and Ann Phoenix. 2004. "Ain't I A Woman? Revisiting Intersectionality." *Journal of International Women's Studies* 5 (3): 75–86.

Braxton, Richard. 1999. "Culture, Family and Chinese and Korean American Student Achievement." *College Student Journal* 33: 250–56.

Brereton, Bridget. 1981. *History of Modern Trinidad, 1783–1962*. Port of Spain: Heinemann Press.

Brereton, Bridget. 2002. *Race Relations in Colonial Trinidad 1870–1900*. Cambridge: Cambridge University Press.

Bressey, Caroline. 2009. "The Legacies of 2007: Remapping the Black Presence in Britain." *Geography Compass* 3 (3): 903–17.

Bristol, Travis. 2018. "To Be Alone or in a Group: An Exploration Into How the School-Based Experiences Differ for Black Male Teachers Across One Urban School District." *Urban Education* 53 (3): 334–54.

Bristol, Travis, and Marcelle Mentor. 2018. "Policing and Teaching: The Positioning of Black Male Teachers as Agents in the Universal Carceral Apparatus." *The Urban Review* 50 (2): 218–34.

Bristol, Travis, and Matthew Shirrell. 2019. "Who Is Here to Help Me? The Work-Related Social Networks of Staff of Color in Two Mid-Sized Districts." *American Educational Research Journal* 56 (3): 868–98.

British Cabinet Office. 2018. "Race Disparity Audit: Summary Findings from the Ethnicity Facts and Figures Website." London.

Brockenbrough, Ed. 2012. "'You Ain't My Daddy!': Black Male Teachers and the Politics of Surrogate Fatherhood." *International Journal of Inclusive Education* 16 (4): 357–72.

Brown, Jacqueline Nassy. 2005. *Dropping Anchor, Setting Sail: Geographies of Race in Black Liverpool*. Princeton, NJ: Princeton University Press.

Bryce-Laporte, Roy Simon. 1972. "Black Immigrant Invisibility: The Experience of Inequality." *Journal of Black Studies* 3: 29–56.

Bryce-Laporte, Roy Simon. 1979. "Introduction: New York City and the New Caribbean Immigration: A Contextual Statement." *International Migration Review* 13 (2): 214–34.

Buckley, Roger Norman. 1979. *Slaves in Red Coats: The British West India Regiments 1795–1815*. New Haven, CT: Yale University Press.

Bureau of the Census. 1918. *Negro Population of the United States, 1790–1915*. Washington, D.C.

Butterfield, Sherri-Ann. 2004. "'We're Just Black': The Racial and Ethnic Identities of Second-Generation West Indians in New York." In *Becoming New Yorkers: Ethnographies of the New Second Generation*, edited by Philip Kasinitz, John H. Mollenkopf, and Mary C. Waters, 288–312. New York: Russell Sage Foundation.

Byrne, Bridget, Claire Alexander, Omar Khan, James Nazroo, and William Shankley. 2020. *Ethnicity, Race and Inequality in the UK: State of the Union*. Bristol: Policy Press.

Calarco, Jessica McCrory. 2014. "Coached for the Classroom: Parents' Cultural Transmission and Children's Reproduction of Educational Inequalities." *American Sociological Review* 79 (5): 1015–37.

Campbell, Carl. 1967. "Toward an Imperial Policy for the Education of Negroes in the West Indies after Emancipation." *Jamaican Historical Review* 7 (1): 68–102.

Cantres, James. 2020. *Blackening Britain: Caribbean Radicalism from Windrush to Decolonization*. Lanham, MD: Rowman & Littlefield Publishers.

Carby, Hazel. 2019. *Imperial Intimacies: A Tale of Two Islands*. London: Verso Books.

Carey, Roderick. 2014. "A Cultural Analysis of the Achievement Gap Discourse: Challenging the Language and Labels Used in the Work of School Reform." *Urban Education* 49 (4): 440–68.

Carrington, Ben. 1998. "Sport, Masculinity, and Black Cultural Resistance." *Journal of Sport and Social Issues* 22 (3): 275–98.

Carrington, Ben. 2010. *Race, Sport and Politics: The Sporting Black Diaspora*. London: SAGE.

Carrington, Ben. 2019. "Remembering Stuart Hall: Learning to Think Differently." *New Formations: A Journal of Culture/Theory/Politics* 96 (1): 248–54.

Carter, Prudence. 2005. *Keepin' It Real: School Success Beyond Black and White*. Oxford: Oxford University Press.

Carter, Prudence. 2012. *Stubborn Roots: Race, Culture & Inequality in U.S. and South African Schools*. Oxford: Oxford University Press.

Carter, Prudence, and Kevin Welner. 2013. *Closing the Opportunity Gap: What America Must Do to Give Every Child an Even Chance*. Oxford: Oxford University Press.

Charles, Camille, Mary Fischer, Margarita Mooney, and Douglas S. Massey. 2009. *Taming the River: Negotiating the Academic, Financial, and Social Currents at Selective Colleges and Universities*. Princeton, NJ: Princeton University Press.

Chiswick, Barry. 1979. "The Economic Progress of Immigrants: Some Apparently Universal Patterns." *Contemporary Economic Problems* 1979: 357–99.

Clergé, Orly. 2012. "Balancing Stigma and Status: Racial and Class Identities among Middle-Class Haitian Youth." *Racial and Ethnic Studies* 37 (6): 958–77.

Clergé, Orly. 2019. *The New Noir: Race, Identity & Diaspora in Black Suburbia*. Berkeley, CA: University of California Press.

Coard, Bernard. 1971. *How the West Indian Child Is Made Educationally Sub-normal in the British School System*. London: New Beacon Books.

Cohen, Cathy. 2010. *Democracy Remixed: Black Youth and the Future of American Politics*. Oxford: Oxford University Press.

Coleman-King, Chonika. 2014. *The (Re-)Making of a Black American: Tracing the Racial and Ethnic Socialization of Caribbean American Youth*. New York: Peter Lang.

Collins, Patricia Hill. 2000. *Black Feminist Thought: Knowledge, Consciousness and the Politics of Empowerment*. 2nd ed. New York: Routledge.

Collins, Patricia Hill. 2004. *Black Sexual Politics: African Americans, Gender and the New Racism*. New York: Routledge.

Collins, Patricia Hill. 2006. "A Telling Difference: Dominance, Strength and Black Masculinities." In *Progressive Black Masculinities*, edited by Athena D. Mutua, 73–97. New York: Routledge.

Conchas, Gilberto. 2006. *The Color of Success: Race and High-Achieving Urban Youth*. New York: Teachers College Press.

Connell, Raewyn. 1995. *Masculinities*. Cambridge: Polity Press.

Connolly, Paul, Becky Taylor, Becky Francis, Louise Archer, Jeremy Hodgen, Anna Mazenod, and Antonia Tereshchenko. 2019. "The Misallocation of Students to Academic Sets in Maths: A Study of Secondary Schools in England." *British Education Research Journal* 45 (4): 873–97.

Coombs, Orde. 1970. "West Indians in New York: Moving Beyond the Limbo Pole." *New York Magazine*, (13): 28–32.

Cox, Aimee Meredith. 2015. *Shapeshifters: Black Girls and the Choreography of Citizenship.* Durham, NC: Duke University Press.

Crenshaw, Kimberlé. 1991. "Mapping the Margins: Intersectionality, Identity Politics, and Violence against Women of Color." *Stanford Law Review* 43 (6): 1241–99.

Crenshaw, Kimberlé. 1993. "Demarginalizing the Intersection of Race and Sex: A Black Feminist Critique of Antidiscrimination Doctrine, Feminist Theory and Antiracist Politics." In *Feminist Legal Theory*, edited by D. Weisberg, 383–411. Philadelphia: Temple University Press.

Crenshaw, Kimberlé, Priscilla Ocen, and Jyoti Nanda. 2015. "Black Girls Matter: Pushed out, Overpoliced, and Underprotected." New York: African American Policy Forum. https://www.law.columbia.edu/sites/default/files/legacy/files/public_affairs/2015/february_2015/black_girls_matter_report_2.4.15.pdf.

Dabydeen, David, John Gilmore, and Cecily Jones. 2008. *The Oxford Companion to Black British History.* Edited by David Dabydeen, John Gilmore, and Cecily Jones. Oxford: Oxford University Press.

Daniels, John. 1914. *In Freedom's Birthplace: A Study of the Boston Negroes.* Boston: Houghton Mifflin.

Dawson, Michael. 1994. *Behind the Mule: Race and Class in African-American Politics.* Princeton, NJ: Princeton University Press.

Dawson, Michael. 2001. *Black Visions: The Roots of Contemporary African-Americans Political Ideologies.* Chicago: University of Chicago Press.

de Noronha, Luke. 2020. *Deporting Black Britons: Portraits of Deportation to Jamaica.* Manchester: Manchester University Press.

Delpit, Lisa. 2012. *Multiplication Is for White People: Raising Expectations for Other People's Children.* New York: The New Press.

Demie, Feyisa. 2005. "Achievement of Black Caribbean Pupils: Good Practice in Lambeth Schools." *British Educational Research Journal* 31 (4): 481–508.

Demie, Feyisa. 2019. *Educational Inequality: Closing the Gap.* London: IOE Press.

Demie, Feyisa. 2021. "The Experience of Black Caribbean Pupils in School Exclusion in England." *Educational Review* 73 (1): 55–70.

Demuth, Clare. 1978. "'Sus' a Report on the Vagrancy Act 1824." *A Runnymede Trust Report*, 1–65. London.

Desmond, Matthew, and Mustafa Emirbayer. 2009a. *Racial Domination, Racial Progress: The Sociology of Race in America.* New York: McGraw Hill.

Desmond, Matthew, and Mustafa Emirbayer. 2009b. "What Is Racial Domination?" *Du Bois Review* 6 (2): 335–55.

Dhondy, Farrukh. 1982. "Who's Afraid of Ghetto Schools?" In *The Black Explosion in British Schools*, edited by Farrukh Dhondy, Barbara Beese, and Leila Hassan, 54–78. London: Race Today Publications.

Diamond, John, Antonia Randolph, and James Spillane. 2004. "Teachers' Expectations and Sense of Responsibility for Student Learning: The Importance of Race, Class, and Organizational Habitus." *Anthropology & Education Quarterly* 35 (1): 75–98.

Dillabough, Jo-Anne. 2004. "Class, Culture and the 'Predicaments of Masculine Domination': Encountering Pierre Bourdieu." *British Journal of Sociology of Education* 25 (4): 489–506.

Dillabough, Jo-Anne, and Jacqueline Kennelly. 2010. *Lost Youth in the Global City: Class, Culture and the Global Imaginary.* New York: RoutledgeFalmer.

Doharty, Nadena. 2015. "Hard Time Pressure Inna Babylon': Why Black History in Schools Is Failing to Meet the Needs of BME Students at Key Stage 3." In *The Runnymede School Report: Race, Education and Inequality in Britain*, edited by Claire Alexander, Debbie Weekes-Bernard, and Jason Arday. London: Runnymede Trust.

Doharty, Nadena. 2019. "'I Felt Dead': Applying a Racial Microaggressions Framework to Black Students' Experiences of Black History Month and Black History." *Race Ethnicity and Education* 22 (1): 110–29.

Domina, Thurston, Andrew McEachin, Paul Hanselman, Priyanka Agarwal, NaYoung Hwang, and Ryan Lewis. 2019. "Beyond Tracking and Detracking: The Dimensions of Organizational Differentiation in Schools." *Sociology of Education* 92 (3): 293–322.

Dornan, Inge. 2019. "'Book Don't Feed Our Children': Nonconformist Missionaries and the British and Foreign School Society in the Development of Elementary Education in the British West Indies before and after Emancipation." *Slavery & Abolition* 40 (1): 109–29.

Du Bois, W. E. B. 1899. *The Philadelphia Negro*. Philadelphia: University of Pennsylvania Press.

Du Bois, W. E. B. 1903. *The Souls of Black Folk*. Oxford: Oxford University Press.

Du Bois, W. E. B. 1920. "The Rise of the West Indian." *Crisis*, September 1920, XXI: 214–15.

Dumas, Michael. 2014. "Losing an Arm: Schooling as a Site of Black Suffering." *Race, Ethnicity and Education* 17 (1): 1–29.

Dumas, Michael, and Joseph Nelson. 2016. "(Re)Imagining Black Boyhood: Toward a Critical Framework for Educational Research." *Harvard Educational Review* 86 (1): 27–47.

Dunn, Hopeton. 1994. "Caribbean Telecommunications Policy: Fashioned by Debt, Dependency and Under-Development." *Caribbean Quarterly: A Journal of Caribbean Culture* 40 (2): 33–56.

Elliott-Cooper, Adam. 2021. *Black Resistance to British Policing*. Manchester: Manchester University Press.

Emejulu, Akwugo. 2011. "Re-Theorizing Feminist Community Development: Towards a Radical Democratic Citizenship." *Community Development Journal* 46 (3): 378–90.

Evans-Winters, Venus E. 2005. *Teaching Black Girls: Resiliency in Urban Classrooms*. New York: Peter Lang.

Evans-Winters, Venus E., and Jennifer Esposito. 2010. "Other People's Daughters: Critical Race Feminism and Black Girls' Education." *Educational Foundations* 24 (1): 11–24.

Fanon, Franz. 1959. *A Dying Colonialism*. New York: Grove Press.

Feliciano, Cynthia. 2005. "Does Selective Migration Matter? Explaining Ethnic Disparities in Educational Attainment among Immigrants' Children." *International Migration Review* 39 (4): 841–71.

Feliciano, Cynthia. 2018. "How Family, Immigrant Group and School Contexts Shape Ethnic Educational Disparities." *Ethnic and Racial Studies* 41 (2): 189–209.

Ferguson, Ann. 2000. *Bad Boys: Public Schools in The Making of Black Masculinity*. Ann Arbor: University of Michigan.

Figueroa, Esther, and Peter Patrick. 2002. "The Meaning of Kiss-Teeth." Department of Language and Linguistics: University of Essex. http://repository.essex.ac.uk/167/1/KSTpapwww.pdf.

File, Nigel, and Chris Power. 1981. *Black Settlers in Britain 1555–1958*. London: Heinemann.

Flood, Sarah, Miriam King, Renae Rodgers, Steven Ruggles, J. Robert Warren, and Michael Westberry. 2021. *Integrated Public Use Microdata Series, Current Population Survey: Version 9.0* [dataset]. Minneapolis, MN: IPUMS.

Foner, Nancy. 1979. "West Indians in New York City and London: A Comparative Analysis." *International Migration Review* 13 (2): 284–97.

Foner, Nancy. 2005. *In a New Land: A Comparative View of Immigration*. New York: New York University Press.

Foner, Nancy. 2009. *Across Generations: Immigrant Families in America*. Edited by Nancy Foner. New York: New York University Press.

Foner, Nancy. 2018. "Race in an Era of Mass Migration: Black Migrants in Europe and the United States." *Ethnic & Racial Studies* 41 (6): 1113–30.

Fordham, Signithia. 1996. *Blacked Out: Dilemmas of Race, Identity, and Success at Capital High*. Chicago: University of Chicago Press.

Fordham, Signithia, and John Ogbu. 1986. "Black Students' School Success: Coping with the 'Burden of "Acting White."'" *The Urban Review* 18 (3): 176–206.

Forsythe, Dennis. 1976. "Black Immigrants and the American Ethos: Theories and Observations." In *Caribbean Immigration to the United States*, edited by Roy Bryce-Laporte and Delores Mortimer, 55–82. Washington, D.C.: Smithsonian Institution.

Francis, Becky, Becky Taylor, and Antonia Tareshchenko. 2020. *Reassessing "Ability" Grouping: Improving Practice for Equity and Attainment*. London: Routledge.

Fraser, Nancy. 1992. "Rethinking the Public Sphere: A Contribution to the Critique of Actually Existing Democracy." In *Habermas and the Public Sphere*, edited by C. Calhoun, 109–42. Cambridge, MA: MIT Press.

Fryer, Peter. 1984. *Staying Power: The History of Black People in Britain*. New York: Pluto Press.

Gamoran, Adam. 2009. "Tracking and Inequality: New Directions for Research and Practice." In *The Routledge International Handbook of the Sociology of Education*, edited by Michael W. Apple, Stephen J. Ball, and Luis Armando Gandin, 22–45. London: Routledge.

Gans, Herbert. 2012. "Against Culture versus Structure." *Identities: Global Studies in Culture and Power* 19 (2): 125–34.

Gerrard, Jessica. 2013. "Self Help and Protest: The Emergence of Black Supplementary Schooling in England." *Race Ethnicity and Education* 16 (1): 32–58.

Gibson, Margaret, and John Ogbu. 1991. *Minority Status and Schooling: A Comparative Study of Immigrant and Involuntary Minorities*. New York: Garland Publishing Inc.

Gillborn, David. 1997. "Ethnicity and Educational Performance in the United Kingdom: Racism, Ethnicity, and Variability in Achievement." *Anthropology & Education* 28 (3): 375–93.

Gillborn, David. 2005. "Education Policy as an Act of White Supremacy: Whiteness, Critical Race Theory and Education Reform." *Journal of Education Policy* 20 (4): 485–505.

Gillborn, David. 2008. *Racism and Education. Racism and Education: Coincidence or Conspiracy?* London: Routledge.

Gillborn, David. 2011. "Race, Class and Disability: The Wrong Kind of 'Special'?" In *British Education Research Association Working Paper*, 1–14. London: BERA.

Gillborn, David, and Heidi Safia Mirza. 2000. "Educational Inequality: Mapping Race, Class and Gender. A Synthesis of Research Evidence." London: Office for Standards in Education.

Gilroy, Paul. 1990. "One Nation under a Groove: The Cultural Politics of 'Race' and Racism in Britain." In *Anatomy of Racism*, edited by David Theo Goldberg, 263–82. Minneapolis: University of Minnesota Press.

Gilroy, Paul. 1987. *There Ain't No Black in the Union Jack*. 2nd ed. London: Routledge.

Gilroy, Paul. 1993. *Small Acts: Thoughts on The Politics of Black Cultures*. London: Serpent's Tail.

Gilroy, Paul. 2004. *Between Camps: Nations, Cultures and the Allure of Race*. London: Routledge.

Gilroy, Paul. 2012. "'My Britain Is Fuck All': Zombie Multiculturalism and the Race Politics of Citizenship." *Identities: Global Studies in Culture and Power* 19 (4): 380–97.

Gilroy, Paul. 2013. "'We Got to Get Over Before We Go Under': Fragments for a History of Black Vernacular Neoliberalism." *New Formations* 201 (Winter): 23–38.

Giroux, Henry. 2002. *Breaking into Movies: Film and the Culture of Politics*. Malden, MA: Blackwell Publishers.

Giroux, Henry. 2008. "Hollywood Film as Public Pedagogy: Education in the Crossfire." *Afterimage* 35 (5): 7–13.

Givens, Jarvis R. 2021. *Fugitive Pedagogy: Carter G. Woodson and the Art of Black Teaching*. Cambridge, MA: Harvard University Press.

Glazer, Nathan, and Daniel Moynihan. 1963. *Beyond the Melting Pot: The Negroes, Puerto Ricans, Jews, Italians and Irish of New York City*. Cambridge, MA: MIT Press.

Go, Julian. 2011. *Patterns of Empire: The British and American Empires, 1688 to the Present*. Cambridge: Cambridge University Press.

Gordon, Shirley. 1958. "The Negro Education Grant, 1835–45: Its Application to Jamaica." *British Journal of Educational Studies* 6 (1): 140–50.

Gordon, Shirley. 1963. *A Century of West Indian Education: A Source Book*. London: Longmans Press.

Goulbourne, Harry, and John Solomos. 2004. "The Caribbean Diaspora: Some Introductory Remarks." *Ethnic and Racial Studies* 27 (4): 533–43.

Government, UK. 2021. "Commission on Race and Ethnic Disparities: The Report." *Commission on Race and Ethnic Disparities*. London. https://www.gov.uk/government/publications/the-report-of-the-commission-on-race-and-ethnic-disparities

Greene, Jack. 1987. "Colonial South Carolina and the Caribbean Connection." *South Carolina Historical Magazine* 88 (4): 192–210.

Greer, Christina. 2013. *Black Ethnics: Race, Immigration and the Pursuit of the American Dream*. Oxford: Oxford University Press.

Grenfell, Michael. 2008. *Pierre Bourdieu: Key Concepts*. Stockfield: Acumen.

Griffin, Farah Jasmine. 2000. "Black Feminists and Du Bois: Respectability, Protection, and Beyond." *The Annals of the American Academy of Political and Social Science* 568 (1): 28–40.

Grosvenor, Ian. 1997. *Assimilating Identities: Racism and Educational Policy in Post 1945 Britain*. London: Lawrence and Wishart.

Grundy, Saida. 2021. "Lifting the Veil on Campus Sexual Assault: Morehouse College, Hegemonic Masculinity, and Revealing Racialized Rape Culture through the Du Boisian Lens." *Social Problems* 68 (2): 226–49.

Hall, Catherine. 2008. "Making Colonial Subjects: Education in the Age of Empire." *History of Education* 37 (6): 773–87.

Hall, Stuart. 1986. "Gramsci's Relevance for the Study of Race and Ethnicity." *Journal of Communication Inquiry* 10 (2): 5–27.

Hall, Stuart. 1990. "Cultural Identity & Diaspora." In *Identity, Community, Culture, Difference*, edited by J. Rutherford, 222–37. London: Lawrence and Wishart.

Hall, Stuart. 1993a. "Negotiating Caribbean Identities." *Walter Rodney Memorial Lecture.* Coventry: Warwick University Centre for Caribbean Studies, 1–13.

Hall, Stuart. 1993b. "What Is This 'Black' in Black Popular Culture?" *Social Justice* 20 (1–2): 101–14.

Hall, Stuart. 1994. "Cultural Identity and Diaspora." In *Colonial Discourse and Post-Colonial Theory: A Reader*, edited by Patrick Williams and Laura Chrisman, 392–403. New York: Columbia University Press.

Hall, Stuart. 1996a. "Introduction: Who Needs Identity." In *Questions of Cultural Identity*, edited by Stuart Hall and Paul du Gray, 12th ed., 1–17. London: SAGE Publications.

Hall, Stuart. 1996b. "New Ethnicities." In *Stuart Hall: Critical Dialogues in Cultural Studies*, edited by David Morley and Kuan-Hsing Chen, 442–51. London: Routledge.

Hall, Stuart. 1996c. "The After-Life of Franz Fanon: Why Fanon? Why Now?" In *The Fact of Blackness: Frantz Fanon and Visual Representation*, edited by Alan Read, 12–37. London: Institute of Contemporary Arts.

Hall, Stuart. 1997a. "Introduction." In *Representation: Cultural Representations and Signifying Practices*, edited by Stuart Hall, 1–7. London: SAGE.

Hall, Stuart. 1997b. "The Local and the Global: Globalisation and Ethnicity." In *Dangerous Liaisons: Gender, Nation & Postcolonial Perspectives*, edited by Anne McClintock, Aamir Mufti, and Ella Shohat, 173–87. Minneapolis: University of Minnesota Press.

Hall, Stuart. 1999. "From Scarman to Stephen Lawrence." *History Workshop Journal* 48 (Autumn): 187–97.

Hall, Stuart. 2011. "The Neo-Liberal Revolution." *Cultural Studies* 25 (6): 705–28.

Hall, Stuart. 2012. "Postcolonialism and Cosmopolitanism: Towards a Worldly Understanding of Fascism and Europe's Colonial Crimes." In *After Cosmopolitanism*, edited by Paul Gilroy, 111–31. Abingdon: Routledge.

Hall, Stuart. 2016. "Old and New Identities, Old and New Ethnicities." In *Culture, Globalization and the World-System*, edited by Anthony D. King, 84–110. London: Macmillan.

Hall, Stuart. 2017a. *Familiar Stranger: A Life Between Two Islands*. Durham, NC: Duke University Press.

Hall, Stuart. 2017b. *The Fateful Triangle: Race, Ethnicity and Nation*. Cambridge, MA: Harvard University Press.

Hall, Stuart. 2017c. "Racism and Reaction." In *Selected Political Writings: The Great Moving Right Show and Other Essays*, edited by Sally Davison, David Featherstone, Michael Rustin, and Bill Schwarz, 142–57. Durham, NC: Duke University Press.

Hall, Stuart, Chas Critcher, Tony Jefferson, John Clarke, and Brian Roberts. 1978. *Policing the Crisis: Mugging, the State and Law and Order*. Basingstoke: Macmillan.

Hall, Stuart, and Tony Jefferson. 1993. *Resistance through Rituals: Youth Subcultures in Post-War Britain*. Edited by Stuart Hall and Tony Jefferson. London: Routledge.

Hamilton, LaMont. 2014. "Five on the Black Hand Side: Origins and Evolutions of the Dap." *Folklife Magazine*, September 22. https://folklife.si.edu/talkstory/2014/five-on-the-black-hand-sideorigins-and-evolutions-of-the-dap

Hamilton, Tod. 2019. *Immigration and the Remaking of Black America*. New York: Russell Sage Foundation.

Hamilton, Tod, Janeria Easley, and Angela Dixson. 2018. "Black Immigration, Occupational Niches, and Earnings Disparities Between U.S.-Born and Foriegn-Born

Black in the United States." *RSF: The Russell Sage Foundation Journal of the Social Sciences* 4 (1): 60–77.

Harper, Shaun, and Collin D. Wright Jr. 2013. "Succeeding in the City: A Report from the New York City Black and Latino Male High School Achievement Study." Philadelphia, PA: Center for the Study of Race and Equity in Education, University of Pennsylvania Graduate School of Education.

Haque, Zubaida. 2017. "Visible Minorities, Invisible Teachers: BME Teachers in the Education System in England." London: Runnymede Trust.

Harris, Angel. 2011. *Kids Don't Want to Fail: Oppositional Culture and the Black-White Achievement Gap*. Cambridge, MA: Harvard University Press.

Hickling-Hudson, Anne. 2006. "Cultural Complexity, Post-Colonialism and Education Change: Challenges for Comparative Educators." *International Review of Education* 52 (1): 201–18.

Hickman, Mary. 2005. "Ruling an Empire, Governing a Multinational State: The Impact of Britain's Historical Legacy on the Contemporary Ethno-Racial Regime." In *Ethnicity, Social Mobility and Public Policy: Comparing the US and UK*, edited by Glenn Loury, Tariq Modood, and Steven Teles, 21–49. Cambridge: Cambridge University Press.

Higginbotham, Evelyn Brooks. 1993. *Righteous Discontent: The Women's Movement in the Black Baptist Church, 1880–1920*. Cambridge, MA: Harvard University Press.

Hinzten, Percy. 2001. *West Indian in the West*. New York: New York University Press.

Hochschild, Jennifer, and John H. Mollenkopf. 2009. *Bringing Outsiders In: Transatlantic Perspectives on Immigrant Political Incorporation*. Edited by Jennifer Hochschild and John H. Mollenkopf. Ithaca, NY: Cornell University Press.

Hollins, Etta, and Maria Torres Guzman. 2005. "Research on Preparing Teachers for Diverse Populations." In *Studying Teacher Education: The Report of the AERA Panel on Research and Teacher Education*, 477–548. Mahwah, NJ: AERA/Lawrence Erlbaum Associates.

Holt, Thomas. 2000. *The Problem of Race in the Twenty-First Century*. Cambridge, MA: Harvard University Press.

Horton, James. 1993. *Free People of Color: Inside the African American Community*. Washington, D.C.: Smithsonian Institution Press.

Howard, Tyrone. 2010. *Why Race and Culture Matter in Schools: Closing the Achievement Gap in America's Classrooms*. New York: Teachers College Press.

Huberman, A. Michael, and Matthew B. Miles. 2002. *The Qualitative Researcher's Companion*. London: SAGE Publications.

Hudson, Brian. 1994. "Geography in Colonial Schools: The Classroom Experience in West Indian Literature." *Geography* 79 (4): 322–29.

Hunter, Marcus Anthony, and Zandria Robinson. 2018. *Chocolate Cities: The Black Map of American Life*. Oakland: University of California Press.

Ifantunji, Mosi. 2016. "A Test of the Afro Caribbean Model Minority Hypothesis: Exploring the Role of Cultural Attributes in Labor Market Disparities Between African Americans and Afro Caribbeans." *Du Bois Review: Social Science Research on Race* 31 (1): 109–38..

Ifantunji, Mosi. 2017. "Labor Market Disparities Between African Americans and Afro Caribbeans: Reexamining the Role of Immigrant Selectivity." *Sociological Forum* 32 (3): 522–43.

Imoagene, Onoso. 2012. "Being British vs. Being American: Identification Choices among the Nigerian Second-Generation." *Ethnic and Racial Studies* 35 (12): 2153–73.

Imoagene, Onoso. 2017. *Beyond Expectations: Second-Generation Nigerians in the United States and Britain*. Oakland: University of California Press.

Ingram, Nicola. 2011. "Within School and Beyond the Gate: The Complexities of Being Educationally Successful and Working Class." *Sociology* 45 (2): 278–302.

James, Winston. 1998. *Holding Aloft the Banner of Ethiopia: Caribbean Radicalism in Early Twentieth-Century America*. New York: Verso.

James, Winston. 2002. "Explaining Afro-Caribbean Social Mobility in the United States: Beyond the Sowell Thesis." *Comparative Studies in Society and History* 44 (2): 218–62.

Jenkins, Destin, and Justin Leroy. 2021. *Histories of Racial Capitalism*. New York: Columbia University Press.

Jensz, Felicity. 2012. "Missionaries and Indigenous Education in the 19th Century British Empire. Part II: Race, Class, and Gender." *History Compass* 10 (4): 310–21.

Jiménez, Tomás. 2010. *Replenished Ethnicity: Mexican Americans, Immigration, and Identity*. Berkeley: University of California Press.

Johnson, Fenton. 1919. "Credit Is Due the West Indian." *The Favorite Magazine*, December, 209–10.

Johnson, James Weldon. 1930. *Black Manhattan*. New York: Da Capo.

Jones, Ken. 2016. *Education in Britain: 1944 to the Present*. 2nd ed. Cambridge: Polity Press.

Jones, Nikki. 2009. *Between Good and Ghetto: African American Girls and Inner-City Violence*. New Brunswick, NJ: Rutgers University Press.

Joseph-Salisbury, Remi. 2020. "Race and Racism in English Secondary Schools." London: Runnymede Trust.

Kao, Grace. 1995. "Asian Americans as Model Minorities? A Look at Their Academic Performance." *Journal of Education Policy* 103: 121–59.

Kao, Grace, and Marta Tienda. 1998. "Educational Aspirations of Minority Youth." *American Journal of Education* 106 (3): 349–84.

Kasinitz, Philip. 1992. *Caribbean New York*. Ithaca, NY: Cornell University Press.

Kasinitz, Philip, John H. Mollenkopf, Mary C. Waters, and Jennifer Holdaway. 2008. *Inheriting the City: The Children of Immigrants Come of Age*. New York: Russell Sage Foundation.

Kasinitz, Philip, Juan Battle, and Ines Miyares. 2001. "Fade to Black? The Children of West Indian Immigrants in South Florida." In *Ethnicities*, edited by Ruben Rambaut and Alejandro Portes, 267–300. Berkeley: University of California Press.

Kasinitz, Philip, and Milton Vickerman. 2001. "Ethnic Niches & Racial Traps: Jamaicans in the New York Regional Economy." In *Migration, Transnationalization & Race in a Changing New York*, edited by Héctor R. Cordero-Guzmán, Robert C. Smith, and Ramón Grosfoguel, 191–211. Philadelphia: Temple University Press.

Kaufman, Miranda. 2017. *Black Tudors*. London: One World.

Kelley, Robin D. G. 2002. *Freedom Dreams: The Black Radical Imagination*. Boston: Beacon Press.

Kelly, Gail. 1979. "The Relation Between Colonial and Metropolitan Schools: A Structural Analysis." *Comparative Education* 15 (2): 209–15.

Kennedy, Margaret, and Martin Power. 2010. "'The Smokescreen of Meritocracy': Elite Education in Ireland and the Reproduction of Class Privilege." *Journal of Critical Educational Policy Studies* 8 (2): 223–48.

Kincaid, Jamaica. 1991. "On Seeing England for the First Time." *Transitions* 51 (1): 32–40.

Kirkland, David. 2010. "English(Es) in Urban Contexts: Politics, Pluralism, and Possibilities." *English Education* 42 (3): 293–306.

Koh, Aaron. 2014. "Doing Class Analysis in Singapore's Elite Education: Unraveling the Smokescreen of 'Meritocratic Talk.'" *Globalisation, Societies and Education* 12 (2): 196–210.

Korthagen, Fred, Jos Kessels, Bob Koster, Bram Lagerwerf, and Theo Wubbels. 2001. *Linking Theory and Practice: The Pedagogy of Realistic Teacher Education.* Mahwah, NJ: Lawrence Erlbaum Associates.

LaBennett, Oneka. 2011. *She's Mad Real: Popular Culture and West Indian Girls in Brooklyn.* New York: New York University Press.

LaBennett, Oneka, and Brian Purnell. 2009. "Special Issue: The Bronx African American History Project." *Afro-Americans in New York Life and History* 33 (2): 7–23.

Lacy, Karyn. 2007. *Blue-Chip Black: Race, Class and Status in the New Black Middle Class.* Berkeley: University of California Press.

Lammy, David. 2010. "The Oxbridge Whitewash." *The Guardian*, December 6, 2010. https://www.theguardian.com/commentisfree/2010/dec/06/the-oxbridge-whitewash-black-students.

Lamont, Michèle, Graziella Silva, Jessica Welburn, Joshua Guetzkow, Nissim Mizrachi, Hanna Herzog, and Elisa Reis. 2016. *Getting Respect: Responding to Stigma and Discrimination in the United States, Brazil and Israel.* Princeton, NJ: Princeton University Press.

Lamson, Peggy. 1973. *The Glorious Failure: Black Congressman Robert Brown Elliott and the Reconstruction in South Carolina.* New York: Norton.

Lareau, Annette. 2011. *Unequal Childhoods: Race, Class, and Family Life. A Decade Later.* Berkeley: University of California Press.

Lareau, Annette. 2021. *Listening to People: A Practical Guide to Interviewing, Participant Observation, Data Analysis, and Writing It All Up.* Chicago: University of Chicago Press.

Law, Ian, and Sarah Swann. 2011. *Ethnicity and Education in England and Europe: Gangstas, Geeks and Gorjas.* Aldershot: Ashgate.

Lee, Changdoo, and George DeVos. 1981. *Koreans in Japan.* Berkeley: University of California Press.

Lee, Jennifer, and Min Zhou. 2015. *The Asian American Achievement Paradox.* New York: Russell Sage Foundation.

Lee, Jennifer, and Min Zhou. 2016. "Unravelling the Link between Culture and Achievement." *Ethnic and Racial Studies* 39 (13): 2404–11.

Lee, Jennifer, and Min Zhou. 2017. "Why Class Matters Less for Asian-American Academic Achievement." *Journal of Ethnic and Migration Studies* 43 (14): 2316–30.

Lee, Stacey. 2005. *Up Against Whiteness: Race, School and Immigrant Youth.* New York: Teachers College Press.

Lee, Stacey. 2009. *Unraveling the "Model Minority" Stereotype: Listening to Asian American Youth.* 2nd ed. New York: Teachers College Press.

Lee, Yun. 1991. "Koreans in Japan and the United States." In *Minority Status and Schooling: A Comparative Study of Immigrant and Involuntary Minorities,* edited by Margaret Gibson and John Ogbu, 3–33. New York: Garland Press.

LeTendre, Gerald, Barbara Hofer, and Hidetada Shimizu. 2003. "What Is Tracking? Cultural Expectations in the United States, Germany and Japan." *American Educational Research Journal* 40 (1): 43–89.

Lew, Jamie. 2006. *Asian Americans in Class: Charting the Achievement Gap Among Korean American Youth*. New York: Teachers College Press.

Lewis, Amanda. 2003. "Everyday Race-Making: Navigating Racial Boundaries in Schools." *American Behavioral Scientist* 47 (3): 283–305.

Lewis, Amanda, and John Diamond. 2015. *Despite the Best Intentions: How Racial Inequality Thrives in Good Schools*. New York: Oxford University Press.

Lewis, Gail. 2013. "Unsafe Travel: Experiencing Intersectionality and Feminist Displacements." *Signs: Journal of Women in Culture and Society* 38 (4): 869–92.

Lewis-McCoy, L'Heureux. 2010. "Shadow Boxing the Self: Confronting Black Male Privilege." Presented at the Founder's Day Symposium, Morehouse College. https://www.youtube.com/watch?v=BfYvL4wnWeY.

Lewis-McCoy, L'Heureux. 2016. "Confronting Black Male Privilege." In *Hyper Sexual, Hyper Masculine: Gender, Race and Sexuality in the Identities of Contemporary Black Men*, edited By Brittany C. Slatton, Kamesha Spates, 75–84. London: Routledge.

Light, Ivan. 1972. *Ethnic Enterprise in America: Business and Welfare among Chinese, Japanese and Blacks*. Berkeley: University of California Press.

López, Nancy. 2002. "Race-Gender Experiences and Schooling: Second-Generation Dominican, West Indian, and Haitian Youth in New York City." *Race Ethnicity and Education* 5 (1): 37–41.

Lougheed, Kevin. 2021. "'Teach the Mutual Interests of the Mother Country and Her Dependencies': Education and Reshaping Colonial Governance in Trinidad." *History of Education* 50 (60): 745–63.

Loury, Glenn C., Tariq Modood, and Steven M. Teles. 2005. *Ethnicity, Social Mobility and Public Policy: Comparing US and UK*. Edited by Glenn C. Loury, Tariq Modood, and Steven M. Teles. Cambridge: Cambridge University Press.

Love, Bettina. 2012. *Hip Hop's Li'l Sistas Speak: Negotiating Hip Hop Identities and Politics in the New South*. New York: Peter Lang.

Lucas, Samuel Roundfield. 1999. *Tracking Inequality: Stratification and Mobility in American High Schools. Sociology of Education Series*. Teachers College Press.

Luna, Zakiya, and Whitney Pirtle. 2021. *Black Feminist Sociology: Perspectives and Praxis*. New York: Routledge.

Lyiscott, Jamila, Limarys Caraballo, and Ernest Morrell. 2018. "An Anticolonial Framework for Urban Teacher Preparation." *The New Educator* 14 (3): 231–51.

Mac an Ghaill, Máirtín. 1988. *Young, Gifted and Black: Student-Teacher Relations in the Schooling of Black Youth*. Milton Keynes: Open University Press.

Maddox, Tyesha. 2018. "More Than Auxiliary: Caribbean Women and Social Organizations in the Interwar Period." *Caribbean Review of Gender Studies* 12: 67–94.

Malliet, A. M. Wendell. 1938. British West Indians Outnumber All Other Groups in Harlem. *Amsterdam News*, March 5, 7–20.

Massey, Douglas S., Margarita Mooney, Kimberly Torres, and Camille Charles. 2007. "Black Immigrants and Black Natives Attending Selective Colleges and Universities in the United States." *American Journal of Education* 113: 243–71.

Matory, J. Lorand. 2015. *Stigma and Culture: Last-Place Anxiety in Black America*. Chicago: University of Chicago Press.

Maurer, Bill. 2001. "Islands in the Net: Rewiring Technological and Financial Circuits in the 'Offshore' Caribbean." *Comparative Studies in Society and History* 43 (3): 467–501.

Mayblin, Lucy. 2017. *Asylum after Empire: Colonial Legacies in the Politics of Asylum Seeking*. London: Rowman & Littlefield Publishers.

Maylor, Uvanney. 2009a. "Is It Because I'm Black? A Black Female Research Experience." *Race Ethnicity and Education* 12 (1): 53–64.

Maylor, Uvanney. 2009b. "'They Do Not Relate to Black People like Us': Black Teachers as Role Models for Black Pupils." *Journal of Education Policy* 24 (1): 1–21.

McKay, Claude. 1912. *Songs of Jamaica*. Kingston: Aston W. Gardner.

McQueen, Steve. 2020. "Education." *Small Axe*: British Broadcasting Corporation.

Medford, Marcelle. 2019. "Racialization and Black Multiplicity: Generative Paradigms for Understanding Black Immigrants." *Sociology Compass* 13 (7): e12717.

Mickelson, Roslyn. 1990. "The Attitude-Achievement Paradox among Black Adolescents." *Sociology of Education* 63 (January): 44–61.

Mills, C. Wright. 2000. *The Sociological Imagination*. Oxford: Oxford University Press.

Mirza, Heidi Safia. 1992. *Young, Female, and Black*. New York: Routledge.

Mirza, Heidi Safia. 2006. "'Race,' Gender and Educational Desire." *Race Ethnicity and Education* 9 (2): 137–58.

Mirza, Heidi Safia. 2009. *Race, Gender and Educational Desire: Why Black Women Succeed and Fail*. London: Routledge.

Mirza, Heidi, and Veena Meetoo. 2012. *Respecting Difference: Race, Faith and Culture for Teacher Educators*. London: Institute of Education Press.

Mirza, Heidi Safia, and Diane Reay. 2000. "Spaces and Places of Black Educational Desire: Rethinking Black Supplementary Schools as a New Social Movement." *Sociology* 34 (3): 521–44.

Mirza, Heidi Safia, and Diane Reay. 2005. "Doing Parental Involvement Differently: Black Women's Participation as Educators and Mothers in Black Supplementary Schooling." In *Activating Participation: Parents and Teachers Working Towards Partnership*, edited by Gill Crozier and Diane Reay, 48–62. Stoke-on-Trent: Trentham Books.

Mittelberg, David, and Mary Waters. 1992. "The Process of Ethnogenesis among Haitian and Israeli Immigrants in the United States." *Ethnic & Racial Studies* 15 (1): 412–35.

Model, Suzanne. 1991. "Caribbean Immigrants: A Black Success Story?" *International Migration Review* 25: 248–76.

Model, Suzanne. 1997. "An Occupational Tale of Two Cities: Minorities in London and New York." *Demography* 34: 539–50.

Model, Suzanne. 2008. *West Indian Immigrants: A Black Success Story?* New York: Russell Sage Foundation.

Model, Suzanne. 2018. "Selectivity Is Still in the Running: A Comment on Ifatunji's 'Labor Market Disparities." *Sociological Forum* 33 (2): 1–6.

Modood, Tariq. 1992. *Not Easy Being British: Colour, Culture Citizenship*. Stoke-on-Trent: Runnymede Trust and Trentham Books.

Morris, Monique. 2016. *Pushout: The Criminalization of Black Girls in Schools*. New York: The New Press.

Morrison, Mosi. 2011. "Are Black Immigrants A Model Minority: Race, Ethnicity and Social Mobility in the United States." Ph.D. Dissertation: University of Illinois at Chicago.

Mose, Tamara. 2011. *Raising Brooklyn: Nannies, Childcare and Caribbeans Creating Community*. New York: New York University Press.

Museus, Samuel, Shaun Harper, and Andrew Nicols. 2010. "Racial Differences in the Formation of Postsecondary Educational Expectations: A Structural Model." *Teachers College Record* 112 (3): 811–42.

Nayak, Anoop. 2003. "Last of the 'Real Geordies'? White Masculinities and the Subcultural Response to De-industrialisation." *Environment and Planning* 21 (1): 7–26.

Neckerman, Kathryn, Prudence Carter, and Jennifer Lee. 1999. "Segmented Assimilation and Minority Cultures of Mobility." *Ethnic and Racial Studies* 22 (6): 945–65.

Newham Monitoring Project. 1991. "Newham: The Forging of a Black Community." *Working Paper 304*: 1–34. London.

Nigel Bollano, O. 1987. "United States Cultural Influences on Belize: Television and Education as 'Vehicles of Import.'" *Caribbean Quarterly* 33 (3–4): 60–74.

Noguera, Pedro. 2008. *The Trouble with Black Boys: . . . And Other Reflections on Race, Equity and the Future of Public Education*. San Francisco: John Wiley & Sons.

Nubia, Onyeka. 2019. *England's Other Countrymen: Black Tudor Society*. London: Zed Books.

Oakes, Jeannie. 1985. *Keeping Track: How Schools Structure Inequality*. New Haven, CT: Yale University Press.

Ochoa, Gilda. 2013. *Academic Profiling: Latinos, Asian Americans and the Achievement Gap*. Minneapolis: University of Minnesota Press.

O'Connor, Carla, Jennifer Mueller, L'Heureux Lewis-McCoy, Deborah Rivas-Drake, and Seneca Rosenberg. 2011. "'Being' Black and Strategizing for Excellence in a Racially Stratified Academic Hierarchy." *American Education Research Journal* 48 (6): 1232–57.

OECD. 2014. "Are Grouping and Selecting Students for Different Schools Related to Students' Motivation to Learn? Pisa in Focus." *Organisation for Economic Cooperation and Development Working Paper 1030*: Paris.

Office of Equity and Access. 2021. "AP for All." New York City: New York City Department of Education. https://apforallnyc.com/.

Office of National Statistics. 2011. "2011 Census: Key Statistics and Quick Statistics for Local Authorities in the United Kingdom." https://www.ons.gov.uk/peoplepopulationa ndcommunity/populationandmigration/populationestimates/bulletins/keystatisticsa ndquickstatisticsforlocalauthoritiesintheunitedkingdom/2013-10-11

Ogbu, John. 1974. *The Next Generation: An Ethnography of Education in an Urban Neighborhood*. New York: Academic Press.

Ogbu, John. 1978. *Minority Education and Caste*. New York: Academic Press.

Oliver, Caroline, and Karen O'Reilly. 2010. "A Bourdieusian Analysis of Class and Migration: Habitus and the Individualizing Process." *Sociology* 44 (1): 49–66.

Olusoga, David. 2016. *Black and British: A Forgotten History*. London: Macmillian Press.

Olwig, Karen Fog. 1993. *Global Culture, Island Identity: Continuity and Change in the Afro-Caribbean Community of Nevis*. New York: Harwood Academic Publishers.

Omi, Michael, and Howard Winant. 1994. *Racial Formation in the United States: From the 1960s to the 1990s*. 2nd ed. New York: Routledge.

Oyěwùmí, Oyèrónké. 2003. *African Women & Feminism: Reflecting on the Politics of Sisterhood*. Trenton, NJ: Africa World Press.

Parascandola, Louis J. 2005. *Look for Me All Around You: Anglophone Caribbean Immigrants in the Harlem Renaissance*. Wayne State University Press.

Paris, Django, and H. Samy Alim. 2017. *Culturally Sustaining Pedagogies: Teaching and Learning for Justice in a Changing World*. New York: Teachers College Press.

Patillo-McCoy, Mary. 1999. *Black Picket Fences: Privilege and Peril in the Black Middle Class*. Chicago: University of Chicago Press.

Patterson, Orlando. 1982. *Slavery and Social Death*. Cambridge, MA: Harvard University Press.

Patterson, Orlando. 2005. "Four Modes of Ethnosomatic Stratification: Blacks in Europe and the Americas." In *Ethnicity and Social Mobility in the United States and the United Kingdom*, edited by Glenn Loury, Tariq Modood, and Steven M. Teles, 67–122. Cambridge: Cambridge University Press.

Patterson, Orlando, and Ethan Fosse. 2015. *The Cultural Matrix: Understanding Black Youth*. Cambridge, MA: Harvard University Press.

Paulle, Bowen. 2013. *Toxic Schools: High Poverty Education in New York and Amsterdam*. Chicago: University of Chicago Press.

Peach, Ceri. 1995. "Profile of the Black Caribbean Population in Great Britian." In *Profile of the Ethnic Minority Populations in Great Britain*. London: Office of the Population Census and Surveys.

Perry, Kennetta. 2016. *London Is the Place for Me: Black Britons, Citizenship and the Politics of Race*. Oxford: Oxford University Press.

Phillips, Glenn O. 1981. "The Response of a West Indian Activist: D. A. Straker, 1842–1908." *Journal of Negro History* 66 (2): 128–39.

Phillips, Mike, and Trevor Phillips. 1998. *Windrush: The Irresistible Rise of Multi-Racial Britain*. London: Harper Collins Publishers.

Phoenix, Ann. 2009. "De-colonising Practices: Negotiating Narratives from Racialised and Gendered Experiences of Education." *Race Ethnicity and Education* 12 (1): 101–14.

Pierre, Jemima. 2004. "Black Immigrants in the United States and the 'Cultural Narratives' of Ethnicity." *Identities: Global Studies in Culture and Power* 11 (1): 141–70.

Pilkington, Edward. 1988. *Beyond the Mother Country: West Indians and the Notting Hill White Riots*. London: IB Tauris.

Portes, Alejandro, and Ramon Grosfoguel. 1994. "Caribbean Diasporas: Migration and Ethnic Communities." *The ANNALS of the American Academy of Political and Social Science* 533 (1): 48–69.

Rampton, Anthony. 1981. *West Indian Children in Our Schools: Interim Report of the Committee of Inquiry into the Education of Children from Ethnic Minority Groups*. London: Her Majesty's Stationery Office.

Randolph, Antonia. 2015. *The Wrong Kind of Different: Challenging the Meaning of Diversity in American Classrooms*. New York: Teachers College Press.

Ransby, Barbara. 2003. *Ella Baker and the Black Freedom Movement: A Radical Democratic Vision*. Chapel Hill: University of North Carolina Press.

Ray, Ranita. 2017. *The Making of a Teenage Service Class: Poverty and Mobility in an American City*. Berkeley: University of California Press.

Ray, Ranita. 2022. "School as a Hostile Institution: How Black and Immigrant Girls of Color Experience the Classroom." *Gender & Society* 36 (1): 88–111.

Reay, Diane. 2001. "Finding or Losing Yourself? Working Class Relationships to Education." *Journal of Education Policy* 16 (4): 333–46.

Reay, Diane. 2004a. "Education and Cultural Capital: The Implications of Changing Trends in Education Policies." *Cultural Trends* 13 (50): 73–86.

Reay, Diane, 2004b. "'It's all becoming a habitus': Beyond the habitual use of habitus in educational research." *British Journal of Sociology of Education* 25 (4): 431–44.

Reay, Diane. 2004c. "'Mostly Roughs and Toughs': Social Class, Race and Representation in Inner City Schooling." *Sociology* 38 (5): 1005–23.

Reay, Diane. 2005. "Thinking Class, Making Class." *British Journal of Sociology of Education* 26 (1): 139–43.

Reay, Diane. 2007. "Unruly Places: Inner-City Comprehensives, Middle-Class Imaginaries and Working-Class Children." *Urban Studies* 44 (7): 1191–1203.

Reay, Diane. 2009. *Making Sense of White Working Class Educational Underachievement. Who Cares about the White Working Class?*. Runnymede Trust: London.

Reay, Diane. 2017. *Miseducation: Inequality, Education and the Working Classes.* Bristol: Policy Press.

Reay, Diane, and Heidi Safia Mirza. 1997. "Uncovering Genealogies of the Margins: Black Supplementary Schooling." *British Journal of Sociology* 18 (4): 477–99.

Reay, Diane, Miriam David, and Stephen Ball. 2005. *Degrees of Choice: Social Class, Race and Gender in Higher Education.* Stoke-on-Trent: Trentham Press.

Reid, Ira. 1938. "Negro Immigration to the United States." *Social Forces* 16 (3): 411–17.

Reid, Ira. 1939. *The Negro Immigrant: His Background Characteristics and Social Adjustment, 1899–1937.* New York: Columbia University Press.

Reddock, Rhoda. 2007. "Diversity, Difference and Caribbean Feminism: The Challenge of Anti-Racism." *Caribbean Review of Gender Studies* 1 (1): 1–24.

Reddock, Rhoda. 2010. "Gender and Achievement in Higher Education." *Journal of Education and Development in the Caribbean* 12 (1): 1–21.

Reddock, Rhoda. 2014. "Radical Caribbean Social Thought: Race, Class Identity and the Postcolonial Nation." *Current Sociology* 62 (4): 493–511.

Reynolds, Tracey. 2009. "Exploring the Absent/Present Dilemma: Black Fathers, Family Relationships, and Social Capital in Britain." *The Annals of the American Academy of Political and Social Science* 624 (1): 12–28.

Reynolds, Tracey. 2010a. "Single Mothers Not the Cause of Black Boy's Underachievement." London: Runnymede Trust. https://www.runnymedetrust.org/events-conferences/econferences/econference/alias-3.html.

Reynolds, Tracey. 2010b. "Transnational Family Networks, Cultural Belonging and Social Capital among Second-Generation British-Caribbean 'Returning' Migrants." *Ethnic and Racial Studies* 33 (5): 797–815.

Rich, Paul. 1987. "The Black Diaspora in Britain: Afro-Caribbean Students and the Struggle for a Political Identity, 1900–1950." *Immigrants & Minorities: Historical Studies in Ethnicity, Migration and Diaspora* 6 (2): 151–73.

Richards, Bedelia. 2007. "West Indian Roots & American Branches: Ethnicity, School Context & Academic Engagement among Afro-Caribbean Students." Doctoral Dissertation. Baltimore: Johns Hopkins University.

Richards, Bedelia. 2013. "Ethnic Identity on Display: West Indian Youth and the Creation of Ethnic Boundaries in High School." *Ethnic and Racial Studies* 11 (1): 1–20.

Richards, Bedelia. 2017. "Tracking and Racialization in Schools: The Experiences of Second-Generation West Indians in New York City." *Sociology of Race and Ethnicity* 3 (1): 126–40.

Richardson, Brian. 2007. *Tell It Like It Is: How Our Schools Fail Black Children.* Edited by Brian Richardson. 2nd ed. London: Trentham Books.

Rickford, John, and Angela Rickford. 1999. "Cut-Eye and Suck-Teeth: African Words and Gestures in New World Guise." In *African American Vernacular English: Features, Evolution, Educational Implications*, edited by John R. Rickford, 157–73. Oxford: Blackwell Publishers.

Ridgeway, Cecilia. 1982. "Status in Groups: The Importance of Motivation." *American Sociological Review.* February: 76–88.

Ridgeway, Cecilia. 2011. *Framed by Gender: How Gender Inequality Persists in the Modern World.* Oxford: Oxford University Press.

Ridgeway, Cecilia. 2019. *Status: Why Is It Everywhere? Why Does It Matter?* New York: Russell Sage Foundation.

Ridgeway, Cecilia, and Shelley Correll. 2006. "Consensus and the Creation of Status Beliefs." *Social Forces* 85 (1): 431–53.

Roberts, David, and Minelle Mahtani. 2010. "Neoliberalizing Race, Racing Neoliberalism: Placing 'Race' in Neoliberal Discourses." *Antidope* 42 (2): 248–57.

Robinson, Cedric. 2000 [1983]. *Black Marxism: The Making of the Black Radical Tradition.* Chapel Hill: University of North Carolina Press.

Robinson, Cedric. 2020. *Black Marxism, Revised and Updated Third Edition: The Making of the Black Radical Tradition.* 3rd ed. Chapel Hill: University of North Carolina Press.

Rodgers, Daniel T. 2000. *Atlantic Crossings: Social Politics in a Progressive Age.* Cambridge,, MA: Harvard University Press.

Rogers, Reuel. 2006. *Afro-Caribbean Immigrants and the Politics of Incorporation.* Cambridge and New York: Cambridge University Press.

Rollock, Nicola. 2007. "Why Black Girls Don't Matter: Exploring How Race and Gender Shape Academic Success in an Inner City School." *Support for Learning* 22 (4): 197–202.

Rollock, Nicola, David Gillborn, Carol Vincent, and Stephen Ball. 2015. *The Colour of Class: The Educational Strategies of the Black Middle Classes.* New York: Routledge.

Rong, Xue Lan, and Frank Brown. 2001. "The Effects of Immigrant Generation and Ethnicity on Educational Attainment among Young African and Caribbean Blacks in the United States." *Harvard Educational Review* 71 (3): 536–66.

Rooke, Patricia. 1978. "The Pedagogy of Conversion: Missionary Education to Slaves in the British West Indies, 1800–33." *Paedagogica Historica* 18 (1): 356–74.

Rooke, Patricia. 1980. "Missionaries as Pedagogies: A Reconsideration of the Significance of Education for Slaves and Apprentices in the British West Indies, 1800–1838." *History of Education* 9 (1): 75–87.

Ruggles, Steven, Sarah Flood, Ronald Goeken, Megan Schouweiler, and Matthew Sobek. 2022. *IPUMS USA: Version 12.0* [dataset]. Minneapolis, MN: IPUMS.

Scott, David. 2004. *Conscripts of Modernity: The Tragedy of Colonial Englightenment.* Durham, NC: Duke University Press.

Scott, David. 2017. *Stuart Hall's Voice: Intimations of an Ethics of Receptive Generosity.* Durham, NC: Duke University Press.

Sealey-Ruiz, Yolanda. 2022. "An Archaeology of the Self for Our Times: Another Talk to Teachers." *English Journal* 111 (5): 21–26.

Sewell, Tony, and Richard Majors. 2001. "Black Boys and Schooling: An Intervention Framework for Understanding the Dilemmas of Masculinity, Identity and Underachievement." In *Educating Our Black Children: New Directions and Radical Approaches,* edited by Richard Majors, 197–216. London: Routledge.

Sharpe, Jenny. 2003. *Ghosts of Slavery: A Literary Archaeology of Black Women's Lives.* Minneapolis: University of Minnesota Press.

Shedd, Carla. 2015. *Unequal City: Race, Schools, and Perceptions of Injustice.* New York: Russell Sage Foundation.

Shepherd, Verene, and Carleen Payne. 2003. "Comparisons: The Caribbean." In *A Companion to Colonial America*, edited by Daniel Vickers, 425–30. London: Blackwell Publishers.

Shilliam, Robbie. 2010. *International Relations and Non-Western Thought: Imperialism, Colonialism and Investigations of Global Modernity*. London: Routledge.

Showunmi, Victoria. 2017. "The Role of the "Black Girls' Club": Challenging the Status Quo." In *Feminist Pedagogy, Practice, and Activism*, edited by Jennifer L. Martin, Ashley E. Nickels, and Martina Sharp-Grier, 229–46. London: Routledge.

Shyllon, Folarin. 1977. *Black People in Britain 1555–1833*. London: Oxford University Press for The Institute of Race Relations.

Silverman, David. 2010. *Doing Qualitative Research*. 3rd ed. London: SAGE Publications.

Simko, Christina, and Jeffrey Olick. 2021. "What We Talk about When We Talk about Culture: A Multi-Facet Approach." *American Journal of Cultural Sociology* 9: 431–59.

Simon, David. 2002. *The Wire: The Complete Series*. An HBO Production, DVD, 23 discs (2002–8).

Sivanandan, Ambalaner. 2008. "Race and Resistance: The IRR Story." *Race and Class* 50 (2): 1–30.

Small, Mario, David Harding, and Michèle Lamont. 2010. "Reconsidering Culture and Poverty Reconsidering Culture and Poverty." *The Annals of the American Academy of Political and Social Science* 629: 6–27.

Smith, Faith. 2002. *Creole Recitations: John Jacob Thomas and Colonial Formation in the Late Nineteenth-Century Caribbean*. Charlottesville: University of Virginia Press.

Smith, Owens. 1985. "The Politics of Income and Education Differences between Blacks and West Indians." *Journal of Ethnic Studies* 13 (3): 17–30.

Snyder, Donald. 1983. "Caribbean Television in the Caribbean: The Case of Jamaica." *Atlantic Economic Journal* 11 (3): 56–62.

Solomon, R. Patrick. 1992. *Black Resistance in High School: Forging a Separatist Culture*. New York: State University of New York Press.

Solomos, John. 2003. *Race and Racism in Britain*. 3rd ed. New York: Palgrave Macmillan.

Solomos, John. 2019. "'Strangers in Their Own Land': Powellism's Policy Impact." *Patterns of Prejudice* 53 (4): 321–36.

Sowell, Thomas. 1975. *Race and Economics*. New York: David McKay.

Sowell, Thomas. 1978. "Three Black Histories." In *Essays and Data on American Ethnic Groups*, edited by Thomas Sowell, 45–73. Washington, D.C.: The Urban Institute.

Steele, Claude, and Joshua Aronson. 1995. "Stereotype Threat and the Intellectual Test Performance of African Americans." *Journal of Personality and Social Psychology* 69 (5): 797.

Steinbock-Pratt, Sarah. 2019. *Educating the Empire: American Teachers and Contested Colonization in the Philippines*. Cambridge: Cambridge University Press.

Strand, Steve. 2010. "Do Some Schools Narrow the Gap? Differential School Effectiveness by Ethnicity, Gender, Poverty and Prior Achievement." *School Effectiveness and School Improvement* 21 (3): 289–314.

Strand, Steve. 2012. "The White British—Black Caribbean Achievement Gap: Tests, Tiers and Teacher Expectations." *British Educational Research Journal* 38 (1): 75–101.

Strand, Steve. 2014. "Ethnicity, Gender, Social Class and Achievement Gaps at Age 16: Intersectionality and 'Getting It' for the White Working Class." *Research Papers in Education* 29 (2): 131–71.

Swann, Michael. 1985. "Education for All: Report of the Committee of Enquiry into the Education of Children from Ethnic Minority Groups." *Committee of Inquiry into the Education of Children from Ethnic Minority Groups Committee appointed by the Department of Education and Science under the chairmanship of Lord Swann.* London: HM Stationery Office.

Swidler, Ann. 1986. "Culture in Action: Symbols and Strategies." *American Sociological Review* 51 (2): 273–86.

Thomas, Deborah A. 2007. "Blackness Across Borders: Jamaican Diasporas and New Politics of Citizenship." *Identities: Global Studies in Culture and Power.* 14 (1–2): 111–33.

Thomas, Deborah A. 2019. *Political Life in the Wake of the Plantation Sovereignty, Witnessing, Repair.* Durham, NC: Duke University Press.

Thomas, Kevin J. A. 2012. "A Demographic Profile of Black Caribbean Immigrants in the United States." Washington, D.C.: Policy.

Thomas, Todne. 2021. *Kincraft: The Making of Black Evangelical Sociality.* Durham, NC: Duke University Press.

Thomson, Pat. 2005. "Bringing Bourdieu to Policy Sociology: Codification, Misrecognition and Exchange Value in the UK Context." *Journal of Education Policy* 20 (6): 741–58.

Tikly, Leon. 2022. "Racial Formation and Education: A Critical Analysis of the Sewell Report." *Ethnicities* OnlineFirst: 1–25.

Tikly, Leon, Jo Haynes, Chamion Caballero, John Hill, and David Gillborn. 2006. "Evaluation of Aiming High: African Caribbean Achievement Project." London.

Tomlinson, Sally. 1977. "Race and Education in Britain 1960–77: An Overview of the Literature." *Sage Race Relations Abstracts* 2 (4): 3–30.

Tomlinson, Sally. 1978. "West Indian Children and ESN Schooling." *Journal of Ethnic and Migration Studies* 6 (3): 235–42.

Tomlinson, Sally. 1981. *Educational Subnormality: A Study in Decision-Making.* London: Routledge & Kegan Paul.

Tomlinson, Sally. 1991. "Ethnicity & Educational Attainment in England: An Overview." *Anthropology & Education* 22 (2): 121–39.

Tomlinson, Sally. 2019. *Education and Race: From Empire to Brexit.* Bristol: Policy Press.

Treitler, Vilna Bashi. 2007. *Survival of the Knitted: Immigrant Social Networks in a Stratified World.* Stanford, CA: Stanford University Press.

Treitler, Vilna Bashi. 2013. *The Ethnic Project: Transforming Racial Fiction into Ethnic Faction.* Stanford, CA: Stanford University Press.

Troyna, Barry. 1984. "Fact or Artefact?: The 'Educational Underachievement' of Black Pupils." *British Journal of Sociology of Education* 5 (2): 153–66.

Troyna, Barry. 1993. *Racism and Education: Research Perspectives.* Buckingham: Open University Press.

Troyna, Barry, and Jenny Williams. 1986. *Racism, Education and the State: The Racialization of Education Policy.* London: Croom Helm.

Turner, Mary. 1982. *Slaves and Missionaries: The Disintegration of Jamaican Slave Society 1787–1834.* Urbana: University of Illinois Press.

Turner, Trevor. 1977. "The Socialisation Intent in Colonial Jamaican Education, 1867–1911." *Caribbean Journal of Education* 4 (1): 50–83.

Tyler, Tom, Jeffrey Fagan, and Amanda Geller. 2014. "Street Stops and Police Legitimacy: Teachable Moments in Young Urban Men's Legal Socialization." *Journal of Empirical Legal Studies* 11 (4): 751–85.

Tyson, Karolyn. 2012. *Integration Interrupted: Tracking, Black Students, and Acting White after Brown*. Oxford: Oxford University Press.

Tyson, Karolyn, William Darity, and Domini R. Castellino. 2005. "It's Not 'a Black Thing': Understanding the Burden of Acting White and Other Dilemmas of High Achievement." *American Sociological Review* 70 (4): 582–605.

Valenzuela, Angela. 1999. *Subtractive Schooling: U.S.-Mexican Youth and the Politics of Caring*. Albany: State University of New York Press.

Van Praag, Lore, Simon Boone, Peter Stevens, and Mieke Van Houtte. 2015. "How Tracking Structures Attitudes toward Ethnic Out-Groups and Interethnic Interactions in the Classroom: An Ethnographic Study in Belgium." *Social Psychology of Education* 18 (1): 165–84.

Vickerman, Milton. 1999. *Crosscurrents: West Indian Immigrants and Race*. New York: Oxford University Press.

Vincent, Carol, Stephen Ball, Nicola Rollock, and David Gillborn. 2013. "Three Generations of Racism: Black Middle Class Children and Schooling." *British Journal of Sociology of Education* 34 (5–6): 929–46.

Virdee, Satnam. 2014. *Racism, Class and the Racialized Outsider*. London: Palgrave Macmillan.

Walker, Vanessa Siddle. 1996. *Their Highest Potential: An African American School Community in the Segregated South*. Chapel Hill: University of North Carolina Press.

Wallace, Derron. 2017a. "Distinctiveness, Deference and Dominance in Black Caribbean Fathers' Engagement with Public Schools in London and New York City." *Gender and Education* 29 (5): 594–613.

Wallace, Derron. 2017b. "Reading 'Race' in Bourdieu? Examining Black Cultural Capital Among Black Caribbean Youth in South London." *Sociology* 51 (5): 907–23.

Wallace, Derron. 2018a. "Cultural Capital as Whiteness? Examining Logics of Ethno-Racial Representation and Resistance." *British Journal of Sociology of Education* 39 (4): 466–82.

Wallace, Derron. 2018b. "Safe Routes to School? Black Caribbean Youth Negotiating Police Surveillance in London and New York City." *Harvard Educational Review* 88 (3): 261–86.

Wallace, Derron. 2019a. "Making Moral Migrants? Exploring the Educational Aspirations of Black African and Caribbean Boys in a New York City Public School." *International Studies in Sociology of Education* 28 (3–4): 237–58.

Wallace, Derron. 2019b. "The Racial Politics of Cultural Capital: Perspectives from Black Middle Class Pupils and Parents in a London Comprehensive." *Cultural Sociology* 13 (2): 159–77.

Wallace, Derron, and Remi Joseph-Salisbury. 2022. "How, Still, Is the Black Caribbean Child Made Educationally Subnormal?" *Ethnic & Racial Studies* 45 (8): 1426–52.

Walter, John. 1981. "West Indian Immigrants: Those Arrogant Bastards." *New England Journal of Black Studies* 2 (1): 17–27.

Walvin, James. 1973. *Black and White: The Negro and English Society 1555–1945*. London: Allen Lane the Penguin Press.

Ward, Howard. 2008. "More Caribbeans Classified as EBD." *Times Educational Supplement*, July 11, 2008, 12–13.

Warikoo, Natasha. 2007. "Racial Authenticity among Second Generation Youth in Multiethnic New York and London." *Poetics* 35: 388–408.

Warikoo, Natasha. 2010a. "Symbolic Boundaries and School Structure in New York and London Schools." *American Journal of Education* 116 (3): 423–51.

Warikoo, Natasha. 2010b. "Youth Culture and Peer Status among Children of Immigrants in New York and London: Assessing the Cultural Explanation for Downward Assimilation." In *Beyond Stereotypes: Minority Children of Immigrants in Urban Schools*, edited by R. Saran and R. Diaz, 183–214. Rotterdam: Sense Publishers.

Warikoo, Natasha. 2011. *Balancing Acts: Youth Culture in the Global City*. Berkeley: University of California Press.

Warikoo, Natasha. 2016. *The Diversity Bargain and Other Dilemmas of Race, Admissions, and Meritocracy at Elite Universities*. Chicago: University of Chicago Press.

Warikoo, Natasha, and Prudence Carter. 2009. "Cultural Explanations for Racial and Ethnic Stratification in Academic Achievement: A Call for a New and Improved Theory." *Review of Educational Research* 79 (1): 366–94.

Watkins-Owens, Irma. 1996. *Blood Relations: Caribbean Immigrants and the Harlem Community, 1900–1930*. Bloomington: Indiana University Press.

Waters, Mary C. 1999. *Black Identities: West Indian Immigrant Dreams and American Realities*. Cambridge and New York: Harvard University Press and Russell Sage Foundation.

Waters, Mary C., Philip Kasinitz, and Asad Asad. 2014. "Immigrants and African Americans." *Annual Review of Sociology* 40 (1): 369–90.

Watkins-Owens, Irma. 1996. *Blood Relations: Caribbean Immigrants and the Harlem Community, 1900–1930*. Bloomington: Indiana University Press.

Weekes, Debbie, and Cecile Wright. 1998. *Improving Practice: A Whole School Approach to Raising the Achievement of African Caribbean Youth*. London: Runnymede Trust.

Whittall, David James. 2012. "Creolising London: Black West Indian Activism and the Politics of Race and Empire in Britain, 1931–1948." Royal Hollowar, University of London.

Willis, Paul. 1977. *Learning to Labor: How Working Class Kids Get Working Class Jobs*. New York: Columbia University Press.

Wilson, Annabel, Diane Reay, Kirsty Morrin, and Jessie Abrahams. 2021. "'The Still-Moving Position' of the 'Working-Class' Feminist Academic: Dealing with Disloyalty, Dislocation and Discomfort." *Discourse: Studies in the Cultural Politics of Education* 42 (1): 30–44.

Wilson, William Julius. 2010. "Why Both Social Structure and Culture Matter in a Holistic Analysis of Inner-City Poverty." *The Annals of the American Academy of Political and Social Science* 629: 200–19.

Winder, Robert. 2004. *Bloody Foreigners: The Story of Immigration to Britain*. London: Abacus Publishers.

Woodson, Carter G. 1933. *The Mis-Education of the Negro*. Washington, D.C.: Association for the Study of African American Life & History.

Wun, Connie. 2016. "Unaccounted Foundations: Black Girls, Anti-Black Racism, and Punishment in Schools." *Critical Sociology* 42 (4–5): 737–50.

Wynter, Sylvia. 2003. "Unsettling the Coloniality of Being/Power/Truth/Freedom: Towards the Human, after Man, Its Overrepresentation—an Argument." *The New Centennial Review* 3 (3): 237–57.

Youdell, Deborah. 2004. "Engineering School Markets, Constituting Schools and Subjectivating Students: The Bureaucratic, Institutional and Classroom Dimensions of Educational Triage." *Journal of Education Policy* 19 (4): 407–31.

Young, Jr., Alford. 2004. *The Minds of Marginalized Black Men: Making Sense of Mobility, Opportunity and Future Life Chances*. Princeton, NJ: Princeton University Press.

Younge, Gary. 2017. "Beyond the Blade: The Truth about Knife Crime in Britain." *The Guardian*, March 28, 2017: https://www.theguardian.com/uk-news/2017/mar/28/beyond-the-blade-the-truth-about-knife-in-britain.

Index

For the benefit of digital users, indexed terms that span two pages (e.g., 52–53) may, on occasion, appear on only one of those pages.

Tables and figures are indicated by *t* and *f* following the page number

Behavior
  complimentary deference strategies
    of British Black Caribbean male
    students, 140–43, 243n.20
  compulsory deference, British
    Black Caribbean female student
    perspectives on, 146–49, 157–60
  cultural framing of, 163
  deference strategy and, 138–40
  ethnic expectations' regulation
    of, 8, 199
  gendered expectations for, 137–40,
    151–52, 199–200, 248n.24, 248n.27
  rewards for complimentary deference
    by British Black Caribbean male
    students, 143–45, 243n.20
Benson, Susan, 11–12, 47–48
Beyond the Melting Pot: The Negroes,
    Puerto Ricans, Jews, Italians and Irish
    (Glazer & Moynihan), 35–36
Bhopal, Kalwant, 191–92
Black Africans, in United Kingdom, 42–43
Black Caribbean enrollment, in US
    universities, xvi–xvii, 196–97
Black Caribbeans
  achievement paradox for, xviii–xix
  barriers to university education for,
    xv–xvii, 193
  Black ethnic imaginary and, 247n.6
  British university enrollment by,
    xvi–xvii
  cultural myths about, 116–18
  distinctiveness as cultural logic
    for, 111–13
  ethnic expectations of, 6–7, 99–102
  terminology, 220n.2
  UK educational expectations of, 2–4, 8
  US college enrollment by, xvi–
    xvii, 219n.7
  US educational expectations of, 1–2
Black ethnic imaginary, Black Caribbeans
    and, 247n.6
Black feminist theory
  Black Caribbean scholarship and, 32
  gendered expectations of deference and,
    243–44n.26
  habitus and, 244–45n.35
  politics of Black girlhood and, 150

race-gender double consciousness
    in, 141
  racial and ethnic politics and, 92
Black Identities (Waters), 14, 60–61,
    68, 78, 113–14, 116–17, 135, 167–
    68, 196–97
Black Lives Matter, 202
Black Manhattan (Johnson), 33
Black Marxism: The Making of a Black
    Radical Tradition (Robinson),
    236n.76
Black model minority myth, 30, 38–39, 185
  ethnic expectations' reinforcement of,
    5–6, 8–9
  racialized hierarchies of intelligence
    and, 39
Black Parents Movement, 50–51, 66–67
Black pathology myth, ethnic expectations
    and, 10
Black supplementary schools
  Black Caribbean student
    enrollment in, 27
  enrollment as institutional defiance
    in, 174–78
  establishment of, xvii, 219n.9,
    231n.122
  resistance to culture trap by, 45–48
Black Supplementary Schools
    Movement, 50–51
Bonilla-Silva, Eduardo, 245n.2
Bourdieu, Pierre
  on colonial entanglement,
    233n.3, 233n.7
  on culture, 15–16, 19, 225n.75
  on distinction, 30, 76, 226n.13, 236n.75,
    239n.3, 240n.28
  on economic, social and cultural capital,
    227n.30
  on habitus, 244–45n.35
  on language and power, 129
  on misrecognition, 163
  on resistance, 12–13, 223n.52
  on social capital, 154, 168–69
  on symbolic violence, 148
Boys. See male students
British Nationality Act of 1948, 43
Britishness
  Black Caribbean perceptions of, 62